REGNUM STUDIES IN GLOBAL CHRISTIANITY

Christianity and Education

Shaping Christian Thinking in Context

REGNUM STUDIES IN GLOBAL CHRISITANITY

Series Preface

The latter part of the twentieth century witnessed a global level change in Christian dynamics. One significant development was the rise of the churches in the global south, not only in their number but also in their engagement with their socio-cultural contexts. As theology is a dynamic interaction between the Christian message and the contemporary life of God's people and the world, it is natural to expect creative theological reflections from the southern churches. Global Theological Voices is a Regnum series exclusively dedicated to such theological explorations by the churches in Africa, Asia, Latin America and Eastern Europe. Through the provision of this credible international platform, the series empowers southern theological scholars whose voices are often not granted space by western publishers. The editors, therefore, invite theological seminaries and universities both in the West and in the 'South' to submit relevant scholarly dissertations for possible publication in the series. Global Theological Voices will serve the global church by bringing the creative southern theological voices into a global dialogue with the existing western theological voices. Ultimately the editors and the publisher pray that the publications in this series will encourage the southern churches to make an important contribution to the shaping of a healthy future for global Christianity.

Series Editors

REGNUM STUDIES IN GLOBAL CHRISTIANITY

Christianity and Education

Shaping Christian Thinking in Context

Edited by

David Emmanuel Singh

Bernard C. Farr

First published in 2011 by Regnum International

Regnum is an imprint of the Oxford Centre for Mission Studies
St. Philip and St. James Church
Woodstock Road
Oxford, OX2 6HR, UK
www.ocms.ac.uk/regnum

09 08 07 06 05 04 03 8 7 6 5 4 3 2 1

British Library Cataloguing in Publication Data
A catalogue record for this book is available from the British Library

ISBN 978-1-506475-24-0

Typeset by Words by Design
www.wordsbydesign.co.uk

The publication of this volume was made possible through the kind financial assistance made by Brian (Suk-hwan) Kim of Miracle Mile Mission, Los Angeles, California, USA

Distributed by 1517 Media in the US and Canada

Contents

FOREWORD

Since the events of September 11th, 2001 when Islamic extremists attacked and destroyed the Twin Towers in New York, the spotlight has been turned on what is being taught in the name of religion. Religious education, as well as religion's role within education systems, has suddenly become important once again. Not only is what is being taught in the schools and *madrassas* in Islamic societies and in the mosques in many European societies coming under scrutiny (Rizvi, 2004) but also what is being taught in many Christian theological institutions around the world.

This book, therefore, is very timely as it lifts the lid on what is being taught in Christian seminaries , universities and theological colleges.

Even international agencies such as the World Bank, and the United Kingdom's Department for International Development, have recognised that the religious and cultural aspects of societies have for too long been ignored and have been subsumed under the rhetoric of economic and social development.[1] Although this is a rather belated recognition it is, nevertheless, to be welcomed for, as Belshaw et al have shown, the role of the churches in African development has often been crucial. [2]

From earliest times it was religious leaders, whether Jewish rabbis, Brahmin priests, Confucian philosophers, Buddhist monks or Christian priests who were responsible not only for imparting religious beliefs to the people but also for teaching literacy skills. In terms of formal education, however, it is the Christian church that has played the greatest role. Although the Jews were the first people to develop formal schooling for both boys and girls, and although both Greece and Rome also developed some formal schooling, it was not until the Emperor Constantine embraced Christianity in 313AD and as that faith spread across the Roman Empire that formal [religious] schooling developed.[3] Indeed, it can truthfully be said that the church was the founder of most formal education throughout Europe and later, via the missionary movement, in most of Africa, Latin America and parts of Asia. As Tulasiewicz and Brock

---

[1] Marshall, K. (2010) 'Education for All: Where does religion fit in?' *Comparative Education, 46.3 (forthcoming)*

[2] Belshaw, D., R. Calderisi, and C. Sugden (eds. 2001) *Faith in Development: Partnership between the World Bank and the churches in Africa.* Washington, Dc and Milton Keynes: World Bank and Regnum Books.

[3] Castle, E.B. (1961) *Ancient education and today.* Harmondsworth, UK: Penguin Books.

observed:

> The historical role of the Christian church in the development of European nations' political and education systems makes the Christian tradition a powerful agent in shaping cultural and national identity.[4]

Norman Davies, in his masterly history of Europe, goes even further.[5] He argues that there can be no proper understanding of European civilisation, or of Europe as an entity, without a recognition of 'the centrality of the Christian tradition, which subsumes within itself the legacy of Greece and Rome, and Israel.'

It is this tradition that motivated the missionary movement and it was this tradition that shaped much of the colonial thinking, rightly or wrongly, as it helped to spread Western ideas about governance, law and order, education and healthcare throughout a large part of the world. It is helpful to remember this at a time when Christianity is being challenged *externally* as never before by the forces of secularism, individualism, economic materialism and technological change. While in the West, in Europe especially, Christianity seems to be in decline it is increasing dramatically in other parts of the world, especially where there is persecution.

Globalisation also poses a challenge since there is a growing emphasis on local communities while at the same time there are global forces pushing for a common economic, cultural, even linguistic conformity. In due course these same forces may well push for a common all-embracing religion. The revolution in the ways in which we communicate with each other, 24 hours a day; the growth of personal blogs and websites; the Internet; the self-centredness of so many; the short concentration spans- all pose a challenge to how the Christian Gospel is presented.

Nor must we ignore the fact that there are more Christians facing persecution and unjust imprisonment than at any previous time in history. How should the church respond globally to what are often local or regional issues?

There are also challenges *within* the church in many different cultural contexts. How to disciple those converts from a Muslim background [MBBs – Muslim Background Believers]. How to resolve, compassionately, those issues that are in danger of tearing the Christian community apart in many countries and regions – homosexuality; the ordination of women as priests, let alone as bishops; the breakdown of families and communities. How to embrace new means of communication without becoming enslaved by it. How to take a balanced view of the Israel – Palestine issue. How to teach about the injustices in the world. Amongst these are the disparities between North and South; the

---

[4] Tulasiewicz, W. and C. Brock (eds. 1988) Christianity and educational provision in international perspective. London: Routledge, p. 9.

[5] Davies, N. (1997) *Europe: A history.* London: Pimlico, p. 9.

growing issue of child prostitution and pornography; the sensitive issues of AIDS and migration and so on. How should different denominations relate to each other, especially where there are fundamental theological differences? How does the church come to terms with political regimes that are openly hostile? These are all issues that need to be faced in the twenty-first century either globally or at a local level.

Christianity thus faces a problem of how to present the Gospel in a rapidly changing age as well as how to come to terms with the many challenges, both internal as well as external, in contemporary society. How it does this is partly down to how clergy are trained, whether in some isolated institution or through practical work in difficult situations or through a combination of both. It is also how far new insights in theology can inspire new leaders without compromising the core Christian message. Above all, while the Christian Gospel is universally applicable, its presentation and outworking is very context specific.

All the above issues, and many more, are dealt with in this valuable book that brings together some of the more important writings on theological education over the past twenty years from the journal, *Transformation: An International Journal of Holistic Mission Studies.* The chapters deal with such themes as different institutional approaches to theological training, mission in a changing and 'globalising' world, theology in different cultural contexts, different methodologies in approaching theological studies, the place of Christian teaching in state universities as well as private ones. There is a wealth of information, ideas, reflections, and practical insights that should make this a basic textbook on theology and mission for years to come.

I wholeheartedly commend it to all readers interested in mission, the best ways of training future church leaders and pastors, and the presentation of Christianity in the twenty-first century.

Keith Watson
Emeritus Professor of Comparative and International Education
University of Reading, UK

Preface

Abstracts

David Emmanuel Singh

Dr. David Emmanuel Singh is Research Tutor at the Oxford Centre for Mission Studies.

The papers in this book have been drawn from *Transformation.* They cover the following broad areas: Institutional development for theological education, theological studies in the context of global mission, education that is contextually aware/informed, academies which deliver such education and methodologies. The book ends with a section on personal reflections.

Tim Dearborn, Horace Russell and Bernhardt Ott's papers form Part I which focuses on the institutional development issues in theological education. Dearborn asks how the new leaders for the church of the future are prepared. Would a collaborative and multi-institutional partnership work better than education through institutions working all by themselves? Seminary education, he argues, is widely perceived not to be fulfilling its role of preparing graduates for ministry. It almost seems like the graduates actually begin to learn when they begin their ministry out side the seminary. It is no wonder that many of these graduates often feel 'spiritually cold, theologically confused, biblically uncertain, relationally calloused and professionally unprepared'.

Horace Russell focuses on the seminary leadership and asks, are Presidents or Principals of seminaries engaged in the work of preparing leaders equipped to motivate those working with him to prepare leaders and the constituencies to which he is accountable? He believes leaderships of institutions anywhere in the world have certain common characteristics but their differences stem from their particular locations and opportunities. The college/seminary principal has the tough role to play as a representative symbol. His/her own prior training and continuing self-discipline is crucial for this to happen among those he serves.

Bernhard Ott reminds those engaged in Christian colleges/seminaries that the main purpose of it all is mission. Mission is used as a broad term encompassing all of what Dearborn also talks about. Ott's purpose is not however on calling his readers back to the past where somehow a perfect model remains preserved for all time but it is to challenge institutions to move beyond traditional models of theological education. Ott examines earlier educational traditions that relate mission to theological education, and their influence on current models and practice. He calls for a mission-oriented transformation of theological education, involving the integration of a mission dimension into all areas of study as well as an intentional focus on missiology.

Part 2 builds on the emphasis on Mission as being the purpose of theological education. It argues that since the scope of Mission is global, theological education needs to adapt – not in the sense of synthesizing a single system but a system that appreciates the global reality and is also local context sensitive.

Hwa Yung particularly highlights some critical issues facing theological education in Asia. He suggests that some of these may owe partly to the rapid growth in numbers in Asian churches within a short span of time and partly to the increasing self-awareness and Asian identity. Thus, one of the central critical issues facing the churches in Asia concerns its varied contexts which are not intentionally covered by theological education. This obviously leads to leaders being prepared for Asia using models and contents from the West. This leads to what Dearborn's article calls leaders who are 'theologically confused' and 'professionally unprepared'. Growth of the churches has understandably led a higher demand for theological education. Institutions of all sorts have been appearing all over the continent, but it is not clear if any effective fresh thinking is happening. In this context, this paper represents an important attempt at defining some of the problems facing theological education in Asia today which need new solutions.

Vinay Samuel's paper approaches the topic from a different perspective. That is, if globalization is a current reality, how does that impact theological education? He does not consider the possibility of the continued validity of the Western model as a whole in the face of globalization but rather focuses on a single process or manner of programme delivery, namely, distance education. Globalization challenges our view of time and space. Samuel asks, how does this challenge our thinking on theological education and how is it affecting our view of the foreign and local elements in theological education? What sort of new initiatives can a new understanding of globalization's relationship to the local contexts bring about? Could education by distance adapt what is distant to the climate of the local?

Tom Houston refreshingly reviews the synoptic Gospels to construct a basis for a discussion on theological education. His approach to the Gospel is person centric rather than text or doctrine/theology centric. He asks, how can the New Testament itself can be used as model for how theological education is delivered anywhere? Interestingly, in his attempt at such a 'translocal' approach he looks at the discipleship of Jesus (particularly the Twelve) as the principal model of theological education for it is concerned with 'the needs of the student', the 'curriculum' and its 'delivery', 'resourcing open access' and 'planning outcomes'. Whether an interpretation can ever be translocal is an academic matter. The more significant question would be whether this points to something that will be acknowledged by theological schools in Asia and Africa as something reflecting the flavour of the local.

Part 3 reviews the question, how should theology be taught in specific contexts such as the Islamic, Latin America, Central and Eastern Europe, or in Pastoral practice in Western Europe? Europe was the traditional centre of the Christian missions in Asia and Africa. It might appear that Christianity is on the decline in Europe, but not so in other parts of the world. Christianity is one of the fastest growing religions in these regions. Despite challenges, the Bartlotti paper argues that the number of 'Muslim background believers' is on the increase. If this is true then there is a need for culturally relevant theological education. It is not an easy matter to deal with because neither Islam, as a religion, nor Muslims, as followers, is monolithic. Although, those who subscribe to it may exhibit certain traits which are similar or common, ethnicity, language etc. complicate by the diversity. This diversity is the subject of enquiry in this paper especially as it relates to the challenges of globalization and the Internet and more importantly from this paper's point of view, to theological education in Islamic contexts.

The Pentecostals from contexts of oppression present one with another specific context for thinking on theological education as the two papers by Cheryl Bridges Johns, Cheryle Brown and Wesley Brown demonstrate. Is it fine to propose subversive theological education as the 'Praxis of Liberation' in contexts where people suffer different types of oppressions? The post communist region of Central and Eastern Europe serves as yet another context for fresh thinking on theological education. These are regions where religious institutions including seminaries and Bible schools were largely forbidden. However, great strides have been made here towards establishing a contextualized theological education. Many such centres need help with libraries and faculty development but more importantly, as these centres have been developed so far with the assistance of the West, they need time to evolve independently of western theological and cultural influence.

The use of Scripture in 'Pastoral Practice' in Churches is yet another context for theological education. Based on his involvement in a project between the Bible Society and the religious and theological faculty of the Cardiff University, Ballard gives his personal reflection on the theme, 'the Bible in Pastoral Practice'. Scholars and professionals have their own concerns about the application of critical thinking on the Bible. This problem is compounded by the particular use of the Bible by the 'contextual' and 'liberation' theologies.

This paper is an attempt at the recovery of the Bible as a resource for pastoral practice unencumbered by its ideological use.

Ian Randall's paper completes this section by giving the readers an actual example of training at a Baptist seminary. Some scholars have written about mission and theological education and Mission orientated theological education and others have commented on theological education for its lack of a holistic mission strategy or have reviewed the issue of the priority for mission in theological education or the 'praxis-based' theological education, which conduces to ministry and mission. This paper contributes to this ongoing discussion by using one theological institution as a lens for examining the connection between theological education and mission.

Part 4 addresses the question, how does theological education actually work in specific academic contexts of university education? The Development of a Masters Degree programme at the St Petersburg Christian University is another example of what Penner calls 'the contextual theological education'. The paper assumes that theology is culturally and historically shaped and this awareness must inform theological education at all levels. The freedom to explore this radical departure from traditional way of doing theological studies, owes much to external academic links the local Christian university was able to develop through the Oxford centre for Mission Studies. Its validation by a British university ensured its international validation. Penner presents this case as a model for theological education programmes with potential relevance to both the global and local contexts.

Darrel Cosden and Donald Fairbairn address the important issue of the centrality of context in shaping theology. An illustration of this is presented in the form of the 'Post-Soviet Protestantism' and 'western conservative Protestantism'. Both groups have certain basic similarities but both seem ignorant of the way their backgrounds and experiences shape their theology. Their ignorance often leads to an absolute theology. The clash is inevitable. The paper however, presents an interesting case of theology as taught at the Donetsk Christian University at the Master's level. In contradistinction to the conflicting and absolute views on theology, the MA course being taught at this university acknowledges the contextual and relative nature of theologies and this is seen as a way forward.

Whilst the private universities in the developing worlds may be creating space for doing theology in the university environment, the fate of theology and theological studies is far from settled in western universities as D'Costa shows in his 'On Theologizing Theology within the Secular University'. In many of the secular universities, theology is 'held captive to an Enlightenment view of its foundations in the modern university setting, restricting it to something resembling religious studies'. The author argues that faiths must be free from this straight-jacket and, hence, various theologies should be allowed to be honest about their starting points and interact freely in the academic setting.

The author recognizes many different models but favours what he calls the 'theological option' whereby theology is allowed to operate freely in the setting of 'Christian universities'.

Jan Jongeneel explores the question of whether the particular study of missions and its theology can be an academic discipline. Clearly, religious and theological studies have different underlying motivations and assumptions. Theological students cannot distance themselves from the study of theology in the sense required of students of religions. Is there then space for missiology in a university? If so, how does it fit in the academic programmes of the university? The author acknowledges questions on the lack of unambiguous academic pedigree of the theology of missions but this does not detract from the fact that theology as a broader discipline and missiology relatively recently have been part of the western universities for ages. What is needed is not to reject missiology as unacademic but a renewed and concerted effort by missiologists to adopt a rigorous academic approach. His own examples come from the universities on the continent of Europe and particularly the Netherlands.

Michael Schultheis' paper explores in this context the role of the private universities where a way in which theology/missiology is making a new beginning as a discipline incorporating the notion of 'transformational development'. There is a phenomenal growth of private universities in Africa many of which are set up by Christian churches. The Catholic University in Beira, Mozambique, for instance, was established in 1996, and the Catholic University of Ghana in 1998. These are principal centres where a new way of studying theology – one that takes mission beyond simplistic caricature of mission to its broader meanings in poverty ridden contexts of Africa.

Part 5 focuses on the important question of methodologies for theological studies. In 'Pentecostal Theological Method and Intercultural Theology', Cartledge explores recent Pentecostal scholarship in its attempt to articulate a Pentecostal theological method. In order to appreciate the roots of the academic study of Pentecostalism more broadly this study refers to the field of intercultural theology. Intercultural theology denotes the creative dialogue that local theologies have one with another. Two very different approaches to theology are considered in particular which have engaged with the Pentecostal tradition. The paper suggests an integration of Pentecostal-Charismatic spirituality, as per the insights of Pentecostal theological method, within the process of practical theology as an intercultural and comparative empirical discipline.

The Methodology of Dalit Theology from India is different. Jeyakiran Sebastian's paper interrogates it in a context where Dalit studies are making a comeback. This is also reflected in the field of Indian Christian theology where Dalit theology has emerged as a separate discipline and not simply as a branch of theology. Dominant forms of discourse have the disconcerting habit of raising questions like 'relevance' and 'viability' which forces people to enter into the 'bypass mode'. Questions raising issues like 'reality' and 'representation', often lead to internecine conflicts that help no one but the dominant discourses. Although much has been achieved, including major interventions in the field of biblical studies and hermeneutics and the rediscovery of Dalit literature, there is much that still needs to be done in the field of Dalit theology.

Continuing the discussion on the transcendental but centred in the human realm, Davies argues that theology concerns itself with human awareness of something that transcends humanity. It starts where we are and involves a given-ness which forms its fundamental basis. Human experience or awareness of God is interpreted from within this agreed framework. Theology is a way of experiencing and interpreting life but it is also dynamic body of knowledge. Within the Christian tradition, this can be seen in the theologies from the so-called 'margins'. The study of such a dynamic body of knowledge has been the concern of theology and religious studies degree programmes in modern Universities. Theology is however, not the preserve of the elite professionals. The professional theologians need to stand alongside ordinary people and learning from their experiences as much as theirs.

David Adams and Bernard Farr's paper on 'Researching Christian Action' concludes this section. It argues that the traditional approach of the academy to research requires the practitioner to locate their inquiries in an academic discipline, inevitably restricting the study to a limited aspect of the challenges of practice and requiring an objectivity that removes the researcher from the action. This paper describes a fresh response to this question – a Post-graduate Programme in Professional Practice. The programme, offered by the Oxford Centre for Mission Studies, draws on work-based learning and reflective practice and facilitates a process of critical inquiry and transformative action in the scholar-practitioner's own context

Part 6 ends with three personal reflections. For all contextual theologies, experience plays a central role as a significant source of inputs. What role should religious experience be playing in learning contexts? Unfortunately, contextual theologies can assign a rather subsidiary space to the latter; this needs to be recovered from its marginalization. Jarvis argues that some experiences, especially the ones that generate in the subject a feeling of creature-consciousness can be described as nothing less than awe-inspiring. Otto spoke of such experiences in relation to the notion of the numinous. Experiences have levels. Reaching the level where we are made aware of our true identity as creatures can gainfully inform our choices and learning. We remain however at the point where we can recognize that such experiences themselves point to the logic of meaning. The meanings that we place upon our experiences may be an expression of faith but the gap between meaning, faith and truth remains unbridgeable.

The D.P. Davies paper draws on his experience as a Welsh educator to comment on various issues involved in extension education and the validation of external degree programmes, in particular, questions related to the quality and validity of programs assessed in languages other than English.

David Adams in his paper explores the relationship between his research and his personal development. He highlights the need for recognizing multiple identities and 'inter-disciplines' involved in research which can then lead to the development of the community as whole. The main question it seeks to intentionally address is: What kind of person-in-community am I becoming through research?

Introduction: On Being Theologically Educated: Ten Key Characteristics

Bernard C. Farr

Dr. Bernard C. Farr is Senior Residentiary Fellow at the Oxford Centre for Mission Studies.

Introduction

The papers in this book provide many insights into theological education. They offer an account of where we have been in the recent past. This Preface is written as a challenge to move forward. Such progress depends, perhaps, on sorting out what is the right question to ask in relation to 'theological education'. And how to answer it.

The hinterlands of Christian theological education are many and diverse. This diversity can be represented in a series of questions. Who needs theological education? Who should provide it? Where should it be provided? How should its delivery be institutionally organized? Is there an ideal theological curriculum? What makes theological education fit for purpose? How might its impact be measured, and is measurement appropriate? Can meaningful theological education be delivered outside the community of faith – in academic University departments, for example – or is something essential lost if that is done? Do the numerous kinds of theological education diverge so much that it is no longer meaningful to apply the term 'theological education' to them all? Is personal formation an essential ingredient of theological education, or an additional matter that only becomes important in certain contexts such as training for Christian ministry?

This diversity of theological education has two sources: on the one hand differing approaches to and understandings of 'theology'; and on the other hand, differing approaches to and understandings of 'education'.

Consider 'theology'. There is an ever-increasing plethora of kinds of theology. Consequently, it is not apparent that the qualifier 'theological' in 'theological education' can be given any obvious or agreed meaning. A meta-question arises, therefore, as to what makes any of these approaches to theology 'theological' as against, say, philosophical or historical or political. What, as Wittgenstein might have asked, is the 'family resemblance'?

It is likewise with 'education': competing understandings are just as numerous and divergent, and can be similarly catalogued. Again, what is the 'family resemblance'?

When such varieties of 'theology' and of 'education' are cross-fertilized, the resulting concepts of 'theological education' are bewilderingly complex and impenetrable. It is not surprising that each year there are an increasing number of conferences, papers, books, blogs, seminars, commissions, resolutions, and pronouncements at the interface of 'theology' and 'education' where 'theological education' resides. This constant activity and endeavour can be likened to a new quest for a holy grail, namely *the* answer to the question: 'What *is* theological education?' Whether this quest is useful is a topic this Preface will now address.

The Problem of 'Theological Education'

To the average person the answer to the question 'What *is* theological education?' is quick and easy: 'Who cares?' The debate is not one that naturally quickens their pulse, excites their heart, nor captures their interest and attention. There is a noticeable glazing of the eyes, a blocking of the ears, and desire to move on to the next business because whatever it is, it must be for someone else but 'not for me'. Such a typical response is partly due to the way the word 'theological' is popularly used to separate off its subject matter (whatever that is) from the main business of life. Furthermore the question provokes the feeling that it is a question about something essentially for 'them' — the 'religious', the 'other worldly', the vicar or the Religious Education teacher. It is decidedly not for the majority who live in the real world with all its pressing concerns! Indeed, some people use the word 'theological' in a decidedly derogatory way. For example, a former Prime Minister of the UK, Harold Wilson, was given to using the adjective 'theological' in his political discourse to mean 'dense', 'impenetrable', 'useless' and 'time-wasting'. Such people see it as characteristic of the 'theological' mind to debate with seriousness such matters as the number of angels who/that can be balanced on the head of a pin. Wilson's political opponents' arguments were thought by him to be sufficiently refuted and dismissed by deeming them 'theological'.

To make matters worse, many adults have an ambiguous relationship with the term 'education'. They do not have particularly pleasant or happy memories of 'education' and think of it as now fortunately consigned to their distant past. What chance does the term 'theological education' have with such burdens to bear?

But let us not despair! Let us re-phrase the question addressed in this Preface thus: 'In what ways can theological education be made a lively, attractive and relevant option for *everyone* and not just for the few?' And in attending to this question, let us more especially ask what characteristics and defining features might, and perhaps should, grace both theological education and the theologically educated person. What could make theological education exciting and desired?

This last question itself raises an underlying issue, namely whether theological education has any useful point or purpose which could be perceived as relevant and therefore excite the ordinary person. Too often theological education, of whatever kind, has been conducted as an end in itself; parallel to 'art for art's sake', theology has been undertaken for theology's sake. If it is the case that utility is essential for the average person to become interested in theological education, should theological education be always a means to something else, and if so, what?

Two Preliminary Suggestions

My first suggestion in response to such considerations is that for the foreseeable future we should avoid using the substantive term 'theological education' altogether – I have used it too much already! As a consequence we would also cease asking the associated substantive question: 'What *is* theological education?' I propose these heuristic moves since the term 'theological education' is clearly, for the reasons set out above, not fit for purpose in respect of taking our understanding forward. There is little point, therefore, in using the term as such or asking questions about it.

My second heuristic suggestion is that we come at the question 'In what ways can theological education be made a lively, attractive and relevant option for *everyone* and not just for the few?' by asking this even more personal question: 'What is it to be a theologically educated person and what characteristics would such a person exhibit?'

Taking the second of these questions first, this Preface assumes that the question is addressed to the Christian community at large, and that the answer is that all kinds of Christian should be theologically educated. Indeed, not only all kinds of Christian, but all Christians without exception. The reason for this assumption is that I am also assuming that 'theology' is not an esoteric discourse, nor a professionalized discourse, nor an academic discourse, nor any kind of discourse which sets theology apart from the 'speech acts' and 'speech forms' of the Christian community.[1] I am instead assuming that 'theology' is any discourse in which, and through which, Christians seek to make sense of this world and their lives in relation to their God who is the Father of the Lord Jesus Christ (Ephesians 1:3; cp. John 14:6). And conversely but in like manner, it is any discourse through which these same people seek to make sense of the

---

[1] This question, it must be noted, implies a prior question: 'What kind(s) of person should be theologically educated person(s)?' I am assuming that the answer to this question is that all kinds of person should as a base threshold be theologically educated to the degree that is fit for the purpose of their being as fully as possible mature in their faith.

God and Father of their Lord Jesus Christ in relation to their lived experience of the 'thrownness' of being human.[2]

Theology taken in this way can be more or less technical, more or less coherent, more or less attached to 'big' names, more or less taught and learned, more or less subject to formalization, approval and correctness. It is a speaking-out by the Christian community from their constant struggles to wrestle with the twin realities of themselves and God through experience(s), deed(s), thought(s) and then word(s). In these struggles they can access the Christian Scriptures and Christian history, doctrine, liturgy, and lives. However, they cannot wear second-hand clothes, nor mouth second-hand formulas, nor depend on second-hand experts. Theology is their own account, in their own words, albeit reflectively and deliberatively informed by what has gone before and hopeful of what may yet be. It is the child's 'Abba', the supplicant's 'Help thou my unbelief', the agonizing cry of the sufferer 'Why?' when addressed to God. To be a theologically educated person is, therefore, never an achieved state. Perhaps, indeed, I should revise the question further and ask not 'What is to be a theologically educated person?' but 'What is the journey for becoming a more theologically educated person?' and 'What signs might there be of progress towards this goal?' But I shall settle for this one: 'What would it be like to be in the presence of, and engage with, a theologically educated person?'

Rowan Williams had similar considerations in mind when he raised the issue in his 2004 CEFACS lecture on the nature of theological education. 'I want to think about what a theologically educated person might be like', Williams says. He answers:

> [Theology] is, yes, a practical discipline, a discipline about acquiring skills for living – to use the contemporary jargon. But those skills for living are shaped by a whole set, a whole heritage of narratives, perspectives, images, metaphors – each one of them traceable to some great upheaval in human understanding which create a responsibility, a sense of, let's use the word, obedience in those who are drawn in by them, which is to say the least unusual in the intellectual world. Theology is about personal transformation, theology is about holiness, theology is about obedience and in a sense in which that last rather contentious idea might be true…[3]

[2] For more on 'thrownness' See M. Inwood, 'Thrownness and Facticity', (1999), http://www.blackwellreference.com/public/tocnode?id=g9780631190950_chunk_g978063119095021_ss1-6. Accessed on 18.02.10.

[3] R. Williams, 'CEFACS Lecture, Birmingham', http://www.archbishopofcanterbury.org/1048. Accessed on 18.02.10. Williams' lecture should be read as a complement to this Preface as it expands on topics I can thus leave aside.

Becoming Theologically Lively, Attractive, Relevant and...

With this question in mind – 'What would it be like to be in the presence of, and engage with, a theologically educated person?' – I shall now consider in what ways the theologically educated person can be a lively and attractive theological companion for everyone, and propose a minimum set of ten characteristics that the theologically educated person needs to possess and exhibit if they are to fulfil this challenge. These are not placed in any particular order since, like the facets of a diamond, the reflection from each adds to the glitter of the whole. The reader may wish to order these characteristics in a preferred sequence, and there is no harm in that. My preference, however, is to ignore the logic of a list and see them as dynamically and internally, not sequentially and externally, related – a point I come to in the tenth characteristic. They should be regarded as existing within a web, with possibilities of multi-directional movement of thought, rather than tabulated and serial.

So here are my proposed ten characteristics:

Being Theologically Knowledgeable... and More

Perhaps the main focus and strength of traditional theological education has been its emphasis on knowledge; as the Apostle Paul put it, 'that which was delivered to me, that I have delivered to you' (1 Corinthians 15:3). The weakness of this emphasis, however, has been that this knowledge has been understood for the most part as essentially propositional in form: the 'facts' of Israelite and Church history, the 'contents' of doctrines, the 'vocabulary and grammar' of Greek and Hebrew, the 'history of ideas', and so on make up 'theological education'. This can remain the case where propositional approaches to theological knowledge are apparently rejected in favour of some other epistemological basis for theology, for example, 'metaphorical', 'expressive' or 'poetic'. The knowledge content remains the same even if a different *status* is given to it as knowledge. Knowledge is conceived as 'know what' rather than 'know how'.

But this approach hardly begins to provide for all that is needed if one is to be a theologically educated person, where 'theology' is taken in the sense set out earlier, namely that theology is 'that discourse in which, and through which, Christians seek to make sense of this world and their lives in relation to their God who is the Father of the Lord Jesus Christ and conversely, but in like manner, that discourse though which these same Christians seek to make sense of the God and Father of their Lord Jesus Christ in relation to their lived experience of the 'thrownness' of being'. The specific and peculiar feature of such theological 'knowledge' is that it is not fundamentally or merely an epistemology of reference, reference beyond oneself to some external reality, cast in propositional form. Nor is it fundamentally or merely an epistemology of accumulation of 'facts' as though theology were some kind of encyclopaedic knowledge. It is inescapably a 'personal knowing' – it is fundamentally and quintessentially 'knowing who', one might say. Jesus himself is remembered to have said, 'If you have seen me, you have seen the Father. How can you ask me to show you the Father?' (John 14:9). Paul takes this further in 1 Cor 13:12 in linking knowing with *being known* and comments on this further in 1 Cor 2: 11 thus: 'For who among men knows the thoughts of a man except the man's spirit within him? In the same way no one knows the thoughts of God except the Spirit of God'. It is then an epistemological and not just a spiritualizing comment when he then adds, 'We have not received the spirit of the world but the Spirit who is from God, that we may understand what God has freely given us'. (1 Cor 2:12). Being theologically educated therefore requires attention to internal and not just external relations-of-knowing. It is not just 'knowing' *per se*. It is the movement from 'knowing' to understanding through the personalizing work of God's spirit.[4]

For my own part, I remain hugely indebted to the extensive and thorough grounding in cognitive-propositional knowledge which I received in my early theological development, whether in Sunday School or as a theology undergraduate. However, the inadequacy of my theological education in this mode was made clear to me in a critical incident in my professional career as a theological educator. I had been lecturing to post-graduate students training to teach Religious Education in UK schools on 'The Use of the Bible in the Classroom'. I had considered with them the uses made of the Bible outside the classroom – for personal devotion, liturgical performance, legitimating doctrine, understanding Christian origins, expression in the Arts and such like. Then I asked the students to discuss whether any of these uses had a place in the classroom of a state school. At the end, a student raised her hand and asked to comment on the lecture and discussion. What she said was a key moment in my own development. She remarked that although she held a good honours degree in Theology and had completed a well-regarded MA in Biblical Studies, she could not remember ever having been asked to *think theologically* about the Bible. However, she said, this session had forced her to do just that, and for the first time. In that moment I realized that this was also true, at least overtly true, in my case. I thought I had been giving a lecture in education, not theology, but actually, no. I had been working with the student theologically on the significance of the Bible. My understanding of what was involved in doing

---

[4] The pietists took this too far. In educational terms it is interesting to look at Rousseau and Pestalozzi as they thought through how educational theory may be re-worked with such considerations in view, though of course they each went their own distinctive way when proposing answers. On 'personal knowledge', see 'Religion', (2007), http://www.heinrich-pestalozzi.de/en/documentation/fundamental-ideas/religion/ Also see M. Polanyi, *Personal Knowledge: Towards a Post-Critical Philosophy* (Chicago: University of Chicago Press, 1958).

theology changed in that moment. I saw that the first step in being theologically educated is to be able to, and required to, think theologically rather than to 'do the knowledge' – although the former skill depends on the latter being in place. But even so, it is only a first step, because there is 'more' to theological knowing than knowing what and knowing how as has been shown above.

Thus, my first characteristic of being theologically educated is to be able to think theologically for oneself and with others in a personal mode about what (who) one 'knows', whatever (whoever) that 'knowing' is. The knowledge contents of theology are, in this way, as large as life itself and not containable in a particular body of words. It is a personal mode of knowing leading to understanding.

Being Theologically Skilled... and More... or Less

A heartfelt complaint of traditionally-minded educators is that modern education is all about *skills* at the expense of *content.* There is some truth in this complaint. It is too easy in education for attention to *process* to eliminate attention to *product* – for emphasis on education as being about the 'births of readers' to be undertaken in a way that leads to the 'deaths of the authors', for 'lighting candles' in the class to be an entire substitute to filling heads as though 'filling buckets'.[5] But the theologically educated Christian is above all a person who thinks skill-fully when thinking theologically.

A wry anecdote bears on this point. An English aristocrat was showing a visitor his magnificent library with its twenty thousand volumes. The awed visitor politely observed that his host must be a very educated man to have such a library and so easily to hand. The lord replied, 'Well, I think I am an educated man but I have only read one of them'. The visitor protested that surely an educated man must have read more than just one book. 'Ah', said the lord, 'you have missed the point. Although I have read only one, I read it *very carefully*!' And so it is with being theologically educated. It is not the quantum of 'know what', or even the number of skills at one's disposal, but the ability to *pay attention* in the sense developed by Simone Weil.[6]

Perhaps this is the lesson of the Gospel vignette of Mary and Martha where one was encumbered in many things but the other chose the 'better part' of

---

[5] The quote 'Education is not filling a bucket, but lighting a fire.' See for more on the source of this quote, 'Education Is Not Filling a Bucket, but Lighting a Fire', *i202 Fall 2009*, http://courses.ischool.berkeley.edu/i202/f09/blog/education-not-filling-a-bucket-lighting-a-fire Accessed on 18.02.10.

[6] It is worth attending to everything that Simone Weil says on the topic of 'attention'. See, for example, S. Cameron, 'The Practice of Attention: Simone Weil's Performance of Impersonality', *Critical Inquiry* 29, no. 2, Winter (2003), http://www.journals.uchicago.edu/doi/abs/10.1086/374026.; accessed on 18.02.10; M. von der Ruhr, *An Apprenticeship in Attention*, Outstanding Christian Thinkers (Continuum, 2007). Accessed on 18.02.10.

paying attention. Put differently, this is the old battle between more and less, breadth and depth, surface and deep knowing, thin and thick text, having skills and being skilful. The 'know all' has never had a good press. The point is not to know it all, but to be able to bring out of one's treasures that focused knowledge which is required at that moment – or as the Japanese have taught us, just enough, just in time.[7] There is a world of difference between 'knowing' and 'knowing about'. Was it more than a witticism for Rabbi Lionel Blue to observe in a radio broadcast that he went to Oxford University thinking he would sit at the feet of the wise, but all too often found that he sat only at the feet of the clever?[8]

My second desired characteristic of the theologically educated person is therefore that however much they know – and they should know a very great deal – they can practise knowledge as a skill, not just possess it as content. The essence of the matter is not that they have more knowledge. The essence is that they *dwell* in their knowledge skill-fully whilst the knowledge *dwells* in them. What this means will be developed in the points below.

Theological Application as 'Sensing' God's World

We have perhaps eight senses by which we apprehend the world: sight – hearing – smell – taste – touch – time awareness – temperature awareness – balance. But I have in mind something different from these. It is the creative (constructive) ability to *make* sense of the world. It is also the sensitivity (receptiveness) to *take* sense from the world.

Let me start with some personal observations. In many years experience of various institutions, I have found that an emphasis on theological application to life is far removed from many theology curricula. An exception may be made for institutions specializing in the cognate area of ministerial education, but not wholly so. (One faculty member I met in such an institution proposed that about 60 per cent of a theological degree for people intending for Christian ministry should be devoted to biblical languages.) Recently (2010) a blogger who was interested in attending a course on the nature of lay theology was indignant to discover that the course would be delivered by a professional theologian, the Rev'd Dr Prof 'x' from a University department. How could such a person, he exploded, have anything relevant to offer to *practical* theology? I have myself blogged under the heading 'I would not want to be a Professor of Unapplied Theology'. There are indeed University departments of theology where no faculty has an expressed interest in, nor evident experience

[7] Just in Time (JIT) is the Japanese quality practice of *kaizen*. See SPAEF, 'A Review of the Adoption of Just in Time Method and Its Effect on Efficiency', (2008), http://www.spaef.com/article.php?id=118. Accessed on 18.02.10

[8] On his years at Oxford see his autobiography, L. Blue, *Hitching to Heaven: An Autobiography* (Hodder and Stoughton, 2004).

of, theological application. Don Cupitt some years ago complained to me in conversation that nothing in his theological training had equipped him to make visits to suffering patients on a hospital ward. The long story behind this separation of theology from life dates back in a significant way to Schleiermacher, but that is a topic addressed by others.

Against this background, I see it as an irremovable characteristic of any theologically educated person (the person who is seeking to make simultaneous sense of God and the world) that for them the world is as essential to theology as is God. Sensing the presence of God (both making and taking) is for the believer a primary means of 'sensing' the world, since the world is made sensible by believing in God. But taking sense from the world is a necessary looping back, as the Psalmist knew (Psalm 8:3). And that is what I mean by theological application – making both God and the world bear on and illuminate the other in ways which cannot be other than practical in outcome. This is not the same, I hasten to make clear, as the application of theology *to* the world, whereby a theological student starts with the doctrine of God and proceeds, through this and related topics, until finally she faces the question: 'How can all this knowledge be applied to life?' (This is how an eminent UK theologian once explained the shape of a good applied theological curriculum to me.) Instead, theological application takes seriously that the God of the Old and New Testaments is quintessentially a God who *acts in and through* the world, not just a God who *speaks to* it. The malaise in theological education arises, I am suggesting, because academic theology can seriously suppose that what God has said, and what people have said about what God has said, is the true subject matter of theology. Traditional Christology, remember, makes a distinction between Word (John 1; God is speaking to us through Christ) and Work (consider Mark's urgent narrative of Jesus doing/acting), and typically treats them separately.[9] But the God of the Testaments is not so. He spoke, *and it was* – word issued in work. It is for this reason that attending to the work(s) of God is to hear the word(s) of God.[10] To be theologically educated, therefore, is to maintain a biblical emphasis on both the word(s) and the way(s) of God. It is to take seriously the Christian doctrine of that creation of which we are an embedded part, as is God. As has been said, Christianity is the most materialist of the religions.[11] Theological application is the skilling of the Christian mind in ways that enable it through 'sensing' the world to know God. This is my third characteristic.

---

[9] See for an example, G.C. Berkouwer, *Studies in Dogmatics: The Work of Christ* (Kampen: J.H. Kok N.V., 1965).

[10] Cameron, 'The Practice of Attention: Simone Weil's Performance of Impersonality'; von der Ruhr, *An Apprenticeship*.

[11] A comment usually attributed to William Temple, former Archbishop of Canterbury who is reported a saying over and over, 'Christianity is the most materialistic religion.'

Theologizing Contextually

I was once seeking institutional permission to appoint a lecturer in contextual theology. At first this appointment was refused on the grounds that the title of the post contains a redundancy – all theology is contextual by nature. Actually, it is not, and after argument the title was approved. Some Christian theology transcends all contexts. Some does not. The problem is in knowing what should be in one category and what in the other. In some theological circles it is fashionable to talk of the long European imprisonment of theology, and how theology done in other contexts should be free from – and free itself from – this bondage. This perception is amplified in a post-modern way by reference to the controlling power of the languages within which theology has been done and how other languages should be free to be themselves. This contention that the gospel can be imprisoned in cultural and linguistic forms appears to suppose that there is a non-historical, non-contextual core to the Gospel which can be accessed anew and directly on a local basis. I am inclined to sympathize with this view, but only somewhat and in a different way. The central non-contextual elements of the Gospel relate to the form rather than the contents of Christian experience, and the form rather than the contents of Christian theology.

Thus, for all Christians in whatever time and context, Jesus is Lord. For all Christians in whatever time and context, the Bible has a pivotal and classic role as a text. These irreducible centralities, however, carry no particularities as to what it means for Jesus to be 'Lord' or for the Bible to be pivotal and classic. Such context-transcending aspects of the Gospel are what the Christian community agrees universally to disagree about locally. It is the responsibility of the theologically educated Christian to engage in contextualizing these elements of the gospel into their culture, society, community, and personal life. In this way theological application actually occurs, theological thinking is brought to bear, and life itself provides resistance to flights of local theological fancy.

This then is my fourth characteristic of the theologically educated person: that such a person seeks to make sense of this world and their life and the lives of those they love in the 'here' and 'now' of their existence – what Heidegger calls their 'facticity'.[12] They do this in relation to their God – a God who is in all their 'heres' and 'nows' – the God who is the Father of the Lord Jesus Christ. And conversely but in like manner, these same people seek to make sense of the context-transcending God and Father of their Lord Jesus Christ in relation to their lived experience of the 'thrownness' of being human.

[12] On 'facticity', see Inwood, 'Thrownness and Facticity'.

Experiential Primacy and Theology As Biography

However this activity of contextualizing theology – or to re-phrase that, thinking theologically through context – is not to reduce theology to anthropology, sociology or psychology. But it is to say that the crucible within which sense is made of God and the world (theology) is inescapably experiential. The Old Testament is scarcely understandable otherwise, whether it be Abram/Abraham on his trek of faith, Jacob wrestling at Jabbok, Israel in the wilderness, David in his psalm-making, Elijah on Mount Carmel, Hosea in his family trials, Habakkuk in his tower. So also in the New Testament, which is nothing if not experience in search of meaning within the terms available to those making the meaning.

And so theological education should remain – as an invitation to pilgrimage from life to meaning, from the world to God. This pilgrimage demands that theological educators do not insert barriers of technical language or now-distant concepts or ancient conceptualities [13] between people and their theological sense-making.[14] John Hick once told me that in his first ministry appointment in rural England he was determined to teach his congregation the great salvific doctrines of the Christian faith. However, he found that his congregation did not have available to them the conceptual worlds of the first Christian centuries or Reformation Europe which are needed to access these doctrines – and why should they? Similarly, an Anglican MA student of mine studied two of his congregations that apparently differed in their theological abilities, only to find that he had been unable to hear the theological skilfulness of one congregation because he himself could only hear technical theology as being theological. He learned in his research that theology can be done in ordinary language which is conceptualized within the given experience of the people. This is akin to the

---

[13] David Jenkins persistently recommended that in reading the Bible the reader has always to ask 'How did people think then which led them to put it like that?' He provided the following as an example. The writers of the gospels lived at a time when demon possession was the available conceptuality if a person fell to the ground writhing and foaming at the mouth. In the middle ages, the conceptuality within which explanation arose was that of the humours of the body and the cure would have been blood-letting. In medicalized twenty-first century conceptuality it would be said that the person was having an epileptic fit and the needed response is to keep calm and re-assure.

[14] There is a case, however, for seeing research as necessarily being involved in its first stage in 'strangemaking'. It is only by making the commonplace first of all 'strange' that one can attain the critical distance required for research to proceed. Ethnomethodology makes this its primary mode of practice. Garfinkel, its originator, analysed in detail the methods used by people in everyday life to account for (make sense of) their activities for themselves and for others. He thus saw ethnomethodology as the study of commonsense knowledge of social structures so as to make sociological reasoning analysable. Ethnomethodology was the subject of fierce debate within sociology departments. Some of its insights have been taken into mainstream sociological theory, particularly through the work of Anthony Giddens.

realization by educators that 'school language' can be the cause of pupils' apparent failure to progress. It is not that the pupils are stupid but that 'school language' is an unwelcome barrier to learning.[15] Indeed, the language of the street and even the ghetto has its own strict grammar which teachers do not know how to access. So who need to be the learners?[16]

My fifth characteristic for being theologically educated is being able to speak of, and speak to, God within and from our own experience using our own language, concepts, conceptualities; as well as to understand how others have spoken from theirs. Perhaps one way of saying this is that to be theologically educated is to take one's own experience(s) and biography seriously when theologizing. We cannot and must not do theology 'secondhand'. It is the constant call to journey into the extra-ordinary (God) through the ordinary (ourselves in the world). For what has God made clear?

> He has made clear to you, O man, what is good; and what is desired from you by the Lord; only doing what is right, and loving mercy, and walking without pride before your God. (Micah 6:8 [Bible In Basic English])

Becoming Progressive and Playful and Experimental

What I have just said is a fundamental challenge to the idea that God's revelation is either complete or contained – whether in scripture, doctrine, moral action or creed. There are not only treasures old, but also treasures new.[17] This freedom to live with God in the 'now' allows for degrees of playfulness

---

[15] See the classic study, D. Barnes et al., *Language, the Learner, and the School* (Boynton/Cook, 1989). It argues that stress on 'proper English' can inhibit non-middle-class children from expressing themselves in the kind of language they use at home, while 'learning' for all too many students means guessing what answers the teacher expects - in 'school language' of course. The final section makes important recommendations on the major issue of language across the curriculum - what sort of language is really appropriate in multicultural schools? A charismatic evangelical teacher-training student I supervised some years ago was convinced that modern teenagers can understand Christian doctrine if only the teacher can find the right teaching methods including exciting visual aids. He admitted failure having tried.

[16] See R. C. Miller. 'The Language Gap and God: Religious Language and Christian Education'. (Place Published, 2010), http://www.religiononline.org/showchapter.asp?title=2300&C=2266. Accessed on 18.02.10. Chapter 5, 'Discernment and Commitment' is based on I. T. Ramsey who argued that religious language is grounded in personal experience and personal disclosure. This understanding of religious language is experientially grounded in that when we communicate with each other personal disclosure occurs. Ramsey argued that we come to encounter God it is also by way of personal disclosure. Ramsey's theological work thus continues the traditional theological view that all religious language is analogical, and the religious vocabulary that we create always involves the language of analogy.

[17] Matthew 13:52.

that make thinking theologically a constructive business. The word 'playfulness' is used here deliberately. Conforming to the given, learning by instruction, being only passive, valuing the past above the present, finding no voice of one's own, may be fine for catechumens but not for Christians seeking to live with God from day to day in ways that are relevant and powerful. There is a need to pose 'what if…', to say 'not so', to become as a child in the midst.

We see this in Jesus' life as he plays with ideas through parables, teases the disciples with riddles and puzzles, replies to questions with questions, performs miracles without explanations, and asks the disciples to speculate about who he is. The disciples learned by living with Jesus from day to day in the home, the fields and the synagogue, not sitting in a rabbinic-type school of instruction or learning the truth by rote. And so also for us now, as we 'play before God'.[18]

Perceiving what it is to be theologically educated as 'being at play before God' is also knowing what it is to be a fool for Christ's sake, I very much like this review of Edward Hays' *Holy Fools & Mad Hatters: A Handbook for Hobbyhorse Holiness*: 'Is it possible for us to defossilize St. Paul's call for each of us to become a fool for Christ's sake?' asks spiritual writer Edward Hays. The answer is a resounding yes! *Holy Fools and Mad Hatters: A Handbook for Hobbyhorse Holiness* is designed for all those who want to cultivate their inner clown. Time, practice, and patience are needed to walk the Christian Way which is, according to Hays, 'narrow as a razor's edge'. Those who follow Jesus are bound to be eccentric. He stood outside the conventions of his day and demonstrated a defiant belief in God's presence here and now. Hays writes: 'In some way every disciple is ordained to servanthood and foolhood, ordained to be a jester to the world'. How does this play itself out? It begins with a daily consciousness of death. In ancient times it was customary for monks and other religious to keep a human skull on their desks. Becoming a Holy Fool continues by acknowledging our indebtedness to others and by living mindfully. Our spiritual lives are enriched when we 'fertilize our faith'. Hays suggests risk-taking, loving those whom we take for granted, practising meaningful rituals, and keeping hope alive. He also proposes that instead of being immobilized by fear, we learn how to play around with our troubles. This Mad Hatter procedure exercises our creativity and imagination. Holy Fools are challenged to reap the harvest of solitude so they can forge their conscience in everyday life. Instead of looking for magic, become a miracle worker. Realize that humour is at the heart of a zestful response to life. This handbook is cleverly designed and filled with whimsical stories and practical exercises. In

[18] See 'Playing before God: Theology and Play in Dialogue', http://forum.llc.ed.ac.uk/si2/gabelman.pdf. Accessed on 18.02.10.

the spirit of St. Francis, Edward Hays comes across as a spiritual jester with serious things to say in a playfully meditative way.[19]

My sixth characteristic is then that the theologically educated person learns to play skill-fully and enjoys the fun of the 'game'.[20]

Becoming Communicative, Social and Relational – and Challenging

There are games that are played on one's own, and sometimes theological activity is indeed a lonely and personal business. But more often games are played with others and this is also the case with theological activity. Put more grandly, we are talking of communities of discourse within which otherwise solipsistic tendencies prevail. Even more decisively, at the end of the day these games must be within the public arena. Here I agree with David Tracy when he writes:

> I have come to believe that anyone making a theological statement that claims to be more than the private-language of a person or a group (i.e., *any theological* statement) must be willing to have that statement judged by two sets of criteria. The first set of criteria seems obvious: a Christian theological statement must be appropriate to the central motifs of the Christian tradition. *What* those central motifs are can and should be argued on purely historical and hermeneutical grounds. If a Roman Catholic manualist theologian informs us that the papal office is central to the New Testament, we want to know what exegetical and historical evidence can count for and against this claim. If no such evidence is forthcoming, then one may fairly conclude that the real backing for the warrant must be found elsewhere than in a public realm of discourse - for example, in the personal belief of the theologian. If a radical theologian informs us that only Christians know and celebrate the death of God, we want to know how this interpretation of Christianity is the correct interpretation of its symbol system. Or

---

[19] See review by F. Brussat and M.A. Brussat, 'Review of E. Hays Holy Fools & Mad Hatters:A Handbook for Hobbyhorse Holiness ', (2009), http://www.spiritualityandpractice.com/books/books.php?id=7089.

[20] This is partly an allusion to Wittgenstein on language games but I am emphasising the sense of play to add to what he says of games, life and travel. On language games, see 'Stanford Encyclopedia of Philosophy', http://plato.stanford.edu/entries/feminist-religion/. Accessed on 18.02.10: 'Some properties of language-games can be noticed in Wittgenstein's several examples and comments. They are, first, a part of a broader context termed by Wittgenstein a form of life (see below). Secondly, the concept of language-games points at the rule-governed character of language. This does not entail strict and definite systems of rules for each and every language-game, but points to the conventional nature of this sort of human activity. Finally, Wittgenstein's choice of "game" is based on the over-all analogy between language and game, assuming that we have a clearer perception of what games are. Still, just as we cannot give a final, essential definition of "game", so we cannot find "what is common to all these activities and what makes them into language or parts of language."'

> is the real backing for that warrant the personal creative vision of the individual religious thinker? Although all can agree that the theologian is to be held responsible for showing how his or her theological statements are appropriate interpretations of the Christian tradition, not all seem able to agree that these conclusions must be defended on public - here historical and hermeneutical - grounds. Until that agreement occurs, theology will not serve its public function of authentic communication.[21]

Even so, there is the danger of becoming trapped within the discourse of the 'public' community as one goes about being suitably and dutifully social, relational and communicative. This puts at risk the ability to play *beyond* the sometimes visible, sometimes invisible, boundaries drawn round that community by that community. It is to experience the pressure towards orthodoxy and against heterodoxy, the expectation to be similar rather than different, to conform and not rebel. But to succumb is to forget that the biblical tradition could not escape the need for the disruptive prophetic voice over against the continuities of ritual and myth celebrated by the priestly class. As Brueggemann commented:

> The task of prophetic ministry is to nurture, nourish and evoke a consciousness and perception alternative to the consciousness and perception of the dominant culture around us. Thus I suggest that prophetic ministry has to do not primarily with addressing specific public crises but with addressing, in season and out of season, the dominant crisis that is enduring and resilient, of having our alternative vocation co-opted and domesticated.[22]

Membership of *any* discourse community can, perhaps always does, impair the habit of radical critique and deny opportunities for neo- and hetero-glossic discourse.[23]

But is it possible to live within yet also beyond the boundaries? This is a question directly addressed in *Being as Communion* when it asks, 'Communion and otherness: how can these be reconciled?'[24] It emphasizes the importance of communion for life and for unity. In the companion volume *Communion and Otherness: Further Studies in Personhood and the Church*[25] he takes on board the complementary fact that communion is the basis for true otherness and identity. He probes the Christian tradition and highlights the existential

---

[21] D. Tracy, 'Theology as Public Discourse', *The Christian Century* (March 1975).

[22] W. Brueggemann, *The Prophetic Imagination* (Philadelphia, PA: Fortress Press, 1978), 13.

[23] M. Little et al., 'Discourse Communities and the Discourse of Experience', *Health* 7:1 (2003).

[24] J.D. Zizioulas, *Being as Communion* (New York: St. Vladimir's Seminary Press, 1985).

[25] J.D. Zizioulas, *Communion and Otherness: Further Studies in Personhood and the Church* (T. & T. Clark Publishers, 2007).

concerns that already underlay the writings of the Greek fathers and the definitions of the early ecumenical councils, and he defends the freedom to be 'other' as an intrinsic characteristic of personhood, fulfilled only in communion.

Thus, whilst my seventh characteristic is that we have responsibilities, as Tracy claims, to be communicative, social and relational rather than controlled, hierarchical and judgmental, there is more to be said than that and more to be gained. Was it Bernard Shaw who remarked that all human progress has come from those who are difficult?[26] But there is obviously a need for a balance to be found here.

Becoming Theologically Aesthetic and Expressive

It is, as noted above, a besetting weakness of traditional theology to give priority of attention to Word(s) over Act(s), the head over the heart, and so on. Consequently the lecture, the seminar, the tutorial, the discussion, the sermon, the talk, the essay, the book, the paper, the conference, and the blog predominate as the means by which theological expression, engagement, communication, sociality and relationships occur. This is a decidedly strange way of proceeding since 'being Church' emphasizes fellowship, compassion, service, worship and other forms of action through which Christians express their faith. Being communicative, social, relational, and being theological thereby transcend (though do not leave behind) the verbal, propositional and cognitive.

Perhaps, then, the term 'academic theology' is a grand term for a truncation of theology which risks missing the point: that, as said above, 'theology' is any 'discourse' in which, and through which, Christians seek to make sense of this world and their lives in relation to their God who is the Father of the Lord Jesus Christ. And conversely but in like manner, it is any 'discourse' though which these same people seek to make sense of the God and Father of their Lord Jesus Christ in relation to their lived experience of the thrownness of being human.

But, if so, then it has to be the case that theological 'discourse' must always seek to remember that it is not sufficient to have the tongues even of angels. Prophecies will cease, tongues will be stilled, knowledge will pass away but the basic theological acts of trust, perseverance, faith, hope and love will remain, and above all, love – through which comes what it is to know fully in being

---

[26] I have been sent for review a book on queer Christology (Christology beyond the orthodox margins). It is interesting to note reactions when I have left the book on the table to see whether people comment. Perhaps the most common reaction is that such a book should not even be in my reading list - such is the fear of the margin and beyond. The study of belief revision (expansion, revision, contraction) has become a branch of philosophy. See P. Gardenfors, *Belief Revision* (Cambridge: Cambridge University Press, 1992).

fully known (I Corinthians 13). Here is a deep challenge to our understanding of what it really is to be theologically educated. There is an aesthetic balance of word and act, of the active and the passive, of the objective and the subjective, of saying and seeing. And this is, perhaps, what we mean by beauty. Gregory Cootsona helps us to bring together theology as the study of God and science as the study of the world when he writes in relation to A.N. Whitehead:

> The twentieth-century mathematician and philosopher, Alfred North Whitehead, offered this provocative statement in his mature philosophical work, *Adventures in Ideas*: 'The teleology of the Universe is directed toward the production of Beauty'. This sentence from Whitehead points toward a rich and stimulating conception of beauty – not as mere ornamentation (ultimately as *cosmetics*), which one can place at the periphery or which possesses merely commercial important - but astonishingly as the central purpose of the universe. With this provocative assertion, Whitehead points toward the *purposive or teleological* element of beauty - what I will call the telos of beauty. As Whitehead is wont to do, he extends his claim as far as possible: beauty structures and directs the final aim of the universe. Or more simply, beauty directs the universe. Whitehead makes an assertion that combines beauty in science with art and metaphysics, *which is not a far distance from theology.*[27]

But where is theology in relation to the beauty of the world and the beauty of God? How should the theologically educated person think into this issue? In this spirit, the following question was put to Pope Benedict XVI:

> Holy Father, my name is Willibald Hopfgartner, and I am a Franciscan. In your address in Regensburg, you emphasized the substantial connection between the divine Spirit and human reason. On the other hand, you have also always emphasized the importance of art and beauty. So then, together with conceptual dialogue about God in theology, should there not always be a new presentation of the aesthetic experience of the faith within the Church, through proclamation and the liturgy?

Pope Benedict XVI answered (I have omitted some text less related to my topic):

> Yes, I think that the two things go together: reason, precision, honesty in the reflection on truth, and beauty. A form of reason that in any way wanted to strip itself of beauty would be depleted, it would be blind. Only when the two are united do they form the whole, and this union is important precisely for the faith....

[27] G.S. Cootsona, 'The Telos of Beauty: A Common Quest for Theologians and Scientists', *The Global Spiral, an e-publication of Metanexus Institute* (2007), http://www.metanexus.net/Magazine/tabid/68/id/10032/Default.aspx Accessed on 18.02.10. My italics.

In his first letter, St. Peter wrote...: 'Always be ready to give an explanation to anyone who asks you for a reason for your hope' – an apologia for the 'logos' of hope, meaning a transformation of the 'logos', the reason for hope, into an apologia, an answer addressed to men. He was clearly convinced of the fact that faith is 'logos', that it is a form of reason.... This is why it is universal, and for this reason it can be communicated to all.

But this creating 'Logos' is not a merely technical 'logos'. It is broader than this, it is a 'logos' that is love, and therefore to be expressed in beauty and goodness. And in reality, for me art and the saints are the greatest apologia for our faith...

...if we contemplate the created beauties of the faith, these simply are, I would say, the living proof of faith. Take this beautiful cathedral: it is a living proclamation! It speaks to us on its own, and beginning with the beauty of the cathedral we are able to proclaim in a visible way God, Christ and all of his mysteries: here these have taken shape, and are gazing back at us. All of the great works of art, the cathedrals – the Gothic cathedrals, and the splendid Baroque churches – all of them are a luminous sign of God, and therefore truly a manifestation, an epiphany of God.

...I think that the great music born within the Church is an audible and perceptible rendering of the truth of our faith: ...Listening to all of these great works – the Passions by Bach, his Mass in B minor, and the great spiritual compositions of 16th century polyphony, of the Viennese school, of all of this music, even by minor composers – suddenly we feel: it is true! Wherever things like these are created, there is Truth.

Without an intuition capable of discovering the true creative center of the world, this beauty cannot be created. For this reason, I think that we must always act in such a way that these two things go together, we must present them together. When, in our own time, we discuss the reasonableness of the faith, we are discussing precisely the fact that reason does not end where experimental discoveries end, it does not end in positivism; the theory of evolution sees the truth, but sees only half of it: it does not see that behind this is the Spirit of creation. We are fighting for the expansion of reason, and therefore for a form of reason that, exactly to the point, is open to beauty as well, and does not have to leave it aside as something completely different and irrational.

Christian art is a rational form of art – we think of Gothic art, great music, or the Baroque art right here – but this is the artistic expression of a much broader form of reason, in which the heart and reason come together. This is the point. This, I think, is in some way the proof of the truth of Christianity: the heart and reason come together, beauty and truth touch. And to the extent that we are able to live in the beauty of truth, so much more will faith again be able to be creative, in our own time as well, and to express itself in a convincing artistic form.[28]

So my eighth characteristic of the theologically educated person is that that their theology expresses itself aesthetically as a fully embodied theology of action, as a performing art, as the heart and the reason coming together in creativity and expression. Living before God in the world is itself the prime expression of being humanly aesthetic.

I now turn to consider the place of creativity in being theologically educated.

Hermeneutics of Action: Theology as Expressive Response

There is a difference between saying, as I have just done, that theology *expresses itself* aesthetically as a performing art, and claiming that theology is a *hermeneutic of action*[29] – that it is in itself, and through and through, *expressive response*. I have three modes of expressive response in mind as constituting how theology operates. The first is expressive response towards God, namely worship. The second is expressive response towards the world as we hold it before God. (This importantly includes our expressive response to the world as ambiguous between good and evil or even frequently hostile.) The third is expressive response towards each other in solidarity. Taken together I am terming these a 'hermeneutic of action'.

The first of these, expressive response towards God, is undoubtedly a problem for anyone dealing with theology as a subject in the humanities, which is where it is usually located in Universities. This is too large a topic to treat here except to say that to the extent to which this paper is cogent, to that same extent what passes for theology in Universities is lacking in the precise dimension which makes theology what it is when it is at home, namely, in the Christian community of worship. An example of this is found in the way Anselm's Ontological argument is typically located within the philosophy of religion courses whereas, in fact, it was set within Anselm's prayer life as he worshipped. As he knelt before God, he pondered the nature of the God he worshipped. It is Anselm's expressive response through an aesthetic balance, within an act of worship, of the needs of the mind and the needs of the heart. It needs to be read and pondered in the same mode. It is an endemic problem in University theology that theology is handled academically apart from the worshipping heart.

---

[28] S. Magister, 'Pope: The Proof of God Is Beauty' (2008), http://www.catholic.org/international/international_story.php?id=30760. Accessed on 18.02.10.

[29] This is of course a term associated with Paul Ricoeur. I share much of what he is aiming for but I use the term here independently of his use. See R. Kearney, ed., *Paul Ricoeur: The Hermeneutics of Action* (London: Sage Publications Ltd., 1996).

The second, expressive response – to the world, including its ambiguities and evils – requires of the theologically educated person that they do theology 'on the ground' and not 'in the air'.[30] I use the word 'do' here with some reluctance but also with deliberation. In a PhD seminar a student was presenting a paper on liturgical reform and constantly using the expression 'doing Church'. At the time I winced, but I have come to see that there is an important point being made here, namely that theology, doctrine and liturgy are all 'in the air' unless they are conceived and perceived as a 'doing'. They all need to come within a hermeneutic of action. The gospel is God's call: it demands response. God is 'Our Father': we respond as children. To be theologically educated is to know how to go into the world as those who have been called by the God whose world it is. And to express therein the character of that God as revealed in Jesus Christ, his firstborn.

The third expressive response is that of solidarity in Christ as Christians respond to each other. This is an inbuilt bias to ecumenism and against factionalism (to use a hard word for denominational theology). It is a gospel that embraces and includes. It is the expressive response of love. But, again, this is a large topic that will not be treated further here.

It has been argued in papers elsewhere in this book, for example by Bernhard Ott, that theology must be thoroughly missional and I take this to mean thoroughly based in action. That is well said by Ott. The exegesis/hermeneutic of *any* text given centrality within theology will in this way, be through a hermeneutic of action. Such texts can only justify their centrality in Christian thought if they illuminate how God has acted among us and through us, and in turn how we should act before and for God. The theological critique becomes the extent to which such texts make action with and for God possible. And the theological reflection becomes how the action they provoke is best performed. The ninth characteristic of being theologically educated, therefore, is that of the 'action turn'[31] through which the nature of the

---

[30] I am indebted for this distinction to colleagues at St Paul's Limuru, Kenya who offer an MA in Community Care and HIV/AIDS which delivers actual care and training of carers as an intrinsic part of the qualification. The terms were used by a visiting party from Cote d'Ivoire who were comparing their own theology curriculum with that of the SPL MA which is premised on theology being expressive response to the world as it is held before God. OCMS led the design of this MA.

[31] 'The action turn' stands over against 'the linguistic turn' that was a development in western philosophy during the 20th century. Its most important characteristic is its focus on philosophy and language. Ludwig Wittgenstein's influence is strong as the term follows from his claim that philosophical problems arise from a misunderstanding of the logic of language and his later comments on language games. See P. Reason and W.R. Torbert, 'The Action Turn: Toward a Transformational Social Science', *Toward a Transformational Science: a further look at the scientific merits of action research. Concepts and Transformations* 6:1 (2001). Also see R.M. Rorty, ed., *The Linguistic*

God who acts becomes our nature also. It adds the hand of toil and the foot of travel to the heart and reason to which Pope Benedict referred (see above). To be theologically educated is to understand that hermeneutics is an orientation to action and not just an interpretation of text.

Phronesis – Theology as the Practice of Wisdom

Phronesis is practical wisdom, or knowledge of the proper ends of life. Aristotle distinguished this from theoretical knowledge and mere means-end reasoning or craft, and considered it to be a necessary and sufficient condition of virtue. It can perhaps be associated with Wittgenstein's definition of understanding as 'knowing what to do next'.[32]

Consider the definitional statement: 'God is love'. This is knowledge, but it does not necessitate understanding in the sense of phronesis. Similarly, 'the loving God' (adjectival) is descriptive and informative, but it does not demand phronesis. 'However, God acts lovingly' (active) does call for phronesis. It simultaneously shows and demands the proper ends of life for God and therefore also for us, as we are drawn into His love.

Therefore I would say that the tenth characteristic of 'thinking' theologically and of being theologically educated, is that of making all the other nine characteristics dynamically cohere *as an act of phronesis* – as practical wisdom that brings coherence to the other nine characteristics.

Conclusion

By way of reminder, these characteristics are:

Being theologically knowledgeable… and more
Being theologically skilled… more… and less
'Sensing' God's world
Theologizing contextually
Allowing experiential primacy and seeing theology as biography
Becoming progressive and playful and experimental
Becoming communicative, social and relational – and challenging
Becoming theologically aesthetic and expressive
Hermeneutics of action: Theology as expressive response

To be able to engage in theology that has these characteristics, and to be able to hold them together as practical wisdom, is what it is to become theologically educated. Which point and conclusion bring us full circle to my opening sentences. The papers in this book provide many insights into theological

---

Turn: Essays in Philosophical Method (Chicago: The University of Chicago Press, 1992).

[32] G.P. Baker and P.M.S. Hacker, *Wittgenstein: Understanding and Meaning*, 2 ed. (Oxford: Blackwell Publishing, 2005).

education. They offer an account of where we have been in the recent past. This Preface is written as a challenge to move forward. Such progress depends, perhaps, on sorting out what is the right question to ask in relation to 'theological education'.

And how to answer it.

PART 1

Institutional Development for Theological Education

Transforming Theological Education through Multi-Institutional Partnerships

Timothy Dearborn

The Rev. Dr. Timothy Dearborn is Associate Director for Faith and Development with World Vision International.

Introduction

We have entrusted to our seminaries and theological schools a daunting responsibility. They are expected to prepare wise, compassionate, theologically astute and pastorally proficient servants who can lead the church and our societies through the crises of the twenty-first century. However, during this century, the theological schools of the Western world have adopted methods for fulfilling this responsibility which, some would say, guarantee their failure. Others, who are more gracious, would admit that current methods at least make success difficult. If the goal is indeed to prepare creative, visionary, dynamic leaders who love God, love people and love God's purposes in the world with a contagious passion, we could not have intentionally chosen more inadequate means.

To state the problem in extreme terms, I am coming to the conclusion that there is no other professional organization in the world which allows its primary professional training institutions to produce graduates who are generally as functionally incompetent as the church permits her seminaries. Most pastors feel unprepared by their seminary education for the demands of pastoral ministry. Can you imagine a medical school retaining its certification if its graduates' first exposure to surgery was as the surgeons? They may have had brilliant lectures on anatomy and oncology. They may even have seen colour slides of brain surgery. Possibly they were provided with cadavers upon which they could practice. They successfully complete difficult written examinations, and at graduation are given their first stethoscopes and scalpels. Now, for the first time in their life, they see human flesh being cut into. They watch surgical saws cut through human skull bones. And their hands are wielding the weapons! Tragically, that's the scenario most of our seminaries and theological schools are still following. The first memorial service I ever attended in my life was as the officiant. The first time I had ever seen someone die in the hospital was as their pastor. The first sermon I ever preached was before a congregation. The first couple in marriage crisis I ever encountered was as their supposed therapist. The first budget I ever saw developed was as a programme administrator.

I may have been able to write 20-page papers on heaven, prepare brilliant strategies for church growth and articulate a clear understanding of marriage. I knew great theories of communication and the servant role of the pastor. However, no one had ever guided me in how to live out these truths. Even worse, many people emerge from seminary less equipped for ministry than they entered. Eager students entrust three years of their lives to a seminary in order to be better equipped to love God, people and the world with all their hearts, soul, strength and mind. Yet too often they graduate feeling spiritually cold, theologically confused, biblically uncertain, relationally calloused and professionally unprepared.

Tragic Consequences

The results of this are obvious. It has rightly been said that the church is like Columbus: going to a destination he knew not where, seeking something he would not recognize once he found it, and doing it all on someone else's money. There is an extraordinary absence of clarity regarding the role of pastors. During 1994, I assisted the Murdock Charitable Trust of Vancouver, WA in conducting a study of the future of theological education in the Pacific Northwest of the U.S. One component of the study was to survey hundreds of laypersons, pastors and seminary professors regarding the qualities of a good pastor. No suggestions were given. Rather, participants described their own perceptions. The discrepancy among the three groups is very revealing. Especially interesting is the different priority placed on spirituality (first for laypersons, fourth for clergy, non-existent for professors); on theological knowledge (first for professors, and fifth for laity and clergy); that only laypersons esteemed relational skills among clergy; that clergy placed highest priority on their position as role models (a role that neither laypersons nor professors valued for pastors); and that pastors omitted placing a priority on their own character!

No wonder there exists the most serious disenchantment of seminaries, pastors and laypersons with one another in history. Many churches are deciding that they can more adequately prepare leaders themselves, and are not sending students to seminaries. Some denominations are altering their degree requirements and determining that an MDiv, the traditional North American degree required for clergy, is not necessary. A growing number of laypersons are questioning the importance of ordination and the specialized role of pastors. Further, they are becoming disillusioned with large churches which function more like poorly run corporations than the Body of Christ. Laypersons feel under-valued and under-equipped. I have interviewed over 150 laypersons from various occupations over the past three years. More than 90 per cent indicated that they have never received any significant support, guidance or even interest regarding their jobs from their pastor. The church is more interested in their volunteer time than in their occupations. Their jobs are validated as means to other ends: income to contribute to Christian causes, places of evangelism, ways to deepen the credibility of the church. Few find from their church significant support or guidance in integrating their work into their faith, and in addressing the complex ethical, economic and leadership issues they face at work with the resources of the Gospel. Furthermore, professors feel under attack. The rules for their roles have changed without anyone telling them. It used to be that the sole requirement was for them to be outstanding academicians. Now, they are being criticized by their administrators, students and the church for failing to do that which they did not know they were supposed to, and for which they feel very unequipped. In addition to being brilliant scholars in their fields, professors are now expected to be enthusiastic classroom performers – able to hold the attention of tired adult students in evening lectures; experienced and veteran pastors; compassionate counsellors able to help students through complex personal crises; seasoned missionaries and urban evangelists; spiritual directors for their students; and skilled mentors in ministry of students as well as graduates.

A final consequence is the tragic fact that our Christian institutions – schools and seminaries, churches and mission societies are more driven by the dictates of the market than by the force of their vision for the coming Kingdom. Our major Christian magazines would go out of business if it were not for the revenue gained by advertisements from seminaries. The number of MDiv students in North America has remained static over the past ten years, about 28,000 students. The number of institutions and programmes has increased dramatically. Thus, institutions (and churches are no exception), are relentlessly seeking to be seeker-sensitive, providing people what they want before their competitors get to them

Simple Solution: Five-fold Transformation

The solution to this tragedy is obvious and simple. For the last three years, I have had the privilege of leading an innovative effort to provide an alternative. When I say 'obvious', I must admit that not everyone is convinced; and when I say 'simple', I do not mean 'easy'. The political and organizational complexities of the solution we are developing create the most demanding challenge I have ever encountered. Friends who are executives in major corporations indicate to me that they have never encountered in business anything as complex as that in which I am engaged, theological education. However, I still insist that the solution is simple and obvious. I will illustrate it by looking at a very different professional education system.

In 1911, the U.S. government concluded a major survey of physician competency in the U.S. They determined that the graduates of two medical schools were significantly better prepared than those from all others. Johns Hopkins and Harvard were more effective for one reason: they were the only medical schools in partnership with teaching hospitals. Within five years of the publication of this study, every medical school in the U.S. had entered into partnerships with hospitals. This is precisely what we are doing in Seattle – developing partnerships between theological schools and teaching churches. I will describe how it is being developed by contrasting the current seminary approach with the one we are implementing, which I audaciously will call the approach of the future. I am convinced that if we can successfully develop this model, then in the years to come, most graduate theological education programmes will be partnerships between schools and churches. I will describe what this looks like as a five-fold transformation in theological education through multi-institutional partnerships. The transformation is fundamentally simple, for all it involves us: transforming the institution; transforming the curriculum; transforming the faculty; transforming the student; and, transforming the process!

Transforming the Institution: Who Provides Theological Education?

I believe I have said enough about the separation that exists between churches and seminaries. However, more needs to be said about the separation among seminaries themselves. One of the objectives of seminary education is to prepare leaders who can participate in the Holy Spirit's work of building the Body up into unity in Christ. Yet, seminaries exist in fierce competition one with another. Each guards its best programme secrets as if confronted with the worst forms of corporate espionage. Bidding for premier faculty members rivals that between professional sports teams. The marketing of institutions is increasingly expensive and slick, spending millions of dollars to employ ad agencies who market seminaries as they would tennis shoes and new model cars.

As in business, the future of theological education rests in creative partnerships between multiple institutions that enter into joint ventures in order to design and deliver a better 'product' that could be done autonomously. Instead of competition existing extrinsically, between rival institutions, those which are the most successfully creative invite an element of healthy competition within their enterprise through joint ventures. The Seattle Association is a joint venture between three academic institutions and over 45 churches which seeks to unite the best of academia and the best of the parish in instructional partnerships. This overcomes both the captivity of theological education to theory, and the intrinsic resistance to change found among all academicians. Similarly, it overcomes the pragmatic and parochial bias of the parish, giving churches an opportunity to benefit from wider vistas. We believe that just as accreditation by the academy is indispensable for theological education, it must become equally indispensable to receive accreditation by the churches.

Several convictions are foundational to this approach. First, theological education is the privileged responsibility of the whole people of God. Church and seminary, professors and pastors, laypersons and religious 'professionals' all have vital contributions in the formation of people for pastoral ministry. Churches have always been expected to own the 'product' of theological education. Now they need to own their share of the 'process'. We've implemented through boards and advisory bodies, processes through which decisions about faculty, curriculum, and academic policies are made mutually by representatives from the academy, the parish and the workplace. Further, we have implemented mentoring relationships through which pastors and laypersons are involved directly in providing instruction. Second, theological education is best provided to part-time students who are full-time Christian servants. Training for ministry should occur in ministry, rather than before ministry. Students need the time to integrate into their lives that which they are learning. Third, the location in which instruction occurs should reflect the goal of the instruction. Rather than having the majority of classes in the academy, which reflects a world of theory and even detachment from ordinary life, we have our course in churches, office buildings, prisons, and drop-in centres for prostitutes. We want the very walls to teach, calling students to the integration of theory and praxis. We offer 50 courses a year, and use over 20 different locations for classes.

As a result of these convictions, we believe that the academy and the church must be knit together so that each can contribute its distinctive roles to the formation of people for ministry. We believe there is a five-fold community which must be formed between the church and the seminary in order to maximize each other's unique contribution to the formation of people for ministry. First, they exist as a spiritual community, for each is part of the Body of Christ. The prime role for each is indeed as a 'seminary' – a 'seedbed for piety', and each participates in the Spirit's work of equipping the people of God to be built up into unity in Christ. Second, they form a hermeneutical community. Each has a distinct contribution in enabling Christians to reflect about the biblical-theological-historical 'text', and to reflect about our present cultural-social 'context'. Such reflection is deficient without the input of the other partner. Third, they provide a community of critical inquiry. Both have roles in submitting the people of God to a loving, critical reflection about their faith and practice. The academy's critical reflection without being rooted in the realities of the parish and world can be esoteric and fantastical. The church's self-criticism, without the objective detachment of the academy, can be culturally captive and narcissistic. Fourth, they exist as a praxiological community. Each provokes the other to envision and implement ever more faithful expressions of the coming Kingdom of God. The church calls the academy to be faithful to God's mission in people's lives. The academy calls the church to ministry with biblical and theological integrity. Fifth, they provide the world with expressions of a community of cooperation. Our balkanized, militarized world, in which religious people are tragically on the frontline of schisms, distrust and separatism, urgently needs visible expressions of community in diversity. In our programmes, students, laypersons and pastors gather from over fifty different denominations to study, pray and reflect together. There is no similar gathering point that draws the people of God in all their diversity around the Person of Christ. Though disagreements over ecclesiology, eschatology and missiology are usually intense, though personality and ethnic differences often provoke challenging tensions, it is thrilling to see God manifest the coming oneness of his people.

Transforming the Curriculum: What Is Studied?

Typically, the curriculum of theological education is retrospective. It is assumed that by gaining some mastery of the past, we will inevitably be better equipped to face the complexities of the future. There is some truth to this. We have all repeated the 'those who are ignorant of the errors of the past are destined to repeat them' axiom. However, the leadership crisis in our Church and our societies more than merely suggests that studying ancient languages, ancient events, ancient sages, and ancient responses to ancient problems is not sufficient. I have reviewed the curriculum of a dozen major theological schools. On average, they require 5000 hours of a student's life over three to four years to prepare them for ministry. The average investment of this time is as follows: Electives 17%, Theology 16%, Greek and Hebrew 15%, Bible 15%, Field education 15%, Ministry Skills 10%, Church History 6%, Communication 4%, Church and Society 2%. Greek and Hebrew, Church History and Historical Theology all have important places in the seminary curriculum. Leaders must clearly understand where we have been and who we are. That is true. However, they also must have a sense of where we are going. Leaders who are past, rather than future-focused, are a contradiction in terms.

Rather than designing a curriculum around required bodies of knowledge, we believe the curriculum needs to help students develop areas of competency. One component of the Murdock study was a conference with seminary deans, faculty and clergy and lay leaders. The aim of this was to begin with a 'blank sheet' and design an ideal curriculum to prepare people for pastoral ministry. After assessing present needs and future trends, we then set out to describe the leadership qualities required to lead the church into the twenty-first century. Beginning with the prioritized lists of qualities provided through the above-mentioned survey of laity, clergy and professors, we developed a much more exhaustive (and exhausting) set of competencies. They are not prioritized, for all were recognized to be essential. These include an ability to: accept and express the grace of God; accept one's own inadequacies, to ask for help and to admit need; embrace life in Christ before service of Christ with mature patterns of discipleship and prayer; live as one member of the community of faith; reflect theologically in the context of ministry; engage in an incarnational approach to ministry; enable people to grow towards maturity in Christ; build up rather than merely maintain; deal with lack of response and with burnout;

equip and inspire laypersons to live as missionaries; discern a clear direction and to inspire and lead others toward those objectives; teach biblical truth with clarity and relevance; speak the language of one's surrounding culture; live comfortably in one's surrounding culture; relate to diverse people; to help people discover their worth in Christ; to make do, to improvise and; focus on what one can do - not expect to solve all problems.

We then asked, 'In light of these qualities, if you could only teach students one course, what course would be the highest priority?' After composing our lists, we then asked, 'If you could offer ten courses, what would you require?' Our prioritized list was as follows: Ministry and Spirituality; English Bible; Historical Overview of Christianity; Christianity and Culture; Evangelism and Mission; Spiritual Leadership; Hermeneutics; Theology of Ministry; Personal Growth and Skill Development; and Communication.

It was noted that few, if any, of these courses are currently required as foundational in most seminaries' curricula. We are taking these insights seriously in the programme we are implementing in Seattle. Students begin their studies by engaging in an assessment of their own understanding and abilities in the qualities listed above. This is administered as a self-assessment, as well as an assessment made by several friends and the pastor of the student. From this, some insight is provided into the student's learning needs, and aspects of the curriculum can be 'custom-designed' around what the student requires to grow into greater maturity in Christ and effectiveness as a leader. We have begun to revise one-third of the traditional MDiv curriculum in accordance with the need for students to develop areas of competence. However, because of the deep sensitivity faculty feel over curriculum reform, so far our prime focus has been on the other three aspects of transformation: who teaches, who is taught and on how teaching is provided.

Transforming the Faculty: Who Teaches?

Seminary professors are usually expected to be experts in four spheres. First, through their doctoral studies and on-going research, they have cultivated expertise on some dimension of the past. Second, they have focused their study on some minute, specific aspect of the past: a portion of Scripture, an event or figure in history, a disputed point in theology. Their credentials are gained through a microscopic attentiveness to detail. Third, they are experts with ideas. Ideas captivate their curiosity and compel their most intense reflection. Fourth, they are experts on words. Words are their primary tools. Each one must be carefully selected. These are commendable strengths. The Body of Christ relies on the depth of insight and the thorough ways in which the Gospel, the church and the world can be examined with these forms of expertise. However, as has already been suggested, a retrospective focus is not sufficient if we are to be prepared for the future; a grasp of minutiae does not help us notice major trends; microscopic analysis can never help us see the 'big picture'; words and ideas alone will not equip us to be better lovers. It is increasingly being recognized that theological faculty must also be selected because of their pastoral experience, their personal spirituality and character, and their capacity to motivate and mobilize the people of God for the challenges of the future.

The curriculum conference which I described earlier continued by discussing the qualities of faculty members which would be required to teach the kind of curriculum we had outlined. We developed a prioritized list of ten qualities: Spirituality: passion for Jesus, personal godliness; Vision: ability to inspire, instil vision in others; Pastoral gifts and ministry experience; Communication ability; Scholarship: Research, analysis, reflection, publication; Servant mentality; Personal transparency; Love for the church; Love of culture; Love of diversity among people.

Though all theological schools need to have some research scholars on their faculties, we are recognizing that a seminary requires a mixture of gifts within its faculty team. Not everyone will be strong in all the desired qualities. A faculty team needs to be formed, not simply by filling needed positions in academic disciplines, but by filling needed positions in personal qualities and experience. We advertised for one faculty position this year in Seattle, and had over 180 applicants. Within our selection committee, we agreed upon five qualities we desired in a candidate: 'PhD and solid academic expertise; spiritual and relational maturity; adaptability and openness to innovation; pastoral and cross-cultural experience; excellence as an educator'. Out of that number of applicants, less than 20 had significant pastoral experience.

An even smaller number demonstrated insightful understanding of the needs for innovation in theological education. We are seeking a balance in our faculty between people who are insightful academicians, and people who are seasoned practitioners of the faith and adept at guiding others in personal growth. One way we are doing this is through team-teaching classes. For one-fourth of the MDiv curriculum in Seattle, half of the class sessions are taught by the seminary professor, and half are taught by students meeting in small groups with pastoral mentors. Mentors are selected because of their practical experience in living out the topic of the particular course, and because in their character and spirituality they embody qualities from which students could benefit. Through this, we are restoring to theological education the use of 'apprenticeships', which up until the mid-nineteenth century, had been the primary approach. This will be discussed more fully in our examination of transforming the process of theological education.

Transforming the Students: Who Studies?

Typically, students engage in theological studies with four motives. First, they have individually perceived a 'call' to pastoral ministry. Second, they are seeking personal growth and answers to personal questions. Third, they are undergoing a vocational transition. Possibly, they have lost their job, and are wondering if their lives might be more fruitful as pastors. Fourth, they may be frustrated with their current lay vocation, and are seeking more immediate integration of their work and their faith. Seminaries thus are dealing with 'raw material' which may need extensive preparation. Faculty members are frequently commenting that a significant portion of their time must be spent on helping students face areas of deep personal brokenness, helping them develop basic spiritual disciplines, and helping them discern direction for their lives and ministry. In the past, it was assumed that these personal needs had already been met in a student's life, prior to beginning theological studies. That can no longer be assumed. The church has suffered because of the long-standing misunderstanding it has held that the seminaries were preparing people for ministry; for seminaries have assumed that the church was dosing that, and that their responsibility was solely theological education. Furthermore, the Body of Christ invests millions of dollars per year to subsidize theological education. On average, student tuition pays 50 per cent of the cost of the education. Probably the most important factor in theological education, more important than institution, faculty or curriculum, is the student. Because others are paying for the individual's education, the selection of students must be more than an individual concern. However, because of the market-driven education, and the need to maintain enrolment, very few seminaries are significantly selective in their admission policy. Any applicant with an adequate educational background, with reasonable psychological stability, and with the ability to pay is accepted.

In response to this, many seminaries (ours included), have introduced a two-tiered admission process. Students with adequate qualifications can be admitted to begin their theological studies. However, only students with a call to pastoral ministry which is confirmed by the Body of Christ, with proven ministry experience and skills, and with significant personal maturity are admitted to complete the MDiv degree programme. These students are assessed at entrance, in order to discern their learning needs. They are given constant assessment by professors, mentors and ministry supervisors regarding their preparation for ministry; and upon graduation we intend to provide them with a profile describing their readiness for various areas of ministry. Because of this, there is a significant attrition rate. This is not viewed as a failure, but as a positive step in enabling students to discern God's leading in their life. Throughout their studies, students are in a learning support group, composed of a pastor and two laypersons who the student selects, who are charged with the responsibility of supporting and evaluating the student's progress. As friends of the student, they are entrusted with helping the student evaluate his or her call to pastoral ministry. This is another example of the absolute necessity of a church/seminary partnership. Only those who know a student outside of the academic context can adequately assess his or her total giftedness and readiness for ministry. Those within the academic context, who are involved in a student's theological and cognitive growth and development, can most adequately assess his or her growth in and understanding of the Gospel, the church and God's mission in the world. It is imperative that people form both the church and the seminary work together in a student's formation.

Transforming the Process: How Do People Study?

Five qualities characterize our typical, current process of theological education. First, it is primarily theoretical. Students listen to lectures, read and write about Scripture, theology, history and ministry. We expect them to be able on their own to make the transition from theory to application. The supervision received for field education experiences often is unrelated to the theoretical perspectives taught in the classroom. Second, it is primarily mono-focused and designed for full-time students. In fact, most seminary faculty covet the full-time attention of their students, and struggle deeply with the distractions students experience from part-time jobs and ministry experiences. Faculty lament students' difficulty in concentrating on their studies. Third, it is individualized and competitive. Students study and are evaluated according to their individual performance. Even though seminaries may value student community life, often this is extraneous and superficial. Fourth, it is institution- rather than learner-centred. The theological school dictates what a student must learn, without much regard for past experience. Fifth, it is expensive. Most students have to go into debt even to fund the portion of the instructional costs they pay through tuition. Yet, they are entering relatively low-income professions.

In Seattle, we believe that the traditional process is inadequate on all five counts. First, the process must be integrated. Full attention must be given to all aspects of formation: academic and intellectual, spiritual and personal, pastoral and relational. Students must be constantly encouraged to apply what they are learning. For example, one idea we are seeking to implement in Seattle is to have students teach what they have learned through a seminary course in a church adult education class. Part of a course requirement will be to design a five-week adult class which teaches the central ideas of the course in a church. During the quarter following the seminary class, students will work with a church pastor and adult education coordinator to refine and then teach the class. Participants in the church adult class will be evaluated to determine what they actually learned. This will be incorporated into the students' assessment. Two other aspects of integration we are incorporating in Seattle have already been mentioned. Eight courses are team-taught by the seminary professor and by pastor mentors. Students do the theological equivalent of medical students' 'rotations'. In this case, rather than paediatrics, oncology and geriatrics being the topics, students follow pastors on 'rounds' studying Christian education, urban evangelism, pastoral counselling, world mission, pastoral theology, worship, homiletics and church leadership. In addition, the students' 'learning support groups' perform important integrative roles in their personal formation.

Second, the process must reflect real life. No one, and especially no pastor, has the luxury of being mono-focused. The art of life, and particularly, of pastoral ministry is the art of juggling multiple responsibilities and conflicting expectations. Therefore, we believe it is optimal for students to study part-time, so that they can more effectively integrate into their lives that which they are learning. Though it creates extraordinary tension, we also believe it is preferable for students to prepare for ministry while being in ministry. Thus, part-time work and part-time involvement in ministry are highly valued components of a student's learning process. Rather than being distractions from studies, they are embraced as additional classrooms. Not only do students learn more about life through this, they also develop their scheduling, prioritizing and life-management skills.

Third, the process must be relational. We embrace a relational theology: God exists in community and has reconciled us to himself and one another in Jesus Christ. The only process which can adequately teach that theology is relational. Therefore, we accept students into classes of 25 people, and they study together as a community for one-third of their curriculum. The mutual support, reconciliation after conflict, and capacity to deal fruitfully with differences which students experience in these 'cohort' groups are unquestionably some of the most helpful results of their experience as theological students.

Fourth, the process must address students' learning needs. The average age of our students is almost forty. They do not all need to learn the same things. Mandating a pre-arranged curriculum is foolish stewardship of a student's time and life. By incorporating pastoral and lay mentors, and providing extensive opportunities for the assessment of students' learning needs prior to a course, we can custom-design many aspects of the learning experience.

Fifth, the process must be less expensive. The Body of Christ and our global economy cannot afford the proliferation of our expensive, competitive, institution-centred theological education programmes. We must provide high-quality, but lower-cost approaches to formation for ministry. So far, we have found four means to facilitate this in Seattle. First, though we have 450 students and offer 50 courses per year, we do not have a campus. We rely on rented office space, and on churches as our classrooms. Second, through multiple academic institutions cooperating and offering courses jointly, the net costs to each institution can be reduced. Third, we rely heavily on volunteers. This year, over 300 people volunteered to participate in the ministry formation of some of our 450 students. If the institutions or the students had to pay for this, the costs would be astronomical. Finally, by encouraging students to study part-time, they can remain employed and 'pay as they go'. Thus, it is not necessary for students to go into debt, or to depend upon donations to pay their tuition and living expenses.

Conclusion

From my perspective, much of what I have said is self-evident. There is nothing surprising. It seems so logical. From the vantage point of established approaches to theological education however, it is scandalous. The surrender of institutional autonomy through partnerships with churches and other academic institutions is challenging. The potential loss of an institution's 'market share' by working with 'rival' educational institutions is threatening. Allowing 'non-academicians' to exercise instructional roles calls into question the job security, and the years of preparation of professors. Yet, from the perspective of the Kingdom of God and the qualities needed to lead the people of God into the twenty-first century, we have no other option. The creative synergy which is unleashed when inherently competitive and dissimilar organizations cooperate is dynamically fruitful. The enhancement of students' readiness for ministry through an intentionally integrated approach to formation is evident. We live in cultures which are preoccupied with power, autonomy and control.

The Body of Christ needs leaders for the church and workplace who understand the world-transforming power of life in community, where personhood is treasured, but individual autonomy and control are not. If the goal of theological education is not propagating information, but rather enabling transformation in community, then the process must reflect that goal. Furthermore, if that transformation is for the church and society, then the recipients of the process need to be clerical as well as lay leaders. Though I have focused this report on theological education for clergy, we are devoting nearly equal time in Seattle to providing educational opportunities for business people, educators, doctors and labourers. As Lesslie Newbigin so aptly says, we must ask 'what kind of training is specifically needed to enable a psychiatrist, teacher, executive, lawyer or civil servant to discern the ways which her profession could be subverted from its allegiances to other principles and become an area where the saving work of Christ is acknowledged?' Finally, the heart of theological-education-in-community, like the heart of life, is worship. We are seeking transformation for passion. Life in Christ, and life through Christ in ministry only does honour to God if it is a love affair. We will never outlive the *Shema* of Israel and its call 'to love the Lord our God with all our heart, soul, strength and mind' and to love our neighbour as ourselves. Education which does not help us grow to be better lovers is heretical and indeed, blasphemous. If that capacity to love one another in Christ cannot be explicitly and tangibly manifest in our theological education institutions, curriculum, faculty, students and process, then we are not qualified to be theological educators.

Presidency or Principalship with Special Reference to the Two-Third World

Horace O. Russell

Dr. Horace O. Russell is Dean of Chapel and Professor of Historical Theology at the Eastern Baptist Theological Seminary in Philadelphia, USA..

There is a sense in which leaderships of institutions anywhere in the world have certain common characteristics. What makes them different is time, place and opportunity. Leadership, of which the College or Seminary President is one form, has to be a representative symbol. He or she has to be able to motivate not only the institution over which he or she presides but also those who support it and this will include overseas mission boards, foundations and the churches. He or she must be able to exert discipline and be self-disciplined and must also be able to provide continuity in the replacement of himself or herself. In the Two-Thirds World these values are often intricately intertwined with the values of the society in which the institution is set. These values are religious values which are a mixture, at times an amalgam, of traditional religious values with an overlay of imposed Christian values, values derived from the Christian colonizer.

This is not to say that the personal Christian faith is not real. It is to say that the institutions created, and the theological institutions and universities are not excluded, bear the marks of the colonizer. Thus, where European nations were in control the institutions bear their national marks, and similarly where the United States of America has been, the same things are apparent. When there is added the new or transnational, global and inter-church organizations like the Theological Education Fund and the Theological Commissions of various sorts, the issues are even more complex. In short, leadership in the Two-Thirds World has the great difficulty of not only relating authentically to the local situation but discovering new models which must refashion the legacies of the past within the current pressures of post colonialism, neo-colonialism and post-modernity. Despite what appears to be a rather gloomy and daunting picture, there are a few observations which might be made.

The Presidency has a ministry which is representational and relational. The Presidency or Principalship must reflect the ethos and meaning of the institution both intramurally and extramurally. Sooner rather than later, what the President does becomes 'who' the President is. In a world where 'function' is interpreted as 'being', it is easy for the Presidency to become a beehive of activity. And because the institution over which he or she presides is one of learning and training the activity takes on these foci. The Presidency is the place to promote the academic integrity of the institution. It widens its programs. It creates diverse curricula so that funds are attracted. If due care is not taken, however, and the annual report can become a catalogue of how much money has been raised and how many new programs added. This should be avoided. There is also a great danger for the Presidency to overlook the aspect that it is also a representative of the training or spiritual formation being given in this institution. If the Presidency is to minister adequately, a proper balance must be struck between 'function' and 'being'. The spiritual demeanour of the President is as important or even more important than the academic or administrative credentials manifested. For it is this that students take with them into ministry.

Thus the President must be seen to worship and be in worship, leading and participating, and indeed as important is the participation in the ongoing life of the church as one who loves the Lord. While the foregoing seems quite obvious there are huge difficulties. The Presidency at times robs the incumbent of these very opportunities. There is the need to travel to raise money, generally overseas, in the Two-Thirds World context. These prolonged absences in the line of duty play havoc with relationships and with personal integrity. Grant-writing and proposals can dull the sensitivity to truth and objectivity and can develop a dependency quite inimical to sustainable theological education. This blunting of the enthusiasm of Christian witness and the undermining of spirituality has been the bane of many a Presidency and institution and must be guarded against.

The Presidency must in its ministry provide enablement to faculty, staff, administration, the governing boards, the churches and the community. This is a tall order but nothing less will do. That is why the President must be a motivator. It is a motivation which comes from the communication of a communal vision and planning. The secret of this ministry lies in developing a common mind around achievable tasks. It has to be a mind to which all components of the community have contributed. It is not enough to develop a mind within the academic community only. Ministry take place everywhere and this mind should also include spiritual concerns. The Presidency must be concerned with the faith question, as regards faculty, administration, staff and students. There is no suggestion here of a test or a witch hunt, but, to put it another way – spiritual formation must be the concern of all. This means that the President must model in himself or herself and the family the 'faith' with which the institution has been entrusted. The Presidency must motivate the community in this direction. This means among other things discipline and self-discipline. It means that in the administration of the institution there is the discipline of love which in turn must derive from the discipleship of obedience. No Presidency exists for itself but in order that the church and fellow believers might be obedient to the call and the will of God. So then, it is rooted in discipleship and as such is servant and enabler of the theological community for academic and spiritual matters.

The Presidency also provides continuity. It links the past and the future within the continuum of the present. While the present incumbent is valued and important, it is always good to recognize that the Presidency is a part of Christian tradition. In the Two-Thirds World where the church is very young, Christian tradition does not have the same appeal. Yet the church has been around for a long time and as such has developed traditions which we dismiss at our peril. She has given to us not only our theologies in print but our hymns and liturgical forms. Thus despite the strangeness of what was inherited and the modifications made daily there must yet be an eye to the past. But the future is also important and this is where a Mission Statement in the hands of a President is helpful. It helps to bridge the gap between the already gone and the not yet. But it cannot be written in stone despite the temptations. Not only are theological institutions not Sinai nor Horeb, Presidents, though at times they might think so, are not Moses. But God still speaks. It is here that the ministry of continuity begins. The Presidency is set where it has always been – around the Lord's Table. Justin Martyr alluded to this as he describes how the President took bread and wine and rehearsing the words of St. Paul would say, 'For I have received of the Lord that which I give to you' (1 Cor. 11:23 and *Apology I, Lxv-Lxvii*). This reciprocity of receipt and gift lie at the root of the Presidency. The Presidency is a reminder of the 'openness' of the Faith. It is a reminder that theological institutions are open and not final. There is a limitedness in the reciprocity for it is 'until He comes' (1 Cor. 11:26). This is an antidote for any inflated ideas of the achievement of a Presidency and allows for a modest understanding of one's place in the scheme of things.

The most difficult task of the Presidency is how to terminate it or when is it time to go. Most institutions possess regulations about this but despite this there are problems. These problems do not all the time derive from bad motives. At times there is a good Presidency which contributes to the well-being of the communities it serves and because of this it is kept, but inevitably it corrupts. In some instances this corruption derives from the fact that colleges and seminaries provide a scarce resource, education. It derives from the fact that in some places the Presidency is the highest paid job in the church and provides both prestige and propinquity to political and economic power. These are in themselves powerful seducers and when taken together are highly tempting. It is here that the Presidency must exercise its episcopal function by not succumbing to these things by remembering the model of Jesus.

In a word, the ministry of the Presidency is one of interpretation. It interprets the institution to the church/churches and the church/churches to the institution and both to the academic community and the world at large. The Presidency, therefore, can never be seen in individualistic or personal terms only. Where there is a cabinet or executive that is the Presidency and at times it also includes the faculty and the student body as well. Unless there is this collective understanding of the Presidency, especially in a Two-Thirds World setting the Presidency will not function well. This view of ecclesiastical leadership will at times be in conflict with the established practices of some ancient churches and some societies but let the consequences be as they may. Gone are the days of the patriarchal hierarchy for reasons with which we are all familiar and in its place has come collegiality. This does not mean that all decision-making has been taken away from the Presidency. There will always be the lonely times but at times like these it is good to know there is goodwill and prayerful support. It was St. Paul who reminded the Philippian Christians, 'Let your bearing towards one another arise out of your life in Christ Jesus. For the divine nature was his from the first, yet he did not think to snatch at equality with God but made himself nothing assuming the nature of a slave. Bearing the human likeness, revealed in human shape, he humbled himself and in obedience accepted even death – death on the Cross' (Phil. 2.5-8). This is the ultimate ministry of the Presidency and the rest is in the hands of God.

Mission Oriented Theological Education: Moving Beyond Traditional Models of Theological Education

Bernhard Ott

Dr. Bernhard Ott is Director of Studies at Theological Seminary Bienenberg, Liestal, Switzerland.

Introduction

In this paper, I would like to recommend four steps that can help lead us toward more fully mission oriented theological education. First of all, I will look at where we have come from in theological education. Secondly, I want us to consider the wider context of our culture. Thirdly, I explore theological criteria, before finally, outlining possible avenues into the future.

Pilgrimage: Where Are We Coming From?

We are here as theological educators. This certainly is not the first time we have reflected upon theological education. We all have our personal pilgrimage with theological education: as students at various stages and in different institutions; perhaps also as church leaders and/or missionaries experiencing the output of theological education; and as teachers and leaders of educational institutions. In our memories, we have good experiences and models to follow, but probably also bad experiences, examples of failure, models not to be followed. It would be interesting to listen to and to reflect upon all the different pilgrimages represented in this room. I want to stimulate personal reflection and perhaps informal discussion by pointing to our common pilgrimage. Most contemporary evangelical institutions of theological education draw from three educational traditions:

The so-called Bible school movement must be seen in close relation to *the modern missionary movement*, especially the faith mission movement.[38] Early schools of this tradition were St. Chrischona in Basel, Switzerland, established 1840 (sometimes considered the first Bible school of this movement world-wide;[39] Spurgeon's Pastors' College, founded in 1856, and East London Institute for Home and Foreign Mission, established in 1873, both in England; and in North America, the New York Mission Training College (1883), Prairie

---

[38] K. Fiedler, *The Story of Faith Missions from Hudson Taylor to Present Day Africa* (Oxford: Regnum, 1994), 144ff.

[39] Fiedler, *The Story*, 145.

Bible Institute (1888), and Moody Bible Institute (1889).[40] The spirit of the missionary movement of the nineteenth century was the driving force in the early days of the Bible school movement. It is therefore beyond doubt that the early Bible schools were mission oriented. In order to estimate the contribution of the Bible school movement, we have to identify its specific ethos. Cheesman,[41] Fiedler,[42] Ferris and Enlow[43] and others have identified the following features of the Bible school ethos:

1. 'To train Christian workers without the "corrupting" influence of universities or liberal denominational colleges'.[44] The Bible school movement must be understood as 'a conservative response to the forfeiture of main-line seminaries to theological liberalism between 1890 and 1930'.[45]

2. 'To prepare non-ordained missionaries'.[46] Bible schools were mission schools by nature. According to Fiedler, 'they were to provide the new (faith) missions with trained missionaries.... Bible schools were uniquely intended for the training of missionaries/ evangelists abroad and at home'.[47]

3. 'To train lay people for witness'.[48] Bible schools expanded ministerial training beyond the limited circle of the academic elite studying in universities and seminaries. 'They were to provide missionary training for those who had no chance of receiving any theological training in the existing institutions, because they were not qualified and/or not wealthy enough to be accepted in them'.[49]

4. 'To emphasize spiritual development as key to equipping Christian workers'. A 'warm spiritual environment' as the context of theological education, 'created by scheduling numerous prayer meetings and worship services through the week', was at the centre of the Bible school ethos.[50] In one way or another, all evangelical institutions for theological education stand in this tradition.

---

[40] Fiedler, *The Story*, 145f.

[41] G. Cheesman, 'Competing Paradigms in Theological Education Today', *Evangelical Review of Theology* 17:4 (1993).

[42] Fiedler, *The Story*.

[43] R.W. Ferris and Ralph E. Enlow, *Reassessing Bible College Distinctives* (American Association of Bible Colleges: Unpublished manuscript, 1995); R.W. Ferris, 'The Future of Theological Education', *Evangelical Review of Theology* 19:July (1995).

[44] Cheesman, 'Competing Paradigms', 488.

[45] Ferris and Enlow, *Reassessing*; Ferris, 'The Future', 3.

[46] Cheesman, 'Competing Paradigms', 488.

[47] Fiedler, *The Story*, 144f.

[48] Cheesman, 'Competing Paradigms', 488.

[49] Fiedler, *The Story*, 144.

[50] Cheesman, 'Competing Paradigms', 488.

However, the Bible schools have experienced fundamental changes in the last 40 to 50 years. Most American Bible schools became Bible institutes and later 'Bible colleges'; some have even added a 'seminary'. In the second half of the twentieth century, the Bible school model has become increasingly inadequate for the training for Christian ministry.[51]

On the one hand, the positive potential of the Bible school model lay in its emphasis on personality formation, somewhat removed from the world, focusing on spiritual formation and community life. This, according to Cheesman, can be a very powerful model of education. On the other hand, it creates an artificial atmosphere in which spirituality and community are scheduled by the institution in a way which has little correspondence with the world the students will later enter.

The Bible schools were established with the goal of training young, committed people for mission and Christian service. This intention was based on two presuppositions: (1) one, two or three years in the 'training camp' situation of the Bible school would be an adequate preparation for overseas mission work or full-time church service, and (2) young and single people would attend such schools. Thus, Bible schools had the status of vocational schools. But these assumptions have changed: (1) preparation for full-time service in the church and in mission work requires in most cases more education. Bachelors and even Masters degrees are now required; (2) at the same time, the age of students has increased and many married students with families now seek preparation for full-time ministry.[52]

In response to new needs, Bible schools started to gain accreditation – but this deeply affected their traditional character. The strength of the Bible school model (spirituality and community) suffered a continuing decrease as Bible schools developed in the direction of academic colleges. The priority of the academic timetable and the pressure of academic work swamped community life and removed time for spiritual disciplines. Furthermore, it turned out to be difficult to fit community and spiritual formation in a measurable way into the accrediting structure. In most cases, the academics (lectures, study time, papers, books) set the pace.[53]

At the same time, the increasing number of older, married students, some even with families, has challenged the closed and structured community life of residential Bible schools. Marriage and family responsibilities, often combined with external living and even part time studies, have made it impossible to fit everyone into the 'monastic' schedule of the Bible school. Despite all the

---

[51] Ferris and Enlow, *Reassessing*, 3ff; Cheesman, 'Competing Paradigms', 488; Fiedler, *The Story*, 148; H. Egelkraut, 'Theological Education in Europe', *Evangelical Review of Theology* 14:1 (1990), 33f.

[52] Cheesman, 'Competing Paradigms', 489; Ferris and Enlow, *Reassessing*.

[53] Cheesman, 'Competing Paradigms', 489.

changes, Ferris and Enlow[54] claim that the Bible school heritage is still alive in many characteristics of contemporary evangelical Bible colleges: (1) commitment to undergraduate preparation for vocational Christian service, (2) commitment to the priority of biblical formation – both mastery of the Bible and mastery by the Bible, (3) commitment to spiritual and ministerial development through the requirement to engage in practical ministry during training, (4) emphasis on Christian character development through setting and enforcing standards, (5) emphasis on indoctrination in orthodoxy as a safeguard to doctrinal purity, (6) emphasis on teaching practical ministry techniques and (7) emphasis on a view of leadership that stresses the intrinsic authority which accompanies divine appointment and guidance. Perhaps the two terms *devotion* and *passion* best summarize the character of the Bible school tradition. In one way this tradition is certainly mission oriented. But the mission orientation focuses on passion and practical evangelistic skills. It does not engage in what today would be called missiological studies with all that this includes.

The University Tradition

But our schools are also shaped by the university tradition. This is the case even when Bible schools and colleges understand themselves in opposition to the university. We are shaped by the university tradition simply because the modern university has shaped the entire understanding of education in our western culture. Thus, we have to look more carefully at the university if we want to understand where we are coming from. The modern university is an institution of the Enlightenment. Jaspers defines it as follows: 'The university is a community of scholars and students engaged in the task of seeking truth'.[55] This search for truth is based on a number of presuppositions which constitute the ethos of the modern university. At least four features can be identified.[56]

1. *The 'academic ethos' of the university*:[57] the fact that the modern university is an institution of the Enlightenment includes a threefold commitment: (1) the commitment to truth, in the sense of the free and rational search for an appropriate understanding and knowledge of reality, is the basic axiom of academic research, carried out in a disciplined, methodological and verifiable way; (2) the commitment to the freedom of teaching and research, as independence from any kind of affiliation with the state, economy, religion or any other power, includes the freedom to study without pragmatism. Only in

---

[54] Ferris and Enlow, *Reassessing*, 3.

[55] K. Jaspers, *The Idea of the University* (London: Peter Owen, 1959), 19.

[56] Jaspers, *The Idea of the University*, 1170; J. Zumstein, 'Theologische Fakultäten an staatlichen Hochschulen', in *Kirche Und Staat*, ed. A. Schindler (Zürich: TVZ, 1994); *Religion in Geschichte Und Gegenwart*, ed. K. Galling, vol. IV (Tübingen: J.C.B. Mohr, 1986).

[57] Zumstein, 'Theologische', 84-89; Jaspers, *The Idea of the University*, 23-43.

this way can the university fulfil its task as the 'conscience of society'; (3) the commitment to human dignity. Freedom of studies does not imply a lack of purpose and meaning. The university is committed to responsible research in the service of human dignity.

2. *The sociological role of the university*: universities are training centres of the academic elite. The entrance requirements are purely academic.[58] Only a selected minority of the population gain university training and they make up the academic elite of society.

3. As the universities grew toward an increasing number of highly specialized academic disciplines, each one with its own set of methodologies, they encountered the problem of *dispersion and fragmentation*. Theology could not escape this development. As it sought its place as an academic discipline of the university, it was forced to base theology upon scientific reasoning.[59] Academic theological studies must be conducted according to the rules of science in other relevant fields: biblical studies according to the rules of historical and linguistic studies; church history according to the rules of historical investigation; systematic theology according to the rules of philosophical studies; and practical theology according to the rules of the social sciences. One result of this is the *encyclopaedic pattern* of theological education, consisting of a broad variety of only loosely related disciplines and subjects. The traditional fourfold pattern (Bible, theology, history, pastoral praxis) has made room for an even greater fragmentation into different fields of specialist studies, each with its own methodology, history of research, problems and literature. The result is an immense fragmentation of theological studies.[60]

4. *The dissociation of academic theological education from ministerial formation*: there is an inherent tension between the church's desire to be in control of theological education and the ethos of the university.[61] Strictly speaking, the university is not interested in ministerial formation. Its purpose is not professional training, but pure academic research. This means that the church must provide means for ministerial formation outside the university structures for the preparation of its future leadership.[62] Traditionally,

---

[58] Zumstein, 'Theologische', 90.

[59] H. Hempelmann, *Kritischer Rationalismus und Theologie als Wissenschaft: Zur Frage nach dem Wirklichkeitsbezug des christlichen Glaubens*, 2 ed. (Wuppertal: Brockhaus, 1987); N. Murphy, *Theology in the Age of Scientific Reasoning* (New York: Cornell University, 1990).

[60] E. Farley, *Theologia - the Fragmentation and Unity of Theoogical Education* (Philadelphia: Fortress, 1983).

[61] Zumstein, 'Theologische', 92-94, 98-100.

[62] J. Nicole, 'Brief History of the So-Called "Classical Model" For Theological Education', *Ministarial Form* 67 (1994), 34; M. Lange and K. Schmid, 'The Council of Students of Protestant Theology (Seth) on Theological Education in Germany', *Minesterial Form* 76 (1997), 37f; T. Hafner, 'Versuche zur Reform des Theologiestudiums', in *Studienreform – Kirchenreform*, ed. W. Bittner, *Idea*

theological education in the university model has not been missionary at all. It was mainly an enterprise of the established European churches, and their focus was maintenance not mission. The issue of mission studies in theological education in the university context first came on the table through German Pietism in the seventeenth century.

In the nineteenth century, Schleiermacher gave missions a place in the curriculum as part of practical theology. In the late nineteenth century, people such as Karl Graul (1814-1864) of Leibzig, Alexander Duff (1806-1878) of Edinburgh, Gustav Warneck (1834-1910) of Halle, as well as the Catholic Joseph Schmidlin (1876-1944) of Münster, tried to introduce the science of mission as a discipline in its own right. Since then, missiology has struggled to find its place in the context of the university, with more or less success. Myklebust summarizes: 'The development of mission studies since 1950... has been characterized by two contrasting tendencies: the increasing recognition of the relevance of missiology for theological study, and the reluctance on the part of the majority of theological institutions to secure for it a separate and permanent place in their curricula'.[63] And David Bosch complains:

> The gradual disappearance of missions or missiology from the curriculum of one theological institution after another further emphasises the malaise. In some of the older European and American faculties of theology, where in the early part of this century missiology appeared to be firmly entrenched, the chairs have been abolished or converted into others for world Christianity, ecumenical studies, Third World theologies, world religions and the like. This development has been linked with the rapid decrease in the number of missionaries from the Roman Catholic church and the World Council of Churches.[64]

It is, therefore, no surprise that Bosch, Myklebust, Kasdorf and others observe that the centre of gravity of missiological interest moved from the ecumenical-oriented universities to the evangelically-oriented schools. For evangelical theological educators it is important to notice that in this shift of missiological studies from main-line universities to evangelical schools, evangelicals have adopted the university concept of missiological studies as science. This has shaped the missiology departments of evangelical seminaries. At this point, I want to summarize that in the university model, theology is understood as *academic research* and theological education means learning to conduct

---

Dokumention 141 (Luzern: Idea-Schweiz, 1993), 11-13; D. Werner, 'Theologie zum Leben bringen. Anforderungen an eine zukunftsorientierte Ausbildungb', in *Emw-Informationen 105* (Hamburg: Evan- gelisches Missionswerk, 1995), 15-17.

[63] O.G. Myklebust, 'Mission in Contemporary Theological Education: A Factual Survey', *Mission Studies* 7:2 (1989), 98.

[64] D. Bosch, 'Theological Education in Missionary Perspective', *Missiology* 10:1 (1982), 13f.

academic research.[65] Theological education in the university context is not mission oriented, however mission studies – or missiology – became an established discipline on its own right in the academic world.

The Seminary Tradition

Finally, we turn briefly to the seminary tradition. It must be understood as representing a third model of theological education with its own characteristics. On the one hand, it has in common with the Bible school model its aim to equip persons for service in church and mission. But it goes beyond the Bible schools in theological reflection and academic work. On the other hand, while it intends to be part of the academic world of the university, its ultimate goal, however, is not independent scientific research. The key feature of the seminary model is its professional aim. It has, therefore, been called the *clerical, ministerial or professional model.*[66] The focus is on the professional training of the clergy. This became the dominant model for the North American seminary.[67]

Where are these seminaries in terms of mission? Exactly along the lines I have outlined. Depending on the tradition in which a seminary stands, it will emphasize a high level of missionary passion. At the same time, it will strive for academic missiological research. However, its main focus will be on training skills for the professional missionary. After all, a seminary is a professional school. It is precisely the tension between these three dimensions which has led many seminaries into a severe crisis in recent years. The following problem areas have been identified:[68] The tension between the academic competencies in research, reflection and writing and the practical demands of the pastoral task; The tension between academic performance and the spiritual life of the students; The tension 'between those curricula and programmes which are mandated by the school mission and those curriculum and programmes which are driven by the market'.[69]

Looking back at the pilgrimage of theological education that I have outlined, we encounter three emphases. One is on 'devotion and passion', the second is on 'scholarship', and the third on 'professional competencies'. This may help people look at their own pilgrimage and at every institution more critically, identifying the emphases experienced and those being promoted in its current

---

[65] Farley, *Theologia*, 39-44.

[66] Farley, *Theologia*, 85ff; D.S. Schipani, 'The Church and Its Theological Education: A Vision', in *Theological Education on Five Continents: Anabaptist Perspectives*, ed. N.R. Heisey and D.S. Schipani (Strasbourg: Mennonite World Conference, 1997), 34ff; C. Duraisingh, 'Ministerial Formation for Mission: Implications for Theological Education', *International Review of Missions* LXXXI:321 (1992), 37.

[67] Farley, *Theologia*, 11f., 44.

[68] B.C. Stewart, 'Tensions in North American Theoligical Education', *Evangelical Review of Theology* 14:1 (1990).

[69] Stewart, 'Tensions', 47.

work. In all of this, we should be aware that none of these models secures the missionary orientation of theological education, even though each one can be oriented towards mission. This means that the decision to conduct mission oriented theological education cannot be reduced to a decision between the three models. We need decisions at a much deeper level. However, first I want to direct our attention to another reality which shapes our understanding and practice of education.

Analysis: What Is Going On in Education?

Doing theological education is not just a matter of internal church business. We are conducting education in the context of the wider western culture. In this sense, the three traditions outlined in the previous section belong, despite all the differences, to the same culture, viz. they are all shaped by the enlightenment paradigm. Traditional western education has faced challenges and has been undergoing tremendous changes in the second half of the twentieth century. Many educators speak of a revolution, of a paradigmatic shift. Many of the issues which are on the table when we discuss theological education cannot be understood without a certain knowledge of this paradigmatic shift in education. This has significant consequences for Christian mission. Let me outline how six elements of the enlightenment paradigm affect theological education and mission.

The concept is that theory and practice are separable and that theory (thinking) precedes practice (action); or the other way around, that practice (action) is applied theory (thinking). This means also that theory can be understood and acquired cognitively, detached from practice. Practice, on the other hand, is the second step, the application of the theory. Practice can follow, but it *does not have* to follow. Theory stands on its own feet. This understanding of theory and practice has deeply influenced our entire understanding and practice of education. The consequences are as follows:

First of all, this view of theory and practice leads to a concept of learning which Lengrand has described with the following words: ‘Up until now, the basic aim of primary, secondary, and university education was dictated by the traditional view that life was divided into distinct parts: a period of preparation, followed by a period of action’.[70] This means that the theory-practice separation has led to an educational system which assumes that the basic theories for the entire lifetime can and must be learned in the early years of life. Again Lengrand: ‘As a result, the whole education system was designed to cram the pupils’ heads with all kinds of facts, and they were supposed to draw on this accumulated capital as best they could to lead to a satisfactory life’. He continues, ‘But if, on the contrary, people can and should continue to learn and

[70] P. Lengrand, ‘Lifelong Education: Growth of the Concept’, in *Lifelong Education for Adults: An International Handbook*, ed. C.J. Titmus (Oxford: Pergamon, 1989), 6.

to educate themselves throughout their life [sic], there is no reason to overburden their brains as children'.[71]

This leads to a further consequence: in a system where theory precedes practice, where initial education plays a predominant role, knowledge is mainly transmitted in a deductive way. In this concept the teacher transmits to the student an abstract theory, which the student has to absorb as abstract theory. The point where teacher and student meet is abstract theory. The teacher may transmit a theory which he or she has developed inductively from personal, practical experience; and may also transmit a theory already received as tradition but applied personally in practical life and now spoken 'out of experience'; and finally, he or she may also transmit a theory received as tradition yet never applied to practical life. The student, on the other hand, has to absorb an abstract theory as a set of pre-packed knowledge and is left with the task of applying it to practical life.

Furthermore, the enlightenment paradigm of science is characterized by a 'logical empiristic, or "positivist", approach to knowledge'.[72] It is based on the assumption that 'reality' can be known objectively. Knowledge is seen as a 'copy of reality'.[73] Hiebert speaks of a 'photographic view of knowledge'.[74] Of course, such an epistemological view has been severely criticized in the academic world of the modern university, and new approaches have been put forward such as instrumentalism, idealism and several post-modern theories. Many of these theories are raising more new questions than answering old ones. But this is not the issue here. What we have to realize is the fact that evangelical theology – and especially its conservative, fundamentalist wing – still holds to a positivist epistemology, and this with the following effect: reading the Bible with a positivist mind set leads to the formulation of a theology which presumes to give a copy of God's word, a photographic view of the biblical reality. In theological education this leads to the transmission of truth in the form of propositional theological statements.

Another component of the enlightenment paradigm of education is an analytical mindset. Analysis means taking the whole apart and defining the isolated components. This is part of the western enlightenment way of thinking. We are trained to take the whole texture of life and pull out every single thread of the texture in order to analyse it. Then we assume that if we have gained an understanding of each isolated single part of life we understand life. However, we have destroyed the texture of life, we have lost the wholeness of life, and end up with fragmentation. The entire enterprise of education is based on the concept of analysis. We have different fields of study, different departments in

[71] Lengrand, 'Lifelong', 6.

[72] P. Hiebert, *Missiological Implications of Epistemological Shifts: Affirming Truth in a Modern/Postmodern World* (Valley Forge: Trinity Press International, 1999), 3.

[73] Hiebert, *Missiological Implications*, 3.

[74] Hiebert, *Missiological Implications*, 11.

our schools, different traditions of research. We offer different areas of study and different majors in our programmes. We have different subjects in our curriculum, and a vast amount of courses and modules. I know that for practical didactic reasons we somehow have to divide the wholeness of life in order to make it teachable. But this is not the key issue. The real problem lies much deeper. In our western thinking we are trained to believe that the sum of the parts makes up the whole.

This leads to the assumption that the mere accumulation of courses and modules will lead automatically to a deeper understanding of the whole. The credit system we are used to in higher education, especially in the American system, has pushed this thinking to the peak. We collect the required number of often unrelated and disconnected courses in order to get a Masters degree. But to master a field or a subject is much more than acquiring pieces of knowledge from within a certain field. To say it in one word: the educational paradigm of traditional western education lacks *integration*. As Gerhard Ebeling[75] states in his introduction to the study of theology: The study of theology is beset by a crisis in orientation. Because our access to the unity and totality that constitutes the subject matter of theology is disrupted, the main domain of its subject matter and task has broken apart and crumbled into a bewildering conglomeration of individual items.

Finally, as a further consequence of what has been said so far, we end up with individualism. Individualism is one form of fragmentation. If theory precedes practice; and if theory is a set of truth statements which can be transmitted deductively, and therefore, can be acquired by the individual mind; and if the wholeness of life, or at least of one area of life, can be mastered through the accumulation of single and isolated parts of reality, then education is a purely individualistic matter. Any person can anywhere acquire and accumulate the necessary knowledge to earn a degree, if only he or she has access to the information. However this is a defective understanding of reality, of knowledge and of education.

Challenges to the Traditional Paradigm

This traditional educational paradigm has been severely challenged in the last century, first of all by Marxist social theory, but even more by people from non-western cultures, who have a much more integrated understanding of reflection and action. It is especially the field of adult education that has challenged many of the assumptions of the old paradigm. Terms such as 'life-long learning', 'self-active learning', 'self-responsible learning' and 'self-directed learning' were coined to describe the features of a new paradigm.[76]

[75] G. Ebeling, *The Study of Theology* (Philadelphia: Fortress, 1978), 1.

[76] E. Prokop and K.A. Geissler, *Erwachsenenbildung. Modelle und Methoden* (Munich/Basel: Reinhardt, 1974), 7.

Many of the recent developments in theological education draw from these new concepts in secular adult education. The disadvantages of traditional education are obvious and common knowledge: Education is reduced to the transmission of theory and the appropriation of abstract knowledge. It is difficult for the students to relate abstract theory to real life in a classroom situation, especially when they have no previous experience in the area of the taught subject; Students rapidly lose their motivation to study if they cannot connect the learned abstract theory with real life situations. There is a tendency to remain in the realm of abstraction and to conduct abstract reflection as an end in itself. There is usually a large surplus of abstract theory at the end of a course taught by the traditional paradigm of learning. Examinations focus on the correct reproduction of abstract theory by the student. The whole system is built on the presupposition that cognitively appropriated, abstract truth can later be applied successfully to life. It is also evident that traditional education has the potential for domination, because the teacher who has the knowledge is in control of the educational process. The student depends fully on the expertise of the teacher.

Paulo Freire, in his critique of the dominant paradigm of western education, speaks of the 'Bankers-Concept of Education',[77] because the teacher makes a deposit of knowledge in the students' minds which should yield interest in the future. Freire speaks of education as 'praxis of domination', because it presupposes that people are empty vessels which ought to be filled with the pre-defined knowledge handed down by the established tradition of a given society. Kinsler has adapted Freire's pedagogy to theological education and criticizes traditional models of theological education for their dominant and oppressive role. Similarly, Henri Nouwen[78] has pointed to the fact that traditional education is a unilateral process in which the teacher is strong and the student weak. The teacher knows, the student does not know. The whole movement is from the strong to the weak. Nouwen rightly calls this 'teaching as a violent process'. What has all of this to do with mission? The church carries out its mission in a world that is in the midst of dramatic changes.

Scherer and Bevans[79] have summarized these changes as follows: (1) We now live in a pluricentric, rather than a western-dominated world; (2) structures of oppression and exploitation are today being challenged as never before; (3) a profound feeling of ambiguity exists about the value of western technology and development and the older idea of 'progress'; (4) we inhabit a shrinking global village with finite resources, and this calls for growing mutual interdependence; (5) humans are for the first time aware of their capacity to destroy the earth and make it uninhabitable for future generations; (6) societies everywhere now seek

---

[77] P. Freire, *Erziehung Als Praxis Der Freiheit* (Stuttgart: Kreuz Verlag, 1974).

[78] Henri Nouwen, *Creative Ministry* (New York: Doubleday, 1971).

[79] J. A. Scherer and S. Bevans, *New Directions in Mission and Evangelization: Basic Statement 1974-1991*, vol. 1 (Maryknoll, NY: Orbis, 1992), ix.

their own local cultural identities and reject slavish imitation of western models; (7) freedom of religion and greater awareness of other faiths force Christians to re-evaluate their own earlier attitudes toward other faiths. In this context, the church in mission is required to be dynamic, to learn as it moves across cultural boundaries. It must be able to theologize contextually, to think in different paradigms, and to reformulate the gospel in new settings. It needs a wholistic approach to reality and must be able to dialogue with different worldviews and religions.

This requires a range of competencies for which a student must receive preparation during his/her time of studies. The outlined traditional ways of education do not equip persons adequately to serve the church as it carries out its mission in a changing world. What we need is a transformation of theological education and this on the theological, on the epistemological, and on the pedagogical level. How can this transformation be achieved? What we need are criteria for conducting theological education according to God's intention. This leads to the next step:

In order to move into the future in a way which corresponds with God's intention, we are first of all in need of a theology of theological education. This subject can only be introduced in this paper. I will briefly address two issues, one is methodological in nature, the other theological.

'Sanctifying' the Structures of the World

Theological education can only be performed in earthen vessels. There are no heavenly models and structures for theological education. We do theological education in the structures of our cultures. In principle, there is nothing wrong with this. However, not all structures of our cultures are appropriate and helpful to contain what we, theologically speaking, are called to do when we engage in theological education. Methodologically, what we need to do can be observed in Deuteronomy 17:14-21. There, Israel wants to introduce into its own culture the social and political structure of an ancient monarchy from the surrounding cultures. God allows Israel to do this. They probably had no other choice since nations were structured this way at that time. However, the ancient monarchy was not quite suitable for what the people of God was intended to be. So God gives certain criteria for the introduction of the monarchy. In some ways, he helped Israel to sanctify the monarchy so that it might be useful for God's people. This is the process we need in theological education. When we engage in theological education we draw from many sources of our history and our culture. We seek university validation. We adopt modern educational theories. We learn from professional training in other professions. We learn to use modern technology for more effective teaching and communication. All these vessels from our culture can be useful, however they also may carry their own dynamics, and these may not always be in agreement with God's intentions. What we also need are theological criteria which help us to adapt educational models, theories, methodologies and techniques in such a way that they help us in carrying out as faithfully as possible the mission God has given to us.

Toward a Theology of Theological Education

As I said earlier, this is not the place fully to develop a theology of theological education. However, I want to point to one central criterion which helps us to test educational theories and methods regarding their usefulness for God's people. Fig. 1 below shows the rationale of the theology of theological education I am proposing here: It begins with God and the statement that God is missionary by his very nature. As David Shenk has put it: 'God seeking us, this is mission'. Since the 1950s, the term *Missio Dei* has been used to refer to this theological claim. The chart uses the terms dimension and intention. They are significant for the theological rationale being suggested here. Hans-Werner Gensichen, who has applied the dimension/intention concept to God, makes the point that God is missionary in his very being, but that this cannot be understood as a static and passive status of being. God is also acting in an intentionally missionary manner by sending his Son and the Spirit. On the second line the chart moves to the church. Like God the church has a missionary dimension as well as a missionary intention. Lesslie Newbigin introduced the 'dimension/intention' concept to ecclesiology in the 1950s – even before Gensichen used it in terms of God – when he was asked to provide a theological foundation for the integration of the IMC with the WCC. On the one hand, the conviction had grown within the ecumenical movement that mission can no longer be a task delegated to mission societies, but that the whole church must become missionary by its very nature and being, and that therefore the IMC must be integrated into the WCC.

On the other hand was the fear of the mission societies, that if the churches take responsibility for missions, then everything becomes mission, and the passion to evangelize the world will be paralysed. In this context Newbigin proposed an understanding of church and mission which says, on the one hand, that the church as a whole, and following this, every aspect of the church's life, has a missionary 'dimension'. In this sense, everything the church is and does has to be seen from the perspective of the church's mission. To be sent – to be in mission – is part of the church's identity. The church is by nature missionary. On the other hand, there must be a missionary intention, i.e. specific missionary actions. With this, Newbigin was able to keep two things together and at the same time to avoid two possible pitfalls. He could maintain that every single aspect of the church's being and acting must be seen through missionary glasses, without swallowing particular missionary actions in such a way that mission gets paralysed. He was also able to maintain the specific and concrete missionary activities without isolating them from the church's missionary being. From this theological and ecclesiological concept we can derive theological criteria to define the task of theology (line three of the chart) and to formulate a theological rationale for theological education (line four of the chart). This will be developed in the final section of my presentation.

Fig.1

Dimension Intention
Missio Dei God's missionary nature God's act of sending his Son and ⇓ His Spirit
Ecclesiology The missionary nature The church's specific ⇓ of the church missionary actions
Theology The missionary nature Specific reflection on ⇓ of all theology the church in mission
Theological The missionary centre Specific, mission-oriented training **education** of all theological education

Integrating Mission into Theology and Theological Education

The first concept is based on David Bosch's proposal for a missionary theology. Bosch has applied the concept of dimension and intention introduced by Newbigin and Gensichen (see chart above) to theology, claiming that all of theology needs to become mission oriented. This means that every theological reflection, every research, and every formulation must be done in view of the church in mission. What we need, says Bosch, are not necessarily more mission courses but a more missionary theology. However, Bosch sees the danger of this concept, namely that, when all theology becomes mission oriented, missiology as a discipline of its own right will be swallowed by general theological studies, and with this, specific missiological research and studies will be weakened. Drawing on Newbigin's concept he therefore calls for a missionary intention, i.e. specific missiological studies. I am suggesting we take Bosch's proposal even one step further and apply it to theological education. This would mean that theological education as a whole needs a missionary orientation. Everything, every programme aim, every course objective, every assignment, every research paper, every test must be developed in view of the church in mission.

On the other hand, there is also the need for specific programmes, courses and research projects which focus intentionally on missiological issues. If we manage to develop a curriculum along the dimension/intention concept, we will be able to solve several of the problems outlined in this presentation: 1. It helps to give the entire enterprise of theological education a missionary orientation without necessarily concentrating only on specific missiological subjects. In this way, an MA in Biblical Studies, or in Pastoral Ministries or in Pentecostal Studies can become fully mission oriented. 2. It also provides a unifying centre for the entire curriculum. This means that the programme does not consist of a variety of more or less related courses according to the divisions of the traditional curriculum. Maybe the professors of the Bible department want to have at least three biblical courses in the programme. The systematic theologians and historians will fight for several theological and historical courses, while the people of the practical departments try to secure some space for counselling, mission, pastoral leadership, or church development. But what is the rationale which holds all of these together? The missionary dimension of all theology and of all theological education can provide this rationale. 3. As soon as we have established such a unifying centre we will find open doors for the kind of integrated curriculum in which the different courses can be linked and interrelated in a meaningful way. The courses are no longer pointing in many different directions in a centrifugal way, rather they point to the centre in a centripetal way. But let us be even more precise:

Clarifying the Task of Theology and the Structure of Theological Education

In his little booklet 'The Mission of Theology and Theology as Mission',[80] Andrew Kirk has outlined a concept of theology and theological education which transcends many of the traditional principles and structures and opens promising avenues for the future of theological education. Kirk defines the nature and the task of theology in a twofold way. First, the first task of theology is to make sense of the whole of life by reference to God. This purpose statement directs our attention towards the world. It is missionary in its approach without using the term mission. Its ultimate focus is not the Bible, not the church and its tradition, not even Jesus Christ, the Holy Spirit or God the father. Here the theologian does not stand in front of God, looking at God, he is rather standing beside God and looking *with* God into the world. I emphasize: *with God!* This is an immense missionary perspective: To stand beside God and look at life under the direction of God. If we stay with the image, we may say that the theologian must keep his/her eyes directed towards the world, and at the same time he must open his ears to listen carefully to God's explanations. This first task of theology is more explanatory in nature, and is conducted from a certain distance. Kirk uses the biblical term 'prophetic' to describe this part of the theologian's task. The second task of theology is to be an agent of transformation, so that the whole of life may reflect God's intention. This now pushes toward action. If God's purpose and mission is the transformation of the whole of life towards shalom, then theology has to put itself in the service of this mission. Based on this twofold task of theology, Kirk suggests a structure of theological education which focuses on the three steps 'see, judge, act'.[81]

[80] A. Kirk, *The Mission of Theology and the Theology of Mission* (Valley Forge: Trinity Press International, 1997).

[81] Kirk, *The Mission*, 58.

From this he outlines a curriculum design in four stages, in which the first two stages focus on 'seeing', the third on 'judging', and the fourth on 'acting':

The first stage focuses on the *pilgrimage of the student*. It is based on the conviction that no one starts as an empty sheet of paper when he or she enters theological training and this prehistory of the student will determine or at least influence much of his or her theological thinking. It is, therefore, extremely important to help students to get in touch with their pilgrimage. The emphasis is not so much on explaining their past, but teaching them the tools to engage in a self-critical analysis of their history. Students who have not been enabled to become aware of their own history and integrate it in a healthy way into their identity will show little awareness of their own and other peoples' history and identity being conditioned when they enter into any kind of church ministry, not to speak of cross-cultural mission work.

The second stage consists of *cultural and social analysis*. The objective of this stage is to help the student to understand better the world in which he or she lives and works. Again, this contains not only teaching about culture and society, but rather teaching tools of cultural analysis, in order to enable students to engage in critical interaction with their world. Students who have not learned to 'read' culture will enter church and mission ministries without the necessary understanding of the world in which she/he lives and works.

The third stage focuses upon *judge*. In this stage the student learns to look critically at what he or she has observed in stage one and two. Of course, according to the twofold task outlined earlier, this will be done from God's point of view. Therefore, understanding Scripture, hearing the voice of the Spirit and listening to the community of believers become central at this stage. Students have to learn how they can articulate normative theology and apply it to their cultural context. Again, the task is not to teach them a once for all defined true interpretation of the Bible, but to teach them hermeneutics, exegetical methods and the steps of theological thinking – in short: to teach them to theologize.

The fourth and final stage is *action*. Here students are taught to theologize in such a way that it leads to action. By now you may have realized that my presentation has followed a certain outline. We moved from 'pilgrimage' to 'cultural analysis', we tried to 'judge' from God's point of view, and finally we moved to 'action'. No, we have not yet really moved to action. But we will encounter many possibilities to act – to put into practice what it means to develop a curriculum for mission oriented theological education. As we approach this task we should not forget that designing a mission oriented curriculum is not primarily a matter of adding some mission courses nor decorating our curriculum with some missiological flowers here and there. No, we are challenged to design programmes which are mission oriented at their very heart. To use the image again: we stand beside God and look into the world. Our eyes are wide open towards the world to understand what is going on there, and at the same time, our ears are wide open towards God to hear his interpretation. And then we are called to become agents of transformation. I believe this is the kind of theological education that God wants, our churches desire, and the world needs.

PART 2

Global Mission and Theological Studies

Critical Issues Facing Theological Education in Asia

Hwa Yung

The Rt. Rev. Dr. Hwa Yung is the bishop of the Methodist Church at Petaling Jaya in Malaysia. He is also the chairperson of the Oxford Centre for Mission Studies, UK.

Introduction

With the rapid growth in numbers within the Asian church in recent years, together with its gradually increasing sense of self-identity, it is inevitable that there has been a growing demand for theological education in Asia. Institutions of all sorts have been sprouting all over the continent. But it is uncertain how much fresh thinking there has been on the subject as a whole in Asia. Many of the institutions appear to have followed, by and large, the existing model or models of Western theological education in more ways than one. This paper is an attempt to define some of the problems confronting theological education in Asia today which need some thinking through, and to propose some suggestions for dealing with them. These problems are best classified into three categories. The first is theological problems. They concern the differences in the ways that theology is done in the West and Asia, and how these differences necessarily affect how theological education should be approached. The second group of problems concerns the underlying philosophy of theological education, the what, why, and who of training. The third group deals with issues of a more practical nature like the problems created as a result of the proliferation of colleges because of denominational differences or Western mission control, finance, brain drain, etc. We will deal with each set of problems in turn.

Theological Issues

The overwhelming dominance of Western thought in the modern world has meant that by and large much of theological education in Asia has been conditioned by the methodologies, agenda, and content of Western theology. Increasingly, it is now recognized that this approach must be changed if the Asian church is to come to terms more adequately with its own identity, context, and mission. At least three broad issues are involved: the foundational problems within modern Western theologies itself, the relevance of culture in theologizing, and the content of Asian theology.

The Underlying Problems of Western Theologies

From a non-Western perspective, three problems can be seen at the foundation of modern Western theology. To begin with, much of the Western theology has been controlled by the autonomous rationalism and the narrow empiricism of the Enlightenment, which together have produced a climate of scepticism that hampers the genuine expression of biblical faith.[82] The emphasis on reason began in the seventeenth century with the concern to affirm the basic rationality of the universe, and not with debunking belief in God. Descartes' famous *Cogito, ergo sum,* it is generally perceived, represents a shift towards making the individual self-consciousness as the final criterion of truth. What began as an emphasis on the proper use of reason to understand a rational universe ended up in the elevation of instrumental theoretical reason into an autonomous principle by which all claims to truth side by side with the above development is the impact of empiricism, the view that the sole source of knowledge comes from sense perception. It arose in part out of the reaction to philosophical rationalism, and its belief that reason was the basis of certain knowledge. But what began as a proper emphasis on the importance of scientific experimentation and sense perception in knowing, often ended up as a 'mitigated scepticism' (David Hume's phrase for his own approach) which effectively denies any objectivity to any knowledge that is not empirically derived. This narrow empiricism prevailed from Hume to the 'Verification Principle' of the Logical Positivists, and Bultmann's rejection of all miracles on the grounds that they supposedly violate the scientific laws of a closed universe.

The combined result of the above, in the words of Newbigin, is that pluralism, which relativizes everything not strictly scientifically provable, is now the reigning 'plausibility structure' in the West today. And Christians are thus forced to defend their faith as 'reasonable' on the basis of the former's assumptions. Inevitably, within such an environment doubt becomes more respectable than faith.[83] This is obviously not the place for a detailed critique of Enlightenment thought. For the moment, it suffices to draw attention to what Diogenes Allen, amongst others, has to say on this. He notes the massive revolution taking place at the present moment as we enter into the postmodern world. The principles of the Enlightenment which formed the foundations of the modern intellectual framework are now rapidly breaking down.[84] Admittedly the future is rather uncertain, 'but it is clear that a fundamental re-evaluation of the Christian faith, free of the assumptions of the modern

---

[82] A.I.C. Heron, *A Century of Protestant Theology* (Guildford and London: Lutterworth, 1980); L. Newbigin, *The Gospel in a Pluralistic Society* (Grand Rapids/Geneva: Eerdmans/WCC, 1989); D.J. Bosch, *Transforming Mission: Paradigm Shifts in Theology and Missions* (Maryknoll, NY: Orbis, 1991).

[83] Newbigin, *The Gospel*, 1-26.

[84] D. Allen, *Christian Belief in a Modern World: The Full Wealth of Conviction* (Louisville, KY: Westminster and John Knox, 1989), 2-6.

mentality that are generally hostile to a religious outlook, is called for'.[85] He goes on to argue that, as the barriers to the Christian faith erected by the modern mentality collapse both philosophy and science, which were once seen as inimical to religious belief, are now in some respects seen to be pointing the way back to it.[86] Given the above, and the fact that much of Western theology has been heavily shaped by the modern mentality which even Western scholars themselves are now beginning to seriously question, there is therefore even less reason for non-Western Christians today to allow their theologies to be domesticated by Enlightenment thinking, something which Western Christians themselves find increasingly dissatisfying. The second major problem is the pervasiveness of dualism within Western theology.

The Chinese scholar, Carver Yu, has pointed out that the root of this dualism goes all the way back to the absorption of Greek philosophy into Christian theology.[87] This gave rise to individualism which became fully established in Western thought.[88] This individualism in turn further helped to accentuate the individualization and spiritualization of salvation, a tendency which has been endemic in Western theology since salvation is thus perceived as both other-worldly and individualistic, with primary emphasis given to the redemption of the individual soul rather than the reconciliation of the world.[89] This, as Bosch puts it, 'could not but spawn a dualistic view of reality, which became second nature in Western Christianity – the tendency to regard salvation as a private matter and to ignore the world'.[90] Thus, eventually the Platonic body-soul dichotomy combined together with individualistic thinking to firmly establish the dualistic view of reality in Western thought, as well as the individualization and spiritualization of Christian salvation in Western theology. The overall result of these developments is that the universe is perceived in dualistic categories at every point: the individual mind and the external world, soul and body, spirit and matter, the religious as against the secular, evangelism versus sociopolitical concerns, and so on.

The consequences of this on theology and ethics is plain. Instead of holistic thinking, we begin to ask: Is the soul more important or the body? Is salvation spiritual (saving the soul) or physical and sociopolitical (saving the body and society)? Generally speaking, if liberals have tended to be guilty of 'horizontalizing' the gospel and mission, conservative Christians have tended to be guilty of spiritualizing the same. In other words, both have been domesticated by the same dualism – only that they tend to opt for opposite

---

[85] Allen, *Christian Belief*, 2.

[86] Allen, *Christian Belief*, 23-96.

[87] C.T. Yu, *Being and Relation: A Theological Critique of Western Dualism and Individualism* (Edinburgh: Scottish Academic Press, 1987).

[88] Yu, *Being and Relation*, 98-105.

[89] Bosch, *Transforming Mission*, 215-17.

[90] Bosch, *Transforming Mission*, 216.

sides of the divide. A third problem perceived in Western theology arises out of the secularized worldview of the Western mind. It concerns the differences between the Western worldview and that shared by the bible and must of the Two-Thirds World. Paul G. Hiebert writing out of his experiences in India, in a penetrating article, 'The Flaw of the Excluded Middle',[91] argues that the former has a blind spot which makes it difficult for the Western mind to understand, let alone deal with problems related to astrology, ancestors and spirits. The Western mind has a two-tiered view of reality. The upper level is that of 'High Religion' which deals with theistic answers to life, and rational beliefs concerning God and other beings who act in the spiritual (and other) world. The lower level is that of the empirical sciences which perceives this world as being controlled by lifeless and impersonal forces.

In contrast, the Indian and biblical worldview consist of three tiers. The upper and lower tiers are similar, at least formally if not materially, to that of the West. However, there is also a middle level of 'Folk or Low Religion' which consists of beliefs in the local deities, ancestral and other spirits, demons, astrology, and the like who or which act in this world. Because this middle level is absent in the Western mind, Western theology has no answers for the problems arising therein. Obviously, what Hiebert describes of the biblical and Indian worldviews, actually applies throughout much of the Two-Thirds world, even among those who seemingly have been secularized by Western education.[92] In particular, the 'excluded middle', wherein the spirit and the physical worlds intersect actively, is an essential component of Asian worldview.[93] That being the case, what is needed in the communication of the Christian faith in the Asian context is not just a 'truth encounter' at the 'High Religion' level, but also a 'power encounter' at the 'Folk Religion' level.[94] Otherwise, Christianity will be perceived as evangelistically powerless, and pastorally irrelevant, in dealing with many of the questions posed by Asian worldviews.[95]

---

[91] P.G. Hiebert, 'The Flaw of the Excluded Middle', *Missiology* 10:1 (1982).

[92] Gerrie ter Harr, *The Healing Ministry of Archbishop Milingo of Zambia* (London: Hurst & Co., 1992); O. Imasogie, *Guidelines for Christian Theology in Africa* (Ghana: African Christian Press, 1983).

[93] F. Bloomfield, *The Book of Chinese Beliefs. A Journey in the Chinese Inner World* (London: Arrow, 1983); B.H. Earhart, *Religions of Japan: Many Traditions within One Sacred Way* (New York: Harper Collins, 1984), 47-100; D.L. Overmyer, *Religions of China: The World as a Living System* (New York: Harper Collins, 1986), 11-16, 57-102; N. Tapp, 'Karma and Cosmology. Anthropology and Religion', in *Asia's Cultural Mosaic: An Anthropological Introduction*, ed. Grant Evans (New York: Prentice-Hall, 1993), 287-300.

[94] Hiebert, 'The Flaw', 45ff.

[95] C. Kraft, *Christianity with Power. Your Worldview and Your Experience of the Supernatural* (Ann Arbor, MI: Servant Publications, 1989), 37-50.

The combined effect of these three foundational problems has resulted in a crippling of Western theology through an intellectual scepticism that weakens faith and exalts doubt, and a secularized worldview which cannot cope with the intermediate spiritual realm (the 'excluded middle') in life. Further it is marred by an underlying dualism which repeatedly 'puts asunder what God has put together', thus preventing us from perceiving both the gospel and the world in holistic terms. Because Asian Christians have generally learnt so well from their Western teachers, much of what is taught and written in Asian theological circles – both ecumenical and conservative – are likewise crippled by the same three factors.[96] In other words, one of the most critical issues facing theological education in Asia is the need for models of theological thinking which will enable the church to transcend the foundational problems found in Western theology today.

The Relevance of Culture

A second area where theological education in Asia must come to terms with is the need to theologize within Asian cultural categories. One example of this is already suggested in the preceding discussion, the contrast between the Western and the Asian worldview. Because the former in modern times have not taken seriously the 'excluded middle', Western theology often fails to help the church deal with problems of occultism, demon possession, healing, and the like. Yet in Asia, without adequate answers at this level (which often involve 'power encounters'), there can be little advance in evangelism and mission.

A second example concerns the ways of thinking. It is now generally accepted that every culture has its own way of thinking, which may be quite different from another's. Edmund Perry, in a lecture at the University of Manchester, May 2, 1950, draws attention to the three basic cognitive approaches that are found in different cultures.[97] A differentiation is proposed between the 'conceptual', corresponding to Northrop's cognition by 'postulation', the 'psychical', corresponding to Northrop's cognition by 'intuition', and the 'concrete relational' in which life and reality are seen pictorially in terms of active emotional relationships present in a concrete situation.[98] The West, India and China respectively represent the preponderance of these three ways of knowing.

On the basis of the above he proposes, with slight modifications, the three models for the Western, Chinese and Indian minds. In each model, the primary mode of cognition is represented by the innermost circle, with the others being

[96] Hwa Yung, "D.Miss. Dissertation" (Asbury Theological Seminary, 1994).

[97] E. Perry, *The Gospel in Dispute: The Relation of Christian Faith to Other Missionary Religions* (New York: Doubleday and Co., 1958).

[98] Perry, *The Gospel*, 99; F.S.C. Northrop, *The Meeting of East and West: An Inquiry Concerning World Understanding* (London: Macmillan, 1950).

secondary and tertiary respectively. The different primary modes of cognition can be illustrated by the different approaches taken by each culture towards, say, the question of veracity of reported miracles. With respect to the first, the Western mind focuses on critical conceptual and analytical issues like, 'How can miracles be possible in a scientific age?' The Chinese mind is likely to ask, 'Can I trust the person who reportedly witnessed and told me of the miracle?', thus focusing on the relationship between the teller and the listener. The Indian mind is likely to say, 'I will accept its truthfulness if I can experience it for myself'. Of course, these are matters of relative emphases within each culture. But they do end up shaping the predominant theological questions asked and approaches taken from within each culture differently.

In our efforts to communicate the gospel cross-culturally in Asia, we must take seriously the differing ways of thinking.[99] For example, given the penchant for concrete relational thinking and a preference for nonlinear logic among Chinese, Japanese and other East Asians,[100] for the purpose of expressing the Christian faith in these contexts, much more emphasis ought to be given to stories, parables, pictures, narratives, poetry, songs and the like, instead of rational apologetics, systematic theologies build upon inductive and deductive logic, and cold analytical approaches to biblical studies.[101] But it is precisely issues of this nature that have not been taken up with sufficient seriousness in theologizing and theological education in Asia.

It should be noted that the above are not just two isolated examples. Other examples wherein the relationship between theology and Asian cultures needs deeper exploration abound. For example, in cultures that do not give primacy to linear logic is the doctrine of inerrancy a helpful way to defend biblical authority? Western theology focuses primarily on the concept of guilt (e.g. justification), but how is the Cross to be interpreted in shame-cultures? How are biblical teachings on servant leadership to be applied in cultures (e.g. Korea) where authoritarian leadership patterns prevail? Again, is the issue between adult and infant baptism to be decided on purely historical, biblical and theological grounds? Or, does it ultimately hinge on how decisions are made within a particular cultural context? Yet these issues are hardly, if ever, raised – again because of the overwhelming dominance of Western theology, whether liberal or conservative.

---

[99] J.C. Condon and F. Yousef, *An Introduction to Intercultural Communication* (New York/London: MacMillan/Collier MacMillan, 1975), 209-49; D.J. Hesselgrave, *Communicating Christ Cross-Culturally: An Introduction to Missionary Communication* (Grand Rapid, MI: Zondervan, 1978).

[100] R.B. Kaplan, 'Cultural Thought Patterns in Intercultural Education', *Language Learning* 16:1-2 (1970), 1-20.

[101] Hesselgrave, *Communicating Christ*, 206.

Content of the Theological Curricula

The above leads to the third broad issue. Quite apart from the fact that theological education in Asia is burdened with the foundational problems of Western theology, and the lack of serious interaction with Asian cultural categories, there is at present a dire lack of material to allow the theological student to focus on more specifically Asian content in his/her theological studies. Three examples with suffice.

One of the most important books to be published recently is Moffett's *A History* of *Christianity in Asia,*[102] because this is the first up-to-date, critical, and comprehensive work on Asia in the first fifteen centuries of the Christian era. Further, it deals with a number of issues which are crucial for the self-understanding of the church in Asia. For example, it treats in great detail the life of the Nestorian church of Persia and its brilliant missionary advances from the sixth to the tenth centuries throughout Asia, including India, Tibet, China, and even Outer Mongolia – all these at a time when the Western church was going through the Dark Ages. To the Asian Christian, who is accustomed to being told that all the Christian wisdom he or she now possesses comes from the West, such a reminder of the Asian church's own history gives him or her a lot more confidence in wanting to develop a clearer sense of self identity. Again in his treatment of John of Damascus and the Nestorian Patriarch, Timothy I, Moffett draws attention to models of Christian-Muslim interactions which have the greatest relevance for Asian Christians living under Islam.[103] Yet apart from Moffett's book, there is hardly any other comprehensive history text that covers the similar ground, and draws attention to similar issues.

A second example can be found in the fact that there are no really good biographies of some of Asia's greatest leaders of past generations like Pastor Hsi, Sadhu Sundar Singh and John Sung – despite the fact that there are lots of material available. What are presently available tend to be written from the perspective of Western missions, and none of the three listed above can claim to be solid critical biographies, like Bainton's on Martin Luther. A church without its own heroes will invariably end up as a church without its own identity!

A third example is found in a paper by Cracknell.[104] Writing out of the British context, he argues that the teaching of the various core theological disciplines, including biblical studies, church history and systematic theology, would be enriched by the introduction of the multi-faith dimension. One does not have to agree with the specifics of Cracknell's suggestion to accept the

---

[102] Samuel H. Moffett, *A History of Christianity in Asia: Beginnings to 1500*, vol. 1 (New York: Harper San Francisco, 1992).

[103] Moffett, *A History*, 324-73.

[104] K. Cracknell, 'A Response from Another Context', in *Ministerial Formation in a Multi-Faith Milieu. Implications of Interfaith Dialogue for Theological Education*, ed. Sam Amirtham and S. Wesley Ariarajah (Geneva: WCC, 1986), 36-47.

validity of his point. And if this is necessary in Britain, how much more indeed would it be necessary in Asia where non-Christian religions predominate. Yet the truth is that again there are hardly any textbooks, especially in systematic theology or biblical studies, written from a multi-faith (and a multi-cultural) dimension.

To sum up this section, the three broad theological issues discussed in this section point to the very urgent need for the production of a whole new generation of theological literature. These will be characterized by a refusal to be domesticated by Western philosophical and theological categories, a much closer interaction with the multi-cultural and multi-religious contexts of Asia, and a concern to deal more directly with Asian issues. This may well be the most crucial issue facing theological education in Asia.

Training Philosophy: What? Why? Who?

The second set of problems deal with the underlying philosophy of our training process. We will look at some of the issues.

Content of the Training: Theology as Speculative versus Theology as Pastoral and Missiological

Much of theology taught in both Western and non-Western seminaries have tended to be rather academic in nature. But the question that must be asked is whether theology ultimately should be academic and speculative, or pastoral and missiological. It appears that increasingly the emerging consensus is that the nature of theology should rather be the latter than the former.

To begin with, it is beyond any reasonable doubt that the foundational documents of the Christian church, the New Testament books, were all written in the context of mission and pastoral practice. As David Bosch has noted, these records were not written by the equivalent of modern-day scholars with the luxury of leisurely research, but 'in the context of an "emergency situation", of a church which, because of its missionary encounter with the world, was forced to theologize'.[105] Further, historically speaking, the speculative approach to theology is an aberration, rather than the norm. Except for the scholastics among the medieval scholars, and the modern period, theology has always been controlled by the pastoral and missiological needs of the church.

Thirdly, it is now increasingly recognized that the modern tendency to treat theology as speculative can only be sustained in the context of the Enlightenment bifurcation of knowledge into the two poles of truth and practice (what liberation theologians call an 'epistemological split'), with the former being primary. Once this epistemological approach is rejected, then the

---

[105] Bosch, *Transforming Mission*, 16.

speculative approach to theology must be set aside. Hence the critique of Liberation Theology of Western theology as being 'unengaged'.[106]

If then theology is fundamentally pastoral and missiological in nature, how is theological education to be effected? Some will try to solve the problem by adding more pastoral and missiological course. But that may merely serve to reinforce the already existing academic and pastoral-missiological divide in theology. It appears that new ways must be found to teach theological subjects pastorally and missiologically. For example, exegesis courses must not be ends in themselves. Rather, they must be taught in a way that leads to sound sermon preparation and good preaching. Systematic theology courses must be inseparably linked with apologetic concerns in evangelism and with pastoral problems. The difficulty with this sort of approach is that, despite some real efforts being made in this direction, few existing textbooks are written in this way?[107]

Why Do We Train? The Goal That We Seek

Closely related to the first question is the question of the goal of training. If theology is fundamentally pastoral and missiological, then the primary emphasis cannot be academic training and inculcation of skills alone. It must also pay at least equal attention to the moulding of the character and spirituality of the trainee. This is not just a biblical emphasis (1 Tim. 3; Tit. 1:5ff), but it is particularly important in Asia culture. Both the concept of the Chinese scholar gentleman and the Indian guru are not merely academically learned individuals, but who also actualize and embody in their own persons and lives their learning.

That this goal has not been easily achieved is evident from the statements of concern expressed in various quarters. One report from India describes the pastors as follows: 'They seem to be well equipped to perform as institutional functionaries and technicians but do not present the image of "men of God" with a passionate concern for people'.[108] But much of theological education is moulded on the Western model which grew up in the period when theology was largely perceived as academic and speculative. Unless we can remodel our educational approaches, we may be doomed from the start to reproduce pastors in the academic and technical mould, who may not have experienced a parallel growth in their spirituality. Yet probably more than anything else in the Asian church today is the need for leaders with genuine Christian character!

---

[106] R.L. Maddox, 'John Wesley - Practical Theologian?', *Wesley Theological Journal* 23:Spring-Fall (1988), 123-26.

[107] J.M. Bonino, *Doing Theology in a Revolutionary Situation* (Philadelphia: Fortress, 1975), 99.

[108] J.A. Bergquist and P.K. Manickam, *The Crisis of Dependency in Third World Ministries. A Critique of Inherited Mission Forms in India* (Madras: Madras: Christian Literature Society, 1974), 63.

Who Are We Training?

The third question concerns 'who' we are seeking to train? In many churches left behind by the missionaries, there is often a strong tendency towards clericalism, with all the associated problems. Some churches, especially evangelical-charismatic ones, have reacted against this, and place their hopes in a predominantly lay leadership instead. But this generates another set of problems. For one, not many lay leaders have sufficiently theological training, formal or informal, to really help their people grow deep in the faith. Further, many of these lay leaders, especially in the big cities, are also too busy to do the necessary homework to produce good sermons and teaching material for their flocks. Worse still is the fact some of these lay leaders, because they tend to be successful leaders in society, often imagine that the reasons for that are quite adequate to ensure that their outside success will be repeated within the church. They therefore can sometimes be blind to their own weaknesses, spiritual and otherwise, and, ignoring their inadequate grasp of the gospel, they often end up dominating in the church, sometimes at the expense of those who have undertaken theological training. Such a 'tyranny of the laity' can be as stifling to the growth of the church as clericalism. The result is that in many areas where the churches have grown rapidly, there has often been no corresponding maturity in the life of individuals and churches. This means that theological education must be geared towards both clergy and laity alike. There is a need to plan more effective part-time courses and other TEE-type of programs, and not just concentrate on fulltime residential training.[109] Moreover, because of the different level of the needs of those seeking training among the laity, the courses available must be geared differently too.[110]

Finally, the laity must be challenged to face their own inadequacies and be willing to seriously undertake training. There is another related question. Given the fact that there is increasing diversification in the modern world, the question of who we are seeking to train must also be answered in relation to the specialized ministries needed to reach different sub-cultures and groups in our society. This would imply different approaches in training for those called to different types of ministry. To cite just one example, the China Graduate School of Theology (CGST) in Hong Kong has been working at specialized approaches to reach blue collar workers. Among other things, these people do not find the more Westernized hymns of the average church appealing at all. One of the things that the CGST group working on this has done is to compose Christian hymns using well known Chinese folk tunes. These songs have been found to be effective not only for Hong Kong Chinese, but Cantonese-speaking

---

[109] F.R. Kinsler, *The Extension Movement in Theological Education* (Pasadena, Ca: William Carey Library, 1981); F.R. Kinsler, ed., *Ministry by the People: Theological Education by Extension* (Geneva/Maryknoll, NY: WCC/Orbis, 1983).

[110] Bergquist and Manickam, *The Crisis of Dependency*, 127-44.

Chinese in rural parts of Malaysia. This example serves to highlight the need to develop specialized training for different forms of ministries in Asia.

The Practical Issues – A Case Study from Malaysia

We come finally to the third group of problems, which are practical in nature. For this section, I will use the Malaysian situation as a case study to illustrate the problems being faced in many Asian countries. I would hesitate to say that the Malaysian situation is representative of all, but I would think that many Asian churches would recognize a fairly high degree of similarity. The Protestant churches in Malaysia do not have many training institutions. Some of these, as in West Malaysia, Sabah and Sarawak are degree granting bodies and, yet, have low numbers of full-time students. When we take into consideration the fact that many of the better qualified students still tend to prefer institutions in Hong Kong, Singapore, Taiwan, and the West for their training, we can begin to grasp the problem.

The consequences of this are many and serious. Given the size of the Malaysian church, there is only a relatively small pool of resources in terms of available finance and faculty from which every college tries to draw. As a result, almost every one of these colleges struggle with the problem of having an adequate faculty, both in numbers and in the level of training. Most have problems with finance because the cost per student tends to be excessive. Because of the inadequate resources, the colleges are not able to give their students the best training possible. And of course, there is gross duplication of each others' efforts. The above problems are further compounded by other factors.

First, the colleges are generally divided along denominational or theological lines. In some cases, these divisions resulted from the desire of western mission boards to retain control! Yet the fact is that most, if not all, of the colleges would be classified as evangelical and/or Pentecostal-charismatic by most Western standards. The point is that in many cases the separation is quite unnecessary.

Secondly, the brain drain of personnel with advanced training is unfortunately very serious in the Malaysian church. There are probably three to four times the number of PhDs or equivalent in theology working outside the country than in it. They have not only gone to Western countries, but also to places like Singapore and Hong Kong where salaries are much more attractive. When you include those with degrees other than PhDs, the numbers would be phenomenal. It has to be said that this is one of the key reasons which have contributed greatly to slow rate of development of good theological institutions in the country.

The third problem is an age-old one in the Asian church, that of the general unwillingness of the church to give her best men and women for the ministry.[111] Although the situation has improved considerably over the past 20 years, the church in Malaysia still has a long way to go. The root problems appear to be threefold: the general level of the maturity of the Malaysian church or its lack of it, the unwillingness to sacrifice for Christ, and the poor image that Christians have of the pastoral ministry in general. Some of the above problems may be soluble from within theological education circles. But many of these are problems of wider consideration and will need to be addressed by the church at large. However, the scope of this paper really precludes any detailed discussion of these. Instead, I shall try to conclude with one thought which I believe to be essential for the way forward.

Conclusion

There is obviously no quick fix for the above problems listed. But I am tempted to suggest that some or even many of these problems will be resolved if the Asian church takes seriously the challenge to contextualize or indigenize, and to move on to a greater spiritual maturity at the same time. For example, if we take seriously the concern to become a truly indigenous church, we would increasingly refuse to allow traditional denominational differences and Western theological divisions to predominate in shaping theological education in Asia. We will, for example, not have our institutions splintered into tiny replicates of much bigger (hence more viable) originals in America and Europe. We would rather ask how our local institutions should be structured, given the smaller and more limited resources of many Asian churches. Or, again, instead of being dominated by the concerns of Western churches, we will want to ask how contextualization must relate to the content.

[111] C.S. Mieo, ed., *Education for Service in the Christian Church in China* (New York: Nanking Theological Seminary, 1935), 15ff., 31.

Globalization and Theological Education

Vinay Samuel

The Rev. Dr. Vinay Samuel is the former Director of the Oxford Centre for Mission Studies, UK.

Introduction

Our focus in this consultation is distance education. In this paper, I want to consider distance education in relation to the larger processes of globalization. Globalization has redefined the very nature of distance. Distance is no longer geographic. Globalization compresses distance, as well as time. We cannot talk about distance without looking at how distance is being redefined by the very process of globalization. Globalization has a particular relevance and challenge to theological education because it affects the way we define distance, education and learning. Global initiatives have been there since Jesus said 'Go into all the world and preach the gospel'. It is part of the very energy of the gospel to be global. How does this global gospel work and how is it unpacked in local contexts? In this paper, we are looking not so much at global institutions and undertakings akin to, say, Imperial Chemical Industries and other transnational enterprises, but at the global effects of a process that is going on all over. What we want to consider are global effects.

Globalization and the Universal in Historical Perspective

Certainly, in the pre-modern world globalization took place, although the word that was used was 'universal'. In the beginning, before Christ, the concept of universal had much more to do with distance and space. It was much more political. Its cultural implications were brought out later. The concept of universality was there, for example, among the Persians. Alexander the Great popularized the concept of universality. He was the first to say that what we have is a global culture. The Romans did the same thing and spread law and order globally. However, from the beginning, the idea of universal was much more politically defined in terms of space and colonization. We see parallels in nineteenth and twentieth century communism, which spread globally, although it was much more geographical and colonial. This unfortunate connotation and link between global and colonial remains even today. Some of my Latin American friends are instinctively suspicious of the 'global' because for them global means colonial and automatically triggers a negative reaction. So you do have the concept of global from the very beginning, even before Christ. Buddhism, also prior to the Christian faith, nurtured the idea that in religion there was a religious and cultural dimension that could be global. This was not understood politically, but in terms of religious and cultural dimensions that could become global. Christianity's 'go into all the world' involved a global or universal vision, and religion as a universal phenomenon. Certainly, Islam combined the two in a very territorial way. But prior to Islam, the emperor Constantine combined conquest with religion, culture and politics. Political space, geography and culture came together in that time. Islam demonstrated that if you extended your territory, it must have the same kind of global culture.

Thus, Bernard Anderson speaks of 'the great trans-continental sodalities of Christendom, Islam, etc'. These were religio-political systems following on from the world empires (the Persian Empire, the Greek Empire, and the Roman Empire). What began to develop was a world system of faiths, viz. the Christian faith, the Islamic faith. Religious world systems started to develop. Even before any economic system developed, religious systems developed which correlated with world systems. We need to take that very seriously. These were examples of distance mediated relationships. The interesting thing was that while these were cultural, and while there was a sense of universal belonging, these processes were initiated in a particular local context. The most interesting thing about Christianity is the way the Christian faith became global (universal). While there was the universality, a sense of belonging to a universal church, there remained the notion of a church in a particular local context. So it combined both local particularity and a sense of universal belonging from the beginning. And that is the magic of the Christian faith. Islam established a similar culture in each place, often by undermining local cultures, though in Islam, too, the global and the local interact in particular ways. But in the Christian faith, the global and the local were there from the very beginning. Universal belonging was always imagined in particular local contexts. We tend to think of life in the ancient, pre-modern times as confined to local situations, inasmuch as travel was very difficult. But who would have thought that there was such a tremendous amount of movement from, for example, the south to the north of Africa? Professor Terry Ranger, a Fellow of OCMS and a retired professor of Race Relations at Oxford University, has demonstrated how much movement there was and how much universality or globalization there was in Africa (and African religions) 1500 years ago. While globalization can be looked at politically in terms of distance, and culturally in terms of universality, it can also be looked at historically, as the end of history. We tend to see history in temporal terms as having no end mark, as going on and on and on. Globalization developed from the idea of colonial geography to the idea of global systems and culture. Now, as we begin the twenty-first century, we have the idea of global as being just contemporary, not even historically rooted. There is an absence of a centre. In this new global order, there is no political or economic centre. Finance flies out from country to country, economies are not controlled. In this environment, information and knowledge, and access to them, also cannot be controlled – nor do people today want, or tolerate, controls.

Globalization – a Definition

Thus far, we have used the term globalization without defining it. What is globalization? Globalization is the intensification of worldwide social relationships which link distant localities. In these processes, local habits are shaped by events that come from many miles away, and vice versa. Thus, when we talk about distance education I think we must focus also on globalization. Globalization is already linking distant localities in such a way that local habits are shaped by global habits and global habits are shaped by the local. It is the globalization of the locals and the localization of the globals. For example, the recent movie about Queen Elizabeth I was nominated for an Oscar and the director was nominated as best director. Now consider the fact that the director is an Indian, and had produced Indian movies from 'Bollywood' (the Indian Hollywood). He produced typical cultural and popular movies. Now, having done a Hollywood movie, he becomes a very wealthy, much sought-after director of Hollywood movies. He was local and now has become global. Do you think he will ever be able to go back and do the same thing? If he does go back to India, he takes the global and all that technology with him. When he directs his next Indian movie, it will be shaped by all that global knowledge and experience.

This illustrates the integral link between the global and the local. It is social events and social relations at distance with local contextualities. Globalization is really a complex sense of connectivity between varieties of local realities distanced from each other. It is a compression of time and space, providing an underlying unity. There is a drive to bring unity to all these things. While there is tremendous assertion of local culture and contexts, there are constant forces taking them into a united culture. Another example is how a local, non-Western Indian dance form, the *Bangda*, has become popular among British Asians. Contemporary British music culture reshapes it, and through satellite TV it is broadcast to its original home. The westernized and globalized *Bangda* now becomes very attractive by the sheer power of its presentation and begins to take root in its local context. What is the authentic *Bangda*? The local authentic one has been reshaped as a global product, with a local name and provenance but globalized. Theologically speaking, we cannot be divorced or protected from this culture. The global environment redefines space and time and anticipates culture. Local is no longer the only authentic culture. A roving culture takes different forms. A scholar once said that material change is localized, political change is internationalized, and symbiotics are globalized. Culture is de-territorialized, freed from the constrictions of face to face interactions of the local situations. Does it mean that they become less material and more imagined? Our relationships are de-territorialized (i.e. freed from having to have face to face communication and interaction in local situations), through the internet and communications. It can never be face to face once we get videos, etc. Actually, it is still face to face, only it is imagined; it is more of an image than a concrete face to face reality.

Mechanisms of Globalization

There are two mechanisms of globalism. Both are global realities; they are not local and are not controlled. One is *symbolic globals*, e.g. money that is interchangeable. That is why there is a tremendous drive to have no restrictions on the exchange of money. Money must be transportable from culture to culture; no boundaries must control it. Another example is computers. We can take a computer from one place to another. It can go across cultures. These are symbolic tokens that can go across all cultures. The second is *exporting systems*. Exporting systems means exporting products and people and systems that are globally transportable. Why is it that from my city in Bangalore we export young people in the age group of 20 to 28, all over to the US, Germany, UK, and elsewhere? It is because their computer expertise on software is now transportable anywhere. So the focus is on connections, communications, speed, contextual inter-changeability. Another characteristic of these mechanisms is their virtuality. What is virtual reality? This is illusion versus concrete reality. The virtual limit does not exist. A person who is working on a chat line may create his own personality. He may be the worst possible person, yet may present his personality in a completely different light. Now these are commodities, and also virtuals. They exchange values symbolically. Even the commodities are virtuals, because you don't even see the money, you only see a symbol of the money. Everything is virtual. Is this the reality that we are in and is this the way theological education is going? Is this the future of distance education? A faculty member at Harvard talks about all these different types of commodities schools are providing. An image, even though it is only virtual, eventually produces its own dynamics. Once you create a virtual thing, don't think you can keep controlling it. They control you back. The things you create start governing you. So then we have that question of where is the issue of power. Virtual reality is only a reference to relationships, not relationships themselves. Does distance education actually build the right type of relationship? If relationships are essential in discipleship, does distance make it worse? Moreover, does virtual reality make it worse yet? Virtual reality is producing only a reference to a relationship, not the relationship itself.

Globalization and the Learning Process

This leads us to the effects of globalization on the learning process. What are the challenges to these learning processes? I think the first is that in the domains of space and local, the nature of distance and the nature of the local are redefined. The very word distance is redefined because distance is no longer distance geographically. Local is no longer local because local is so impregnated, challenged and compressed by the global today. Conversely, the local also shapes the global, such that you can no longer talk about the local and global in the same way as you did twenty-five years ago. So we need to be asking, how does this reality re-shape our learning processes? How do we learn?

The second challenge to the learning process, particularly for those in theological education, is the process of enchantment and disenchantment and re-enchantment. Western modernity disenchanted a world where the spiritual was seen as the real and permanent and the material as passing. The enchanted supernatural world was disenchanted into a modern materialist world dominated by reason. Post-modernity has identified the impoverishment of spirit such disenchantment produced. The contemporary process of globalization is not committed to disenchanting all aspects of life reducing them to the rational and the spiritual. As it draws on esoteric and varied products and experiences, it allows room for everything to be re-enchanted (e.g. biblical Christians in India ask for their new cars to be blessed; material wealth is seen as a blessing).

Globalization, in its drive for the most creative and the newest fashion and product, develops all kinds of hybrid products. In developing a shopping mall for a city in India, the architect draws on shopping malls in the USA, Singapore, adds elements that relate to the local context and produces a hybrid product. Not having emerged organically from the local culture, the shopping mall is alternative and functional, but cannot express the soul of a culture in the way a local bazaar would. Globalization produces hybridity and commodification. This is a challenge is for theological education. Are we looking for a theological education that takes the energy of the African church, the technical finesse of the American church, the cynicism of the British church, and a variety of others, and produces a hybrid thing?

The final challenge to the learning process is ethics. In the midst of this globalization, the real hunger is for ethics, for motivation. So ethics becomes a very important element. At the beginning of the last century we had a breakdown of social institutions with a degree of moral structure. And with that broken down, there comes an ethical vacuum and with an ethical vacuum, violence comes in, because power is the only currency. Fast-changing systems require the development of ethics that meet the challenges of globalization.

Global Learning Resources and the Learners

Another challenge for the learning processes are global resources, that is, the resources are now global and no longer are contained in one place. The learner, too, has become central in the whole globalization context. Thus, the whole learning process is learner driven and learner negotiated. As a consequence, another challenge facing us is how to evaluate and accredit such a learning process. And how to introduce ethical orientation into that learning process. How do we introduce practice and re-introduce locality into that learning process? How does it impact personal relationships when the learning process is so virtual, when the learning process is shaped by the re-definition of distance as virtual? It is no longer just distance, it is virtual distance. How do we introduce the dimensions of personal relationships and care, and their contextual practice? I think large educational institutions like universities are quite happy carrying on blindly ignoring this reality. Yet it will overtake them, and they will begin to realize that they will be losing out very badly if they move into virtual reality the way they want to move into virtual reality. In such a scenario, the Oxford system of learning through one to one mentoring, for example, would be replaced by a learner focused, learner driven, learner negotiated, virtual reality shaped relationship. So how will that shape the learning process? That is the bottom-line challenge that we have before us.

We must consider also the challenge to the very content of theological education. We need to look at what the content is and assess whether the content can cope with these realities. Can the content cope with the forces and the trends that drive globalization? The more I see and meet with seminary students, the more I get depressed about how irrelevant the content they are learning is to the realities of the world they have to assist. We need to look at the content very seriously. Globalization demands that we look at how we should evaluate theological education. How do we evaluate what is happening to individual students? How do we evaluate a student's growth? How do we measure his or her effectiveness? What must he or she achieve to be given this credential of an MA or PhD now? In a globalized educational context, how do you accredit and evaluate courses?

Models of good practice are not confined to just one individual or institution. There are hundreds of models of good practice, each one developing their own model. Good practice must also, therefore, be collaborative. How can we be collaborative in developing good practice? Given the realities of the present context as I have outlined it, good practice has to be global and collaborative. How can we learn from each other? What are the ways in which we can draw on this global context that we are a part of, and benefit from globalization's compression and redefinition of distance?

How can good practice in one place cross boundaries, and affect practice and become a resource elsewhere, and how can we try and work together? In the development world in which I work addressing poverty, we are constantly looking at good practices. Often, for us in the development world, good practice is becoming increasingly scaled up; we are forced to do it in a major way and be more efficient: that is what development is all about. Development is no longer aid and other things, it is also development finance, which is very important. The World Bank, private industries, and private investments are coming in a major way into the poverty business and they are all scaling up their collaborative efforts. Thus, a given Christian group or organization can no longer say that we have to have our own little programme here in this little shanty town in Brazil. It is now a vast field of collaboration. And the development world has gone way ahead there.

The Christians in the development world are still pretty naïve. But the rest are moving ahead in a very dramatic way. I find it encouraging to see some of that as a model for us in theological education. We might ask ourselves, how do we become more collaborative? Do we collaborate locally? Is there global collaboration? How do local collaborators link with the global? A lot of us are passionately and personally committed to bringing about change. We are not just institutionally committed. How, then, do we collaborate? And what kind of partnerships, both local and global, can we bring about? I would add that, foundationally, our contribution must be viewed as not merely for theological education, but for the whole church. Inasmuch as we live in a global culture, the issue of our involvement or non-involvement in issues of globalization is primarily ethical. That is a further challenge that I set before you.

When I first came across programmed instruction in 1969, it involved a different way of instructing students. How can we look at good practice in course writing, which was mentioned as a gap that needs to be addressed? To share an experience of ours with TAFTEE (The Association for Theological Education and Extension), we took material from the SEAN from Argentina for those with seven years of schooling and rewrote it. We just changed the illustrations and the odd area of family issues which were not necessarily important in our context. The framework was generally the same, but it was possible to change it because of the way it was written. In this sense, there is a lot of technological support today and globalization does help us. We need to consider the economics, because he who has the dollar has the power. At the end of the day it is a power issue. This has been one of the struggles in contextualization. We produced about thirty courses between 1975 and 1978 in India. Because of our contextual commitment, we believed they were only for us and completely irrelevant to any other context. Even offering them to other contexts would be seen as a colonial imposition. Globalization questions that way of fencing contexts and contextual products.

The interesting thing was that four years ago, East Africa wanted to use our courses to develop their own. We insisted they must develop their own, even if they based them on our courses. Nothing happened for four years. So in 2000 they expect to use them in their Indian form but let local tutors adapt them to particular contexts. What we should have done, perhaps, using TAFTEE as an example again, was when we were developing some of our courses, to have had people from East Africa joining us in the writing of courses so they could pick up the skills and write it together. Why cannot an international team write that together, including the team in the places that are going to use it? Rather than one group decide and say we will provide a global framework, maybe the next step would be to say, okay, even in the construction of that international framework, let there be collaboration. That is one of our concerns. Thus, collaboration in the development of instructional resources is an example of the way processes of globalization can help us constructively address issues of power, economics, and good practice.

Globalization and Post-Doctoral Study

The Oxford Centre for Mission Studies (OCMS) has been producing an increasing number of doctoral graduates. In the past, OCMS has tried to develop a post-doctoral programme for the graduates. For example, an intensive post-doctorate study programme was developed on 'Evangelicals and Democracy'. A preliminary survey was published by the Cambridge University Press, because they believed there is nothing available on this subject area. The study programme was expected to produce eighteen post-doctorates, all of whom were to be non-Western and collaborating in such a way as to create fabulous resources for research and writing through this process. The main idea was that our ministry was not in simply enabling people to acquire PhDs as a teaching qualification so they can then teach from 'old notes', but it was intended to encourage people to remain active in research learning new skills and producing new material. A need for collaborative action was in this context felt even in the design of international programmes.

As suggested above, we need to focus on the content of curriculum. I draw again from my experiences with TAFTEE. We started developing course writing techniques. I thought we were way ahead of even the secular field in India, only to discover to my horror, as I learned from the people working in development, especially those in secular development, that there are the technologies of course writing. They have drawn on all sorts of new course writing techniques for new course development. I feel like a country cousin, absolutely incapable of matching their sophistication and skill. And yet I thought we were pioneers. Thirty years ago we started this whole process before anybody else. Now it may be that we need to be much more collaborative. Take what happened in Indonesia in the last year. Christian universities, that were mainly part of the ecumenical movement, began to say that they needed to collaborate with evangelical groups who have emerged and with whom they have no real connection. For the first time they will come together. One emphasis they had was that they had enough of their own university standards and accreditations. They began to discover these were no longer adequate in a global world. Indonesian Christians are saying Christian witness is public and we need the best we can get.

And therefore we need something international. It is incredible to hear that from people who have been made to believe for years that anything international is really Western, hegemonic and therefore suspect. International is something we need to relate to and draw on. What kind of mechanism is there for this to happen? If you want to relate to an international university, it is too expensive. British university validations are pretty expensive, and for OCMS to try and do something for them is extremely expensive. How do you devise different methods by which we can assist these who want to have an international framework? We must devise methods by which they can draw on, share with, relate to, and have a reference point with, international learning and accrediting networks and international Christian learners and teachers.

If the best research suggests that the key element is the out of class student/teacher contact, how does distance education integrate that as a practice and what is the best practice in that student and teacher contact? TAFTEE has been training pastors/elders from different parts of India for some years. These pastors/elders are training others in their own regions. A large number of students live where their ministries are located and are not only able to access resources in Bangalore by distance mode but receive help from the TAFTEE trained pastors/elders closer to them. This is how TAFTEE is able to expand its student base an all-India. One elder can be used for the whole process of learning, so that the contact hours actually increase for each student – it is not just face to face contact but also email contact. While the elder provide that kind of regular contact for the duration of two or three years or one full year, the experts based elsewhere can provide technical inputs through email contact.

How can research become part of good practice? It is a very important area. We did this at TAFTEE for years. We did a lot of research on local churches and their histories were written by their own students. We produced hundreds of histories of local churches. Eventually when all that gets put together, the real history of the church in India will probably get written. We teach them research methodology. However, the challenge is to integrate research results into course materials.

Conclusion

So, the issue globalization raises for distance theological education is this: Distance theological education presupposes a connectedness between places. It began as the connectedness between distant places in one nation. Now globalization is the death of distance, so we have connectedness between distant places in the world. Our task as theological educators is to avoid a homogenous one size fits all approach, which is one of the drives of globalization, and instead, both embrace our connectedness and use our resources jointly in such a way as to enhance the significance of Christian public witness in each locality. I am convinced we can use globalization for the benefit of theological education if we take seriously the issues raised above.

Theological Education through the Apostles

Tom Houston

The Rev. Tom Houston is Emeritus Director of the Bible Society of Great Britain, President of World Vision and Director of the Lausanne Committee for World Evangelization.

Introduction

The obvious place to begin talking about theological education is the New Testament. The apostles were the first to receive any form of Christian theological education and so are models that we need to examine. In this paper I am focusing particularly on the following: Models and outcomes – Jesus and the twelve; the needs of the student; Curriculum and delivery; and Resourcing open access.

When They Were Formed

The twelve are not where the gospel story begins. It is important to note at what point they emerge as 'the twelve'. John describes the twelve as in place just after the feeding of the five thousand, and during his teaching on the bread of life. John dates these events just before a Passover. Jesus said, 'Did I not choose you twelve, and one of you is a devil?' (Jn. 6:70). This means that there had been time for the false apostle to reveal his true colours. So the twelve were chosen at least a year before the crucifixion Passover and not in the recent past. Matthew speaks of the twelve for the first time in connection with their mission in Galilee (Mt.10:1). He does not say that they were chosen immediately before that mission. He speaks as if the twelve had been previously in existence. Luke says that the twelve were chosen just before the Sermon on the Mount (Lk.6:12-15). Mark confirms the view that the twelve were called just before the Sermon on the Mount and some time before they were sent forth on their preaching and healing mission.

So, the selection by Jesus of the twelve from the larger band of disciples who had gathered around him divides the ministry of Jesus into two almost equal parts. In the earlier period Jesus worked single-handed. His deeds were confined for the most part to a limited geographical area, and his teaching was on incidental subjects. By the time the twelve were chosen, the seeds of the kingdom had been spread so widely that he needed to pay attention to the future. This he did by selecting the twelve and beginning to teach them what they needed to know to carry on his work when he was gone. There were two sides to this: 'teaching', when he was with them, and 'experience', when he sent them out to preach and heal. This is always how God teaches. The task of teaching and training the twelve was critical for the future work of the kingdom. It has not become any less critical today. They were to learn that they were not just objects of his teaching. They were to become subjects with his teaching in their mouths.

Who They Were

They were adults, who were already in an occupation and earning their daily bread. They were already following him. Mark located their call at a time when people were in the process of sorting themselves out with regard to Jesus. They had heard the demons, which he cast out, cry out that he was the Son of God. They heard him teach with an authority that they had never heard before. They watched him perform miracles of healing. His family was finding it hard to take. The Pharisees and the teachers of the law were hardening against him. Mark describes the circumstances and gives their names (Mk.3:13-l9). Even the men he selected to be an inner circle had not yet made up their mind about Jesus. It is five chapters later (8:27-30) before he asks who they thought he was.

We need to note that he risked appointing the Twelve before all their questions were answered. It was a risky strategy, was it not? Just think of the people he invited. Simon (Jesus gave him the name Peter) – always at the top of the list; always in front. The big fisherman, high blood pressure, tense, blustering, blundering, impulsive, impatient – a daredevil, dictatorial, a big mouth, dominating. He is one of only two, about whose family we know anything of the women. In his case, it was his mother-in-law. She had a temperature and we are not surprised with Peter around. Yet with all that he was warm, genial, generous and loyal. Jesus called him when he was still like that. James and his brother John, the sons of Zebedee, whom Jesus nicknamed Boanerges or the MacThunders, because they were always rumbling about something. They were from an ambitious family, had friends in high places (Jn.18). It would seem that their mother had taught them that if you want to get anywhere in the world, you have to push and the family must stick together. They had little patience with people who got in their way and were implacably hostile to their rivals. Not a pleasant pair to meet in the dark or by broad daylight, yet Jesus called them.

Andrew seems to have been the second fiddle type of person, a shadow to his more impressive brother Peter. Yet he was no fool. In fact he got to Jesus ahead of Peter and effected their introduction. He had a Greek name, Andrew, which comes from the Greek word for 'a man'. He appears once or twice in the company of the other one with a Greek name, Philip, as here. Greek names in Galilee, signified that people or their parents were tired with ultra Jewish ways and felt that the future lay in combining the best elements in their own culture with the new learning and more efficient ways of the west. Jesus chose him.

Philip seems to have been similar to Andrew, for when some Greeks wanted to see Jesus, it was to him and Andrew that they came. He was an enquiring kind of person, wanting answers, but more than that we do not know except that Jesus called him. Matthew, also called Levi, was the collaborator of the bunch getting fat from cooperating with the Roman occupiers. He was a civil servant in the tax department. He worked out his own little racket and with a bribe here and ten per cent there, he was making money and able also to take in the odd girl friend when he fancied one. He had a great memory for connections and family trees. He had a flair with the pen too, in a systematic sort of way, probably because of his familiarity with books in his despised profession. He had many enemies and his friends were as unprincipled as he was. Yet Jesus did not stop to weigh the effect of Matthew's past on his own enterprise. He called him.

Thomas was the opposite of Peter, cautious, suspicious, pessimistic, never the man to be swept off his feet – a damper on other people's enthusiasm. He has two speeds, dead slow and stop but once he gets moving, he's slow but sure. You can just hear this spanner in the works saying, 'It's all very well but seeing is believing'. Don't count your chickens before they're hatched. What has been, is his measure for what will be and yet Jesus saw a role for him on his team. James son of Alphaeus and Thaddeus (Judas) are two nondescripts, so mediocre that all we know is their names and one question one of them asked. Yet they had a function to perform in his kingdom and Jesus called them.

Simon the patriot or zealot was a political revolutionary who believed in using violence for political ends. He was in the movement led by Judas of Galilee, which had attempted one revolution some years earlier and would erupt again later. He was a fanatic nationalist. How he got on with Matthew the collaborator is difficult to imagine. Yet Jesus chose him for the inner circle of disciples to be trained. Judas Iscariot, always the last in the list. He betrayed Jesus and is the enigma of the bunch, the great surprise. His background is obscure. He may have been the only man from the south of the country, if Iscariot means a man from Kerioth, a village in the south. He is the consummate actor, deep, hidden as to his real self, appearing exactly as he wanted to appear to others. He has a mind like an adding machine, a flair for finance and is made the treasurer. He can fiddle the books with the best and commit theft and never get caught; all the time appearing to be generous and thoughtful of others. But for all his bland front, he has dark disturbing thoughts, sometimes even of suicide. Greedy and selfish, Jesus called him and gave him a chance. That is the twelve.

Manual workers, white collar people, extroverts, introverts, conservatives, progressives, political, non-political. Their behaviour as a team left a lot to be desired. They squabbled and quarrelled and made mistakes and none of them scored 100 per cent in loyalty for they all forsook him and fled after one had betrayed and another had denied him. Yet that is how it was. He selected people, before they were convinced that he was the Son of God. The raw material for disciples is not very wonderful. They are men of like passions with ourselves. Yet he chose them to be with him and sent them out. A little more than a year later, they had become of one accord and were turning the world upside down. So they were adults, they were very different and they were twelve. The number twelve was not lost on them. They were the successors of the sons of Jacob the ancestors of the twelve tribes of Israel.

What They Were Taught

I will not try and give a summary of what Jesus taught the twelve. It would take too long and would almost be contrary to the way he taught. He did not teach systematically and it is well nigh impossible to categorize and present what he taught in a neat outline. Let me just make some observations. His overall concept was the kingdom of God. The radical difference was his showing it to be the kingdom of his God whom he called father. Only fifteen times in the Old Testament is God called Father. As we dip into the gospels it is a truth that bursts out on us like a torrent coming to full flood in John's gospel. He taught about attitudes and behaviour, standards and discipline, laws and customs. He had new things to say about marriage and the family, about social behaviour. He spoke of the world of the spirit and dealt with love and faith and fear and hypocrisy. He let them discover who he was and made it clear why he had come and how he would die. But he would rise again and he told how the world would end. These are inadequate notes but it is perhaps more important to consider:

By Example in Context

Mark notes that he called them to be with him and then sent them out. Being with him was essential. He exemplified what he taught. Recently Howard Gardner, a Harvard educational psychologist, wrote a book called *Leading Minds*. He analyses the lives of twenty effective leaders in different fields. In every case, their success depended on what he calls communication by embodiment. They lived their message. Jesus taught nothing he did not demonstrate. He did not teach in specific subjects at stated times. He taught as they went about their work. Nearly all the teaching that the twelve received was either by a question one or several of them asked about something he did or said or something they saw. They asked about prayer, about riches, about faith, about forgiveness. They asked about parables they did not understand, about casting out demons and about salvation. Sometimes they were afraid to ask and he read their minds and taught them anyway. The result of this was that everything that he taught was in context and relevant. It was not abstract and remote.

By Parables

Jesus' parables show he was quick to observe his audiences so that he could speak on subjects that were familiar to them. Jesus' discourse started where people were. He kept his eyes open in people's houses, for home and family are the greater part of any person's life. Jesus is always talking about them. He talks about kitchens where the leaven makes the dough rise. He talks about how children ask for bread. He talks about how the bread came out of the grass fired oven. He talks about fish and eggs, and not without salt. He observed cleanliness and washing up, sometimes obsessive. And he speaks about weddings and how exciting they were, and funerals and how tragic they were. He saw the differences between quarrelling children. He noted sometimes, that there was little love lost between brothers. He knew about the bother of unreliable servants who got drunk or helped themselves to what did not belong to them. He speaks about work situations. He knew about farms, and ploughing, sowing, and weeding, and harvesting. He draws illustrations from sheep, and oxen, and hens, and dogs, and vines, and figs, and mustard trees.

He was familiar with the market place with its pearl merchants, its traders, and its fortune hunters, where adults cannot hear themselves talk for children's endless playing. He is at ease with fishermen, builders, and soldiers; the whole work scene of his audience. He talks about social conditions: crime, the law courts, prisons, the banquets of the rich, and the misery of the poor. He knew about sickness and doctors and their bills. He sensed the impatience with neighbours, and antipathy to strangers, and notices commonplace conversations. The wide world of nature comes into his discourse, with the wind gusting in the trees and the flowers, the sparrows, the eagles, the foxes, the camels, the wolves, the serpents and the doves, and their ways. He left a lot to his hearers. He assumed they knew things and could work them out for themselves. They were left to draw their own conclusions from the parables. The disciples needed to ask what he meant because he did not say what he meant. In this way people ended up by saying things to themselves that they would have resented if he had tried to say them directly to them. Jesus did not have the urge that most preachers have to say it all every time. You remember ten per cent of what you hear and 90 per cent of what you say. If you want them to remember it, get them to say it and that means you not saying it. Jesus did that. Let me add another feature about how the parables secured a hearing. They show that things people know have to be told again in an unpredictable way. The easiest way to lose attention is to be predictable. With Jesus there was always that unexpected turn to the way he took the familiar and used it.

By Overheard Dialogue and Debate

The teaching of Jesus is often his response to the objections and the ideas of those who debated with or opposed him. We have to thank the debater-lawyer for the Good Samaritan. We have to thank his opponents in the Pharisees for the lost sheep, the lost coin and the prodigal son. It was opponents that brought out so clearly that the good news transcends race and class, is not hidebound by legalistic attitudes and is about love and grace and forgiveness, and not about merit and censorious attitudes. In Luke 12 someone came from the land owning class asking the question about dividing their inheritance. Jesus gave that incomparable and uncompromising statement about the rich fool who built the extra barns and his soul was required of him. If it had not been for the opponents, that gem of the gospel would not have been there. In Luke 20 he teaches about authority, about priorities, about taxation. 'Render to Caesar the things that are Caesar's and to God the things that are God's', and about the resurrection. All of this teaching was given in that last great tremendous teaching week of Jesus before his death. They are all examples of the gospel defined over against hard-hearted opponents. Whole chapters of teaching in John's gospel are given in debate with his critics and opponents. The twelve were present and overheard the gems of truth that fell from his lips and they added to their understanding of the gospel.

By Stages

He did not teach one theme all at once. He taught them progressively. His timing arose from his judgment of what they could learn at any given time. He spoke of things he was not able to tell them at the time but indicated that they would learn them later (Jn.16:4-5,12-14). He taught them to observe the same principle. 'Do not cast your pearls before swine or give what is holy to dogs' (Mt.7:6).

By Experience

He sent them out on their own to put into practice what he had told them. He was ready to trust them. In the case of Peter he was ready to allow him to fail, to learn what he could later share with his brothers (Lk. 22:31-32). In all of these ways, Jesus gives us a model which we should follow in our teaching of others.

How They Turned Out

We do not know how they all turned out. In Acts, after chapter 1, only Peter, John and James appear. John is often with Peter as a kind of moral support but he does not open his mouth. James appears only to be executed. Peter has a dynamic career as preacher and pioneer. Peter comes into the picture again towards the end of his life with his letters. John and Matthew gave us a gospel each. The books of the New Testament are living documents. They are works written by specific individuals for specific situations, each gospel having its own characteristics, moulded by these two factors. Who, then, is John Mark, this Jew with a Latin surname?

A Second Generation Christian

John Mark's mother was a prominent Christian in Jerusalem whose name was Mary. Thirteen years after the death and resurrection of Jesus, she owned a house in Jerusalem with servants, and large enough, when Peter was in prison, for 'many to be gathered together praying' (Acts 12:12). It is likely that his mother was a widow as the house is spoken of as hers and not his father's. Mark's cousin was Joseph from the island of Cyprus (Col. 4:10). He was of the tribe of Levi, who originally became priests or helpers in the temple and owned land in Cyprus. The family would seem to have one foot in the diaspora, while still retaining the other foot in Jerusalem. When the early church began to care for the poor, Joseph sold his property in Cyprus and gave the proceeds to the apostles to help meet the needs of the poor. The apostles thought highly of him and nicknamed him Barnabas, which mean someone who encourages people (Acts 5:36-37).

So, Mark was from a prosperous family with a foot in two worlds. Eusebius, the early church historian, tells us that Mark neither followed the Lord nor heard him. Piecing the evidence together, it appears that Mark was too young to be taking notice of things when Jesus came to Jerusalem for the weeks of the Jewish festivals. That makes Mark one of the first second generation Christians, whose mother, at least was a Christian before him. Being brought up in a Christian home has some great advantages. You grow up knowing about Jesus and the Bible and the church. It also has some snares. The snares seemed to figure more prominently in John Mark than the advantages. He shows some of the traits of those who wear the garments of their parents' faith before they find their own. The picture that comes to my mind when I think of a person whose faith has been inherited but not made their own is that of a little girl of about nine or ten, who is playing houses with her friends. She acts the mother. She puts on a dress of her mother's and a hat many sizes too big for her. She clanks around in high heeled shoes, large enough to have her own inside them with room still to spare. They are clothes that are fine for a game. But if there were a fire, and she had to run for her life, the borrowed clothes would only be cumbersome and lead to her tripping up and falling.

How like the faith of some of us who were brought up in a Christian home! It is fine, so long as they can continue to play at being Christians, doing and saying the right things in the right company. But when they are left on their own, or they put out into the storms of life, their faith begins to prove inadequate. It only causes them trouble. God has no grandchildren! It seems as though John Mark started out like this. It may be that those whom you teach are at this stage. Our attitude and our curricula need to take account of this possibility.

A Second Chance Disciple

Mark was taken for a disciple and first encouraged into Christian service by his generous cousin Barnabas. He was taken by Barnabas and Saul from Antioch to Jerusalem after their work of famine relief. They then took him as a junior member of the team on their first missionary journey (Acts13:5). All went well in Cyprus, which after all was home territory for Barnabas and John Mark. When they came into the fever ridden, mountainous, inhospitable region of Pamphilia on mainland Turkey, John turned tail and ran home to his mother, Mary, in Jerusalem (Acts 13:13). We do not know what made him desert the team. It must have been something serious from the scene it caused when Barnabas next tried to take his young cousin along on the second missionary journey. 'Barnabas wanted to take John Mark with them, but Paul did not think it was right to take John Mark with them, because he had not stayed with them to the end of their mission but had turned back and left them in Pamphilia. There was a sharp argument and they separated. Barnabas took Mark and sailed off to Cyprus. Paul chose Silas and left, commended by the believers to the care of God's grace. He went through Syria and Cilicia, strengthening the churches'.

For ten years, John Mark disappears from the story. We do not know what happened to him but we can guess that although Paul took a stern line with him, Barnabas kept him under his wing and must have helped him over whatever difficulties he had. For when he is next mentioned, he is with Paul again in Rome when he was in prison and nearing the end of his ministry (Col. 4:10). Paul speaks of him later also with high commendation at the very end. He tells Timothy, 'Get Mark and bring him with you for he is very useful in serving me' (2 Tim. 4:11). Mark's first following of Christ came to a sticky end, but by the grace of God, it was not the end. He lost one battle but he turned to fight again and to follow again and be a blessing to every generation of Christians from then until now through his gospel. We may have such early failures among those we teach. We may even be in that situation ourselves where our first following of Jesus has come to grief. We may have failed in a test and brought dishonour to our church or family, or to the name we love. Mark's story is that there is a second chance and God can restore your usefulness if you will turn back to him and overcome in the area of weakness.

A Second Fiddle Companion

Mark was always with someone of greater importance than himself. He was a number two. One organization for which I have often been a speaker at their big conferences, has a habit of giving each speaker a 'dogsbody' for the days he is in town. It has two purposes. The leaders do not need to stop what they have to do to pay attention to the needs of the visitor and the visitor gets all his needs attended to promptly and generously, whilst the young man gets the chance to be in the company of an experienced Christian leader for the days of the

Conference. I have the feeling that Mark was a bit of a dogsbody, always looking after someone. Acts 15:39: Barnabas took Mark with him. 2 Tim. 4:11: Paul says, 'Get Mark and bring him with you for he is very useful in serving me'. 1 Pet. 5:13: Peter says. 'My, son Mark, sends greetings'. Mark was always number two, overshadowed by another. He was rather like the grandson of the famous preacher, Jonathan Edwards, who was for ever being complimented on having such a great grandfather, until he became exasperated and used to reply, 'Yes, Sir, but every tub must stand on its own bottom'. We shall see the significance of this before we are finished.

A Second Hand Compiler

Eusebius, the early church historian says, Mark having become the interpreter of Peter, wrote down accurately everything that he remembered without, however, recording in order what was said or done by the Lord. For neither did he hear the Lord or follow him; but afterwards, as I have said, attended Peter who adapted his instructions to the needs of his hearers but had no design of giving a connected account of the Lord's oracles. So then, Mark made no mistake while he thus wrote down things as he remembered them for he made it his care not to omit anything that he heard or to set down any false statement therein. So, the picture of Jesus that we have in his gospel is not Mark's but Peter's. This is all the more remarkable when we have to note again and again how vivid an eyewitness account this is. Yet Mark was not there! Even in the incidents recorded also by Matthew or Luke, Mark always adds something that the others do not have. Yet, he was not there! To the last he was the faithful reproducer of another's story.

So little did he superimpose anything of his own, that to this day, Mark is regarded as the most original of the gospels. It is the shortest but has the most incidents. He had the opportunity to write a great gospel. He knew and was with Peter often. Peter may well have been the one through whom he came to faith in Christ, for Peter calls him my son Mark. In addition he knew Luke and Paul. The verses in Col. 4:10 and Phil. 2:4 both report that these three writers of the New Testament were with Paul when he wrote to the Colossians and sent Onesimus, the runaway slave, back to his master there. I cannot but believe that they talked about their writing about Jesus on occasions like that.

Mark had a nick-name, he was called 'Kolobodaktulos', 'Stumpy Fingers'. He had some deformity that was noticeable in his hands. Perhaps this was often seen when people watched him writing. Maybe he was the kind of person who was always writing things down. Because of this, his deformity was noticed much more than if had kept his hands in his pockets. Do you ever become depressed about your lack of originality? I know I do. Yet what a ministry there is in passing on what others have produced. We would not have had Peter's picture of Jesus had it not been for his faithful original copier. There are many who almost panic when they think about witnessing to Jesus themselves, becoming tongue tied or embarrassed. They could, however, take a leaf out of Mark's book and introduce their friends to someone who could do it better than they. That was essentially Mark's ministry.

The Writer of the Second Gospel

Now there is a final twist to this. It is generally agreed that Mark's was the earliest of the gospels, the first to be written. Yet true to the pattern, it ended up second in the New Testament. Matthew with its genealogies and frequent links with the Old Testament was the obvious one to begin the New Testament and effect the transition from the Old Testament and poor old Mark, though first to write, ends up second again. All of this has something to say to us. Those who have studied the gospels know the characteristics that are usually attributed to each of them. Matthew portrays Jesus as the king; Luke shows us Jesus the man; John reveals the Son of God. And what about Mark? Yes, his is the gospel of the servant messiah, who came not to be served but to serve and give his life a ransom for many (Mk.10:45).

Another interesting thing is that Mark uses the title 'lord' much less than the other gospels. His most common title for Jesus was 'teacher'. When he does use 'lord' it is mostly in Old Testament quotations that he uses to speak about God. That is in keeping with the fact that he was writing in Rome originally for a Roman or Italian audience where 'Kurios' was used for the emperor, Nero and Mark would not want his readers to think that Jesus was like that. Mark's emphasis is on the work of Jesus, what he did. He has nineteen miracles and only four parables. We could call it action packed, yet there is a great emphasis on Jesus having to suffer and die. Indeed the gospel is a bit like a murder story where someone is going to be killed and the author tells the events leading up to the murder, so as to show us who did it and why – and what happened to the body.

How did Mark arrive at these facets of Jesus' character? From his own very real walk with Jesus. He needed to cope with always being in the shadow of someone else. Mark was always the servant and he found his inspiration in Jesus the servant and portrayed him as such to the world. Here we discover a great truth about our witness to Jesus. As we all have a different road to walk, so we are enabled to show forth a distinctive aspect of our Lord's character. You are writing a gospel, a chapter a day; by all that you do and all that you say, Men read what you write whether faithless or true! Say, what is the gospel according to you?

Luke, the Doctor and Companion

When we come to look at curriculum and delivery of distance learning I think Luke, with his exclusive material and different emphases, will help us. He has a particular constituency in mind, represented by His Excellency, Theophilus. I have had to meet heads of state, government ministers and ambassadors as I have gone around the world. You have to think twice if they are your audience. If Luke had a church in mind, when he wrote, it would be one that had Roman officials at least paying attention to their message. We owe a lot to Luke, both for his gospel and for the Acts. Apparently he felt the story was not fully told until he had written about the rise and spread of the early church. Acts had to follow Luke's gospel if Theophilus was to be fully informed. So what kind of person was he? There are only three references to him in the New Testament. I will work from these three very short simple references and his writings to give you my picture of this man, Luke.

In Colossians 4:13 (AV) Paul describes him as 'the beloved physician' or, (GNB) 'the dear doctor'. I call him the diffident doctor. We know him as the patron saint of medicine. There are St. Luke societies named after him. It is worth thinking about that. If Paul had not put this note in Colossians, would we have known of his medical connections? I think not. There is no record of him treating or healing anyone anywhere. Indeed, there is no record of him doing anything anywhere. Titus was sent on special service and received a letter. Silas sings with Paul in prison in Philippi. Luke seems even to have escaped arrest at that time. Timothy is put in charge of a church and gets two letters sent to him. Mark is mentioned both for his deficiencies and his credits. Aristarchus, Epaphroditus all have a known piece of the action, like Priscilla and Aquila, but Luke is not mentioned as having done anything even though he wrote the biggest part of the text of the New Testament. He seems to have been a very retiring doctor. In fact, it was Paul who was the healer. In Acts 14 he heals the lame man at Lystra.

In Acts 16 he heals the possessed girl in Philippi. In Acts 19 handkerchiefs and aprons from him effect healings and people believe. In Acts 20 he seems to raise Eutychus from the dead when he fell out of the window when Paul preached too long. He is presented by Luke as performing signs and wonders in a couple of places. In Acts 28 Paul heals the chief official of Malta, Publius' father, of fever and dysentery. Luke tells the stories, but there is no word of Paul calling in the doctor even when he was present, or at least he never records it. We also know that Paul, himself, was often a sick man. Galatians 4:13 tells us that his coming to Galatia had to do with his sickness. We know in 2 Corinthians 12:7 that he had a thorn in the flesh, which he asked the Lord three times to take away, but was merely given grace to cope with. We do not know what it was:

- The early fathers, Augustine, Jerome, Gregory and Aquinas said it was something sensual.
- Luther and Calvin and the Reformers thought it was something spiritual.
- Chrysostom and Hilary, the Greeks, thought it was something external like opposition or persecution.

- More recently, people have actually thought it was a physical malady and that is how it is translated in the GNB.
- Lightfoot thought it was epilepsy.
- Farrar thought it was acute opthalmia.
- Sir William Ramsey thought it was chronic malarial fever. I think the important thing is that we do not know what it was.

If it had been mine, you would have known. If it had been yours, we would have known. But Paul did not talk about it except under apology and protest in 2 Corinthians 12. Luke, the doctor, does not tell us in the Acts that it was there or what it was. All we know is that he laboured more abundantly than they all in spite of his thorn in the flesh. This Paul modestly says was just another manifestation of grace. No doubt Luke knew what it was. I cannot help feeling that Luke treated Paul as he was able when he had bouts of whatever it was. I guess Paul was grateful. I think that is why he called him the beloved physician or the dear doctor. Was it this factor in Paul that kept Luke going with him? Was this his calling to be the unofficial medical attendant to a wonder-working apostle, just to keep him alive? It is quite a thought.

We note, however, his latent professionalism. There are numerous instances where in his gospel he uses the technical medical words not used in other gospels. The demon-possessed man in the synagogue at Capernaum is 'convulsed'. The father of the epileptic approaches Jesus coming down from the mount of transfiguration with the language of a patient paying a visit to a doctor. The problem of the eye of the needle for rich people in Luke is the surgeon's needle. He has six different words for worry in his gospel, all of which only he uses and all of which are used only once in the New Testament. I cannot help thinking that this shows someone familiar with various aspects of psychosomatic ailments.

There is evidence that he is a physician, but only a 'pro' would spot it. Is it a case of the professional, the specialist, becoming a support staffer, or a private physician but most importantly a caring companion? In 2 Timothy 4:11 Paul has this plaintive note, 'Only Luke is with me'. Paul is in prison. Demas, who had been one of the fellow workers at the end of Philemon in his first imprisonment, has now forsaken him, having loved this present world. Crescens, Titus, Tychicus have all gone on other missions. Now Paul says toward the end, when he is now ready to be offered, 'Only Luke is with me'. He is a faithful, loyal, caring companion about whom Paul thought it worth mentioning just that he was there and that there was no one else. Paul needed support. He often did not get it. You find his nervousness coming out when he does not have support in 2 Corinthians 2:13 when he was agitated at the absence of Titus. He could not rest. You see it in his loneliness in Philippians 2:21, where he says, 'Everyone else is concerned only with his own affairs' – a dramatic sentence. Luke was one that gave him the support and companionship that he needed, and he did it very unobtrusively, but he did it to the end. In Acts, Luke very subtly indicates his presence in what we call the 'we' passages.

The story changes from the third person, 'he', 'she' and 'they', to the first person 'we'. There is a reading in Codex Beza that makes the first 'we' passage, Acts 11:28 where Agabus, the prophet, predicted the famine that was going to come. This led to the first relief exercise from Antioch to Jerusalem. Scholars think it unlikely that he was there at that time or that it is an accurate reading. But it probably gave rise to the tradition that Luke was from Antioch. Incidentally, there is another tradition in the anti-Marcionite prologue to Luke's gospel that says he died unmarried in Boeotia at age 84. We do not know this for sure, but it gives added colour to our picture if we think of him as a single doctor who joins Paul, when he and Barnabas mount the first famine relief programme for the poor in Jerusalem.

The first time we are sure that Luke was with Paul is in Acts 16:10. In Troas Paul saw the vision of the man from Macedonia. Luke joins him as he sets sail for Europe. He is present in Philippi with Lydia, and at the healing of the demoniac girl. But he is not in the arrest. He is not in the prison, and he is not with them when they move on to Thessalonica. We wonder what happened. Some have suggested that he stayed on in Philippi as the pastor, and I can imagine that, but that would be only speculation. In Acts 20:6, he comes from Philippi about three and a half years later and enters the narrative again. He and the others sailed from Philippi to Troas and they go up to Jerusalem as bearers of the great collection, that three-year fund-raising effort in which Paul was involved in the middle of his ministry. He is with Paul when he goes to Miletus and makes the speech to the Ephesian elders. He accompanies him to the Islands of Cos and Rhodes, the land of Tyre. They sail on to Ptolemais, Caesarea, Jerusalem, and back to Caesarea where he is in prison. Then it is Adramyttium, Myra in Lycia, Safe Harbours, Malta, Rhegium, Puteoli and Rome. He is there all the way.

Why do I mention all of the ports? Well, it was a tempestuous time. There were prisons on land and storms at sea. Through them all, Luke was there, the caring companion, no doubt helping Paul with his malady, keeping him alive to reach Rome. All the time he registers the details of their travels and records them for posterity. How eloquent the 'we' passages are about simple companionship. We do not rate this quality as highly today. One of the things that impresses me about the Billy Graham team are the number of men that are still just there with Billy: Cliff Barrows, T.W. Wilson until his death, and Walter Smith. They are there. It is thought that Paul was a widower, not in very good health. If it is so, then we can see how important Luke and these other companions were to him. Can I say here to the spouses also, 'You cannot put a value on caring companionship'?

What a different story Paul's might have been if Luke had not been there. He probably would not have lasted the pace. How different for many of us if our companions also had been missing. We must never underrate the value of people who are always reliably there. Luke then, is the diffident doctor, the symbol of the absence of universal healing in the church; the support staffer, attending to documentation and consistency, valuable both then and now. The careful companion sticking at his God-appointed post by the side of another. It all says to me that the New Testament is not different from today. It is a picture of inter-dependence, where we are all necessary to one another, and together to God and the mission.

Paul and His Letters

In any development today the question of resources must start by making the best use of the resources that are already there, before importing anything from outside. If we do not, we will make projects unsustainable. It would yield some insight on using existing resources if we looked at Paul and his letters.

Thirty-five per cent of the New Testament is made up of 'letters' from five named and one anonymous correspondent. Paul wrote 70 per cent of these letters. Why did Paul adopt this 'method of teaching'? His own learning from Gamaliel was pursued face to face, at set times and in a settled place in Jerusalem. There was already a literary form of letters in Greek and Latin. Cicero in the recent past, Seneca contemporary with Paul and Pliny later used this form of literature. Teachers of rhetoric gave instruction on how to use this literary form. Paul's letters are not like them. If there are parallels from his time, it is in the personal letters found in the Greek papyri. Historically, the first use of letters to the churches, containing the Christian teaching, was after the Council of Jerusalem (Acts 15:22-31). They put the decision about circumcision and the law of Moses in a letter and sent men to tell them, in person, the same things they had written. Paul was one of the people who carried the letter, read it to the churches and explained its contents. I like to think that this is what gave Paul and the others the idea of using letters to teach. By the time of 2 Peter they were regarded as Scriptures (2 Peter 3:16).

Paul says most about his own letter writing in 1 and 2 Corinthians. The first letter to Corinth in the New Testament was not his first letter to them. He had written an earlier letter to which the Corinthians had replied with a set of questions (1 Cor. 5:9). So Paul gives his motive in writing a second time. It was 'not because I want you to feel ashamed, but to instruct you …'. (1 Cor. 4:14). He gave answers to questions they had written about unmarried people etc. (1 Cor. 5:9); food offered to idols (1 Cor. 8:1); spiritual gifts (1 Cor. 12:1); money (1 Cor. 16:1). He protests that he is not writing to claim his rights (1 Cor. 9:15). Sometimes he says that he was giving the Lord's command. In other places he says he was saying this, not the Lord. In 2 Corinthians, he says that he writes only what they would understand (2 Cor. 1:13); to save them from a stormy confrontation with him (2 Cor. 2:3); to make them realize how much he loved them, and to find out how they were standing up to their trials (2 Cor. 7:8).

He says that he was not sorry he wrote, even if it made them sad, because their devotion to him had proved to be really deep (2 Cor. 7:12). Then he says he is writing to stimulate them to keep their promise to send money to God's people in Judea (2 Cor. 9:1). It is clear that some people said harsh things about his letters and their contents. They said that he wrote letters to avoid speaking to them face to face (2 Cor. 10:9-11). Paul denies this. He says that he wants them to have put things right before he arrived and save him from having to deal harshly with them when he came (2 Cor. 13:10). It is a picture of an interactive exchange, not just to share information but to help them adjust their lives to the demands of the truth that he penned.

The definition of theology I use is: 'A theology is a set of answers taken from scripture to the set of questions any generation is asking about God'. This definition shows that Paul was building a theology when he wrote his letters. He answered the specific concerns they or others had conveyed to him about their new found Christian faith. He found an existing medium to convey his theology. It cost very little other than a journey by a bearer to the recipients. It was heard live in church after church. He used the most suitable current medium to convey the Word of God. There are various kinds of letters: those he addressed to Christian congregations in places like Thessalonica, Galatia and Rome, based on reports that reached him about the people there; those that formed part of reciprocal correspondence where questions were asked and replies given.

One addressed to a particular individual, Philemon, expressing his care for the bearer of the letter, a runaway slave. The letters were addressed to a wide geographical area from Rome across the Adriatic, through Macedonia and Greece and over the sea again to what we call Turkey. It really was distance learning! I learned how comprehensive this theology was when I was in the pastoral ministry in Nairobi, Kenya. I remember how it happened. I had just finished one series of Bible expositions and was talking to my wife, Hazel, about what we might do next. She said, 'Why don't you talk about God? Too often it seems that you end up talking about us and our responsibilities'. I felt it was a valid point, so I started to think and pray about it. I ended up doing a series of sermons on 'Paul and his God'. I would start at the beginning and try to trace how Paul discovered what he knew of God. I worked on four principles: it would be biographical, working progressively through Paul's life; it would be based on the language he used about God; it would try and coordinate these two to see if there was any match between them; it would let that speak to our lives at that time in Africa. I ended up doing a series of 67 sermons on 'Paul and his God' that lasted almost two years. It was a stimulating exercise from which both I and the congregation benefited greatly.

I took each phrase that Paul used about God and noted at what periods of his life these phrases were most used by him. (See the exhibit at the end of this article.) The phrases Paul uses about God are in the centre column. The periods of his life in the right-hand column. In the left-hand column are the places in the Acts and his letters where these phrases are used. In the treatment, I tried to cover all that Paul said on that aspect of God in all his letters and not just deal with the biographical episode. Look at 'The gifts of God' about half way down page one. Although it starts with Paul's discovery of Timothy's gift it included what he taught about gifts in Romans, 1 Corinthians and the letters to Timothy, over five Sundays. Note how comprehensively the subjects in the centre column cover the doctrine of God and his work in our lives. It was a fairly rounded theology.

Some Examples

'The Love of God'

Sermon 38 brought us to 'The love of God'. I asked the people to imagine themselves sitting in a house in Ephesus, listening to Paul as he tried to put together and dictate his reply letter to one of the questions the Christians in Corinth had sent him. The day before he had begun to deal with spiritual gifts. These had been a cause of envy, rivalry and strife between the Christians. Their meetings were breaking up in disorder as one and another insisted on holding the floor. In his reply, he had shown in chapter twelve that these are only gifts. It is God who gives them for the common good. He then applied this with the classical philosopher's illustration of the mutual interdependence of the parts of our human bodies.

From the illustration he comes back to the actual gifts and applies what he has said to apostles, prophets (and thirdly) teachers, healers, administrators and practically and psychically gifted people. The argument is moving on relentlessly. Now, strangely, he digresses. His whole tone alters. 'I will show you a more excellent way' and he begins to speak about love. It is soon over, just three paragraphs. Then he carries on where he left off about the priorities they should have with regard to the development of their gifts. It is quite unusual, and most unexpected and yet it has become the best-known passage from Paul's writings. It was read at both the wedding and the death of Diana, Princess of Wales. Yet it was an interjection, a parenthesis, an aside. It does not mention God or Jesus Christ or the Holy Spirit. My methodology showed me that up until this point in his life Paul has not said a lot about love.

There is no record in Acts of his even using the word love, either noun or verb in his preaching. In his writing to the Thessalonians he does not say a lot but what he does say is more about the love between Christians than about the love of God. Thus far in 1 Corinthians he has mentioned love only twice. One was in an Old Testament quote about what God has prepared for those who love him (1 Cor. 2:9). The other was in chapter eight about the relative importance of love and knowledge (1 Cor. 8:1-2). Now suddenly he burst out into these three concentrated paragraphs. It is as though a dam had burst and all he has been pondering about love gushes out at once. In all his later letters, thoughts about the love of God are a steady flow. What burst the dam at this point? I think we can guess. We know the problems in Corinth that were confronting him. He is trying to help a company of Christians whose fellowship is riddled with hostility, rivalry and strife. He is using everything he knows to make a real church out of them. Then it hits him.

The answer is in his own experience. He had once been a religious bigot full of ambition and very hot in doing others down. But he had been changed. How? By the love of God. As he was to write later to Timothy, 'I formerly blasphemed, persecuted and insulted, but I received mercy… and the grace of our Lord overflowed for me with the faith and the love that is in Jesus Christ'. It dawns on him that this is the need of the Corinthian Christians more than anything else if they are to be reconciled and made into one united fellowship. So he launches into the subject and both his first and last paragraphs confirm our view because it puts love in contrast with the whole range of possible gifts. Then I preached two sermons, one on 'love and gifts' and a second on 'love and character'. I could preach them again to you now.

'The Grace of the Lord Jesus'

Sermon 41 brought us to 'The grace of the Lord Jesus'. The grace of God is a phrase that is found in every one of Paul's letters. This comes in the key passage about the great collection (2 Cor. 8:9). There was a remarkable reversal of roles. The Gentile churches collected what they could give, Sunday by Sunday, for about three years and put it aside until a personal representative from each region could assemble and take it together for the relief of the Christians impoverished by famine in Jerusalem and Judea. It is a powerful story that should be told much more often than it is. It took us three weeks to explore. This enabled us in story form to discover that giving is: a secondary matter – a grace or a gift from God; proportionate to income; voluntary; an equalizer between the 'haves' and the 'have nots'; and productive of praise and prayer and personal enrichment of spirit.

'The Man of God'

The third example was in sermon 64 on 'The man of God'. This is such a common phrase in popular speech and occurs about 20 times in the Old Testament. Yet it occurs only twice in Paul and both are in the letters to Timothy (1 Tim. 6:11 & 2 Tim. 3:17). What circumstances then, made him speak of the man of God? These letters cover Paul's two experiences in prison in Rome. First there was his house arrest when people were able to come and see him. Then he was released and visited again some of the places where he had founded churches. Ephesus, Macedonia, Crete, Corinth, Miletus and Troas all crop up again in his writings of this period. Then he was arrested again. This time his imprisonment in Rome was more severe. The fires of persecution were beginning to blaze.

It was in these two periods of enforced inactivity, that he saw the crying need for good leadership. He was not getting any younger. He was 'Paul the aged', to Philemon. He began to think of the situation when he would be gone and the church would no longer have him to turn to. It is not surprising that in these circumstances he should ask himself, what makes a man of God. And in 2 Timothy 3:14-17 we get his weighty answer. It is the man or woman who continually applies himself personally to the Scriptures. The man of God is made by the word of God. The Scriptures effect his conversion, shape his convictions, direct his conduct and make his career fruitful. That is still our need today. To me the most serious matter in the churches is the decline in biblical literacy.

Whatever you do, show those whom you teach how to live on the Scriptures and then how to share them relevantly with others to whom they preach. Have you ever asked why Paul had to spend so many years in prison? Was it not such a waste of talent? I think not. It led to his getting seven more letters written. Perhaps more significant, it led the timid Timothy to stand on his own two feet and Titus and Silas and Mark and all the other men and women we find listed at the end of his letters. Perhaps we need to find a dynamic equivalent to consign some of our greats to let the young come forward and be given their greatest challenges in their prime and not when they are really going down hill.

Exhibit

Paul and his God scheme

Letter	*Subject*	*Incident or episode*
Acts 26:4-18, 1 Timothy 1:12-17	The father of mercies	Paul's conversion
Galatians 1:11-24	The God of hope	Paul in Arabia
Galatians 3:13-22	The promises of God	Activities of the Judaisers
Acts 9:19-31, Galatians 1:18-24	The God of patience	Paul rejected in Jerusalem
Acts 12:25-13:3	God is faithful	Paul's call from God.
Acts 13:4-12	God is true	Elymas the sorcerer
Acts 13:16b-41	The power of God	Preaching at Antioch in Pisidia
Acts 14:8-20	The living God	Preaching at Lystra on idols
Acts 15:1-19, Acts 11:19-30	God over all	
Col.1:11-23	The God of peace - with God	Paul's success at Antioch
Acts 15:30-41	- from God	Paul and reconciliation
Philippians 4:1-9 Col. 3:12-17	- of God	Dispute with Barnabas re Mark
Ac,16:1-3, 2Tim.1:1-7,Tim.4:11-16. Phil.2:19-24	The gifts of God	Paul's resilience
	* Knowing your gifts.	Discovery of Timothy and its
2.Tim.2:1-15	* Knowing your gifts 2 & 3.	outworking and exposition.
2Tim.2:15-26.	* Financial potential	"
1 Timothy 4:1010, 17-20	The will of God - decisions.	"
Acts 16:6-10, 2Cor.1:15-2:4	The work of God	"
Acts 16:11-18, Philp:1-4	The salvation of God	The call from MacedoniaPaul in
Acts 16:11-18, 25-34	The kingdom of God	Philippi, circumstances
Acts 17:1-9	The Word of God.	Paul in Philippi, people.
Acts 17 10ff	The God of all creation	Paul at Thessalonica
Acts 17:(16)22-31(34)	The foolishness of God	Paul in Berea
Acts 18:1-17	The weakness of God	Paul's speech in Athens
		Paul in Corinth
1Cor:18-31		Paul in transit to Ephesus via Antioch
1 Thessalonians 2:1-12	God is witness	Writing in Corinth to Thessalonica
1 Thessalonians 2:1-12	The gospel of God	
2 Thessalonians 22:1-11	The day of the Lord	"
Acts 19:1-7	The Spirit of God	The disciples of John the Baptist
Acts 19:8-20	The name of God	Paul and the Jewish exorcists
Acts 19:23-41	The invisible God.	The riot in Ephesus
1 Corinthians 1:4-17	Followers of God	Paul's baptizing in Corinth
1 Corinthians 2:6-16,	The wisdom of God.	At Ephesus, receiving and sending
1 Corinthians 5:1-5, 6:1-8	The church of God- assembly	letters to Corinth
1 Corinthians 12:12-27	The church of God - body	"
1 Corinthians 13	The love of God 1.	"
	The love of God 2.	"
2 Corinthians 1:3-14	The God of all comfort	Response to slander in Corinth
2 Corinthians 8:1-14	The grace of the Lord Jesus	"
2 Corinthians 8:16-9:5	"	The great collection
2 Corinthians 9:6-15	"	"
Romans 1:1-17 Acts 20:1-6	The righteousness of God	3 months in Corinth waiting for
Romans 1:18-32	The wrath of God	the delegates with the collection
Romans 6:1-11	The life of God	to assemble . Paul devises the let-
Romans 7:21-8:8	The law of God	ter to the Romans as a P.R. docu-
Romans 8:14-23,28-32	The Son of God	ment to explain about himself and
Romans 9:1-8, 11:1-6	The people of God	his teaching, in advance of his
Romans 11:1-25	The kindness & severity of God	going there after Jerusalem.
Romans 12-16		"
Romans 13:1-10	The servant of God-words for.	"
Romans 14:1-4, 10-12, 2:1-11	The servant of God	"
Romans 16:1-20	The judgment of God	"
Acts 20:17-37	The servant of God	Message to Ephesian elders
Acts 24:1-21	The work of God	Arrest in Jerusalem
Acts 27:9-12, 21-25, 33-36	The God of our fathers	Escape from shipwreck
	The providence of God	

PART 3

Contextual Theological Education

Open Access in Closed Societies: Theological Education in Muslim Contexts

Leonard N. Bartlotti

Dr. Leonard N. Bartlotti is Associate Professor of Intercultural Studies at Biola University, USA.

Introduction

The purpose of this paper is to explore issues related to open access theological education in 'closed' societies, or what are sometimes referred to (in Christian mission circles) as 'restricted access' nations. Primarily, I want to look at contextual factors affecting Christian theological education within what is, broadly speaking, a socio-political environment that is restrictive if not hostile to the Christian faith. Partly because of my own experience and research interests, I will confine my reflections to areas where the Islamic tradition is dominant, with the understanding that some of these contextual factors also apply to other situations where faith is under fire. Islam represents the challenge of the Other, the Samaritan who is theologically near and far, both open and closed. Thus, clearly, one of the competencies needed in theological education is the ability to equip the church to relate biblical faith to Islamic and other cultures.

Bernhard Ott has affirmed that mission integrated theological education requires a clear vision of the church in mission, as well as a clear vision of theological education in mission.[112] What are some of the preliminary understandings that might guide theological education in Islamic contexts with a view to a programme of engagement? In this paper I want to explore some of the issues involved, using a restrictive society as a paradigmatic context. Tom Houston defines theology as, 'A set of answers taken from scripture to the set of questions any generation is asking about God'. How do we get at that 'set of questions'?

I would like to put forward a number of issues or contextual realities for discussion. As you will quickly recognize, this is a suggestive, not an exhaustive, treatment of the issues, and they are not presented in terms of priority. Some items could be viewed as barriers to open access or to the learning process; others are related to issues of local relevance and pedagogy. Together they represent some of the realities facing those currently engaged in theological education in these spheres. Before grasping the internet, for

[112] See Ott's paper above.

example, as the answer, or even part of the answer, to theological education in restrictive or closed societies, we need to be willing to consider, at least, some of the questions raised in a particular context. Certain of these theological questions relate to our understanding of the mission task in relation to Islam and other major cultural blocks of 'unreached peoples'.

The Audience: Muslims, Church and Mission

The first reality is the recognition that there is indeed a new audience of learners and potential learners that need resources for theological reflection. In countries and ethnic groups around the world, Muslims are turning to Christ in perhaps greater numbers than ever before. In Iran, to cite just one example, more Muslims have turned to Christ in the last twenty years since the Iranian revolution than in the last one thousand years combined. Similar results can be cited among certain Fulani groups in West Africa, Turkic Muslims in Central Asia, and elsewhere.

This response can be traced in part to a resurgence of prayer and the initiation of new efforts and strategies to make the gospel 'Good News' to Muslims. Until a few years ago, less than two per cent of the global missionary force were working to reach Muslims, despite the fact that the 1.2 billion Muslims comprise one-sixth of the world's population. This startling neglect has been linked to historical prejudices, the perceived difficulties of working in Islamic areas, as well as fear, unbelief, and the fact that missions were quite overwhelmed with the harvest elsewhere in the world. Even now, the amount of money and personnel focused on ministry to Muslims is disproportionately small in comparison with the human need. Islam remains perhaps the church's greatest challenge.

Nevertheless, the exciting reality is this: in Central Asia and Southern Asia, in parts of the Middle East and Southeast Asia, as well as in countries of the West, there are now a growing number of 'Muslim background believers' (MBBs) or 'Muslim followers of Jesus', meeting in cell groups, churches, and 'Christ-centred communities'. Thus, one mission objective of open access theological education must be to develop programs to *train leaders within and for the emerging church in the Muslim world.* 'Within' the emerging church – because there is a new generation of MBBs now a part of the body of Christ. We are dealing with an audience of MBB learners who are, or will be, in desperate need of theological education within their own Islamic cultural context. (We will look at this in more detail below.) We also need to train leaders 'for' the church, because there is still a critical need for greater numbers of national and expatriate Christians from the West and the two-thirds world to engage Islam theologically *and* in terms of holistic mission in these pioneer contexts. I am not aware of any concerted attempts to bring together these two arenas of study.

This suggests two other critical groups of potential learners: a) national Christian leaders and churches (non-MBB), and b) missionaries and NGO workers engaged in holistic ministry. One mission has over 600 workers on some 100 international teams working exclusively among Muslim peoples. Some of the practical problems being engaged include ministry to refugees and displaced persons, micro-economic development, community development, reforestation, appropriate technology, children at risk, women's rights, reconciliation, etc. Many exciting and creative initiatives are taking place – largely *without* the benefit of an integrated network of global theological and missiological and development resources. There are teams of workers, but not teams of learners. One challenge to us as global theological educators is to relate the considerable expertise and resources of theology, development, 'mission as transformation', etc. to helping these learners (MBBs, national leaders, missionaries and NGO workers) address life and death issues related to church and mission in the Muslim world. In many of these contexts, 'church' is still taking shape and viable indigenous church movements have yet to be birthed or are in process.

Christians, churches and Christian NGOs are struggling to relate faith to faith, faith to culture, and to meet human need in areas where Christian activity may be construed as having political or subversive meanings, and where progress is measured by individual lives changed, and sometimes in blood. To give you an example: In one national church in the Middle East, there are perhaps eight to ten Bible teachers for over 150 students presently engaged in undergraduate (BA) programmes; three or four of the teachers are of Muslim background. If we include the diaspora in the West and elsewhere, this Christian community may have thirty to forty students who might be eligible for an MA programme. Most of these students could study in English, though their level of English proficiency varies. In any case, few theological textbooks (beyond the BA level) are available in their language; almost no books are available that would be respected and read by enquiring Islamic theologians. The fastest growing churches have roots in a traditional 'Christian' people, although increasingly, response is from the majority around them with a Muslim background; thus, a separate network of house churches has formed.

What might a curriculum for mission and ministry in this context look like? Another example: In a certain Central Asian context, there are a small number of believers, but all are from a Muslim background. Most believers would come from one or other of the two dominant ethnic groups in the country, groups that are antagonistic to each other. There is no established church, and in contrast to the first example, no room for 'church' in the social structure of the society. Cell groups have formed in a neighbouring country, and leaders are developing. Most teaching is one-on-one or in house groups. Prior to faith, some of these believers, mostly men but some women, attended Western-style universities; almost all are eager to study English, but are fluent (and have done most of their university studies) in the lingua franca of their homeland. Most cannot relate culturally, linguistically or socially to the 'national' church of their present country of domicile, where 'Christian' is a sub-cultural and near 'tribal' identity, more than a designation of faith. These latter 'national' Christians can relate Christian faith to Christian sub-culture, but do not assume a church in mission to the world, or to the millions of Muslims around them. What might a curriculum framework for mission and ministry in this context look like?

Diversity: Islam and Islams

Despite the stereotypes of Western media and the rhetoric of pan-Islamic apologists, by now it is clear to most observers that the notion of an Islamic monolith is myth. Islam is incredibly diverse. Thus, new followers of Christ bring a complex diversity of backgrounds to the educational table. *Doctrinally*, the major divide is between Sunni and Shia Islam (the latter comprise about ten per cent of the Muslim population of the world, mostly in Iraq and Iran). But within this broad division, there are different schools of thought and theological sub-streams, each with a different orientation toward divine law and matters touching faith and practice and culture. *Geographically* and *linguistically*, despite the common association of Islam with the Middle East, only about twenty-five per cent of the world's Muslims are Arabs. The majority of Muslims are therefore outside the Arab-speaking Middle East. In thirty-six countries they form a majority of the population, and in four others they are nearly half the population.

There are many more countries wherein Muslims are a significant minority, for example, India, with over 200 million Muslims. Culturally, there are hundreds of ethno-linguistic groups wherein Islam is dominant. *Politically*, too, the issue of the relationship between Islam, state and society involves a broad spectrum of creative adaptations ranging from the rigid Islam of Saudi Arabia and Afghanistan to the imposed secularity of Turkey. What exactly is a 'Muslim country' or 'Islamic state'? Consequently, according to John Esposito,[113] there are two fundamental questions we must ask in relation to Islam in public life that epitomize the complex issues involved: 'Whose Islam?' and 'What Islam?' We also recognize that there is significant *intracultural variation* in Islamic religious commitment, as well as alternative typologies and scales for measuring it. Within the same ethnolinguistic group in the same city there may be nominal Muslims, secular Muslims, Westernized Muslims, cultural Muslims, devout Muslims, folk Muslims, etc., at any level on the socio-economic ladder.

Every Muslim has his/her own sense of 'Muslim' identity within the larger *ummah* (community) and in relation to the local community. Some from each of these groups have become learners. But the diversity within Islam goes

---

[113] J. Esposito, 'Islam in Asia: An Introduction', in *Islam in Asia: Religion, Politics and Society*, ed. J. Esposito (New York and Oxofrd: Oxford University Press, 1987), 20.

deeper than matters of doctrine, geography, linguistics, culture, politics, and typologies of religious commitment. Studies of 'popular Islam' and 'Islam in context' – Islam as it is embedded in and embodied by local culture – have reinforced the fact that Islam, like Christianity and indeed all ideologies, has been adapted, contested and transformed in the process of transmission. The core of *shared symbols* common to the Islamic tradition over time and space may have very *different meanings* within localized social contexts and meaning systems. Scholars recognize that local circumstances, historical processes, and dynamics of power have shaped even the 'orthodoxy' of Islamic scholasticism.

Thus, practices like pilgrimage or fasting, understandings of suffering (e.g. the Shi'ite passion play commemorating the martyrdom of Hussayn), and notions of religious leadership (e.g. the saint or *shaykh*), may have different meanings and a very different social significance depending on the context. Yet another way of apprehending Islam and Muslims is *phenomenological.* For example, a study of the mystical, literary and poetic traditions within Islam helps us understand how God and man, nature and culture are experienced, represented and embodied in expressive forms. Partly on the basis of this broad diversity and ambiguity within Islam, many scholars challenge the notion that there can be an Islamic 'essence' common to Islam in geographically and historically diverse circumstances. One Egyptian scholar has even suggested that such is the diversity of meaning and expression that we are better to speak of 'islams' – in the plural and without capitalisation – than to speak of 'Islam' in the usual Quran- and text-centred religious studies understanding of that term.

In this perhaps extreme view, 'Islam' does not exist in the real world, only 'islams'. What are the implications of this more particularistic and ethnographically informed understanding of Islam for church and mission, and in particular for open access theological education? In what ways must our theological education and delivery system be adjusted to take account of this diversity within the Islamic tradition? If programmes are to be 'learner-driven', when Muslims from this more complex mix of constituencies and traditions turn to Christ and become a part of his church, what resources and understandings do they bring to the task of theological learning? Will core materials which are 'centrally collated and managed' (as someone has suggested), be relevant to students from an alternative tradition of how to think theologically, of how to handle the 'Text' and 'texts'? If the 'international network' of distance educators represents those of us from a Christian tradition or sub-culture, will we have sufficient linguistic, literary and theological expertise, and nuanced understandings of Islam, to help local believers make the programme locally relevant? What will be gained or lost if they study in English? Will translations of Western texts into national languages or trade languages be sufficient? What are the politics of language in specific areas? How can we train those who learn to think theologically on-line to communicate with those of their own people who live in the face to face world of orality in villages? Will we increase the conceptual gap between these two worlds? Muslim background churches are reported to be emerging among Berbers, Turks, Kurds, Iranians, Tadjiks, Karakalpaks, Kazaks, Uighurs, and many other peoples. What will it take to make global resources not only accessible but locally relevant to these learners, and to the emerging churches they represent? As educator David Goodbourn reminds us, we need to ask, what are the barriers to learning? What are the contextual factors which shape their understanding of God, text, history, identity, etc.? The larger methodological question relates to the relationship and tensions between the universalistic (global) and the particularistic, and the processes by which universalistic and particularistic meanings are transferred, shaped and adapted.

Ethnic Realities and the Church

In many countries that have a predominantly Muslim population and culture, 'national churches' exist which do not reflect the ethnic and demographic realities around them. We label them 'national', despite the fact that such churches may be mono-ethnic churches writ large, with appreciable barriers of language, culture, and prejudice between them and Muslim (and other) ethnic communities. In many cases, despite the presence of converts, or even a few 'multi-ethnic urban conglomerate churches', the denominational and educational structures of the 'national church', and its evangelistic and pedagogical approach, may be dominated by the customs, language, and leadership of one group or other. It may be ill equipped to engage in theological reflection on the nature of the church and its mission.

Thus, in multicultural contexts, if theological education is built upon this network, and perhaps designed with the 'needs' of this 'national church' in view, the disturbing possibility arises that it may unwittingly reinforce the walls between Christians of different faith backgrounds. In a metaphorical sense, it will be another Acts 6 case of the 'Greek-speaking widows being overlooked in the daily distribution'. Another issue arises about the relationship of internet-based theological education to existing national churches, residential Bible schools and leadership certification processes. In some countries, older leaders with less training feel threatened both by theological education and by zealous young leaders. Some national churches expect to exercise a measure of control or supervision over the ministerial training process.

Though these objections may seem petty, and are easily surmounted by a determined individual student with his/her own computer, or an academic consortium with financial resources and prowess, the potential social consequences of an individual 'learner driven' 'always and everywhere' education should not be underestimated. In the East, education and knowledge are as much a matter of honour as of insight. The producers and providers must take care not to undermine inadvertently the very churches such programmes nominally pledge to support. This raises the question whether national church leaders, or in the case of the MBB audience, NGO leaders and mission agencies, are perceived as 'customers', 'observers', or active 'partners' on the 'producing' team? Or the 'learning' team? Does the programme development timeline allow room for some level of joint-ownership? From the point of view of field workers, outcomes must be measured in relation to the growth of existing and emerging Christian communities. Thus, in envisioning theological education in Muslim contexts, we must *envision the church, not just the graduate*.

Local Theology

Depending on the context and their previous religious training and experience, new believers within 'closed' societies bring with them an entirely different set of assumptions about God and man, about the nature of revelation and the divine Word, about Christology, history and the people of God, the dynamics of religious leadership, spirituality, prayer, piety, faith, eschatology – quite apart from a host of other cultural particularities. Despite multiple points of contact between Islam and Christianity, and a similar vocabulary, they know a different narrative. Students will say the right words, but hear different music, or no music at all – as Samuel Zwemer described it, 'Islam is a religion without a song'. Weber says with reference to media and theological education in the West, The pastoral task of the church is also to help redefine an individual's 'story' in the context of the community: to create an *ethical community*. Here the church emphasizes that everyone's individual story, however intimate and personal it may appear, is part of a *negotiated* story.

In other words, living in community involves some give and take of values and ideals. We learn about ourselves from others; we begin to define our existence when we are engaged with others. This challenge is particularly relevant to the Muslim world. Theological education among and for Muslim followers of Jesus, and the larger church in Muslim lands, must help students reflect on their story, and the story of their people, within a new narrative, a new saving faith, negotiating a new sense of history and identity, and a creative new song. We cannot assume that core programmes and materials developed for other contexts, or even a 'Christianized' national church within the same social, geographical or linguistic radius, will work for emerging MBBs and MBB churches. In what ways will they need to be modified? For example, some Arab Christians in the Middle East use the name 'Jesu' for Jesus and avoid Islamic-sounding terms; Muslims refer to Jesus as 'Isa Masih', often preceded by the honorific title *hazrat*, and use other technical religious vocabulary.

In Central Asia, Turkic-background believers do not fit in Russian-speaking congregations. In Pakistan, what will theological education and local tutor networks look like when the small 'national' church is made up of third-generation, Hindu-background, socially marginalized, Punjabi Christians? What is the role of missionaries in this scenario? What does it mean to do theology in a multicultural Islamic context and who will be doing it? This also raises issues of power: who controls the theological education process? Having said this, we must recognize that in some situations, theological contextualization appears a luxury. When the demand for leadership is great, when there are few resources, and pastors and believers risk being beaten, imprisoned, or murdered for their faith, pragmatism and survival count more than missiological idealism. Nevertheless, responsible mission educators can provide the persecuted church with resources to envision its future. As Alexander Malik says, 'Confessing of [sic] Christ in an Islamic context means our Christology' – indeed, every element of theology – 'ought to be developed within an Islamic religio-socio-cultural situation and addressed to it'.

For example, what is the image of God being presented in these materials? What is the image of the church and the dominant metaphors used to envision it? How are Christians and the church perceived in the eyes of the local community, government and media? In the Western media, as one observer has noted, the church is not so much negatively portrayed, as not portrayed at all: it is absent from images of the public square. The same may be the case with certain Muslim societies. However, the larger notion of public religious 'faith' is not absent. In this case, theological education must help the learning community envision what it means to be the 'new creation' people of God in that society, and to relate their identity to the hegemony of Islamic religious, national, and political identities and discourses, as well as the cultural heritage of the people around them. For the suffering church, the notion of a pilgrim church, the corporate suffering servant, may be important. It is also critical that links are forged with other emerging churches or persecuted churches in the region or in other regions. That is, doing theology may involve processing the narratives of the suffering church in Russia and Eastern Europe, Cambodia, Vietnam and Iran, not to mention other historical accounts. Given adequate security protocols, the internet provides the possibility of opening up new avenues for the encouragement and instruction of these suffering churches.

Security and the Persecuted Church

One of the obvious issues related to access to theological education in Islamic contexts is the matter of political uncertainty and security – the security of the delivery system, but more important, the security of the local believers. Any content deemed offensive to Islam, or which appears to make Muslims a missionary target, may put local believers at risk. A high measure of security must be built into the delivery system, without raising suspicions in the process; the security of the downloading computer is yet another problem. The real or perceived threat of hostile disinformation, social and economic discrimination, if not outright persecution unto death, if information related to their presence or activities is insensitively handled, is for some a strong demotivating factor to the learning process.

What are some other factors in the learning environment? Few students apart from the wealthy may have their own room or privacy for study, and students may not own their own computer. Thus, the local church may need to provide a learning centre within their facilities, or better, in a separate 'safe-house'. In some contexts, telephone calls, faxes and emails are monitored. Home visits may raise suspicions. Women students may not be able to leave the home regularly for tutorials or learning centres. Parents and family take a keen interest in the academic progress of individual members. Education is not a purely private concern, but is assumed to be a gateway to economic advancement and financial security, and the enhancement of family honour in the community. Students may have to keep their printed materials hidden or locked in trunks, or may not be able to keep them at home. Political turmoil or localized outbreaks of persecution (e.g. anti-Christian polemics in the press, unusual surveillance, the arrest of a local pastor or believers) occasionally may disrupt the learning process. In the emerging climate of globalization, students in large urban centres will have greater freedom and access to learning resources. But those living in outlying provinces face particular difficulties. Though the problems are not insurmountable, these factors in the learning environment are important to keep in view when establishing learning objectives and assessments.

Identity and Community

As we know, in many non-Western cultures, individuals find their identity not in what they do, but in relation to their social network, viz. extended family, clan or tribe. This is typified by the notion of genealogies: these are significant not as an accurate record of the past (for in fact they are quite malleable and adjustable), but because the past is used to provide identity in the present; a mythic set of past relations gives the individual a kind of 'social map' corresponding to privileges and obligations within that social network. What happens when an individual accepts Christ and – off-line or on-line – undertakes to acquire theological education? He is introduced to a new community of believers, learners and scholars to whom he is not related by kinship, the normal idiom of relationships. He may develop an instrumental relationship, but these individuals are far removed (distance here is determined relationally) from the system of social relations and obligations most relevant in his local context.

The notion of exchange is present, but it may be one divorced from the localized exchange system. How can theology learned on-line and certification achieved on-line, and a reputation achieved on-line, be made relevant to a person who lives every other aspect of his/her life within the tightly knitted fabric of a community? Will we, by virtue of our pedagogical approach, communicate the message, a message common to Western as well as Indian philosophy, that the pathway to truth is an autonomous one, that knowledge and intellectual growth can be achieved by personal effort? That the individual can find identity apart from community, or by rupturing his real ties to his previous community? Which community is the virtual one? Is the goal personal development or the reaching of his/her people? If so, we run the risk of introducing a new form of extractionism, a virtual reality mission compound.

The Problem of Meaning

Reliance on the internet raises certain questions anthropologists have come to call the political economy of meaning. The latter is concerned with how systems of meaning shape, and in turn are shaped by, the political and economic contexts in which they occur. The relationship between politics and economics, on one hand, and belief systems on the other, is extremely complex. By focusing on educational technology and delivery systems, which are inherently related to issues of power, we may be tempted to overlook the historical tensions between Islam and the West which influence relations. So we must study the 'meanings' which help people make sense of their world and inform social action.

These 'alternative' meanings stand in contrast to, or in a multidimensional relationship with, increasingly dominant western meaning systems. We have become used to the elaboration of such thought in relation to cultural blocks, the so-called 'Muslim world', for example. What is less characteristic, in some western mission literature, is a willingness to elaborate the systems of meaning that inhere in specific societies. As Eickelman points out, 'Some meanings are shared, others are challenged or denied, and most are consciously or implicitly altered in the process of transmission'. For example, ideas related to the 'self' in relation to society are shaped by the social location of the actor, dominant and subversive ideologies, class and gender, and the social institutions through which meanings are communicated. In many Middle Eastern tribal societies, for example, the notion of self is related to concepts of what it means to be a 'man of honour'.

Even such a presumably simple notion as that of the self is culturally shaped, contested and negotiated by actors. Such constructions and negotiations may be situational, and involve a skill in verbal artistry, the ability to create and compose poetry or use proverbs. As Caton shows, self may also be historically anchored in genealogical conceptions of tribe and group, most often as the self/group is differentiated from the Other around them; these boundaries may be marked as between town and tribe, centre and periphery, contiguous ethnic groups, or differentiation may be marked by some other symbols and behaviours. The Other is measured against such constructions of self. The implication is simply that we may not be communicating the meaning we think we are communicating. The very process of the transmission of religious knowledge involves symbols which themselves have ambiguous meaning: 'God', 'man', 'woman', 'sin', 'community' – it is their very ambiguity and apparent universality which gives such symbols their power, and deceives us into thinking that individuals understand the same meaning.

For example, we can look at the common Islamic symbol of the veil. In the context of Turkey's ongoing debate regarding the relation of religion to national identity, the headscarf has been seen as a symbol of protest, a means for the assertion of an Islamic identity that has been crowded from the national political scene since the secular democratic reforms under Attaturk. In France, controversy over the right of Muslim schoolgirls to wear the headscarf made it a symbol of minority rights and Islamic identity, stretching and contesting the concept of French identity and what it means to be French. In Afghanistan, the veiling of women is complete, and is associated with true Islam; in this context, women are the primary symbol of Islam, a metaphor for the proper submission and humility of man to God. Complicating the picture, women are a multivocal symbol, representing not only religion but honour – the other primary moral conception governing Afghan society.

However, for some progressive Muslims in the West, this type of symbolization represents a perversion of the true meaning of Islam and a medieval retrogression. To westerners, the veil signifies oppression and gender apartheid, and along with the 'sword', has become one of the stereotypic negative images of Islam. The point is that when we (e.g. as educators) convey a particular narrative or symbol, however normative or abstract in our own minds, meaning – even Islamic meaning – is modified, and is often negotiated and changed, in relation to an individual's context, religious and cultural tradition, and significant others.

A final note on meaning: What is the meaning of the internet, of technology? How is this related to Muslim understandings of faith, culture, modernity, morality, and the West? It surprises some people to learn that the so-called 'medieval' Taliban government of Afghanistan operates its own website, and related sites offer a sensitive portrayal of the Taliban worldview. What does the internet mean? In part, I would suggest, the internet is attractive because it at once represents power and rhetoric – both of which are important elements in many Muslim societies. The internet represents a new social space, a forum for rhetoric, which enables one to do a 'glorious deed of honour' verbally, globally. For an individual, the computer also represents, more than any particular mindset of openness to knowledge, the possibility of a job, the image of a modern person, access to outside resources, a skill that translates into reputation and honour. In one case I am familiar with, the single computer acquired by the university department was lodged in the office of the chairman; he did not know how to use it, but it was placed on a table beside his desk. When offered training, he said that only he and his secretary would need training and would be given permission to use the computer.

What was going on here? In this man's view, knowledge is a form of cultural capital, a form of wealth, like land, women, money, which are used to acquire honour. A computer is the new global symbol of knowledge which enhanced his culturally-shaped image of leadership. How did I suggest training his staff and introducing the notion of 'open access'? In part, I used the logic of honour: his own stature as a man of knowledge would be increased if he allowed his staff to get training – the first department in the entire university to do so. Second, I appealed to tribal notions of relationship: the personal loyalty of his larger teaching staff would increase if he would provide for them to be trained as well. Note that education and access to educational technology and resources here are interpreted with reference to patronage. Unfortunately, the solo computer is still in this man's private office. Is that what we want to do with distance theological education?

Profiles of Higher Islamic Learning

Open or Closed?

One way to approach our subject is to ask questions about what Muslims have done or are doing in the area of theological education. Sociologists point out that schooling, especially higher education, 'implicitly defines and transmits a culturally valued cognitive style, "a set of basic, deeply interiorized master-patterns" of language and thought on the basis of which other patterns are subsequently acquired'. What does Islamic theological education look like and what 'cognitive styles' are associated with it? What are the traditional modes of education? What is the role of the book, the master or teacher, and school (*madrassa*)? What are the popular or informal processes of education? How does Islam and Islamic religious education relate to other local or folk belief systems? What is the role of oral literature and forms of verbal art, e.g. music and ballads, and what are the dynamics of performance? How have western models of education affected traditional modes? In what ways is the Islamic theological system 'closed' or 'open'? What is the effect of new media like faxes, satellite television, and the internet, and how are they shaping learning and communication in relation to traditional styles, authorities and belief systems? If we look at Islamic education there are obviously a variety of patterns and variations on common themes.

Clearly, the introduction of western educational models has affected pedagogy, learning styles, and curriculum. westernized education, and English-medium education, however, is sometimes the preserve of a wealthy, urban elite. There is, however, increasing access to and use of the internet, particularly in the cities; it is here that there is the greatest potential access to online theological resources. ('Access' in this case may not be determined so much by technology (though that may be a factor), but by what may be doable or acceptable socially, without jeopardizing personal security or reputation.)

Knowledge and the Social Paradigm of 'Understanding' in Islamic Cultures

In seeking to profile education in Islamic contexts, it is important not to assume that any one pattern is normative for the entire Islamic world. 'There were several patterns of Islamic education, each of which is appropriately analysed in its particular context', that is, in relation to particular societies at particular periods of time. Eickelman explores the 'social paradigm' at the base of the Islamic education system in his study of Islamic higher education in Morocco in the 1920s-1930s. For example, the *madrassa*-based Islamic learning in Morocco at that time involved three elements: *lesson circles* made up of *shaykhs* teaching 8-12 students; *peer learning* or informal learning processes; and *sponsorship*, by which individual students might be mentored and introduced to a wider network of scholars and so grow in reputation themselves.

The pedagogical style included rigorous discipline, and a lack of explanation of material 'learned'; a student is not to ask questions, and student input is minimized, not maximized. '"Understanding" (*fahm*) in the contexts of such concepts of learning was not measured by any ability to "explain" particular verses', but was implicit. 'Understanding' consists of the ability to use particular Quranic verses in appropriate contexts, in the fashion of oral literature, poetry and proverbs. One acquires 'a demonstrated "understanding" of the Quran through social situations in which Quranic verses and other memorized materials were used'. We note here, too, the complex relation between literacy and orality: in the Moroccan context, despite the dependence on (scarce) printed texts and their symbolic role at the base of the education system, 'only the oral transmission of knowledge was regarded as culturally legitimate... knowledge acquired exclusively from the study of books was regarded as unreliable'. Eickelman also points out that in the Islamic education system in general there is an emphasis on the fixity of knowledge and on memorization.

This cognitive style is in synch with popular understandings and non-religious spheres of knowledge. However, it may be contrasted with the emphasis on personal discovery and 'self'- and learner-centred approaches to learning advocated in the West. Theological educators must ask, then, how does this or that culture view 'knowledge' and the transmission of knowledge? What is the relationship between religious knowledge and local knowledge?

Outside Knowledge and Social Change

Another important consideration is the relation of 'outside knowledge' to local religio-political systems, and the local perception of the outside bearers of this knowledge. Barnes, for example, describes some of these dynamics in her study of ritual, power, and outside knowledge in a pre-colonial African community. She shows that African societies, for example, were neither isolated nor homogeneous; rather they were open to outside experience and outside people and outside ideas. 'The outsider… is a potential agent of change. Like adding to a gene pool, the presence of outsiders in a community adds to the pool of knowledge – to the cultural mix – that exists among its inhabitants'. However, as one explores the way outside knowledge is perceived and related to other domains, one inevitably encounters the issue of power. Outsiders and strangers in a community are not merely acted upon or incorporated into the local community; they are actors who enter into the local competition for power. Barnes points out that 'competition for power – and the socially valued elements that legitimate – involves people in competing for knowledge so as to become dominant'.

Outside knowledge has an advantage because it is easily mystified and easily controlled or co-opted by those who aspire to prominence. Brian Street (1975) provides a complementary perspective in his study of the impact of the introduction of modern education on a village in Iran in the early 1970s. The Shah's government used education as an instrument for the 'modernization' of the entire state, and trained and sent out teachers into rural areas. 'Those being educated in rural areas are thus the recipients of a philosophy which belongs to an alien social group and is being channelled through external institutions consciously devised to alter local life patterns'.[114] This difference, Street says, is at the root of many of the problems elitist educational theorists face in dealing with government- run rural schools; 'The teacher is not integrated with the community but is an outsider; he does not try to teach the village children to integrate but to become outsiders'.

In this case, 'The teacher is outside the system; "he is in the village but not of it"'.[115] Further, viewed through the eyes of the villager rather than those of the developer, education becomes a means by which students 'upgraded' economically and climbed the social ladder out of the village. At the same time, the student finds himself 'in daily conflict with two systems of thought and values' which claim his allegiance. 'He learns the value of certain rituals, such as exams, and of certain symbols, such as pieces of paper stating "qualifications"; and these concrete things he aims to achieve, believing that they will provide economic success, work, security, western goods and status'. Meanwhile, these rewards are subject to forces extraneous to him, in the wider world if not that of the education system, and 'the symbols may not achieve the results he has been led to believe'.

One wonders the degree to which the internet and the content of the web might be viewed in analogous way. Like the teacher in pre-revolutionary Iran, the internet educator is an agent of change. By using it as a (or the) primary delivery mechanism for theological education, will we produce teachers and church leaders who represent, if not an alien philosophy, an alien way of doing

[114] B.V. Street, 'The Mullah, the Shahnameh and the Madrasseh: Some Aspects of Literac in Iran', *Asian Affairs* 62 (1975), 291.
[115] Street, 'The Mullah', 292.

theology, of learning and communicating truth? The outsider and his 'outside knowledge' may be related to a history of western colonial domination (both explicit and subversive) of the Muslim world, and the perceived continuity of this domination in terms of economics, technology and popular culture, if not politics. Thus, Christians must use 'western' technology as a positive instrument of socio-economic change, while at the same time fostering and encouraging 'continuity in the midst of change', rather than the erosion of traditional cultural values.

Inasmuch as a 'stranger' may variously enhance, enliven, benefit, or threaten, a local community, it is important to be sensitive, at least, to the processes by which outside knowledge and resources of theological education are made relevant to, and incorporated into, local communities and their knowledge systems, and to the power dynamics involved in these processes. Are we fully aware of what internet technology and learning may symbolize to people in developing nations? It is possible that, as Street puts it, 'the symbols may not achieve the results he [the student] has been led to believe'. Historical case studies of modernization and change in the Muslim world provide cause for both hope and caution. The convulsive reactions to the Shah of Iran in 1979, or to the earlier modernization programme of King Aminullah in Afghanistan (1919-29), or that of the Afghan communists (1974-78), provides extreme, but instructive, illustrations of the complexity of the dynamics of faith, culture and social change in the Muslim world. Perhaps the latter subject is itself worthy of inclusion in a curriculum of on-line theological education. A theological education that fosters radical spiritual and social change in the name of the kingdom of God must anticipate potential consequences, both 'cross' and 'resurrection'.

Islamic 'Open Access' Theological Education

The very way the title of this paper is phrased suggests a final question, namely, whether Islamic theological education can rightly be described as 'open' or, more stereotypically, 'closed'? To answer this question, let us leave Oxford for a few moments and teleconference to another consultation that took place in the fourteenth century. The Sufis of Andalusia (Spain) have been having a long, intense, verbal (and sometimes physical) debate among themselves about the nature of the distinctive Sufi 'path' or way to knowledge. The Sufis represent a distinctive tradition of learning and spirituality within Islam, sometimes overlapping with, sometimes in contrast or conflict with, the scholastic tradition.

In Sufism, one builds upon knowledge of the externals of divine Law and ritual praxis and progresses to a more intuitive experience of the divine, and unveiling of the spiritual world. As Muhsin Mahdi describes it, here are the contentious questions: Is it sufficient to read what other Sufi masters had written about their own experiences and depend wholly on the guidance of books? Or, is it indispensable to have a living master, a *shaykh*, who explains the signs that appear along the disciple's paths, warns against the dangers that may confront the disciple as he pursues his training, and clears up the uncertainties and confusions that may arise on the way as the disciple attempts to distinguish good from bad and proper from improper among the happenings and states he experiences – a master, therefore, who will perform a function similar to that performed by a physician with respect to the sick[,] and the just leader, the *imam*, with respect to the leaderless and disorderly community? Is it enough, in short, for the disciple to read books and follow written instructions; or is it indispensable that he follow an *imam* or a *shaykh*, listen to his directions, imitate him, and act on his instructions?

In some ways, the debate mirrors our own. The Sufi path involves textual understanding (i.e. use of learning resources), and spiritual experience, as well as the guidance of others, and participation in a larger regional and global network involving men of learning, centres for study. The question is, can an individual become a competent practitioner of the knowledge of God merely by reading books or taking courses on the internet? Or does he need instead, or in addition, to be trained by masters? Related to this are questions of quality – content, modes of delivery, teachers, standards, and outcomes like spiritual formation. The Andalusian Sufis could not solve the matter among themselves, nor could the local jurists to whom they appealed for a decision in this proto-internet forum. Therefore, the question and opposing arguments between camps were formulated and addressed in the form of a letter 'forwarded' to a number of learned men in Fez, the Oxford-like capital of the Marinids, asking for their opinions. At least three men wrote responses and posted them on their version of the world wide web. Note the resourcing going on here, and the access to pious scholars and a scholarly network made up of those from within the Muslim tradition, even if they were outside of a particular Sufi brotherhood.

The jurist Abu al-'Abbas al-Qabbab (d. 1377) sided with the group arguing for the necessity of a master. Arguing by analogy with the other arts of medicine, jurisprudence and grammar, al-Qabbab insists that 'no student can become a competent practitioner merely by reading books; he needs, in addition, to be trained by masters who "possess the keys of the books"'. To al-Qabbab, the Sufi path is like a vast and dangerous desert, if anything, a living master is more necessary in Sufism than in other arts. Like a good jurist, he looks at similar cases, models of learning in other disciplines, formulates a general spiritual and pedagogical principle, and then applies it to theological education, the case at hand. For al-Qabbab, 'continuity and change, correctness and error, and right and wrong, are all invested in the living Sufi master and guide'.

But wait, let's check out another other 'hot link' here: the fourteenth century website of the great Sufi Ibn 'Abbad al-Rundi. According to the prototypical *www.al-Rundi.com*, the master is indeed indispensable. But al-Rundi notes that there are two kinds of Sufi masters. There is the 'teaching master' (*shaykh al-ta'lim*), who teaches the books on Sufism, directs students to the truly knowledgeable authors, and explains what is unclear or not in agreement with the divine law. It is of this kind of master that it is said, 'He who has no master, the devil is his master'. Then there is the 'training master' (*shaykh altarbiya*), whose function is to 'reform the character and improve the minds of those who moral character is defective and whose wits are dull'. Under the regime of the training master, moral qualities are refined, and souls learn recitations, solitude, speaking, abstention from food, and other spiritual disciplines. Somewhat surprisingly, according to al-Rundi, the Andalusian Sufis who insisted on the necessity of a training master were wrong: it is the teaching master who is indispensable. He reminds them that earlier in the Sufi movement (notice the use of history and tradition), spiritual disciplines were self-imposed. Frequenting the company of friends and brothers, and travelling to meet other saints and learned men reinforced these disciplines. (Note the sense of a learning community, and the notion of dispersed learning.)

But times had changed. By al-Rundi's time, laxity had set in; Sufism had become a popular movement and both training masters and serious disciples were extremely rare. Al- Rundi moans, 'I do not know which of these two calamities is the greater one: the fact that one cannot find a training master or the fact that there is not a genuine disciple around'. Thus, al-Rundi's answer to the questions posed by the Andalusians about the technicalities of the path to knowledge does not so much choose sides as offer a general critique of the whole system, both masters and students. The popularization of the Sufi way had led to a decline in morality and intellectual standards, and reliance on the technology – books alone. To al-Rundi this evidenced a lack of purity of intention (*niyyah*), the very basis of the Sufi path. Al-Rundi argues for a third way, saying that the Sufi path is meant not for the masses but for the elect few. 'Books are needed and masters are needed, but neither of these two things is sufficient. Neither should be made the object of exclusive reliance; only God is worthy of exclusive reliance'. The Sufi path is not a wild, dangerous desert, but a solitary path, with a series of helpful stations and resting places where one finds helpers to aid him. Al-Rundi emphasises 'the primacy of reliance on God rather than on books and masters'.

One should set out on his path, fight the enemy of self, worship God in sincerity, and rely upon him; merely reading some manual on Sufism is not enough. If al-Rundi were here today, he might question the assumption that we need to extend theological education to the masses. More importantly, he might raise the question of outcomes and challenge us to envision the graduate: What might a student look like who enters and walks the holy path via the internet? In Islamic society, the proverbial critiques of the mullah (Muslim priest) are one hint that while book knowledge and clerical roles are respected and feared, they are also mocked. As an Afghan proverb puts it, 'As a half-doctor is a danger to health, a half-mullah is a danger to faith'. The great historian and sociologist Ibn Khaldun posts the final reply. He puts things in historical perspective, and concludes that in true Islam, there is no distinction between knowledge of the external demands of the divine law (*fiqh al-zahir*) and knowledge of the internal demands of the divine law (*fiqh al-batin*); the fact that we separate them is an indication of decline and departure from God's original intention.

Ibn Khaldun urges us to envision the various types of learners and sees three alternative skill outcomes of theological education: There is the ability to fight the 'battle for piety', which every Muslim must fight. It requires no master of the teaching or training type, but can be acquired through books and with the aid of teachers and learned men. Skill in the second battle, the 'battle for uprightness' consists in acquiring Quranic and moral virtues; this is not for the masses, but for the few, preferably with a master. It can be acquired by studying the works of learned men, discussions with friends and brothers engaged in the same battle on the same path. Note that the higher outcomes require greater access to learning resources (books), to peer learning, as well as to a master. But for the supreme battle, the 'battle for unveiling', for the vision of God, the disciple must place himself in the hands of a training master.

No one can take such a path alone. According to Mehdi, the book and the master really represent one pole and a common framework for learning. Both are resources. For at the other end is the learner, man – his nature, his capacity to learn, his skill in teaching others, his willingness to seek God. It is humbling to recognize that fourteenth century Muslims and Muslim scholars were debating issues similar to our own, issues relating to 'open access' to theological education resources, to a network of fellow learners and scholars, the most effective path to spiritual formation, and ultimately to the knowledge of God. The image of these Andalusian seekers so long ago should motivate us to provide a way for seekers – of Muslim or other background – in our day to meet and to follow the master we ourselves by grace have come to know.

Conclusion

In this paper we have looked at eight contextual issues that can affect open access theological education in restrictive access Muslim contexts. We have seen that there is a large audience of new potential learners, made up of Muslim background believers, NGO workers, and international Christians from many lands engaged in pioneer wholistic ministry in diverse Islamic contexts. Despite a core of shared symbols, the 'Muslim' contexts for theological education are complex and variated, both within and between cultures. An understanding of the dynamic interplay between the Islamic tradition and local meaning systems, therefore, must affect our approach to communicating Biblical truths. Our understanding of 'church' in Muslim contexts must be broadened to take into account emerging church movements made up of Muslim followers of Jesus, perhaps of a different ethno-linguistic background than the dominant 'national' church structures and leadership. Theological education in such contexts must shape outcomes not simply for the individual learner, but the learner in his/her multifaith community, while envisioning the shape of the emerging church.

Churches in these contexts must be equipped to do theology in context. Resourcing from the wider church is needed which will not jeopardize the security, identity and relational networks that shape local identities. In this era of globalization, open access theological education represents the potential to use new media to reach the 'new publics' emerging throughout the Muslim world. In new venues and via new media, Muslims themselves are using core symbols and traditional values to argue for new interpretations of what it means to 'be Muslim'. For theological educators, the challenge is to ensure that international workers, Muslim followers of Jesus, national churches and 'Christ-centred communities' in Muslim contexts, and millions of other seekers of God in diverse settings around the world, find the social space, resources and 'open access' needed to do theology and mission within and for the benefit of the societies in which they live.

Pentecostals and Praxis of Liberation: A Proposal for Subversive Theological Education

Cheryl Bridges Johns

Dr. Cheryl Bridges Johns is Professor of Discipleship and Christian Formation at the Church of the Church of God (Cleveland) Theological Seminary, Cleveland TN, USA.

During the summer of 1982, I was among those who had gathered at Boston College to learn from and dialogue with the Brazilian educator Paulo Freire. Freire is best known for his revolutionary pedagogical process involving the dynamics of 'conscientization' which may be defined as learning to examine social, political and economic injustices in order to take action to correct them. He has asserted that his educational process is Christian and prophetic and should be part of the church's ongoing educational activity. After class one afternoon, I worked up enough courage to approach Freire in order to dialogue with him regarding the implications of his educational philosophy within the context of Pentecostalism. I vividly remember Freire's response to my inquiry. He threw his hands in the air and stated dramatically, 'Oh you Pentecostals! You don't make history!' I came away from the conversation full of questions regarding my own identity and began a pilgrimage of seeking to give an adequate response to Freire's criticism.

Freire's educational paradigm was developed within the context of the Two-Thirds World, and it reflects a view of education as a tool either for liberation or for oppression. Within this same context was born Liberation Theology, which understands the task of religion as offering freedom to the oppressed. The same revolutionary ferment which gave rise to education for conscientization and a theology for liberation has also been the context for the rapid growth of the Pentecostal movement. For some, the growth of Pentecostalism reflects an attempt by the 'masses' to escape the harsh realities of the world and to form a 'haven' of submerged religious protest. Are Pentecostals in need of a liberating pedagogy toward conscientization, which would move us from being a 'haven of the masses', which is 'paralyzing, alienating and alienated',[116] to becoming a people who 'make history' for the cause of liberation?

It is my contention that Pentecostalism, while benefiting from aspects of a praxis-based model of education, offers its own unique environment and

---

[116] P. Freire, 'Education, Liberation and the Church', *Religious Education* 79:Fall (1984).

epistemological framework for the development of a true pedagogy of the oppressed. There exists within Pentecostalism the dynamics of conscientization; however, these dynamics are initiated and maintained by a transforming encounter with God, which refigures the corresponding action. In this brief essay, I will attempt to discuss some of these dynamics and to, propose a model for Pentecostal theological education which would reflect both a praxis-oriented epistemology and the distinctive of Pentecostalism. Theological education, by its very nature and purpose has both to express and to critique prophetically its particular religious ethos. Pentecostal theological education would, therefore, offer a primary context for both the expression and critical analysis of one of the world's most rapidly growing religious movements.

A Subversive Memory: Historical Precedents for Conscientization

The task of discussing the dynamics of conscientization within Pentecostalism should begin with an awareness of the 'subversive memory' within the movement's history of its radical social implications. From its inception at the turn of the century, Pentecostalism has had a revolutionary and prophetic character. With its roots firmly in black spirituality and in the holiness movement of the nineteenth century, Pentecostalism began as another cry against the abandonment of the historical churches to authentic spirituality and to the cause of the masses. As early as 1906, the Los Angeles revival indicated that the movement had at its heart the dynamics of conscientization.[117] Here, blacks, whites, men, women, Hispanics and Asians were equal. From the holiness revival, Pentecostalism inherited an emphasis upon sanctification. The church was to be a light exhibiting the inherent characteristics of the kingdom of God. From black spirituality, Pentecostalism retained the emphasis upon an oral, ongoing liturgy, a maximum participation of the body and the freedom to include such things as visions and dreams.

The active presence of the Holy Spirit called for a radical equalizing of blacks and whites, males and females, rich and poor. The presence of glossolalia served as a radical social critique, in that it signified that knowledge of God was a gift bestowed to all. Tongues of fire were enabling even the most inarticulate persons to speak the language of heaven, aid served as a witness to the educated and the articulate that they too were inarticulate and voiceless before the face of God.[118] No wonder the Pentecostal revival was a scandal! From the perspective of the participants, it truly turned the known social system on its head. Thus, Pentecostalism stood as a contrast to the dominant order of

---

[117] W.J. Hollenweger, 'After Twenty Years Research on Pentecostalism', *International Review of Mission* 75:January (1986).

[118] F.D. Macchia, 'Sighs Too Deep for Words: Towards a Theology of Glossolalia', *Journal of Pentecostal Theology* 1:October (1992).

its day. It was a subversive and revolutionary movement, neither based upon philosophical ideology nor totally upon critical reflection. It was a movement that experienced through the Holy Spirit God's divine liberation. Since World War II, North American and European Pentecostalism has lost most of its prophetic zeal. Following the sect-church typology, Pentecostalism has lost many of its 'sect-like' characteristics. In the Two-Thirds World, where Pentecostalism is flourishing, one can see many of the revolutionary characteristics found in the beginnings of the movement. Even here, however, there are attempts to 'domesticate the movement', to tame it for political control or for the sake of an ideology.

In spite of these changes and challenges, there exists within Pentecostalism a 'corporate memory' of its revolutionary roots. It is the task of the movement today, especially among those involved in theological education, to reconsider critically its own 'story' and to make itself available to the radicalizing presence of God's Spirit. Thus, the conscientization needed among Pentecostalism is one which would ignite what Walter Brueggemann has labelled as the 'prophetic imagination'. Its task is 'to move back into the deepest memories... of community and activate those very symbols that have always been the basis for contradicting the regnant consciousness'.[119] Thus, conscientization would not be the tacking on of a new ideology but the involving of what Brueggemann has called 'the primal dimension of every memory' of the Pentecostal community. The task of conscientization is a prophetic task. It is the task of offering symbols of hope in order for people to make history. Brueggemann describes this process:

> In offering symbols the prophet has two tasks. One is to mine the memory of this people and educate them to see the tools of hope. The other is to recognize how singularly words, speech, language, and phrase shape consciousness and define reality. The prophet is the one who, by use of these tools of hope, contradicts the presumed world of the kings showing both that that presumed world does not square with the facts and that we have been taught a lie and have believed it because the people with the hardware and the printing press told us it was that way. And so the offering of symbols is a job not for a timid clerk who simply shares the inventory but for people who know something different and are prepared, out of their own anguish and amazement, to know that the closed world of managed reality is false. The prophetic imagination knows that the real world is the one that has its beginning and dynamic in the promising speech of God and that this is true even in a world where kings have tried to banish all speech but their own.[120]

Following the thought of Brueggemann, it can be concluded that conscientization among Pentecostalism begins its dynamic in the 'speech of

---

[119] Brueggemann, *The Prophetic Imagination*, 66.
[120] Brueggemann, *The Prophetic Imagination*, 66-67.

God' (even *glossolalia!).* This speech comes through the presence of the Holy Spirit, actualizing the kingdom of God among a people who know something different and are prepared out of their own anguish and amazement to expose the falseness of the closed world of managed reality and to make God's history upon the earth.

A Subversive Present Reality: Theological Dimensions of Conscientization

There is in Pentecostalism theological precedent for conscientization. This precedent can be found in a praxis-oriented hermeneutic which views knowledge and truth as being fulfilled in life experience. Therefore, truth is not abstracted from reality, but grounded in a covenantal relationship between God and humanity. It is relational, experiential and powerfully transformational. Closely related to an experiential, praxis-oriented hermeneutic is a way of theologizing which may be defined as oral narrative. This mode of doing theology allows for theory to become part of the life of the community of faith. Story becomes the medium of expression in such a community. A narrative theology has implications for the conscientization process, especially when placed within the framework of a larger apocalyptic vision. In such a context, testimonies become more than communal stories or creeds. They are transformed into announcements of holy history.

While many Pentecostal believers may be voiceless in the political realm, they speak with an eloquent passion in the spiritual, and they understand that their actions and prayers are taking down spiritual strongholds. They make holy history, and narrative is thus the language of this historical empowerment. It announces and denounces critiques and uplifts, blesses and curses. The voice of the people is, therefore, empowered by the Holy Spirit to become the speech of God. Consequently, peasant women or textile workers can give expression to their own *magnificat*, which announce the dethroning of worldly powers and the ushering in of a new age. An oral liturgy, involving the participation of everyone, is an equalizing aspect of Pentecostal worship. Rather than becoming an escape, such a context for worship bestows the capacity for action in concrete historical experience. Hollenweger proposes that Pentecostal liturgy is revolutionary and can serve 'for the conscientization of the people of God'.[121] Furthermore, he notes that:

> If the inarticulate peon in Latin America realizes that he has something to say, if the despised Indian of Mexico begins to sing and make music with the instruments of his persecuted ancestors, if the Chilean begins to dance thy dances of his forefathers… if these people realize that what they have is good enough for the worship of God, that God accepts the 'thank offerings of their lips', this seems to me to be of a more revolutionary quality than the copying of western

[121] W.J. Hollenweger, 'Creator Spiritus', *Theology* 81 (1978), 39.

> revolutionary theories, which makes them again puppets of a foreign ideology, albeit a so-called revolutionary ideology.[122]

While it is obvious that Pentecostal congregations are often 'havens for the masses', the radical implications of these havens are often overlooked. David Martin observes that these havens provide for the dispossessed 'a new cell taking over from scarred and broken tissue'.[123] Within these new cells, a new ordering of reality can occur which displaces the destructive forces of human existence. Within these havens, peaceable kingdoms are formed which help to change the template of culture as the latent becomes manifest and the limited free space devised by religion is enlarged. Therefore, the 'havens' may be protean in their potentials.[124] These communities of the Spirit serve as prophetic critiques of the dominant culture. The challenge for Pentecostals in the future will be to maintain a sense of existing as a 'community of the Spirit' while becoming upwardly mobile.

Conversion and Conscientization

Often the conscientization process toward liberation is defined in traditional, metaphorical terms of conversion. In order for oppressors to join in solidarity with the oppressed, they must undergo a radical reorientation. 'Conversion to the people requires a profound rebirth. Those who undergo it no longer remain as they were'.[125] Manoel de Mello, leader of the 'Brazil para Cristo', describes the type of conversion which Pentecostals seek as one which creates a new perspective in the individual: 'This form of evangelism does not produce a Sunday Christian, but rather a believer who is able to witness to the society in which he lives. It… creates a new consciousness. The gospel of the Kingdom is here and now'.[126]

Clearly, the Pentecostal concept of conversion is not antithetical to the liberationist concept of conversion. It is, however, rooted in an historical experience with God who calls people as both a subject of history and as an object of God's forgiving grace. Therefore, conscientization is not self-grounded but grounded in the dynamic of the Holy Spirit. The Pentecostal believer makes history, but the route of the historical journey is determined by God. The dialectic of history is, therefore, not a materialistic dialectic as Marx would propose. But neither is it entirely the dialectic of Hegel's notion of *geist*

---

122 W.J. Hollenweger, 'The Social and Ecumenical Significance of Pentecostal Liturgy', *Studia Liturgics* 8 (1971-1972), 213.

123 D. Martin, *Tongues of Fire: The Explosion of Protestantism in Latin America* (Oxford: Basil Blackwell, 1990), 284.

124 Martin, *Tongues of Fire*, 286-88.

125 P. Freire, *Pedagogy of the Oppressed* (New York: Herder & Herder, 1970), 37.

126 de Mello, 'Participation Is Everything', *International Review of Missions* 60:April (1971), 245-48.

(spirit) in which the human role is that of passive participant. Salvation history becomes a dialectic of humanity's ontological re-creation by the Holy Spirit which consummates in a holy partnership with humankind.

Sanctification is to be the ultimate goal for the world inasmuch as the coming consummation of the kingdom of God will result in all things being brought into a harmony of God's reign. God will one day be all in all, and for many Pentecostal believers, this holy consummation can occur in their lives as a sign of the age to come. Therefore, issues of racism, sexism, oppression and violence are issues of sanctification. It is not within human ability alone that these issues are to be resolved, for greed and the desire for power are always present. There is a need for a faith which joins the human heart with the passion of God and thereby creates the space for utopian visions to be actualized, both individually and corporately.[127]

The ongoing experience of sanctification has created utopian visions among people who do not employ critical-reflective, principled, formal operational thought processes. They have experienced what Craig Dykstra has called 'imaginal transformation'.[128] By experiencing the holy, there is a creative reorganization of the imagination (self) and the emergence of a new *gestalt* (form). The corresponding action, therefore, is directed by this altered perception of the world. In sanctification, orthopathy, as it refers to right affections, is joined with orthopraxis. One's nature is altered and one's affections reflect the heart of God. This experience leads not just to personal piety but also to social transformation inasmuch as the eschatological goals of the kingdom are paralleled on a social level.[129]

In a very real sense, Spirit baptism is the unveiling of a new reality and the realization of an altered consciousness. Rather than being submerged into reality, a person de-centres through a radical reorientation of the self in the face of the holy. A person is thus empowered for service and enabled to experience the paradox of suffering and the power of renunciation. One speaks the language of the new order and envisions epochs of lived justice and peace. Spirit baptism, therefore, signals a radical reorientation and de-centring of the human heart and the empowerment to be subjects of holy history.

A Proposed Model for Subversive Theological Education

Theological education within a Pentecostal context should reflect the definitive ethos of the movement in such a manner as to promote confessional identity while at the same time enable students to reflect critically upon that identity. To

---

[127] S.J. Land, *Pentecostal Spirituality: A Passion for the Kingdom* (Sheffield: Sheffield Academic Press, 1993).

[128] C. Dykstra, *Vision and Character* (New York: Paulist Press, 1981), 81.

[129] T. Runyon, 'Wesley and the Theologies of Liberation', in *Sanctification and Liberation*, ed. T. Runyon (Nashville, TN: Abingdon Press, 1981), 10.

be true to its tradition and its epistemological base the movement must acknowledge that its education can never be elitist, removing people from and placing them over others. Knowledge of God, while enhanced by the power of critical reflection, is never dependent upon this power. Theological education within a Pentecostal context should therefore reflect the speech of God in its amazing power to astonish, radically equalize and empower people to re-make history. It is my contention that Pentecostals are not served well by acritically adopting a praxis-based model of theological education and adding to that model a Pentecostal faith identity. What follows, therefore, is an attempt to construct a model for theological education which incorporates the distinctive nature of conscientization within a Pentecostal context while engaging, in a dialectical sense, the implications of a praxis based model.

A praxis-based model of theological education calls for a major shift in how truth is related to actual historical practice.[130] It is concerned with how knowing and obeying are connected. The classical view of education, which separates theory from practice, fails to join adequately what one must know and what one must do with the knowledge. A praxis epistemology calls for a conscious move away from dichotomizing theory and practice and toward seeing them as twin moments of the same activity that are united dialectically. Instead of theory leading to practice, theory becomes, or is seen in the reflective moment in praxis. Theory arises from praxis to yield further praxis. Within modern interpretations of this term, praxis, there is the implicit understanding that it contains an activity which places humanity as active subjects in the historical process. At best, God is a subjective presence in the ongoing dynamic of reflection-action. There are problems and limitations with a praxis epistemology, especially when compared to a biblical under standing of knowledge. Because a praxis epistemology is grounded in Hellenistic thought, in spite of all efforts to join theory and practice into a singular moment, there remains in practice a fundamental dualism between matter and reason. Because of this dualism, praxis assumes an unbridgeable distance between the knower and the known. While claiming otherwise, the entire system elevates theory (in the form of critical reflective reasoning skills) above all other forms of knowledge. The objectification of others is an unavoidable aspect of this knowledge and the power of transformation is of necessity grounded in the 'spirit' of the individual.

Edward Farley's assessment of praxis as a radical version of the Enlightenment ideal (the critical principle), which elevates the power of human criticism over all truth claims, brings us to the fatal flaw of such an epistemology.[131] Human reflection-action, while important, is distorted and may become self-serving and thereby hinder a true knowledge of reality. Without an

---

[130] C.B. Johns, 'Yielding to the Spirit: A Pentecostal Approach to Group Bible Study', *Journal of Pentecostal Theology* 1:October (1992).

[131] E. Farley, *The Fragility of Knowledge* (Philadelphia, PA: Fortress Press, 1988), 4-9.

authority beyond the self that transcends and even negates reflection-action, we are left, in spite of our worthy intentions for the transformation of society, with sinful praxis. Another problem with praxis springs from our inability, also due to sin, to know ourselves truly as subjects in the world in which we live. Transformation of the knower has to occur before that person can contribute to the righteous transformation of the world. This transformation requires the knowing person to be known and exposed and changed, thereby becoming an object as well as an active subject in the historical process.

This transformational knowledge is captured in the Hebrew word, *yada*, which stresses the interrelatedness of the knower and the known. Within the Hebraic understanding, if a person knew God, he or she was encountered by the one who lived in the midst of history and who initiated a covenant relationship which called for a response of the total person. Knowledge of God is not measured by information one possessed but by how one was living in response to God. The New Testament, while employing Greek terms, continues the Hebraic understanding of 'to know'. Knowing the Lord is still viewed as the result of encountering God in a manner that results in submission to his will but with the focus being on knowing God through Jesus Christ. Realization of the inherent limitations of praxis has caused some liberation theologians to speak of an 'epistemological break' which 'consists in the existential and historical following that yields a praxis knowing which is distinct from "natural understanding" as well as contrary to it'.[132]

Daniel Schipani has reformulated liberationist praxis into an 'epistemology of obedience', which is characterized by discipleship as 'the dynamic, dialogical, and discerning following of Jesus'.[133] He asserts that the liberationist's view of praxis must be evaluated in light of the criteria derived from revelation, and from biblical revelation especially, 'lest doing the truth becomes equivalent to making the truth through historical praxis, rather than practicing the truth which is ultimately being revealed to us'.[134] It is evident that a praxis epistemology must be modified in order to be incorporated into the Pentecostal faith tradition. Schipani's revision would come close to capturing the necessary dynamics. Knowledge of God involves encounter with and participation in the divine nature which results in the transformation of the knower. The praxis that would flow out of such an encounter would generate a fresh vision of the kingdom of God, a vision that incorporates an ethic that is consistent with an epistemology which joins knowing and loving.

---

[132] J. Sobrino, *The True Church and the Poor*, trans. M.J. O'Connell (Maryknoll, NY: Orbis Books, 1984), 25; J. Sobrino, *Jesus in Latin America*, trans. R.R. Barr (Maryknoll, NY: Orbis Books, 1987).

[133] D. Schipani, *Religious Education Encounters Liberation Theology* (Birmingham, AL: Religious Education Press, 1988), 125.

[134] Schipani, *Religious Education*, 136.

Yet, it must, be emphasized that Pentecostals have often neglected the critical reflective dimensions of existence in the world. We have failed to respond appropriately in obedience as historical subjects. The solution may well rest in the integration of praxis methodology within the epistemological framework of yada. Theological education would thus involve the beforementioned dynamics of the Pentecostal faith, with transformation being normative, but it would also involve critical reflection upon lived experience Such a combination would powerfully engage the total person in his or her socio-political environment while calling for the active presence of the Holy Spirit within the learning community. Students would hear and respond to the speech of God, knowing that true conscientization comes by a transformative encounter with the holy.

In such a learning context, the total educational process would temper the illusionary power of education which, while humanizing and liberating, gives a false sense of one's ability to have power over the world. Pentecostal theological education, to be true to a Pentecostal epistemology, must constantly be aware that knowledge of God and reality is a gracious gift bestowed regardless of gender, race, socio-economic standing or educational level. Given these assumptions, I wish to propose what would be the major components of such a model for Pentecostal theological education which would help students to know God[135] and which would 'combine transcendent experience with a commitment to a liberating historical future'.[136]

The Pentecostal faith is foremost a corporate experience. In their mutual koinonia, Pentecostal believers share in the mystery and freedom of God. The community of faith paradigm of theological education best allows for this experience. Theological education in the context of community would have certain characteristics which define its unique process of discipleship. Foremost among these characteristics is the understanding that theological education is to be viewed as formation. In such an environment the intellectual work of a theological community is seen as part of a larger vision of mature Christian discipleship. Theological education from this perspective does not mean that there is no 'ordered learning' or critical inquiry utilizing the best scholarly tools. Hence, theological education as formation is more than mere socialization, and the community of faith is not just a community that worships but a learning community which operates from the posture of worship.[137] Formation in such a context would refer to all factors and processes that contribute to the shaping and moulding of the individual and community into the fullness of Christ. It is a demanding, exacting process and there are no short cuts. It is a radical,

---

[135] D. Kelsey, *To Understand God Truly* (Louisville, KY: Westminster John Knox Press, 1992), 75.

[136] Macchia, 'Sighs Too Deep'.

[137] S. Te Salle McFague, 'Between Athens and Jerusalem: The Seminary in Tension', *The Christian Century* 93:4 (1976).

countercultural endeavour which has at its very core the posturing of persons for ongoing transformation.

Components of Theological Education as Formation

Theological education as formation has three distinct dimensions which interact to form both individuals and community. These dimensions may be labelled as enculturation, education and instruction.

Enculturation may be defined as the formation or moulding into the individual the ethos of the community. One never outgrows the need to be shaped by a community of faith. In Pentecostal theological education, as persons participate in the ritual life of the worshipping community, they are shaped and formed by these processes. Such processes also posture one to receive the grace of God. Conscientization occurs when theological education allows for and facilitates the joining of affective and cognitive dimensions of existence. Theological education should, therefore, involve enculturating actions which facilitate the creation of a unique confessional community of faith, existing as a radical alternative to the dominant order. Hence, a community of learning should also include participation in such rituals as communion, footwashing, testimony, prayer for healing and other forms of Pentecostal faith expression. The total environment is seen as formational and that which facilitates knowledge of God.

Education provides what John Westerhoff describes as 'those critical reflective activities' related to the communal experiences.[138] In this sense, education focuses on developing and actualizing the human potential. It is in this component of theological education that a praxis epistemology is most helpful. Educational processes involving analyzing, forming judgments, discovering and criticizing make possible individuation which is necessary to 'read one's reality' as a subject in the world. Such education is a liberating and humanizing endeavour. Reality becomes the object of critical reflection and action. Scientific analysis should be applied to the complex nature of socio-political dynamics. Within the framework of a relational epistemology, which sees Scripture as agent of encounter and transformation as well as the authoritative base for inquiry, all disciplines would seek to discover their relation to the truth of God's Word as well as their relation to culture, tradition and church experience.

Instruction refers to the 'building in' or formation of the individual through helping him or her to acquire knowledge and skills. Because of an authoritative view of Scripture, which emphasizes its propositional nature, many Evangelicals appear to emphasize instruction over other aspects of formation. In some cases, instruction precludes critical inquiry inherent in education as a

---

[138] J. Westerhoff, 'Formation, Education and Instruction', *Religious Education* 82: Fall (1987), 581.

whole. What results is an acritical assimilation of facts and skills which are useful 'tools' for the Christian faith. In these instances, the theological school is viewed as primarily a place to obtain skills in such areas as exegesis, church growth techniques or church hermeneutics. In such environments, there is little community awareness and very little critical awareness. Unfortunately, many Pentecostals have adopted this approach to instruction, which runs contrary to their own approach to truth. Instruction, while necessary within a Pentecostal context, should have both the authoritative revealed nature and the experiential nature. These two components exist in a dialectical relationship, with experience being evaluated by the norm of Scripture. Also, within the instructional processes there should be openness to and a yielding to the Paraclete-teacher who leads into all truth. Therefore, instruction would be corporate and interactive with the Scriptures and approached as an avenue for personal and corporate engagement with God.

The power of transformation is honoured as people together yield to the Holy Spirit's mission in the world. Perhaps this proposal does not go far enough in re-thinking theological education within a Pentecostal context. It does, however, attempt to conceptualize a framework for honouring the subversive memory and theological precedents for conscientization among Pentecostals while acknowledging the need for astute critical reflection-action found in a praxis based model of theological education. There may need to be totally new wineskins created to educate for ministry those who believe that one can know God truly and join with him in the re-making of history. Such new wineskins would be subversive in their implications for conscientization, just as the Pentecostal movement itself may yet prove to be.

Progress and Challenge in Theological Education in Central and Eastern Europe[139]

Cheryl Brown and Wesley Brown

Dr. Cheryl Brown is Director of Biblical Studies and Lecturer in Old Testament. Dr. Wesley Brown is Chaplain and Adjunct Lecturer at the International Baptist Theological Seminary in Prague, Czech Republic.

Theological education in Central and Eastern Europe has changed phenomenally in the past twelve years since the end of communist rule. A striking example is theological education amongst Russian Baptists. During the Soviet period, despite large numbers of Baptist churches in Russia, no seminary or Bible school was permitted.[140] This has changed today both in terms of the numbers of different denominational schools and cooperation between them.[141] In this article, we will highlight some developments in theological education in Central and Eastern Europe, noting areas in which progress has been made and also obstacles which continue to challenge educators seeking to equip leaders for church-related ministries.

We will organize our survey and analysis under the following three headings: first, contextualization of theological education; second, the praxis of theological education (models, curriculum, resources, validation, and support); and third, cooperative efforts in theological education. For the most part, we will look at theological education amongst Baptists, since this has been our primary context during our years of ministry in Europe, thus enabling us to draw upon personal experiences with new institutions that have opened in the past decade, as well as those which have re-opened or been expanded during those years. Moreover, in many cases, we take as points of reference in our comments specific mandates articulated by the International Councils of Accrediting Agencies (ICAA) for Evangelical Theological Education in their 'Manifesto on the Renewal of Theological Education',[142] as these provide a framework for the globally recognized essential components of evangelical theological education today.

---

[139] The data presented in this paper reflect the period up to 2003.

[140] Egelkraut, 'Theological Education', 35.

[141] P. Penner, 'Contextual Theological Education among Post-Soviet Protestants: The Development of a Masters Degree at St Petersburg Christian University', *Transformation* 18:2, April-June (2001), 119.

[142] 'Manifesto 1995, on the Renewal of Theological Education', *Evangelical Review of Theology* 19:3, July (1995).

Contextualization of Theological Education

The crucial importance of contextualizing theological education is expressed in the Manifesto's first mandate: 'Our programmes of theological education must be designed with deliberate reference to the contexts in which they serve'.[143] Contextualization involves not only content but also modalities of delivery and evaluation. The obstacles to genuine contextualization are particularly formidable in Central and Eastern Europe, in part due to historical circumstances surrounding the establishment of the theological institutions. Most began in the early years following the dissolution of the Soviet Union and the Soviet bloc, when new evangelical churches sprang up very quickly nearly all across the former communist world, thus creating an acute and urgent need for trained leaders.

The majority of these schools were established with the help of western missionaries or mission organizations as an extension of evangelism and church planting ministries, which meant that they were often western 'transplants', following western models and western standards, with western curriculum, western teachers, and western literature Sergei Nikolaev, President of the St. Petersburg Evangelical Theological Academy and Bishop of the Evangelical Churches of North-West Russia, pointed out the challenge within the Russian context in his address to the Euro-Asian Accrediting Association in October 1999:

> The problem of protestantism in Russia lies in the fact that we teach people universal truths, lead them to the ends of the earth but do not notice that they have not learned to walk in their own land.... Conformity of theological education with the historical and cultural roots of the society is a vital and urgent task.[144]

Many educators in Central and Eastern Europe are taking up the challenge, reflecting more intentionally and strategically about ways to tailor theological education to their specific contexts and needs.[145] A crucial aspect of contextualization is the integration of theological education and the life of the churches it seeks to serve. Thus, the second mandate of the 'Manifesto' reads: 'Our programmes of theological education must orient themselves pervasively in terms of the Christian community being served.... Our theological programmes must become manifestly of the church, through the church and for the church'. To be sure, this is a constant challenge in theological education

---

[143] M. Griffiths, 'Contextualization of Overseas Theological Education', *Evangelical Review of Theology* 19:3, July (1995); Penner, 'Contextual Theological'.

[144] S. Nikolaev, 'The Problems of Euro-Asian Theology for the New Millenium: Address Given to the Euro-Asian Accrediting Association (EAAA)', (Kiev, Ukraine: 1999).

[145] J.E. Plueddemann, 'The Future of Evangelical Theological Education', *Evangelical Review of Theology* 14:1 (1990), 21.

globally; but perhaps it is greater in Central and Eastern Europe, where, in most cases, westerners and/or nationals who have lived and studied in the west initially established and now continue to operate and fund theological schools. This has resulted in a widespread perception amongst many of the older generation of national leaders – who, often because of their experiences under communism, are anti-intellectual and fearful of western 'corruption' – that these schools are foreign elements and not to be trusted. Such fears and attitudes are not always unfounded.

Lesslie Newbigin points out that detachment of theological students from the churches has not infrequently led to a form of elitism: 'It has been said that the standard type of seminary training tends to create a professional elite separated from the ordinary membership....'[146] He goes on to conclude that '...true theology can be done only in a community which is committed to faithful discipleship, including both worship and practical obedience'.[147] In our travels throughout Central and Eastern Europe, we have encountered this criticism of residential seminaries, sometimes with good reason and sometimes unfounded. It can happen that students develop an air of superiority because they have had more education than the pastors who mentor them as part of their practical training in ministry. Also, some students who have studied for four or five years refuse to go to rural village churches or smaller churches whose membership consists of a handful or two of mostly older women.

On the other hand, a number of older pastors – many of whom served time in Soviet prisons – lacked any opportunity for an education and feel threatened by a seminarian who may have more knowledge. This insecurity may lead the veteran pastor to express disdain for education and to assert that all a pastor really needs is the Word and the Holy Spirit, or that pastors during the Soviet era did their work just fine without education. Despite the western roots of many institutions, such that they remain virtual transplants from the west, a growing number are reflecting and strategizing, in dialogue with their constituencies, about how they can best integrate academy and church. On several occasions, we have heard theological educators liken the theological school to the medical school, maintaining that it should include both theoretical and practical components, with the greater emphasis upon how theory is applied in real life.

The degrees offered in Baptist and Anabaptist Studies at the International Baptist Theological Seminary (IBTS) in Prague, Czech Republic, illustrate how the seminary seeks to address the needs and concerns of its constituent churches. IBTS was mandated (in September 1997) by the European Baptist Federation (EBF) – comprised of fifty-one Baptist Unions across Europe and the Middle East – to train and equip missionaries, teachers and leaders for their

---

[146] L. Newbigin, 'Theological Education in a World Perspective', *Churchman* 2:93 (1979), 107.

[147] Newbigin, 'Theological Education', 112.

theological institutions and churches. Accordingly, in the past five years the seminary has developed MTh, MPhil or PhD degrees in four subject areas (validated by the University of Wales): Biblical Studies, Baptist and Anabaptist Studies, Contextualized Missiology, and Applied Theology. Students in Baptist and Anabaptist Studies are currently researching, reflecting on and writing the histories of Baptists in their home contexts, much of it original work on oral histories that will pass away with the older generation of believers if not recorded soon. Moreover, in the Journal of European Baptist Studies, inaugurated in 2000, IBTS provides a forum for European Baptists to publish their work in these and other areas pertinent to Baptist and Anabaptist history, faith and practice. An example of the kind of original work being done is Toivo Pilli's work on 'Union of Evangelical Christians – Baptists of Estonia 1945-1989: Survival Techniques, Outreach Efforts, Search for Identity'.[148]

The Praxis of Theological Education

A Variety of Models

Point no. 3 of the 'Manifesto on the Renewal of Theological Education' mandates 'Strategic Flexibility in the forms and content of theological education': '...to take account of all academic levels of need, and not become frozen in serving only one level... [and] embrace a greater flexibility in the educational modes by which we touch the various levels of leadership need, and not limit our approach to a single traditional or radical pattern'. In evangelical seminaries and Bible schools of Central and Eastern Europe today, although a single model – the full-time residential model – continues to predominate, one also can find a variety of creative and innovative models; increasingly, educators are seeking to equip leaders for diverse levels of ministry and to develop and/or adapt better modalities to accomplish their goals. We briefly illustrate with three examples – from Bulgaria, Russia, and Prague (IBTS).

In 1992, Bulgarian Baptists inaugurated the Bulgarian Baptist Theological School, a four-year, part-time, certificate level programme. It was subsequently expanded (1996), in terms of curriculum and structure – new modules were added and four new extension centres were opened – and reconstituted as the Baptist Theological Institute (BTI). The curriculum consists of two components: correspondence courses; and workshops or seminars, which are offered once or twice a year. Any Bulgarian Baptist is eligible to study in BTI's centres, whether as an auditor or for credit toward the certificate or diploma.

---

[148] T. Pilli, 'Union of Evangelical Christians-Baptists of Estonia 1945-1989: Survival Techniques, Outreach Efforts, Search for Identity', *Journal of European Baptist Studies* 1:2, January (2001).

BTI has been quite successful in equipping a large number of leaders relatively inexpensively, while enabling them to remain in their home contexts and ministries. A disadvantage, however, is that it can take a long time to complete their studies for a degree. In 1999, theological education amongst Bulgarian evangelicals moved forward significantly when they established the Bulgarian Evangelical Theological Institute (BETI), a cooperative effort amongst six registered evangelical denominations. While each denomination operates its own school, BETI is jointly directed by a board comprised of representatives from each group. It is a full-time, four and a half year programme leading to a bachelor's degree accredited by the European Evangelical Accrediting Association and recognized by the Bulgarian government.

Baptists in Russia have developed a variety of models for equipping their leaders, on diverse levels. On the master's level, Moscow Theological Seminary offers a five-year (full-time) Master of Divinity, while St. Petersburg Christian University – in which Baptists cooperate – offers a one-year MTh in Biblical Studies and a master's in Missions.[149] On the bachelor's level, both St. Petersburg Christian University and St. Petersburg Evangelical Theological Academy offer a four-year (full-time) degree or a part-time option; while the Moscow Theological Seminary has a four-year, part-time bachelor's degree. At the same time, Russian Baptists have opened more than twenty Bible schools, generally one-year, full-time residential programmes for training pastors and other church leaders already engaged in ministries. At the Siberian Bible School in Irkutsk, for example, several of Wes's students in 1997 were missionaries who had planted churches farther west, around Chita, and were able to study Bible, theology, and applied theology courses only after such practical experience in ministry. Another option for those who must study part-time is the Moscow Theological Institute. The programme is built around two, two-week residential modules per year in Moscow, along with self-directed study, research and/or writing in between the sessions.

Advantages of this format are that it enables church leaders to remain in ministry contexts, does not uproot families, as in a longer residential programme, and provides opportunity for interaction with others likewise actively engaged in ministry. Finally, the Russian Institute of Preachers in Bryansk is the newest (2001) programme, developed jointly by the Russian Baptist Union, the International Baptist Theological Seminary (see below, IBTS), and David Brown of American Baptists' International Ministries, the director. It was founded in response to a specific need to better equip those who teach preaching – in one of the Bible schools or in the Moscow Theological Institute – as well as pastors, evangelists, or missionaries. The Institute is a three-year course, which meets twice a year for two intensive weeks. Students come from as far away as Chita in Eastern Siberia, north of Mongolia.

[149] Penner, 'Contextual Theological', 120.

IBTS, in Prague, Czech Republic, which serves the entire European Baptist family, has developed a variety of educational programmes, in terms of both form (models) and content (subject areas and multiple levels). They now offer MTh, MPhil and PhD degrees – all validated by the University of Wales – in four subject areas: Biblical Studies, Baptist and Anabaptist Studies, Contextualized Missiology and Applied Theology. In every case, the MTh requires three modules, one core and two electives, and a 20,000 word dissertation. The modules are usually two-week intensives, delivered at three time blocks throughout the academic year, with ongoing seminars in each subject area, along with a joint weekly seminar. The modular format enables students to study either full-time or part-time, with part-time students travelling to Prague during the intensives and then writing essays and/or exams while continuing in their home contexts and ministries. Most choose to study part-time. An ongoing challenge is how best to deliver equivalent content to the part time students, since they are unable to participate in the ongoing seminars; there has been some preliminary strategizing about developing interactive seminars on-line, but much work remains to be done before this possibility becomes a reality. The MPhil and PhD, currently only part-time, non-residential, are entirely research degrees, following the pattern of British universities. Under close supervision of a mentor, students must write (more or less) three chapters of the thesis during the first two years of matriculation, whereupon his/her work is evaluated to determine if he/she may then move ahead to the PhD or must terminate study with the MPhil degree.

In the same way, on the MTh level, a student who successfully completes only two of the three modules will be awarded the certificate or, if one completes all three modules minus the dissertation, the post-graduate diploma. IBTS also offers a one-year residential Certificate in Applied Theology (CAT), which combines intensive English language study with survey modules in Biblical Studies and Theology, Church History, Mission and Evangelism, and Applied Theology. Its primary purpose is to train lay leaders, though a number of graduates go on to higher levels of theological education and 'full-time' church-related ministries. Additionally, IBTS sponsors directors' conferences. These are one- two- or three-week non-degree courses held throughout the year, either on campus in Prague or in some other location, to help equip in specific ways pastors, lay leaders, educators and Baptist Union leaders. For example, in August 2001, the Director of Applied Theology, Dr. Parush Parushev, hosted a conference entitled 'Discipleship and Formation of Christian Character: a Radical Reformation Perspective'. The 46 conference participants came from 16 countries and 20 Baptist Unions.

Resources

Facilities

Many new theological institutions have faced the challenge of finding a permanent home. In several cases, they have purchased and remodelled a school or other building, often with significant financial assistance by Overseas Council International and Overseas Council Canada. The following are examples of building projects, supported in large measure by funds from the West, though not all by Overseas Council: St. Petersburg Christian University (SPCU) purchased new facilities in April 1999, renovated classrooms and administrative offices and moved to the new campus in September 2000, thanks in part to Overseas Council Canada. During the current academic year (2001-2002), an adjoining building is being remodelled as a dormitory and is projected to be ready by autumn 2002. Moscow Theological Seminary of Evangelical Christians-Baptists (MTS), after years of renting space in the Russian Baptist Union building, has now been able to purchase a vacated school building; renovations and remodelling are expected to be completed in time for dedication on 1 September 2002. College of Theology and Education (CTE), in Chisinau, Moldova, which has grown dramatically since its inception in 1992, was at first crowded into the Moldova Baptist Union building. The situation has eased considerably since the addition of two stories and, more recently, the construction of a new (adjoining) building with a large dining hall and young women's dormitory space. Latvian Baptist Theological Seminary in Riga, founded in 1922, was housed in a building adjoined to a church. During World War II, first the Russian communists (1940), then the Nazis (1941), and then again the communists (1944) took over the buildings. They destroyed the library and used the seminary auditorium as a communist theatre. Even after the end of communist rule, it was not until 1992 that the building – in extreme disrepair – was finally returned to the Baptist Union and the seminary; and the task of restoring it continues.

Library

Most of the seminaries have had to build their libraries from scratch in the past twelve, or less, years since they were founded or re-established. We have already noted that the Baptist Theological Seminary in Latvia lost its entire library during the communist take-over. For most new seminaries this is one of the most formidable challenges they face, because of both the enormous cost and the lack of available books and journals in Central and Eastern European languages. In one new seminary, the librarian showed Wes two shelves of books in a closet – at least half of which were in English – as its total library. It would be fair to say that most of the Eastern European seminaries' libraries are at least two-thirds in English. In some cases, theological institutions are cooperating jointly in an inter-library loan programme, particularly to make more journals, a major expense, available to a larger coterie of schools.

Computers and the Internet

Every seminary in Central and Eastern Europe has computers available for student use, though, to be sure, of varying quality and quantity from school to school. For example, some have only donated, used IBM 286 or 386 computers, which – not surprisingly – are in constant need of repair; and spare parts are not always available, even if funds were available to purchase them. In one seminary we noted that half the student computers were not functioning. Every seminary has at least one computer with internet access. We know of a seminary in which only graduate students are permitted internet access, while undergraduates may use the computers to type term papers but are denied access to the internet. The internet presents both an excellent potential resource and an enticing temptation for theological students. Since so many articles, books, lectures, and bibliographies are accessible on the internet – in a diversity of languages – it can make it possible for students in more remote areas, or areas with limited educational resources, to participate in theological education.

For many, it is the *only* way they can study, as they can access materials and also maintain contact with teachers or mentors. Since 1997, we have increasingly come to rely upon the internet to network with leaders at theological institutions and to advise students, especially receiving and dialoguing with them about their exams, essays and research papers. An essentially undeveloped area at this time is online education, although some schools are working on this. But at the same time, the temptation to plagiarize is great. Not infrequently, students copy material and present it as their own work; and too often they get away with it, since it is difficult if not impossible, for educators to produce solid proof of plagiarism. Yet, in specific cases, we know of students who were dismissed or denied a degree because of plagiarism.

Curriculum

Mandate no. 5 of the 'Manifesto on the Renewal of Theological Education' delineates the essential components of curriculum development and evaluation: 'Our programmes of theological education must be dominated by a rigorous practice of identifying objectives, assessing outcomes, and adjusting programmes accordingly'. In a 1998 lecture to theological educators in Central and Eastern Europe, Mark Elliott, editor of the East-West Church and Ministry Report, emphasized that the curriculum should be shaped by an institution's mission statement (What do theological educators seek to accomplish?) and highlighted some specific goals that must be addressed: build a solid foundation in the theological disciplines, in communication and preaching, and denominational distinctives; give students tools with which to understand and relate to secular society (contextualization); educate students for analytical thinking rather than mere memorization and unquestioned acceptance (which characterized education under communist rule); and provide for developmental needs of the students.

Unfortunately, during the early and mid 1990s, many seminaries were not able to engage in much serious curriculum planning since they were quite dependent upon visiting teachers from the West. 'Planning' was mostly based upon questions such as, Who was available? When? What subject(s) could he/she teach? Who could pay their own way and perhaps even contribute financially to the seminary? Happily, during the past five years, this pattern has begun to change as more and more nationals have returned to their institutions from study abroad and assumed teaching positions. Not only is there less dependence upon expatriate teachers – and interpreters for them – but these nationals often have brought to curriculum development a fresh perspective and skills gained through their experience in different educational contexts.

The comments about contextualization are especially relevant to the issues of curriculum. One seminary, in response to the multiple contexts of its constituent churches – which includes a large Muslim population – has developed a one year programme for people from Middle Asia, with courses on Islam and reaching the Muslim world alongside more 'traditional' introductory courses. Students who do well may return and enter a degree programme if they prove able to do solid academic work and show spiritual maturity. Mark Elliott recommends that evangelical seminaries in former communist countries introduce more courses on Eastern Orthodoxy and Catholicism and courses on biblical principles of conflict management.[150] As they mature, theological schools are working more intentionally on 'assessing outcomes' of their curriculum development efforts, through establishing a uniform standard by which to evaluate results has proven difficult, due to the very wide diversity of evangelical institutions. Recognition of the need for such standards has led schools to participate in groups such as the European Evangelical Accrediting Association (EEAA), its newest regional member being the Euro-Asian Accrediting Association (EAAA), and/or the Consortium of European Baptist Theological Schools (CEBTS) (see below for more on these organizations). Also, institutions whose degree(s) were validated by the University of Wales (IBTS, SPCU, and Donetsk Christian University, DCU) built into their programmes the same quality assurance controls as were in place in the British University system; this included the 'requirement of externality', which requires assessment not only by two institutional staff, but also by a university-appointed external examiner.[151]

---

[150] M. Elliot, 'Theological Education after Communism: The Mixed Blessing of Western Assistance', *EWCMR* 3:1, Winter (1995), 3.

[151] D.P. Davies, 'Doing Theology in One's Own Language', *Transformation* 8:2, April-June (2001), 135.

Validation

Theological institutions in Central and Eastern Europe have sought accreditation through a variety of organizations or institutions, the main ones being the following:

a. The European Evangelical Accrediting Association (EEAA), an associate region of the International Council of Accrediting Agencies for Evangelical Theological Education (ICAA). The EEAA, part of the World Evangelical Fellowship and the European Evangelical Alliance, was officially constituted (by 23 schools) on October 31, 1979. Amongst its goals are to establish a network of mutual cooperation between the member schools, including establishing common educational standards, and to grant academic certificates and diplomas recognized in Europe and overseas countries. Many of the schools in the East European Schools of Theology (EEST) are validated by EEAA. The newest member region of the EEAA is Euro-Asia, with the establishment of the Euro-Asian Accrediting Association.

b. The Euro-Asian Accrediting Association (EAAA), officially launched on 15 October 1997, began with more than 31 schools from the Confederation of Independent States (CIS = former Soviet Union) and currently has 49 member schools. Most of these schools have been unsuccessful at attaining governmental accreditation[152] and so have joined together as peers to establish and maintain common educational standards. Many schools have been accredited on the bachelor's level: Odessa Theological Seminary, St. Petersburg Christian University, the College of Theology and Education (in Moldova) and Lampados Bible College (in Russia) – with several other schools presently undergoing the review process.

c. 'Foreign' University Validation has been attained for some master's level programmes. The principle universities accrediting degrees are the University of South Africa (SPCU's MTh in Missions) and the University of Wales, which validates IBTS's MTh, MPhil, and PhD degrees in the four subject areas, SPCU's MTh in Biblical Studies, and DCU's MA in Contextualized Theology (originally in partnership with the Oxford Centre for Mission Studies).

d. Governmental validation has been granted to some institutions. For example, the Romanian government fully recognizes the University of Bucharest's Baptist Theological Faculty, which has a highly successful 'double major' programme that allows students to study theological subjects and at the same time literature or a foreign language to prepare for teaching in public schools or universities. We have already noted that the Bulgarian Evangelical Theological Institute is registered with the Bulgarian government.[153] The Lithuania Christian College, in Klaipeda, is in the process of gaining governmental recognition. IBTS in Prague received governmental recognition

---

[152] Penner, 'Contextual Theological', 119.

[153] G. Griffith, 'New Bible Institute Registered in Bulgaria', *EWCMR* 8:1, Winter (2000), 14.

this year. Governmental refusal to validate degrees is an ongoing struggle for some schools, for example, the Latvian Baptist Seminary.

Publishing

Undoubtedly one of the most critical needs amongst evangelicals of Central and Eastern Europe is for literature in their own languages, better yet, produced by their own authors. For the most part, evangelical publishing in many of these areas is a relatively new phenomenon, begun largely after the fall of communism. In the early 1990s, the emphasis was on translating well-known evangelical authors from Britain and North America; and thus certain books (for example: Josh McDowell's *Evidence that Demands a Verdict* and C. S. Lewis's *Mere Christianity*) can be found in almost every language of the region. At the same time, some of the translated books are not sufficiently relevant to the needs and issues of churches in the East. For example, in one country in which Wes taught Christian Ethics, the only ethics book available in the national language, in the entire seminary library of over 7,000 volumes, was on Philosophical Ethics and had absolutely no application to contemporary issues or to issues specific to the seminary's context. Clearly, most progress has been made in Russian language publishing.

The early 1990s saw the establishment of Bibleiskii Kafedra (Bible Pulpit) which has worked creatively and energetically amongst evangelical, pentecostal and charismatic groups to seek broad consensus on what books have been/are most needed in various disciplines and then to facilitate translation and publication of such books into Russian. The entire project, now administered by EAAA, has expanded to include support of publication by indigenous scholars. An example of the superb quality of work being done is the newly-published (2001) massive church history, *A History of Christianity: The Second Millennium* (English translation of the title),[154] by Sergei Sannikov of Ukraine. The volume surveys and analyses church history from Eastern Orthodox, Roman Catholic, and protestant perspectives. Moreover, new Russian language journals continue to appear, for example *Bogomysliye* (by OTS), Khronograf (by SPCU), and *Bogomyslie v internete*. Yet, at the same time, there remains a great need for national authors to write contextually in other subjects, particularly those often subsumed under the general rubric of 'Applied Theology', such as counselling, homiletics, human rights and religious liberty.

Faculty Development

We have noted a significant change in the faculty composition in many of the seminaries and colleges in which we have taught during the past five years. Even in the mid-1990s, the situation remained essentially as Mark Elliot

[154] Bibliographic data unavailable.

described it in 1993: 'Every evangelical school presently relies heavily on short-term western faculty who instruct with the aid of translators'. Now an increasing number of nationals have completed degrees in Theology or Biblical Studies and returned to teach, or seminaries employ their own graduates while allowing them to pursue a graduate degree part-time. Two fairly recent conferences we attended have highlighted this striking transition in theological education. The Conference of European Baptist Theological Educators at IBTS (January 2000) brought together nearly seventy presidents/ rectors, deans and faculty from across Europe and the Middle East; a conspicuous number of them were national leaders from Central or Eastern Europe, and their progress reports gave testimony to the increasing indigenization of theological education in their regions.

Likewise, the European Baptist Theological Teachers' Conference at IBTS (June 2001) reflected these developments. One seminary leader from Western Europe remarked how encouraged he was to become acquainted with new and younger participants from Central and Eastern Europe, who evidenced spiritual maturity and serious reflection about their task. This represents real progress in theological education and at the same time presents some major challenges. People who have earned a graduate degree in North America on scholarship often find it difficult to return to their home country, as much for economic as for cultural reasons. We know of a case in which a national was told that the seminary would be happy to have him on the faculty, but they could not pay him a regular salary. On the other hand, expatriate teachers generally put no strain on the budget; they usually pay their own way in travel and do not require a salary, and many bring a monetary gift for the school – something the national could never match. How can seminaries find a way to transition to their own national faculty and pay them a living wage (vastly less than even their scholarship stipend in North America)?

Another challenge is how the national who has earned a degree abroad will contextualize courses to make them relevant and appropriate. Not infrequently, a new teacher develops a course whose content represents a virtual transplant of one taken in Western Europe or North America. Other challenges stem from the reality that those who go to Western Europe or North America become accustomed to a standard of living that is extremely difficult to leave behind; many simply choose to stay in 'the promised land'. Sometimes even if a student is committed to returning, his spouse and/or children may not share the commitment; or if they do return, they may find it too difficult, even impossible, to integrate or re-integrate into the home culture. For these and other reasons, mostly financial, we generally counsel people to study as close to home, in the European context, as possible. And now with more and more options becoming available, an increasing number are finding ways to remain in Europe.

Partnership, Support, and Dependence

It is no exaggeration to say that every evangelical theological institution in Central and Eastern Europe is dependent upon outside financial assistance. But this assistance is a mixed blessing, as Mark Elliott averred in a 1995 article in EWCMR: …[T]he global commitment and material prosperity of many western evangelical churches, missions, and seminaries have translated into an extraordinary, perhaps unprecedented, outpouring of assistance for fledgling seminaries and Bible institutes all across East Central Europe and the former Soviet Union. In most institutions, western assistance is welcome. The question is what kind of assistance is beneficial and who should make that decision. Our experience bears this out; for, deplorably, Americans frequently attempt to use money to control the theological orientation and curriculum of Central or Eastern European schools. We know of one case in which a western institution initially provided monetary and teaching assistance to a seminary, but promptly terminated all assistance when the seminary could not in good conscience embrace their eschatology and wanted to continue association with sister churches deemed 'liberal' by the supporting institution.

Elsewhere, an American mission organization assured a seminary of its financial support – provided that the Americans could appoint the faculty and bring whomever they wished to teach from North America. Some organizations seem to believe that only they have the correct theology and know with whom the seminary should associate. This desire, or need, to control reveals a certain theological imperialism and distrust in the Holy Spirit's ability to lead Central or Eastern European Christians. Instead, we must wholeheartedly commit to genuine partnership, characterized by mutual respect and openness in sharing perspectives. Too often Eastern European institutions are made to feel as if their contribution to theological education is insignificant, as Judith Berling points out: 'North American money has too often created asymmetry in relationships. A sense of indebtedness or of being the client of a wealthy patron has inhibited international or cross-cultural partners from expressing their needs, concerns, and stakes.… Partners abroad are often too polite to assert their own agenda or challenge the unconscious assertion of privilege, which can easily come with the resources and good intentions of North American institutions'.[155]

Despite the financial challenge due to very low salaries, or unemployment, of constituent church members, a few seminaries have sought to achieve at least some level of self-support, whether financial or otherwise. An excellent example is in the multi-faceted response of churches supporting the Hungarian Baptist Theological Seminary in Cluj, Romania, a full-time residential programme: 1. Every church in the Baptist Union must provide an offering for the seminary. 2. At the fall harvest, churches donate a large quantity of potatoes which are then stored in the seminary cellar for later use. 3. A baker in one of

[155] J.A. Berling, 'Hard-Earned Counsel for Assisting Post-Soviet Seminaries', *East West Church and Ministry Report* 8:4, Fall (2000), 2.

the churches regularly supplies a vanload of bread, some of which is frozen until needed. Not every seminary is on its way to becoming self-supporting, however. We know of an institution that developed a plan to become financially self-sufficient by starting a dairy; Mennonite farmers from the U.S. pledged to donate the cows. Then an American arrived and offered a large amount of money to the institution; and, not surprisingly, the project toward becoming self-supporting was quickly abandoned. Missiologically, western agencies must be challenged to examine their methodology in support of theological education, and what procedures most contribute toward less dependency.

Cooperative Efforts

Mandate no. 12 of the 'Manifesto' asserts: 'Our programmes of theological education must pursue contact and collaboration among themselves for mutual support, encouragement, edification and cross-fertilization.... The biblical notion of mutuality needs to be much more visibly expressed and pragmatically pursued....' It is clear that evangelical theological institutions in Central and Eastern Europe have made significant progress in realizing this goal in the past decade. The following are examples of such cooperative efforts: 1. East European Schools of Theology (EEST) – This, the 'academic arm' of the Council for Eastern European Theological Education (CEETE), is a fellowship to facilitate graduate theological education for post-communist Europe. EEST works primarily to encourage and support contextualized graduate theological programmes and to share library and faculty resources. 2. European Evangelical Accrediting Association (EEAA) (see above). 3. Euro-Asian Accrediting Association (EAAA) (see above). 4. Consortium of European Baptist Theological Schools (CEBTS).

In September, 2001, 18 theological institutions, almost half of them in Central and Eastern Europe, covenanted to work together in equipping leaders for Baptists in Europe and the Middle East, through mutual support and exchange of information and other resources (including faculty). In its first forum held in February 2002, CEBTS addressed pertinent and practical issues such as validation, quality control, curricula (including sharing of course outlines and/or syllabi), lay and specialist education, sabbaticals, fund raising, training of administrative leaders, e-learning, sharing of library resources and faculty exchanges. Task groups were established to continue work in these and other areas. CEBTS plans to meet together biennially, with a leadership council meeting annually.

We mention briefly some recent conferences that have addressed topics of interest to theological educators in Europe: 1. 'The Second Consultation on Theological Education and Leadership Development in Post-Communist Europe in the Context of the Kingdom of God and the Kingdoms of the World', September 1-5, 1998, at the Evangelical Theological Faculty, Osijek, Croatia. 2.

'Theological Education in the Twenty-first Century' (All Nations College, England; September 2000), sponsored by the EAAA. Lectures included topics such as contextualization of theological education, spiritual formation of students, curriculum development, pedagogical methods, cooperating internationally, technology, globalization and post-modernity. 3. 'The Conference of European Baptist Theological Educators' (IBTS, Prague; January 2000). Some of the topics treated were curriculum development, administrative skills for presidents and administrators, use of the internet, teaching methods, financial resourcing, faculty development, library, and building community. 4. 'Doing Theology in a New Europe', 'The European Baptist Theological Educators' Conference (EBTTC) (IBTS, June 2001).

The conference brought together 64 participants from 14 countries, representing 24 seminaries and Bible schools. A western European conferee later reported: It was particularly stimulating to have so many from the Eastern European and Middle Eastern seminaries present and to find such lively optimism and forward thinking both in strategy and theology combined with strengthening church life and leadership in these areas. Some of the younger, extremely young, teachers of theology are giving great hope for the future of scholarship, theological education and pastoral training in the East and Europe as a whole.

Conclusions

We have examined developments in theological education in Central and Eastern Europe since 1989, within the framework of several mandates of the 'Manifesto on the Renewal of Theological Education'. Clearly, significant progress has been made in numerous dimensions of theological education, while at the same time, certain problems continue to challenge educators in this region. In terms of contextualization, some institutions have made specific efforts to adapt to local needs and cultural contexts, and others continue to operate according to western models; most schools fall somewhere in between these two poles. An ongoing task in contextualizing theological education is to nurture its relationship with the local churches. Moreover, excellent progress has been made in all aspects of the praxis of theological education.

A variety of models have been implemented (on diverse levels), many schools have secured their own facilities, libraries are improving, there is increasing implementation of appropriate curricula, more and more nationals are leading, teaching and writing, publishing of textbooks and other resources is expanding, validation efforts serve to establish and maintain standards recognized by peer institutions, and/or governments, and schools are cooperating together more. At the same time, there remain enormous challenges. For example, libraries lack adequate holdings in national languages, and thus cultivation and support of national authors should be a priority. Faculty development still needs careful attention, with strategic planning as to the different teaching positions to be filled and where personnel should earn necessary degrees; remaining in Europe for graduate study has clear advantages on many levels and is the best stewardship of resources. While we applaud the generosity of many western churches and mission organizations in support of theological education, too often this assistance has come at the price of submission to western theological imperialism.

Certainly, institutions and their supporters must seek to forge genuine partnerships, characterized by mutual respect and recognition of the Holy Spirit's presence to guide, but perhaps not always in ways an expatriate may perceive as 'right'. Finally, an ongoing need is for increased cooperation, less reduplication of effort and less competition. Although there is still a proliferation of small, struggling institutions established to promulgate a particular doctrinal perspective – many in countries where the percentage of evangelicals is quite small – it is encouraging to see some evangelical seminaries embracing several denominations, as well as efforts to share resources, such as journals. This transition, perhaps most of all, represents a significant maturing and progress towards healthy peer relationships amongst theological institutions in Central and Eastern Europe.

The Scriptures in Church and Pastoral Practice

Paul Ballard

Professor Paul Ballard is professor in the School of Religious and Theological Studies, Cardiff University, UK.

Introduction

These reflections arise out of an involvement in a project between the Bible Society and the School of Religious and Theological Studies, Cardiff University, on the theme, 'The Bible in Pastoral Practice'. This collaboration came from the discovery that the two bodies had concerns that could be mutually enriching. The Bible Society has, for some time, been wrestling with the problem of how the voice of the Bible can effectively be heard again in an increasingly pluralistic and post-Christian society. One of the ways chosen to forward this purpose has been to work with groups of academics around selected issues. Practical theology, a specialist interest in the Cardiff School, has been, in common with many others in this field in recent years, engaged with questions of how pastoral practice can be more firmly rooted in a theological perspective, which clearly includes the Bible as a major theological resource. This collaboration has enabled Biblical scholars, pastoral theologians and pastoral practitioners to meet in a number of fruitful exchanges and to produce a series of books and other papers and articles, which it is hoped will further the exploration more widely.[156]

This project may seemed to have had a comparatively well defined brief. However, it turned out, as worked progressed, to be more complex and far reaching than at first sight appeared. Each group brought with it, despite their personal commitment to the common enterprise, the unsolved concerns of their scholarly or professional specialisation. On the one hand, there were issues raised by the academic captivity of the Bible and the impact of critical scholarship and exegesis. Pastoral practice, on the other hand, having renewed itself by drawing on the insights, theories and skills of the human sciences and their attendant professions, has been conscious of having lost its theological bearings. At the same time, liberation, feminist and other theological

---

[156] S. Pattison, *A Critique of Pastoral Care* (London: SCM, 2000); P. Ballard and S.R. Holmes, eds., *The Bible in Pastoral Practice: Readings in the Place and Function of Scripture in the Church* (London: Darton, Longman and Todd, 2005); G. Oliver, *Holy Bible: Human Bible. Questions Pastoral Practice Must Ask* (London: Darton, Longman and Todd, 2006); P. Ballard, 'The Bible as Pastor', *A Dedicated Edition of Contact: Practical Theology and Pastoral Care* 150 (2006).

perspectives have not always found the Bible an easy text to live with. Within the everyday pastoral practice of the churches, also, the Bible is not always easily understood or interpreted. How, therefore, is an ancient text, that so often appears to be far removed from contemporary life, to be appropriated and made creatively alive, even in the community of faith? This may seem to be a particular problem for modern or post-modern western culture but these are real and increasingly demanding issues for the life of the whole Church across the globe. This is, in fact, unfinished business, of which we have so far only scratched the surface.

I want in this paper to pick up a particular theme which, though inherent in the very nature of the project, has not really been taken up with sufficient care. As a practical theologian, it is interesting to note that the recovery of the Bible has been most frequently characterised as a dialogue between pastoral practice and practitioners, on the one hand, and the Bible as a pastoral resource, on the other.[157] The Bible is, in this way, taken to be a self-sufficient entity with which it is necessary to deal directly. This reflects the way, especially in the Protestant traditions, the Bible has been treated theologically in the modern Church. This has, ironically, been reinforced by the critical academic scholarship that has grown up in the last two hundred years. In fact, however, the Bible does not exist independently but embedded, in a peculiar and particular way, within and through the community of faith. The Bible is the Christian Scriptures, both constitutive of, and the creative treasure of, the People of God. But, as far as I know, the implication of the notion of the Bible as Scripture as a serious factor in looking at the use of the Bible in pastoral practice has not been, in any systematic way, taken up. If we were to start from the Christian concept and function of Scripture, would that shed additional light and point in useful and creative directions? It would certainly relate to the interest among Biblical scholars at the present as to whether and how to take the canonical nature of the Bible into scholarly account.[158]

So the focus becomes, from a practical pastoral point of view, a question as to how the Bible actually operates as Scriptures within the life of the church. This, too, naturally, brings with it an intricate set of historical, dogmatic and practical questions, not all of which can be taken up adequately in a brief paper. It is only possible to look at, in indicative form, three leading themes that seem most directly to bear on pastoral practice, namely: the nature of the canon; the importance of liturgy; and the interpretive nature of Scripture.

---

[157] R. Hurding, *The Bible and Counselling* (London: London: Hodder ans Stoughton, 1992).

[158] C.E. Braaten and R.W. Jensen, eds., *Reclaiming the Bible for the Church* (Edinburgh: T & T Clark, 1996); P.R. Davies, *Whose Bible Is It Anyway?* (Sheffield: Shefield Academic Press, 1995); J. Barton, *Studies in the Biblical Canon* (London: SPCK, 1997); J. Webster, *Holy Scripture, a Dogmatic Sketch* (Cambridge: Cambridge University Press, 2003).

The Nature of the Canon

The meaning of 'canon', from ancient Egyptian and Greek, is 'rule' or 'measuring rod'; that is, something or someone that comes within a normative regulation or practice. So there are canonical clergy that live under a rule and there is canonical law that governs the practice of the church. Most importantly there is the liturgical canon, the canon of the Mass, which is, in a multitude of forms, at the heart of Christian worship. It is this central act of that makes worship Christian and brings us to the renewing centre of faith. Essentially it is the celebration of the Lord's Supper in the fellowship of the church. Here is the origin of the canonization of the saints as those that are remembered publicly in the mass as founders and examples in the faith. Alongside this, Christian liturgy has always had another canonical element – those Scriptures that are read as the primary witness to the faith. This was taken from Synagogue practice and enlarged to include, over time, the New Testament. This is the canon of the Word. So the issue of the canon is primarily about identity, marking out the essential focus of faith and thus how this community understands itself in the wider culture in which the church is inevitably immersed.

Identity, however, implies also boundaries. Some writings are within the canon and others outside. This may, to some, seem arbitrary, and it is possible to point to writings in the early Church as found in the Roman Empire, which both just crept in and were reluctantly left out of the New Testament. The boundaries, however, were not and have never been so hard and fast as they may seem to us. Nevertheless a rule emerged in the early Church that gradually became more or less universal, witnessed to (e.g.) by the Muratorian canon (c250 in Rome). But the New Testament canon did not come about in a vacuum but out of the battle for a right understanding of the Gospel, crucially in that pivotal period when the church emerged on the full stage of history, roughly from the third to the fifth centuries. These were the writings that witnessed to the fullness of the Apostolic faith, beating off such challenges as posed by Marcion, the Gnostics and Arius. So the Bible, alongside the creeds, embedded in the worship of the church, is a theological reality, born of the furnace of controversy, and set as one of the pillars of the faith.

In recent years, under the influence of such scholars as Brevard Childs and E.P. Sanders, and in reaction to the dominance of critical secular historical scholarship, which tends to treat the Bible simply as an ancient text, there has been a call to take seriously again the canon as a basic factor in Biblical exegesis. Canonical criticism argues that Christian Biblical interpretation must accept the canonical text as the starting point. It exists because it is the Scripture of a believing community. The effect of this is to treat the Bible as a whole and not simply as a series of texts more or less accidentally bound together. This does not, in my view, obviate the need to take seriously the scholarly enquiry both in to the origins and forms of the texts and of the history of reception of the texts down the years. Different questions need different critical instruments. It does mean, however, taking seriously the coherence of the Bible, despite its manifest diversity and sometime problematic form. In a very real way this is an appeal to the long held principle, most clearly articulated by Calvin, that the parts of Scripture are to be interpreted in the light of the whole and the general sense of Scripture.[159] It also has the effect of requiring, exemplified in the Lutheran tradition, the presence of a key hermeneutic perspective, sometimes referred to as 'the canon within the canon', by which the whole may be interpreted. For Luther it was 'justification by faith' that led to his somewhat doubtful rejection of James. There have been a number of other such candidates.[160] Given the diversity of the text, it is not easy to see how such an organizing theme can be identified, certainly not from the text itself. It will, in the end, be a dogmatic decision, yet one that is clearly consonant with the nature of the church's witness. Surely it will point to Jesus Christ as, in Bonhoeffer's words, 'the incarnate, crucified and risen Lord'.[161] This does not necessarily provide an easy clue as to how to read every part of Scripture. The material is so diverse and even sometimes questionable. There are the so-called 'texts of terror'. And do we really assume that God was a party to genocide or colonialization? In every age there have had to be exegetical tools that try to make sense of the obscure and problematic. Nevertheless there is here in the Scriptures a place to which we can turn, and meet again the faith and experience of the Apostolic church and the Gospels, and to learn afresh who he is 'for us today', what it means to follow him and to have our understanding surprisingly and creatively challenged. Jesus Christ is 'the same yesterday, today and for ever' (Heb. 18.8). That steadfastness is the rock of faith. Yet his unchanging nature is his constancy of love, peace, mercy, reconciliation and justice, which may, in the light of circumstances and knowledge, take different yet remarkably consistent forms. The Christian doctrine of revelation is essentially eschatological in form, which means that all will be revealed only in the Kingdom (e.g. I Corinthians 13.12; Philippians 3.12-16; Ephesians 4. 15-16).

What does such a recovery of the canon mean for the use of the Bible in pastoral practice? It means, first, the Bible is primarily a theological and spiritual witness rather than an historical record. Through it, indeed, we find Christ, the Christ who brings us to the Father and who sends the Spirit into the

---

159 D.K. McKim, ed., *John Calvin: A Companion* (Cambridge: Cambridge University Press, 2004).

160 P. Althaus, *The Theology of Martin Luther* (Philadelphia: Fortress, 1966); B.S. Childs, *Biblical Theology of Old and New Testament Texts: Theological Reflection on the Christian Bible* (Minneapolis: Fortress, 1994); F. Watson, *Text and Truth: Redefining Biblical Theology* (Edinburgh: T & T Clark, 1997); J. Barr, *Holy Scripture, Canon, Authority and Criticism* (Oxford: Oxford University Press, 1983); C.H.H. Scobie, *The Ways of Our God: An Approach to Biblical Theology* (Grand Rapids: Eerdmans, 2003).

161 D. Bonhoeffer, *Ethics* (London: SCM, 1955), 89-91.

world and into our hearts. But attention is shifted from the meaning of the text as originally given, which is the preoccupation of both the Biblical historical scholar and the fundamentalist, to the way that the text illuminates and is illuminated by the whole canon and the God to whom it witnesses. There is less interest in the 'teaching' of the Bible, or even of Jesus, as instructions to be obeyed or doctrines to be believed, and more interest in how the words point to a living reality, the dynamic of God's relationship to the world and its redemption. So pastoral practice asks not what does God say but: What sort of God are we dealing with? How can we be faithful before such a God? How do we embrace the God who so embraces us? Not what do we learn but how do we indwell this reality to which the Scriptures witness.

Secondly, it means discovering, in Stephen Fowl's phrase, what it means to be 'wise readers' of Scripture. What is needed is a deep familiarity with the text. This, however, is only the prolegomenon to understanding. To understand the Scriptures theologically is to seek the mind of Christ (Rom. 2.2; Phil.2.5), to have hearts renewed by the Spirit, so that Word and reality are one. 'One of the chief tasks', says Fowl, 'facing Christian communities concerns the formation of their members into being wise readers of Scripture'.[162] What is being sought is *phronesis,* practical wisdom. This is the task of a lifetime, acquiring the 'habit' of love, indwelling the word of Scripture as well as living in the concrete reality of our times. This brings us close to the terminology of literary hermeneutics, of the language of 'the merging of the two horizons'.[163] However, there, also, is a simplicity about it all. We can be glad of and need to use the work of specialist exegetes and Biblical theologians, but in the end it is not about skills or information, though both are vital when it comes to working with people, but character. Spiritual wisdom informs the heart and works with compassionate understanding. We know when we have met saints. They leave us humble but grateful and exalted. The emphasis is on recovering something of what Wycliffe was seeking when he said he wanted even the ploughboy to be able to read Scripture, even though we know it is not that simple. It suggests that it is possible to move beyond critical historical scholarship, not rejecting it, but moving towards the kind of situation the Paul Ricoeur called 'a second naivety'; a simplicity that is replete with wisdom.[164] Such an approach suggests, therefore, that the relationship of the Scripture to the immediate pastoral situation is normally less direct and more about finding out how to live in the present as one whose heart is hid with God in Christ (Col. 3.2).

---

[162] S.E. Fowl, *Engaging Scripture: A Model for Theological Interpretation* (Oxford: Blackwell, 1998), 179.

[163] See A. Thiselton, *New Horizons in Hermeneutics* (London: Harper Collins, 1992); K.V. Vanhoozer, *First Theology: Scripture and Hermeneutics* (Leicester: IVP, 2002).

[164] P. Ricoeur, *The Symbolism of Evil* (New York: Harper Row, 1967); D.R. Stiver, *Theology after Ricoeur: New Directions in Hermeneutic Theology* (Louisville, Westminster: John Knox, 2001).

If this is so, then the overt use of the Bible in pastoral care is less likely to happen at the point of decision or distress, in comforting or challenging, though there will be occasions when the book will be opened with reason and profit. Rather it all points to the fact that pastoral care comes out of the constant growth in grace that is an essential part of church life. Its foundations are laid in the ongoing ministry, woven in to times of prayer, study, discussion, service, places where the foundations of Christian wisdom are laid, so that when the storms come the edifice may be shaken but holds because it is built on a rock[165] (Matt. 7.24-27). And the text of the Bible percolates through this process so that it is a very part of the fabric of the Christian life and Christian service.

The Importance of the Liturgy

The Christian community is created and made visible in and through its worship, expressed in Word and sacrament. This is the public service, the *leitourgia,* or liturgy (Rom. 12.1) that is the hub of all Christian life and action. This is affirmed in every mainstream tradition. As an Orthodox study puts it: 'The Church as an institution points to the eucharistic assembly as its sole genuine image, as the transparent icon of Christ'.[166] In Protestantism, summed up in the Westminster Confession, the visible Church is ' a congregation of men (sic) where the pure Word of God is preached and the sacraments administered according to Christ's ordinance' (1571, art.19).

As we have seen the Scriptures find their true place here at the canonical or definitive heart of the church's existence. Indeed these writings could be said to be truly Scripture only at this point. Outside this context they may indeed carry authority but they can equally be understood as ancient historical texts. They become Scripture because they are both read and heard in the faithful assembly and become the vehicle for the Word of God. All other uses in the church, whether corporate or private, are derivative from this primary use.[167]

The Scriptures are both a given, that is they speak to the church, and are received that is, become the word of God in faith. There has always been this bi-polarity in the doctrine of Scripture. The classical understanding of inspiration (however this is interpreted in detail, which is not under discussion here) asserts that the Holy Spirit is at work both in the formation of Scripture and in the process of interpretation and understanding. Both are necessary, whatever the tension that holds them together or apart. There is here a

---

165 R.A. Lambourne, *Community, Church and Healing* (London: Darton, Longman and Todd, 1963); M. Wilson, *A Coat of Many Colours* (London: Epworth, 1988).

166 I. Bria, ed., *Go Forth in Peace: Orthodox Perspectives on Mission* (Geneva: World Council of Churches, 1986).

167 G. Georgiou, *The Use of Scripture* (Swindon: Bible Society, 2000); D. Kelsey, 'Scripture, Doctrine Of', in *A New Dictionary of Christian Theology (London: SCM)*, ed. Alan Richardson and John Bowden (1983).

fundamental dialectic process, akin to that recognized by modern hermeneutics. It is to be expected, therefore, that there will always be both a sense of givenness (the Bible is there on the lectern) and a fluidity as the exegetical and illuminative response proceeds. The Scriptures are a sign of unity and diversity as the witness to the Christ who is present in and with the fellowship and to each individually, in each time and place.

Such an understanding of the location of canonicity, however, has an interesting and important pastoral consequence. One of the issues in contemporary pastoral care is how the authority of the Bible is to be expressed. The tendency is to have some kind of instrumentalist view of the Bible, whereby it has to be specifically introduced into the pastoral context for it to be effective. This is especially contentious where the pastoral engagement, say in counselling, is on the fringes or beyond the fellowship of faith. How, for example, does the Christian pastor relate to a person of another faith or of no faith? The answer must be to take the canonical nature of the Bible seriously. Where the pastoral conversation takes place clearly within the community of faith all parties will respect the wise use of the Bible, because it is Scripture in and for the church. As the location of care moves further from the centre, so the opportunity and wisdom for appealing to the Scriptures is weakened. For the pastor, of course, the Christian faith, informed by Scripture, will remain normative – but not necessarily publicly acknowledged. The serving, caring stance of the Gospel is to seek the welfare of the needy, the stranger and the oppressed, meeting them where they are. It does not cease to be Christian care if the name has not been named. There is, thus, a kind of gradation from an explicit proclamation of the Gospel to acts of human solidarity, but these are all part of the stuff of the universe, of which Christ is both Lord and Saviour and in whom all things cohere (Col. 1.15-20).

This is, in fact, what actually seems to happen. What we are stressing is that one need not feel guilty about it. It was interesting to find, in a survey, precisely this pattern. Asked how they used their Bible in a number of typical pastoral situations, ministers and church leaders of every ecclesiastical and theological persuasion indicated (i) that they saw the Bible primarily as a resource from which they drew their values, perspective and insights in to the human condition, and that this remained in the background and was not necessarily made explicit; and (ii) that, while the Bible was used or quoted not infrequently, this was clearly more often so when dealing with a Christian and less frequent and even normally absent when dealing with someone outside the church.

It is worth, however, looking further and more closely as to how the Scriptures are embedded in Christian worship. First, Christian worship is Trinitarian, both in form and in essence. That is, it reflects the shape of the Gospel. There is an essentially theological rationale, whatever the historical forces that have influenced its particular expressions and however diverse its expression culturally. It moves from humble access and adoration to the proclamation of the Word. The God of heaven and earth, almighty creator before whom we bow comes to us in gift in Christ. Proclamation of the Word leads to response and trust, culminating in incorporation into the Body of Christ in communion. The Christ who is given to us calls us and makes us his own. But this response and incorporation moves outward into sending, serving and witness. It is by the Spirit that we are made one with Christ and driven out and sustained.

This cycle of receiving and returning reflects the very life of God who exists in the community of the Triune unity. It is into this life that we are caught up.

> When we cry, 'Abba! Father!' it is that very Spirit bearing witness with our spirit that we are children of God, and if children, then heirs, heirs of God and joint heirs with Christ – if in fact we suffer with him so that we may be also glorified with him (Rom. 8.15-17 NRSV).

This Trinitarian form also finds expression in the rehearsal of the Christian year, from creation, through the Gospel to Pentecost and Trinity. This is the framework of Scripture. Moreover the modern, three year lectionary cycle, more or less accepted by Catholics, Anglicans and many Protestant churches, takes us through this story with a wide variety of readings from the Bible. Indeed each of these weekly selections reflects the same pattern, with readings from Old Testament, Epistle and Gospel.

Above all this comes to a climax in the Eucharist. Here we are drawn directly into the drama, the story, of salvation. Narrative theology, of various kinds, has underlined the sweep of God's dealings with the world from creation to consummation. This may seem odd in a post-modern, pluralistic world when cultural meta-narratives are declared dead. But the Biblical witness, for all its oddity and audacity, is that there is a history of redemption at the centre of which is the living Christ. But it is not a story that is imposed by force but on one that is offered in compassion and love. We are invited to join our story to God's story. This comes out most clearly in Eucharistic worship. We are drawn into the drama of 'the night on which he was betrayed' in order to be incorporated into the risen life of Christ, anticipating the gathering together of all things. Our story is joined to and enriched by his story. Indeed our aim is to find its completion in the fullness that is Christ (Eph. 4).

It is against this background of narrative theology and hermeneutics that much recent pastoral care has been interested in story as a therapeutic tool.[168] It is pointed out that the Bible is largely narrative and story. One of the devices is to invite people to set their story alongside the often very human story to be found in the Bible, of brothers and families, of ambition and failure, of wisdom

---

168 H. Anderson and E. Foley, *Mighty Stories, Dangerous Rituals: Weaving Together the Human and the Divine* (San Francisco: Jossey-Bass, 1998); E.P. Wimberly, *Using Scripture in Pastoral Counseling* (Nashville: Abingdon, 1994).

and faithfulness, and to reflect on their juxtaposition. It can be pointed out, however, that the Biblical material is much more diverse and note must be taken of the prophetic, poetic and wisdom texts. There is, however, less problem if, as must happen, all the Biblical material is seen as expressions of and responses to the historical presence of God in the midst of his people. Indeed Biblical texts can only work in this pastoral way because there is already some recognition that the particular story has its significance within the wider God related context, which is his dealings with all people.

In passing it is worth remarking that, at its best, Christian worship is shot through and through with the Scriptures. The Psalter, for instance, has always been part of Christian hymnody, from the monthly cycle of the monastery to the Scottish paraphrases. Hymns and prayers are studded with Biblical quotations and allusions. In other words the weekly round of Bible reading, praise and prayer can immerse the worshipper in an almost sub-conscious engagement with the Bible. It is probably this as much as anything, that shapes our understanding of Scripture. Unfortunately, in our post-Christian context, where few have a living contact with the community of faith, and where alternative ideologies compete for attention, there seems to be a dearth of Biblical awareness. Everyday words and phrases are not recognized as coming from Scripture. Even in the churches there seems to be difficulty in keeping the memory alive. Yet there is hope and signs that the People of God can and will adapt and meet the new circumstances.

The Interpretive Nature of Scripture

The history of the formation of the Christian canon is well attested, in general if not in perfect detail. The early Church accepted the Synagogue practice of reading the Scriptures in worship. This meant, in the first instance, the Hebrew Scriptures or, more probably, the Jewish Greek Scriptures, which we know as the Septuagint (LXX). But these Scriptures, themselves, were emerging in their final form precisely in that same first century CE, with the consolidation of Rabbinic Judaism. It would also seem that very early on Christian material was added. Almost certainly the stories and teaching of Jesus, the so-called Memoirs of the Apostles, were rehearsed; and fairly soon the letters of Paul and other material were incorporated, as we can see from Ignatius' instructions to the Philippians. The Muratorian canon (c250 in Rome), as already noted, is the first clear evidence of the New Testament in roughly its present form. Even so it was not for another hundred years or more that the New Testament canon began to be accepted more or less universally.

The story, however, does not end there. There have always been always been minor differences between the Eastern (Orthodox) and the Western (Catholic) traditions. Outside the Roman Empire other canons also emerged, such as the Ethiopic Bible of eighty-one books. More significantly, at the Reformation there was a considerable divergence, at least in terms of the Old

Testament canon. The Catholic Church continued to use the Greek LXX, translated into Latin by St. Jerome, and known as the Vulgate (or common Bible). It was the Council of Trent, as part of its desire to reform Catholicism in the light of the attacks of the reformers, that was the first council to promulgate an official canon. The Protestants, meanwhile, taking a lead from Luther, only accepted as fully canonical the writings then known in Hebrew and found in the Scriptures of the Synagogue. They did not, however, revert back to the order of the Hebrew Bible – Torah, Prophets, Writings – but kept the LXX order. The rest, only then found in the Greek text, were given a lesser status as the Apocrypha, as useful but not binding. Yet even here there were differences of emphasis. Lutheranism used the Apocrypha more freely than in Calvinism and it is noteworthy that in popular religion there were frequent references to the book of Tobit and the story of Susanah, as witnessed in art and elsewhere. So we have a history that stretches over many centuries and which, in a sense, is still going on.

There is, however, still more. In Judaism there is a history of interpretation – *midrash* – which seeks to uncover the deeper meaning of Scripture and its import for living in the present. From this Rabbinic tradition there emerged the *Mishnah* (the oral teaching) and the *Talmud*, which combines the *Mishnah* with further discussions on the *Mishnah,* called the *Gamara.* For Scripture to keep its relevance in later and often radically different circumstances there has to be a process of reflection. We can find echoes of this in the Gospels, such as when Jesus is asked to take sides in the debate concerning how the Law was to be understood (Mark 12.28-34 and parallels); or when he condemned the fastidious keeping of the minutiae of the Law (Luke 11.42). I can vividly remember the impact of seeing a picture of a mediaeval Jewish MS which showed the Law surrounded by the *Mishnah* and the *Talmud.* Here was the Scripture growing before my eyes. This process continues every time a Rabbi is asked to pronounce whether a new product is *kosher,* or when the Jewish courts relate themselves to British law.

The dynamic, however, is found in the Hebrew Scriptures themselves. The traditional division of the Law, Prophets and Writings are both an indication of the history of the canon and a hierarchy of authority and interpretation. The core of the Hebrew scriptures is the Covenant of God through Moses, set out in the *Torah,* which is probably not best translated as 'law' but as 'way' (see Deut. 30.11-20; Josh. 24.1-18). The prophets thus become a commentary on the *Torah,* the story of how Israel responded to the challenges of her history in the light of that Covenant. So they point back to the foundation and forward into the future with the call to live the Covenant out, but under very different conditions. The writings take this further, though in a looser way, both historically (into the Maccabbees) and prophetically in the wisdom literature.

Indeed, we can see the New Testament itself as a *midrash* on the Old Testament. Jesus, as the new Moses (Matt. 5-7) provides the pivotal key for a fresh interpretation in the light of the new totally radical circumstances.

Certainly Paul works in this way on both the Old Testament and Jesus, seeking to clarify for the Gentile converts what it means to have faith in 'the God and Father of our Lord Jesus Christ'. This included a major re-evaluation of the Law (Gal.4.21-5.15) as well as lesser issues such as meat offered to idols (I Cor. 8; Rom.14).

The process still goes on. In Christianity, there has not been a body of writings such as the *Talmud* but there are authoritative writings from decrees of councils and similar bodies to the revered writings of key theologians according to your tradition, such as Augustine, Thomas Aquinas, Luther, Wesley and Barth, let alone a myriad commentaries and other tomes. Moreover, every Sunday in worship the pattern is rehearsed. The sacrament of the Word is threefold. The Scriptures are read, in canonical order, and then expounded for the present day. This is followed by an affirmation of commitment, which, in many liturgies, takes the form of the creed. Out of this both the Christian community and each one of us enters into and begins to acquire that perspective that is moulded in Christ and which we can call Christian wisdom. Christian truth is not delivered as a set package but through the struggle to live faithfully which means decision, repentance and new steps in faith.

Scripture, therefore, in the Christian tradition is not so much a book as a process of interpretation at the heart of which stands the primary record of the covenant actions of God in Christ. Scripture is, as we have insisted, bi-polar: on one side the canonical documents with which we are in dialogue and on the other our situation within which we are placed and where we have to be responsible not only to God but our neighbour, the creation and ourselves; and these are set within the community of faith created by God. What we have done here is to underline the hermeneutic process as an essential element in the doctrine of Scripture.

There is, however, an important corollary here. Faithful living is indeed set in the context of the creative saving reality that is revealed in the Bible; but it is also having to seek to know what that means for today. This can look very different in practice, according to historical, cultural and socio-economic circumstances. There can be, and indeed have been, some seismic shifts in what is understood as being acceptable Christian belief and behaviour. As suggested earlier this process can be found in the Bible itself. It could be argued, for instance, that the pivotal event in Israelite history is the Exile because they came out of it with a very different understanding about God and the nation than when they went in. Similarly in the New Testament the notion of Israel was universalized. Down history, too, we can see turning points when the Spirit has opened up new insights and opportunities.

This is what Protestants want to claim of the Reformation; but it is as well also to remember the emergence of mediaeval Christendom and the rise in the post-Reformation era of the missionary Church. This year we celebrate two hundred years of the British abolition of the slave trade and soon sixty years of the World Council of Churches, both dramatic turns in the life of the Church.

Nor is it all advance. There is also judgement and failure out of which the Christian community has had to struggle, whether the Crusades or the Holocaust, the suspicion of science or western imperialism. We are indeed living at a time of major challenge in many areas, from the exploitation of the planet to economic justice, from the questions posed by bio-engineering to matters of gender and sexuality. None of these are patient of easy solutions in theory and certainly not in practice. They are all contested areas and we have to live in the mess that is the world and the church. What is being sought, however, is the ability to be true to the fundamental reality of Christ while seeking to embody that truth in and for our time. The result will never be perfect because the Kingdom is not yet here, but we must each work for Kingdom values as we can and where we are.

This is the context for pastoral care, those personal and intimate occasions which seem to be so small in relation to the wider reality. Yet each individual or small group or congregation can and will make a difference. It is here that the struggle for Christ's truth takes place and is enfleshed. These are the places where the burden is really carried and where the shoe pinches, whether by those who are in positions of power and influence or by those who are crushed and disadvantaged. Moreover this is where Christian wisdom is forged and discovered for us today and which becomes the heritage that is passed on to later generations.

Conclusions

From this brief discussion of the Scriptures in the Christian tradition in relation to pastoral practice, which could have been extended in greater detail, two themes perhaps arise.

The first is the very particular way the Scriptures function in relation to the Christian community and its ongoing life. It is very clear that the Judeo-Christian tradition is very different from other religious traditions, not least those that would be described as religions of 'the Book'. The Bible has emerged from and is at the heart of an interpretative process. It is authoritative and normative but, within a wider context of faith, constantly rediscovered and reinterpreted. This leads to a certain openness and fluidity; but not an arbitrariness because there has always to be both a relation to the focal point in Christ and a sense of belonging to a living tradition. The Bible belongs to the church. It is constitutive of it and a resource for it. It finds its truth and reality in the worshipping community. It is there that the Bible comes alive.

Secondly, Christian pastoral care, as part of the witness, service and mission of the church, can only relate to the Bible in ways that are consonant with this understanding of Scripture. Gospel concern and action flows from the centre – from being made one with Christ and being sent out by him. This means that such care will, as part of the interpretive process and within the living tradition, endeavour to enable people to live faithfully at that point where they find themselves. Christian pastoral care is always exploring, looking for those signs that lead people to find Christ, if need be in very new ways and fresh patterns for a new age.

In the end the Bible is but witness; witness to the living God, Father, Son and Holy Spirit, who calls us to be drawn more and more into that life that is both complete in itself but which spills out in love for the creature, becoming complete in communion.

'A Mode of Training': A Baptist Seminary's Missional Vision

Ian M. Randall

Dr. Ian M. Randall is Tutor in Church History and Spirituality, Spurgeon's College, London, and Senior Research Fellow, International Baptist Theological Seminary, Prague.

Introduction

In 2003, Darrell Guder wrote about mission and theological education in an article, 'From Mission and Theology to Missional Theology'. In this illuminating piece he traced the way in which thinking within Princeton Theological Seminary in the USA had developed in the area of mission and theological education from the nineteenth century to the present. Guder stated: 'When we describe theology as missional, then we do imply that the work of theology is not an end in itself but is related to God's mission in the world'.[169] Commenting on this interpretation of the task of theology, Desmond van der Water suggests that although theological institutions include some mission studies, most 'have subscribed to a theological curriculum which is either implicitly or explicitly lacking in a holistic mission agenda'.[170] The question of the priority given to mission within theological education has been tackled at various points in the past. In two articles in *Transformation* in 2001 Bernhard Ott examined 'Mission Orientated Theological Education' and 'Mission and Theological Education'. Ott followed Andrew Kirk's suggestion in *The Mission of Theology and the Theology of Mission* (1997) that the pilgrimage of a student involves seeing, judging and acting.[171] A book which came out two years after Kirk's, *Reenvisioning Theological Education: Exploring a Missional Alternative to Current Models*, by Robert Banks, has also been influential. Banks argues for praxis-based theological education which enhances ministry

---

[169] D. L. Guder, 'From Mission and Theology to Missional Theology', *The Princeton Seminary Bulletin* 24:1, New Series (2003), 36. For background on missional church and missional theology see D.L. Guder and L. Barrett, eds., *Missional Church* (Grand Rapids, Mich.: Eerdmans, 1998).

[170] D.P. van der Water, 'Transforming Theological Education and Ministerial Formation', *International Review of Missions* 94:373 (2005), 207.

[171] B. Ott, 'Mission Orientated Theological Education', *Transformation* 18:2 (2001); B. Ott, 'Mission and Theological Education', *Transformation* 18:2 (2001); cf. Kirk, *The Mission*, 53-58.

and mission.[172] This article will, like Guder's study of Princeton Seminary, use a particular theological institution as a lens through which to examine missional theological education. Spurgeon's College, founded a century and a half ago (1856), has played a significant role within evangelicalism as one of the best known Baptist seminaries in the world. It has also been committed from its beginnings to a missional vision and it is this trajectory which will be analysed here.

Shaping of Missional Pastors

Charles Haddon Spurgeon (1834-1892), the founder of what is now Spurgeon's College in South Norwood, London (previously the Pastors' College), was the most outstanding preacher of the Victorian era, a period that was marked by great pulpiteers who attracted large congregations. J.C. Carlile, a journalist and a Baptist minister trained at the College, who wrote one of the numerous biographies of Spurgeon, suggested that Spurgeon belonged to the category of people who have 'turned the current of religious history into fresh channels'.[173] At the Metropolitan Tabernacle, situated at the Elephant and Castle, London, which was built for Spurgeon's congregation and which opened in 1861, Spurgeon regularly preached each morning and evening to over 5,000 people. Extensive social ministries, notably an orphanage in Stockwell, were a feature of Spurgeon's ministry. During Spurgeon's pastorate at the Tabernacle over 14,000 people were baptised on profession of personal faith and joined the church membership. The sermons preached by Spurgeon also had a powerful international impact. By 1899 over a hundred million copies of his sermons had been produced, in twenty-three languages.[174] Spurgeon's robust evangelical theology was clearly conveyed by these means. He 'frankly admitted' in a report he gave as President of the College that his views about spreading the gospel and about training – 'a mode of training preachers' that was highly practical – were out of line with the thinking generally prevalent in the 1850s.[175] It was his distinctive vision that led him to found a College.[176] Over

[172] R. Banks, *Reenvisioning Theological Education: Exploring a Missional Alternative to Current Models* (Eerdmans: Grand Rapids, Mich., 1999).

[173] J.C. Carlile, *C.H. Spurgeon: An Interpretative Biography* (London: The Kingsgate Press, 1933), 30.

[174] Carlile, *C.H. Spurgeon*, 236-37.

[175] *Outline of the Lord's Work by the Pastors' College, 1869*, (London: Passmore & Alabaster, 1870), 4.

[176] See P.S. Kruppa, *Charles Haddon Spurgeon: A Preacher's Progress* (New York: Garland Pub., 1982); L.A. Drummond, *Spurgeon: Prince of Preachers* (Grand Rapids, Mich.: Kregel, 1992); M. Nicholls, *Lights to the World: A History of Spurgeon's College, 1856-1992* (Harpenden: Nuprint, 1994); D.W. Bebbington, 'Spurgeon and British Evangelical Theological Education', in *Theological Education in the Evangelical Tradition*, ed. D.G. Hart and Jr. R.A. Mohler (Grand Rapids: Baker Books, 1996).

the course of 150 years this College has become known throughout the world as a place where training of effective Christian leaders takes place.[177]

Mission was integral to C.H. Spurgeon's conception of ministry. A concern to equip people to 'preach the gospel', as Spurgeon often put it, characterised the ethos of the College in its early decades and continued thereafter to be a feature of the training the College offered. When Spurgeon began the College it was, he related in his magazine *The Sword and the Trowel*, because he was in contact with a group of 'earnest young men' who had come to Christ under his ministry and who 'felt an irresistible impulse to preach the gospel'. He recognized that they lacked education, and that this could be a serious problem, but he did not want to suppress their zeal. In any case, he realized that if he had tried to stop these budding evangelists 'they would respectfully but conscientiously have ignored my recommendation'. With this in mind, Spurgeon committed himself, through the College, to giving those with an evangelistic as well as a pastoral calling 'an opportunity to educate themselves for the work'.[178] A prime example is Thomas Medhurst, the first student, who had just finished his apprenticeship to a rope-maker when he began his studies. When some people heard Medhurst preaching in the open air they complained to Spurgeon about Medhurst's inadequate English. Spurgeon talked to Medhurst who said: 'I must preach, sir; and I shall preach unless you cut off my head'. The critics agreed then that he must preach.[179] During Medhurst's pastorates – Kingston, Coleraine in Ireland, Glasgow, and Lake Road, Portsmouth – he baptised nearly a thousand people.[180] The College's annual report of 1884-85 re-affirmed that its purpose was to educate those, like Medhurst, called to 'maintain and spread the gospel of the grace of God'.[181]

In the first few decades of the College's life, 'the spread of the gospel' took place largely through students from the College starting new Baptist congregations. In the 1868 College report Spurgeon commented that 'a very large proportion of our brethren have *created their own spheres*, and others have accepted pastorates where the prospects were such as to repel all others'.[182] It was the ethos of the College that encouraged them in this missional

---

[177] See more in I.M. Randall, *A School of the Prophets* (London: Spurgeon's College, 2005).

[178] *The Sword and the Trowel* [hereafter *S and T*], April 1870, 10.

[179] C.H. Spurgeon, *Autobiography; Compiled from His Diary, Letters, and Records by His Wife and His Private Secretary*, 4 vols., vol. 2 (London: Passmore and Alabaster, 1899), 151.

[180] Carlile, *C.H. Spurgeon*, 170; E.W. Bacon, *Spurgeon: Heir of the Puritans* (London: George Allen & Unwin, 1967), 91. Bacon makes an unfortunate error in saying that Thomas Medhurst became the head of a strange sect in America. Bacon is confusing Thomas Medhurst with C.S. Medhurst, his son.

[181] *Annual Paper Concerning the Lord's Work in Connection with the Pastors' College*, (1884-85), 3. Titles vary a little – hereafter *AP*.

[182] C.H. Spurgeon, 'A word of thankfulness from the President', *Outline*, 3.

direction. This church planting phenomenon continued, and in 1881 Spurgeon expressed his enthusiasm in this way:

> It is my greatest pleasure to aid in commencing new churches. The oftener brethren can create their own spheres the more glad shall I be. It is not needful to repeat the details of former reports; but many churches have been founded through the College, and there are more to follow. I announced at the beginning of this enterprise that it was not alone for the education of ministers, but for the general spread of the Gospel; and this has been adhered to, a part of the income being always expended in that direction.[183]

At the time of Spurgeon's death in 1892, the number of students who had been trained at the Pastors' College numbered 863, and 627 of them were serving in the Baptist denomination as pastors, missionaries and evangelists. More than 90,000 people had been baptised in churches led by former students at the College. Over half the new churches founded within the Baptist denomination in England in the period 1865 to 1887 were as a result of the activities of Spurgeon and the students of the College.[184] The missional focus of what happened at the College was clear.

In his study of mission oriented theological education, Bernhard Ott discusses the Bible school movement and its close relationship with the modern missionary movement. Lists of early Bible schools that helped to create this tradition often start with St. Chrischona in Basel, Switzerland, established in 1840, and may include Spurgeon's College as one of the early schools in England, as well as noting the crucial importance of later institutions such as the Bible Training Institute in Scotland and the Moody Bible Institute in North America.[185] However, it is not strictly correct to place Spurgeon's College in this Bible school category. Graham Cheesman, Klaus Fiedler and others have identified a number of features of the Bible school ethos: training that avoided the 'corrupting' influence of liberal theology; the preparation of non-ordained missionaries, training lay people for witness, and an emphasis on spiritual development.[186] At Spurgeon's College spiritual development was certainly a crucial element. In 1870 Spurgeon said regarding the role of the College: 'It appears to us that the maintenance of a truly spiritual College is probably the readiest way in which to bless the churches'.[187] But the other Bible School distinctives were hardly present. Indeed far from thinking in terms of non-ordained overseas missionaries or lay training, the emphasis of the College in

---

[183] *S and T*, June 1881, 305.
[184] *AP*, 1891-92, 12; M. Nicholls, *C.H. Spurgeon: The Pastor Evangelist* (Didcot: Baptist Historical Society, 1992), 99.
[185] Ott, 'Mission Orientated', 75.
[186] Cheesman, 'Competing Paradigms', 484-99. Cf. Fiedler, *The Story*, 144-45. Cheesman has expanded his study of Bible Schools in his unpublished PhD.
[187] *AP*, 1870, 4.

its earliest years was on training ministerial leaders for Baptist congregations 'at home'. Many of these, as noted, were new church plants and Spurgeon described the College in 1873 as a 'Home Missionary Society for the spread of the gospel'.[188]

Not all the College's missional efforts were successful, but many of the new plants that were started by students or former students became established Baptist churches.[189] Outreach which began in Wandsworth, south London, in 1859, for instance, brought into being East Hill Baptist Church. Under John W. Genders, a student at the College who later undertook teaching at the College, meetings were started in the Assembly Rooms of the Spread Eagle Tavern. By the mid-1860s the membership was over 150 and a chapel was erected costing £3,000.[190] An inn was also used as a venue in Bromley, Kent, where meetings were started in 1862 in the Assembly Rooms of the White Hart. Archibald G. Brown, aged nineteen and a student at the College, saw the Bromley congregations grow from about 30 to 200 in a year. In 1863 a church was formed with twenty members and two years later it was reported that a large chapel was being erected.[191] The East London Tabernacle, Stepney Green, which became the second largest Baptist church in London (after the Metropolitan Tabernacle), met in the Beaumont Hall, Mile End Road. Students from the College built up the East London Tabernacle congregation to 200 people in the early 1860s, and a chapel seating 800 was erected in 1864. Archibald Brown moved from Bromley to the East London Tabernacle and under his ministry Sunday evening congregations (which in churches of this period were always larger than Sunday morning congregations) grew to 1,200 people and by 1868 the rapidly-growing membership had reached 500.[192]

What did Spurgeon believe were the crucial elements in producing pastors who were effective 'home missionaries'? He was committed, firstly, to solid theological education. 'Be well instructed in theology', Spurgeon urged, 'and do not regard the sneers of those who rail at it because they are ignorant of it. Many preachers are not theologians, and hence the mistakes which they make'. It is significant, however, that for him theology was linked with mission. He continued: 'It cannot do any hurt to the most lively evangelist to be also a sound theologian, and it may often be the means of saving him from gross blunders'.[193] Spurgeon insisted, secondly, that their training should help students to be effective communicators. All students preached regularly in

---

[188] *S and T*, April 1873, 147.

[189] See I.S. Drummond, 'The Spurgeon Legacy', CNAA BA Dissertation (1990), 44. This is a detailed analysis of the church planting strategy and achievements of Spurgeon.

[190] *Outline*, 1867, 69.

[191] *S and T*, March 1865, 130.

[192] *Outline*, 1868, 21; *East London Tabernacle*, (London: East London Tabernacle, 1956).

[193] *S and T*, May 1874, 221-22.

churches and congregations relayed their opinions of the students back to the College. Spurgeon's concern was to attract 'the working classes', and in typical style he stated: 'Now the devil does not care for your dialectics, and eclectic homiletics, or Germanic objectives and subjectives; but pelt him with Anglo-Saxon in the name of God, and he will shift his quarters'.[194] Spurgeon considered that effective delivery in speaking had often been passed over by universities as 'beneath notice', but it was a professional skill.[195] In the third place he rejected any mode of training that was disconnected from ordinary life. There has been a tradition, one that is now questioned, of creating a monastic type of environment for those in training.[196] Spurgeon opposed that. At the College's commencement Spurgeon argued that it was spiritually healthy for students to lodge with ordinary families. He believed those in training should be 'kept in connection with the struggles and conditions of everyday life'.[197] These three elements continue in the life of Spurgeon's. Since the 1980s congregation-based schemes have become the primary mode of the College's training.

Training of Evangelists

Although most of those who trained at the College in the early period functioned as congregational leaders, Spurgeon also recognized that there was a role for those who were not in settled pastoral leadership. In the 1870s 'The Pastors' College Society of Evangelists' was set up, linked directly with the College. This was designed to further 'mission work in our own country', as W.Y. Fullerton (a Society evangelist – and author of the hymn 'I cannot tell why he whom angels worship') put it. W.Y. Fullerton and J. Manton Smith, who had also trained at the College, were in great demand throughout Britain. Although Fullerton, an Irishman, was the leader, this was a joint ministry, to an extent mirroring in the 'Spurgeonic' context the work of the American evangelist D.L. Moody and his co-evangelist and singer Ira D. Sankey.[198] Fullerton described how Manton Smith's 'Gospel witness, singing, and cornet-playing were renowned all over the kingdom and beyond'.[199] Whereas those students who were planting churches had a clear denominational agenda – their task was to establish Baptist congregations - a Society of Evangelists' report

---

[194] *S and T*, April 1871, 218; cf. *AP*, 1870, 5-6.

[195] *S and T*, May 1882, 260.

[196] See F. King, 'Theological Education and Mission', *Mission Studies* 19:2 (2002), 82-83.

[197] *S and T*, April 1870, 149.

[198] David Bebbington's book, *The Dominance of Evangelicalism* (Leicester: IVP, 2005), is sub-titled 'The age of Spurgeon and Moody'.

[199] W.Y. Fullerton, *C.H. Spurgeon: A Biography* (London: Williams and Norgate, 1920), 239-40. For the songs used see *Evangelical Echoes and Song Services* (London: Passmore and Alabaster, n.d.) - held in the Spurgeon's College Heritage Room.

covering 1890-91 noted that the College evangelists had served not only with Baptists, but also with Congregationalists, Presbyterians, Methodists and the Society of Friends. There had also been missions to young people connected with YMCAs and YWCAs. In many places, said the report, hundreds had professed conversion.[200] This is clear evidence of how the College itself promoted mission.

Leading evangelicals paid tribute to the effectiveness of the work of the College's Society of Evangelists. At Regent's Park Chapel, London, where F.B. Meyer (the leading Baptist speaker at the Keswick Convention) was pastor, Fullerton and Manton held an evangelistic campaign in 1891. The outreach of this church included social ministry, with one of the elders, Dr. Percy Lush, engaged in medical care for the poor.[201] At a Chapel church meeting Meyer, who like Spurgeon had a particular concern for the poor, announced that many people had been affected by the mission. During that year the Chapel welcomed eighty-two new members by profession of faith.[202] Another leading nineteenth-century evangelical, the Earl of Shaftesbury, the most prominent evangelical social reformer of the Victorian age, was enthusiastic about the College evangelists he heard speaking at services in theatres. He praised their colloquial mode of address. Shaftesbury, an evangelical Anglican, had no faith in high church ritual – 'bits of wax candle' and 'gymnastics in the church' – but applauded the evangelistic work of 'the pupils trained in Mr. Spurgeon's College'.[203] Despite this affirmation from such a prominent Anglican, it was noted in 1891 that College evangelists had not preached in any Anglican church. Nor had they spoken in any Brethren meeting room. Nonetheless, Fullerton referred to their ministry as 'truly Catholic; not un-denominational, but inter-denominational'.[204] Spurgeon, although a staunch Baptist, give priority to the gospel, not denominational distinctive. In 1871, speaking of the eighteenth-century Evangelical Revival, Spurgeon stated that although 'we, as Calvinists, gravely question the accuracy of much that the Wesleyan Methodists zealously advocated', nonetheless 'the disciples of Wesley', as well as of George Whitefield, 'brought out very clearly and distinctly the vital truths of the gospel of Jesus Christ'.[205] This was an example for evangelists to follow.

Some within Baptist circles however, questioned the value of evangelists. Spurgeon's missional priorities were not universally accepted. In 1881 Fullerton wrote with a degree of bitterness: 'We magnify our office; not, we

---

[200] R. Shindler, *From the Usher's Desk to the Tabernacle Pulpit* (London: Passmore and Alabaster, 1892), 154-57.

[201] I.M. Randall, *Spirituality and Social Change* (Carlisle: Paternoster Press, 2003), 65.

[202] Minutes of the Regent's Park Chapel Church Meeting held on 26 January 1891: see Randall, *Spirituality*, 119-20.

[203] Shindler, *From the Usher's*, 142-43.

[204] Shindler, *From the Usher's*, 155.

[205] *AP*, 1870, 5.

trust, above what it deserves, but above what it is generally supposed to include. Indeed, it is amusing sometimes to notice the suspicion and prejudice and hostility with which the name... [evangelist] is greeted. "He is an evangelist!" Let us avoid him, and hamper him, and hinder him!'[206] Fullerton argued that evangelists should be trained, organized, and should work for and with the churches, and he even suggested a form of covenant that would bind pastors and evangelists together. 'Evangelist, "Will you have the pastor to be your co-worker...?" Pastor, "Will you welcome this evangelist as your helper?"' [207] Evidently Fullerton and Manton Smith continued to feel undervalued. Spurgeon wrote to Fullerton in 1883: 'I have never had the most distant idea of your ever having been snubbed or tolerated. It may be so, but I have never heard a living soul at the Tabernacle speak of you except with the greatest esteem'.[208] Fullerton, Manton Smith and other College evangelists continued their ministry. In 1893, however, Fullerton was invited to become pastor of Melbourne Hall, Leicester, a church which had been started by F.B. Meyer and which had a congregation of 1,500. The College Trustees offered him £100 per year extra to continue as an evangelist but he decided to take the pastorate.[209] Later Fullerton was to exercise a wider ministry as Home Secretary of the Baptist Missionary Society. [210]

With the death of C.H. Spurgeon it became more difficult to sustain aspects of the evangelistic work which he had supported so vigorously. His brother, James Spurgeon, who took over in 1892 as President of the College, spoke in the 1892-93 College report of the money expended in Home Mission work, in 'aiding the preaching-stations originated by the late President', and also mentioned that he had 'made it a rule to redeem every promise made by the late Pastor...towards any extension of work now being carried on'.[211] This proved to be impossible. New initiatives, however, were apparent. Two brothers, E.A. Carter and F.C. Carter, who trained at the College and imbibed its missional outlook, became involved in church planting in the 1880s. E.A. Carter developed a wider itinerant ministry and in 1889 founded the Pioneer Mission. The aims were to increase weak Baptist churches, to commence new Baptist causes and to evangelize generally. Initially there was a focus on the North-

---

[206] *S and T*, January 1881, 19.

[207] *S and T*, January 1881, 20.

[208] C.H. Spurgeon to W.Y. Fullerton, 1 October 1883 – held in the Spurgeon's College Heritage Room.

[209] Minutes of Pastors' College Trustees, 2 November 1893; Trustees of Pastors' College to W.Y. Fullerton, 3 November 1893; Fullerton to Trustees, 11 November 1893; Fullerton to Trustees, 25 November 1893 (all in Spurgeon's College Minute Book, 1893-98, Box 14).

[210] For his life see his autobiography, W.Y. Fullerton, *At the Sixtieth Milestone: Incidents of the Journey* (London: Marshalls, 1917).

[211] *AP*, 1892-93, 4.

West of England, but their work spread.[212] Whereas earlier the College itself had been the spring-board for mission, by the end of the nineteenth century it was benefiting from the fruit of enterprising former students such as Carter. Later, in 1920, Caradoc Jones from Wales, who had also trained at the College, began work in France (Brittany) as an evangelist with the Pioneer Mission. This led to the founding of a church and an orphanage. During the Second World War Jones spent four years in a concentration camp, and gave himself to ministry there.[213] Mission of all kinds continued, but the inter-wars years were not years of advance for most evangelicals in England, including Baptists.[214]

Immediately after the Second World War, there was evidence of a new evangelistic thrust in Britain. An American Youth for Christ team arrived in Britain in March 1946. Billy Graham was one of its members and he was to become the leading evangelist of the twentieth century. Graham's visits to Britain in the 1940s brought fresh vision in many places, and the contacts that he made led to the massive Harringay Crusade in London during the first three months of 1954. College students were involved.[215] George Beasley-Murray, who was on the College staff from 1950 and was then appointed principal, spoke of the number of students coming to Spurgeon's who had either been converted or called to ministry through Billy Graham meetings.[216] When (in 1964) *The Christian* ran a series of testimonies from Harringay converts, the person featured who had entered pastoral ministry was Peter Pearmain, who trained at Spurgeon's.[217] Another development in this period was the growth of the Inter-Varsity Fellowship (IVF), which drew together Christian Unions in the universities. In November 1947 Spurgeon's College students were involved in the organisation and leadership of a London Inter-Faculty Christian Union (LIFCU) mission designed to reach the thousands of students in London. Nearly 170 meetings were held including five united meetings at King's College London with average attendances of 500-600 students.[218] Spurgeon's College was keen to be part of this new post-war evangelistic impetus.

---

[212] Shindler, *From the Usher's*, 162-63; G.W. Harte, *Historical Tablets* (Southport: Thomas Seddon, 1951), 51; Nicholls, *C.H. Spurgeon*, 108-09.

[213] *College Record*, December 1950, 22-3; cf. W.M. Pearce, *Knight in Royal Service* (London: Pioneer Mission, 1962).

[214] For a study of this period see I.M. Randall, *Evangelical Experiences: A Study in the Spirituality of English Evangelicalism, 1918-1939* (Carlisle: Paternoster, 1999).

[215] I.M. Randall, 'Conservative Constructionist: The Early Influence of Billy Graham in Britain', *The Evangelical Quarterly* 67:4 (1995).

[216] P. Beasley-Murray, *Fearless for Truth: A Personal Portrait of the Life of George Beasley-Murray* (Carlisle: Paternoster Press, 2002), 76.

[217] *The Christian*, 29 May 1964, 4.

[218] *Spurgeon's College Magazine*, Autumn 1947, 25. For the history of the IVF (from 1975 the UCCF – Universities and Colleges Christian Fellowship), see D. Johnson, *Contending for the Faith* (Leicester: IVP, 1979).

One specific area of training in evangelism offered by the College (and by other Colleges) in this period was summer campaigns. In 1954 Raymond Brown, who was then a student and who in 1973 was to become College Principal, reported on encouraging results in six missions.[219] More were planned. Two years later, however, the College students reported that although they had brought vitality to the churches through their missions they had largely failed to reach non-churchgoers. They had found themselves preaching evangelistic sermons to church members. This influenced seven College students to become involved with the Luton Industrial Mission under the leadership of William Gowland. The Industrial Mission aimed not only to win people for Christ but to redeem society. Gradually the emphasis on social action – a holistic emphasis which had been prominent in Spurgeon's own ministry – would again find an important place in local mission undertaken by ministers trained at the College. Spurgeon's students felt they were seeing the church in action in new and dynamic ways.[220] Another new development for the College was the use of skiffle music in evangelism. A music group was formed by Bryan Gilbert, a student with a background in music, to engage in evangelism. Gilbert himself later pioneered 'One Step Forward' evangelism. In 1958 the College faculty (although not Beasley-Murray, the Principal) 'expressed its strong distaste for the use of this kind of music'. The College Council was divided on the issue of the skiffle group.[221] The first half of the twentieth century saw a continuing but rather cautious commitment to the training of evangelists at Spurgeon's College.

Church Renewal, Church Growth and Church Planting

Major changes hit British Christianity in the 1960s. According to Callum Brown in *The Death of Christian Britain*, from 1963 Christianity in Britain went on a downward spiral. More generally, Brown sees the 1960s as the decade in which the Christian-centred culture that had conferred identity on Britain was rejected.[222] This claim, however, which has received much attention, needs to be set alongside David Bebbington's analysis of British Christianity in the 1960s. In *Evangelicalism in Modern Britain*, Bebbington notes that in 1963 charismatic renewal came to an Anglican parish in Beckenham, Kent, when the vicar, George Forester, and some parishioners received the 'baptism of the Holy Spirit' and began to speak in tongues. During the next quarter of a century, Bebbington continues, the charismatic movement

---

[219] [Spurgeon's] *College Record*, May 1955, 29-30.

[220] *College Record*, July 1957, 2-6.

[221] Minutes of the Spurgeon's College Council, 14 April 1958.

[222] C.G. Brown, *The Death of Christian Britain* (London: Routledge, 2001), 1, 193.

became a powerful force in British Christianity.[223] Both Brown and Bebbington view the 1960s as a decade of significant cultural change. Out of that period of upheaval came the decline of cultural Christianity but also the emergence of a new expression of Christian spirituality – charismatic renewal. Spurgeon's College was affected. George Forester spoke about his recent experience of the 'baptism of the Spirit' to a local ministers' fraternal, and Malcolm Piper, a member of the fraternal who had recently completed his studies at Spurgeon's, began to share his conviction that what he had heard from Forester and witnessed in Beckenham had 'the unmistakeable mark of a work of God'.[224] The influence of this stream of spirituality grew and in 1968 the College Council noted: 'A number of students (fourteen in all) have been influenced by the new Pentecostal teaching on the Holy Spirit'. The faculty members had initiated discussion in College. The students involved were described as 'earnest, sincere and restrained'.[225] Experiences of renewal were to lead in many cases to new vision for mission.[226]

In autumn 1963, the College to Dagenham, Essex, which involved the four Dagenham Baptist churches, undertook a mission. The Dagenham group of Baptist churches was an early experiment in team ministry and mission, sponsored by the Baptist Union and the Essex Baptist Association. The 1963 mission included large youth meetings, a coffee bar, talks in schools and factories, and a Saturday morning cinema club which attracted many children. Over fifty College students and staff took part, working with the three ministers, all of whom had trained at Spurgeon's College, and a Deaconess, Sister Margaret.[227] College-related missions in the 1960s often involved events in coffee bars with a music group, The Venturers, which was led initially by Bryan Gilbert and which proved to be an important training ground for evangelistic work. A number of those involved in the group committed themselves to working together in Baptist ministry in Rochdale. Among other initiatives in the 1960s, students participated in 1967 in a 'Church and Society' course in connection with the West Ham Central Mission, under the leadership of Colin Marchant, who studied at Spurgeon's in the early 1950s. Since College students were often from middle-class suburban or small town churches, gaining insights into inner city ministry was of crucial importance.[228] Colin

---

[223] D.W. Bebbington, *Evangelicalism in Modern Britain: A History from the 1730s to the 1980s* (London: Routledge, 1995), 229.

[224] Malcolm Piper to Alec Steen, 9 April 1964: Baptist Revival Fellowship archive, held in Spurgeon's College Heritage Room.

[225] Minutes of College Council, 9 April 1968.

[226] For more on charismatic renewal among Baptists in Britain see D. McBain, *Fire over the Waters: Renewal among Baptists and Others from the 1960s to the 1990s* (London: DLT, 1997).

[227] *College Record*, December 1963, 17-19; *BT*, 17 October 1963, 2.

[228] *College Record*, June 1967, 3-5.

Marchant introduced many College students to issues in urban ministry and wrote on this subject in books such as *Signs in the City.*[229]

George Beasley-Murray used his principal-ship to give evangelism a high profile in the 1960s and early 1970s, and Raymond Brown continued this evangelistic emphasis. In 1967 Beasley-Murray said that when he was asked to summarise the aim of the College his answer was: 'To produce pastor-evangelists who can build up the churches'. The answer, he added, was framed with the example in mind of Spurgeon, who was the pastor-evangelist *par excellence*. In expanding on his thinking, Beasley-Murray, who was one of the leading New Testament scholars of his generation, suggested that pastors needed to preach the whole gospel, grappling with the whole Bible and with the Holy Spirit's illumination in the church though the ages. 'To achieve that on a significant scale', he considered, 'is an immense task. It is complicated by the fact that men and women today are out of touch with the message of the Gospel. Their thought is moulded by agencies which take no account of God, and therefore which, for practical purposes, are atheistic'.[230] Beasley-Murray proposed the creation of a Spurgeon's College lectureship in Evangelism and support from America enabled Lewis Drummond, who had held pastorates in the USA and had a PhD from King's College London, to be appointed at Spurgeon's as lecturer in Evangelism and Pastoral Instruction.[231] Roger Greenway, writing in 2003, observed from his experience lecturing in seminaries in many parts of the world that '[f]ew candidates for the pastoral ministry receive the kind of training they need for effective leadership in evangelism'.[232] From the 1960s Spurgeon's College sought to reconnect with its older evangelistic tradition and to offer specific training in evangelism.

When Raymond Brown became Principal in 1973 he soon engaged with the same issues. In response to the publication by the Baptist Union of Great Britain in 1980 of *A Call to Commitment – Baptist Christians through the 1980s*, Raymond Brown wrote articles about the contribution made by the College to a number of areas of church life, highlighting in 1982 the theme of commitment to mission.[233] The same period saw a new interest in church growth. Paul Beasley-Murray, minister of Altrincham Baptist Church, produced a study entitled *Turning the Tide*, which analysed Baptist churches and

---

[229] C. Marchant, *Signs in the City* (London: Hodder & Stoughton, 1985).

[230] *College Record*, December 1967, 2-4.

[231] Executive Committee Minutes, 29 September 1967; *College Record*, December 1968, 4-5.

[232] R. S. Greenway, 'Evangelists: Recovering a Lost Gift', in *Fullness of Life for All: Challenges for Mission in Early 21st Century* ed. I. Daneel, et al. (Amsterdam: Rodopi, 2003), 39.

[233] *College Record*, December 1982, 15-17; cf. *A Call to Commitment – Baptist Christians through the 1980s*, (London: Baptist Union, 1980).

developed a model of church growth.[234] When Paul Beasley-Murray was appointed Spurgeon's College Principal in 1986 he was committed to church planting and church growth, and to introducing College courses which offered training in these areas.[235] In 1988 it was agreed that the College would start an Evangelism and Church Planting course, in partnership with Oasis Trust, a rapidly-growing agency for evangelism and social concern founded by Steve Chalke, a Spurgeon's student in the later 1970s. A particular emphasis on urban mission developed. Research showed that of the Spurgeon's students who settled in home ministry from the mid-1970s to the mid-1980s one-third settled in inner-city situations.[236] Stuart Christine, who had trained at Spurgeon's and served with the BMS in Brazil (where he had considerable experience in theological education), became a tutor at the College and then the first Oasis Director of Church Planting and Evangelism.[237] There was a significant emphasis, under Paul Beasley-Murray, on the College producing theologically trained evangelists.

Concern for urban and cross-cultural mission led to a number of new developments. A course was started on Asian thought and practice, led by Ram Gidoomal, Director of South Asian Concern,[238] and by Stuart Murray, who succeeded Stuart Christine in 1992 as director of the Church Planting and Evangelism course. Increasingly the College attracted students from Black Majority churches in London. A major initiative, initially in East London, was Urban Expression, launched in 1997 in partnership with the College and Oasis Trust. Stuart Murray, who had been involved in planting a church in Tower Hamlets and who wrote important books on church planting,[239] saw Urban Expression as a vehicle for inner-city ministry. Colin Marchant was also an important facilitator in this area. Juliet Kilpin, who entered Baptist ministry in 1996 having trained at Spurgeon's, became part-time co-coordinator of Urban Expression and an associate lecturer at Spurgeon's. She and her husband Jim led the first Urban Expression church planting team. By the end of 2004 there were seven Urban Expression church planting teams in London and further

---

[234] P. Beasley-Murray and A. Wilkinson, *Turning the Tide* (London: The Bible Society, 1981).

[235] For more on English Baptists developments in the 1980s see I.M. Randall, *The English Baptists of the Twentieth Century* (Didcot: Baptist Historical Society, 2005), chapter 10.

[236] A. Thompson, 'Ministerial Training from a London Perspective', 20 May 1985, with Spurgeon's College Council Executive Committee Minutes of 19 June 1985.

[237] See S. Christine and M. Robinson, *Planting Tomorrow's Churches Today: A Comprehensive Handbook* (Tunbridge Wells: Monarch, 1992).

[238] Ram Gidoomal has written a number of books including R. Gidoomal and R. Thomson, *A Way of Life: Introducing Hinduism* (London: Hodder and Stoughton, 1997).

[239] For example, S. Murray, *Church Planting: Laying Foundations* (Carlisle: Paternoster Press, 1998).

expansion to other parts of the country was envisaged.[240] Former Spurgeon's students led several teams but teams were trans-denominational. The College's innovative forms of training in evangelism and church planting meant that students from a variety of denominations came to the College to train.

From October 2002, under the principal-ship of Nigel Wright, who had seen significant church growth and renewal in his own pastoral ministries, a further new course in evangelism was introduced. Wright's vision was for training 'attractive and evangelical ministers of the Gospel'.[241] The new evangelists' course was intended to train those who would become 'competent and effective advocates of the Christian message in a wide variety of settings'. Although there was an intention to attract students from different denominations and organisations, the course was designed to be a recognized means of training towards accreditation as an evangelist with the Baptist Union. The College was convinced of the need to prepare a generation of evangelists to speak for Christ in a society in which Christianity had been substantially displaced. It was anticipated that trained evangelists might function as full-time, part-time or voluntary workers or might be 'bi-vocational', seeing their present employment as part of their ministry. The communities to be reached by these evangelists were increasingly diverse, and it was considered important that evangelists trained by Spurgeon's should come from diverse and varied contexts. In the view of the College – and here there was an echo of W.Y. Fullerton's thinking - it was important not to operate with a 'stereotype' of what an evangelist was, but rather to seek creative diversity - men and women, black and white, traditional and non-traditional, young and old.[242] Rachel Dutton, who was appointed the course's leader in 2002, had been on the staff of St Andrew's Church, Chorleywood, responsible for evangelism and discipleship. In 2003 Roger Greenway argued for seminaries in the twenty-first century to take as seriously the training of evangelists as they do the training of pastors.[243] Spurgeon's has attempted, in seeking to renew its foundational vision, to address this missional challenge.

Wider World Mission

This article has focussed on home mission since it was with this in mind that Spurgeon's College was originally set up. But the College has also played its part in world mission. Spurgeon felt a particular affinity with the growing 'faith mission' movement of the nineteenth century. In 1858 he expressed his

[240] From the Urban Expression website http://www.urbanexpression.org.uk.
[241] *College Record*, November 2000, 2.
[242] *Training at Spurgeon's College: Evangelists' Course*, 2004, 2-5.
[243] Greenway, 'Evangelists', 39.

sympathy with the 'faith' philosophy of George Müller.[244] In 1863, when the BMS was in financial difficulties, Spurgeon bluntly stated that his 'Utopian and spiritual' views of mission were at odds with the Society's stance. Later he reiterated his belief that mission activities should be 'in the highest degree works of faith', rather than based on fund-raising, and he also argued that the BMS had become an 'interposing medium' between the churches and the missionaries. He wanted churches and missionaries to be 'bound together by ties of mutual relation unknown at the present time'.[245] By 1866, however, the BMS had made some alterations to its constitution and Spurgeon's attitude began to change. The extent of the change is seen in the fact that in 1886 he said the Society was welcome to come to College Conference and 'look out some more heroes' for missionary work.[246] Links between the College and the BMS grew closer during the later 1870s and the 1880s. Former College students became involved in pioneering mission with the BMS and other societies in a number of countries, while others went abroad to become ministers of churches in countries such as the USA, Canada, Australia and New Zealand.

It was in the later 1860s that the call to overseas mission became more prominent in the life of the College and reports began to be published of those 'moved to devote themselves to Missionary work in foreign lands'.[247] Spurgeon commented that he often prayed that the Pastors' College would become 'the mother of missionaries'.[248] By the late 1870s it was noted in *The Sword and the Trowel* that students had gone to such places as China, Japan, India, Italy and Spain.[249] There was great interest in this period in China, especially in the work of the China Inland Mission (CIM, later OMF, the Overseas Missionary Fellowship) which had begun in 1865 under the leadership of Hudson Taylor and which became the largest mission in the world. From the mid-1870s a steady stream of people who had trained at the College or who belonged to the Metropolitan Tabernacle joined the CIM. Spurgeon enjoyed Taylor's company and admired his radical methods.[250] Later the Boxer uprising in China brought about the first martyrdom of someone from the College: Silvester Frank Whitehouse went to China in 1888 with the CIM, returned to England and studied at the College, and served in China for only one year when he and his

---

[244] C. Ray, *The Life of Charles Haddon Spurgeon* (London: Passmore and Alabaster, 1903), 257; B. Stanley, 'C.H. Spurgeon and the Baptist Missionary Society, 1863-1866', *Baptist Quarterly* 28:7 (1982), 320.

[245] Stanley, 'C.H. Spurgeon', 320-21.

[246] Cited by B. Amey, *College Record*, December 1969.

[247] *Outline*, 14.

[248] *S and T*, March 1873, 128-31.

[249] *S and T*, September 1879, 446.

[250] Nicholls, *C.H. Spurgeon*, 80.

wife were killed.[251] On 18 September 1900 a telegram was read to the College from the BMS announcing the massacre of Mr and Mrs Whitehouse.[252] In 1902 Thomas Spurgeon, a son of C.H. Spurgeon, unveiled a marble tablet in honour of the College's first martyr.[253] The College's connection with Japan was much more limited, but reports in 1879 from W.J. White, a former College student serving in Japan, spoke of 1,000 people wanting to be baptised.[254] India would attract a number of College students, especially from the 1880s onwards.

A significant development for Spurgeon was the sending of two African Americans to serve with the BMS in Africa. In 1878 Thomas Johnson and Calvin Richardson, two of the African Americans who trained at the College in this period, went to West Africa. They were not the first African Americans to come to the College. James Magee arrived in 1867 from Toronto, Canada, and later went on to wide-ranging ministry in the USA.[255] By 1874 Spurgeon – like others before him - had in mind the possibility of considerable numbers of African Americans going to Africa as missionaries. Thomas Johnson, who had been a pastor in Denver, Colorado, came to the College a year later. He told his remarkable story in *Twenty-Eight Years a Slave*. Johnson arrived at the College full of anxiety and described how he felt 'so happy in his [Spurgeon's] presence, and so at home with him'. Johnson was assured by Spurgeon that he would have his full support in his desire to go to West Africa.[256] Spurgeon invariably responded with enthusiasm to those whom he encountered personally who fired his imagination with new evangelistic possibilities. In this case possibilities were explored with the BMS. The Society already had a Black missionary in West Africa, Joseph Jackson Fuller, a Jamaican, who had served in the Cameroons since the 1850s.[257]

Thomas Johnson was joined part way through his time at the College by Calvin Richardson, who came from First Baptist Church, Washington, DC, and in October 1878, when they had completed their studies, *The Baptist* reported: 'Special farewell services to the Revs. T. L. Johnson and C. H. Richardson, who are going to Africa as missionaries... were held on Wednesday last week in the Metropolitan Tabernacle. There was a very large attendance, and Mr.

---

[251] B. Stanley, *The History of the Baptist Missionary Society, 1792-1992* (Edinburgh: T&T Clark, 1992), 201. In the Boxer rising twelve BMS missionaries and three missionary children were put to death.

[252] Minutes of the College Students' Missionary Association, 18 September 1900: Minute Book, 1886-1917.

[253] *S and T*, December 1902, 627-8.

[254] *S and T*, September 1879, 446.

[255] See J.H. Magee, *The Night of Affliction and Morning of Recovery: An Autobiography* (Miami, Florida: Mnemosyne Publ., 1969). Facsimile repr., originally publ. Cincinnati: The Author, 1873.

[256] T.L. Johnson, *Twenty-Eight Years a Slave, or the Story of My Life in Three Continents* (Bournemouth: W. Mate & Sons, 1909), 78-90.

[257] Stanley, *The History*, 109.

Spurgeon occupied the chair, introducing Mr. Johnson, who delivered an interesting address upon slave life, mission work in Africa, and his expectations and purposes respecting the future'.[258] Mr and Mrs Johnson and Mr and Mrs Richardson spent time in Freetown, Sierra Leone, and in Monrovia, Liberia, and then settled in the Cameroons, but illness struck the Johnsons. In *The Sword and the Trowel* for January 1880 Spurgeon included a letter which contained, as he said, 'a very touching account' from Johnson of his wife's suffering. The fever which she contracted led to her death. Johnson expressed his thankfulness for the support of the congregation at the Tabernacle and concluded the letter. 'Yours truly, for Africa'.[259] Johnson returned to the USA and had a long ministry among American and English Baptists. C.H. Richardson continued to work in Bakundu, Cameroon, reporting in 1886 that he had distributed (among traders who could speak English) Spurgeon's sermons, sent by Mrs Spurgeon, and that he was also translating them.[260] The College continued to take a keen interest in Africa and in its African American missionaries. The way in which accounts of mission were publicized stimulated other students to offer for mission overseas.

Although the College introduced students to a wide range of missionary activity, Spurgeon wanted the College to have closer contact with missionaries than was sometimes possible through missionary societies. N. Hardingham Patrick, who entered the College in 1886, was taken on in 1889 by the newly-formed Pastor's College Missionary Association, which undertook to provide his financial support.[261] Spurgeon wrote to Patrick: 'I rejoice that the way is cleared for your going to North Africa. As a brother looking to our own funds for support you are the first representative of the Foreign Mission of the College, and I am the more earnest that you should lead the way gloriously'. He continued: 'Aspire to be another "Patrick", – the apostle of North Africa, as he was of Ireland'.[262] The work undertaken by Patrick and his wife, based in Morocco and linked with the North Africa Mission, was initially discouraging. In the College's 1891-92 College *Annual Report* he said that the preaching and the medical work being done seemed to be having no spiritual effect.[263] A year later the picture was different. Although there was opposition, he was now seeing many people of different backgrounds enquiring about faith. These included an older Spanish person, a young girl who wanted to be baptised, a French mother who said 'I believe in Jesus and my sins are all forgiven', and a

---

[258] Johnson, *Twenty-Eight Years*, 101. Citing *The Baptist*, 4 October 1878.
[259] *S and T*, January 1880, 42-3.
[260] *S and T*, February 1886, 92.
[261] *S and T*, January 1889, 44.
[262] C.H. Spurgeon from Mentone, 14 December [1888], Correspondence of Spurgeon, 1863-1886, Spurgeon's College Heritage Room.
[263] *AP*, 1891-92, 4.

young Spanish man.[264] Patrick was able to form a church among Spanish and English people.[265]

Another missionary supported by Pastor's College Missionary Association was Thomas Gillard Churcher, who was a student at the College in the late 1870 and then went to Edinburgh to study medicine. After graduating in 1884 he worked at the Mildmay Mission Hospital, Bethnal Green, and then moved to North Africa, which was the scene of his life's work. Spurgeon strongly supported the Kabyle Mission (later the North African Mission), with which Churcher served. Together with his wife, who was a hospital nurse, Churcher pioneered medical services in Morocco (in Tangier and Fez), where he was the first European medical doctor, and in Sousse, a large city on the coast of Tunisia.[266] In the early 1890s Churcher reported that he was seeing about 100 patients a week, while superintending the Hospital, 'Hope House'. Churcher commented on the religious situation in Morocco, saying that for many people only secret discipleship was possible, since religious liberty was not a concept that was embraced. There were, he said, some secret disciples.[267] A report in 1903 said that during his time in North Africa Churcher had treated up to 70,000 patients and that Christianity was much more favourably viewed as a result of his work.[268] The College was made aware of the challenges of the Islamic world.

In the early decades of the twentieth century, the College's involvement in world mission was not as evident. The College Missionary Association did not survive. There were links across Europe, for example through William Fetler (known also as Basil Malof), an outstanding Latvian who studied at the College from 1903 to 1907. Fetler was supported from 1907 by the Pioneer Mission and saw remarkable results in St Petersburg, Moscow and Riga, the capital of Latvia. As a result of his work in St Petersburg a church building was opened in 1911 seating 2,000 people and in 1927 a similar sized building, the Salvation Temple Revival Baptist Church, was opened in Riga.[269] A new focus of interest for the College opened up in the 1950s when Arthur Elder, who had been born in Argentina and who had studied at Spurgeon's before working with the BMS in China, took up service in South America. The expulsion of missionaries from China meant that BMS personnel and finances were available for new work. By 1965 there were eight BMS couples in Brazil and a strong Spurgeon's connection was evident.[270] Stuart Christine's appointment to the College staff

---

264 *AP*, 1892-93, 43-4.

265 *AP*, 1893-94, 30. He returned to ministry England in 1899.

266 *S and T*, September 1903, 456-60.

267 *AP*, 1892-93, 43.

268 *S and T*, September 1903, 456-60.

269 J.A. Stewart, *A Man in a Hurry* (Asheville, NC: Russian Bible Society, n.d.), 39-40, 90-91, 104. Cf. J. Wood, *Born in the Fire* (privately published, 1998).

270 For fuller details about Brazil see Stanley, *The History*, chapter 15.

helped to strengthen the College's Brazilian links and also enhanced the teaching of mission in the College.[271] The later twentieth century has also seen many links between the College and the countries of Eastern Europe. Students went with the BMS in the 1990s to various parts of Europe, including France, Italy, Croatia, Albania and Bulgaria. From the late 1990s the College has had close links with the International Baptist Theological Seminary, Prague, and the need for theological education 'with an accent on mission' (as proposed by Vladimir Federov) in the Central and Eastern European context has been seen as a priority.[272] World mission continues in different ways to be an important dimension in the life of Spurgeon's College.

Conclusion

From its beginning Spurgeon's College gave high priority to training students to be effective in mission, whether as pastors or as those in full-time evangelistic ministry. John W. Ewing, who trained at the College in the 1880s and had a significant ministry at Rye Lane Chapel, Peckham, which became one of the largest English Baptist churches, spoke in 1906 of how he had received from his training at the College 'a sense of the value of the cross' and 'an impulse towards soul-winning', especially the need 'to speak face to face with my hearers, bringing every power I possess to bear upon the work of leading men and women to Christ'.[273] The emphasis given to effective evangelism in the early decades of the life of the College was evident. Although in the early decades of the twentieth century some of that momentum was lost, George Beasley-Murray made it clear in the 1960s that his aim as Principal was to see the College producing evangelistic pastors. They should, he insisted, be well grounded in academic study, by contrast, as he put it, with those who were 'slick salesmen of religion'.[274] From the 1980s there was increasing emphasis on evangelists being able to advocate the gospel with confidence in a changing culture.[275] The College was aiming to help those who would, in line with C.H. Spurgeon's original vision, be skilled at bringing people to personal faith and discipleship and who would be able to apply the Christian message to the contemporary world.

---

[271] For reflections on teaching mission in seminaries from a Baptist missionary in South America see A. Neely, 'The Teaching of Missions', in *Toward the Twenty-First Century in Christian Mission*, ed. J.M. Phillips and R.T. Coote (Grand Rapids, Mich.: Eerdmans, 1993), 269-83.

[272] V. Federov, 'Ecumenical Missionary Needs and Perspectives in Central and Eastern Europe Today: Theological Education with an Accent on Mission as a First Priority in Our Religious Rebirth', *International Review of Missions* 92 (2003).

[273] *S and T*, June 1906, 286-7.

[274] *College Record*, December 1967, 2-4.

[275] *Training at Spurgeon's College: Evangelists' Course*, 2-3.

In 1992, in an article 'Ministerial Formation for Mission: Implications for Theological Education', Christopher Duraisingh argued that while theological training had to include theological analysis, spiritual formation and development of skills, there was an over-riding need for a missiological paradigm, so that those in training in seminaries would see themselves as persons 'who engage themselves and who enable others to be engaged in the *mission Dei*'.[276] Although in Spurgeon's time the term *missio Dei* was not part of evangelical parlance, Spurgeon's priorities were the same as those expressed by Duraisingh, and these priorities are central to the College's ethos today - with the term *missio Dei* now often being used. In 1881 Spurgeon, drawing from the thinking of American Baptist missionary pioneer, Adoniram Judson, wished 'to make the Pastors' College a seed-garden for the church and for the world'.[277] In 1891, near the end of his life, Spurgeon, drawing from John Wesley, once again enunciated what may properly be considered the College's vision for a mode of training that was missional: 'The world is our parish, and our [College] brethren are not sitting down, waiting to be called to settled charges, and comfortable incomes; but they are willing to go wherever there is an opening for preaching Christ, and gathering a church'.[278]

---

[276] Duraisingh, 'Ministerial Formation', 38.
[277] *S and T*, April 1881, 175.
[278] *AP*, 1890-91, 4.

PART 4

Theological Education and the State University

Postgraduate Theological Education in the Former Soviet Union: A Case of St Petersburg Christian University

Peter Penner

The Rev. Dr. Peter Penner has been in leadership with St. Petersburg Christian University in Russia and is lecturer in Biblical Studies and Missiology at IBTS, Prague.

Introduction

This paper has a two-fold focus. Firstly, it describes the overall context of theological education in the Former Soviet Union (FSU). This includes several aspects: the biblical-missiological context; the historical context of the local church and of theological education in the FSU; the larger context of change in the FSU in the areas of education, philosophy and politics; and the global context, especially the influx of missionary activity from North America, including western ideas of theology, theological education and church life. Secondly, it examines a contextually shaped theological education programme established in St Petersburg, Russia, and its global link with and validation by a British university. This locally delivered course is characterized by its *relevance* to the needs of the church and society in Russia, as well as by its *integration* with and *recognition* by international institutions and educational standards. Thus, this presentation may be viewed as a case study on how local and global perspectives on theological education can converge in particular contexts.

Part I: The General Context of Theological Education in the Former Soviet Union

The following fundamental statements lay the foundation for the second part of the paper. They present results of an evaluation undertaken in my doctoral dissertation, entitled, *Guidelines for the Mission of Theological Education in the FSU*.

The NT background

Theological education is not only preparation of the student for possible entry into mission work, it is mission. Theological education and training are mission work in the narrow as well as in the broad sense. This idea is supported in the

New Testament and throughout Scripture. In the training efforts of Jesus and the Apostle Paul, we see how this concept takes shape within the framework of the emerging church and its mission. Jesus is the teacher of his disciples, and as such, of the church. In Mt. 23: 8-10, the task of the teacher (*rabbi*) becomes associated with the title and work of the triune God. It is affirmed that Christ alone has a right to this position and he teaches with authority. Consequently, it is not appropriate for his followers to call themselves 'teachers' in the same sense, because they are sisters and brothers and disciples of Christ. The mission of the Messiah is 'to teach' and 'to make disciples'. Such an interpretation underlines the importance of education (training) in God's mission. It is a mission that the growing church of the first century took seriously and continued to promote. Faith in Christ is the faith of a trained (educated) disciple, and not a faith that promotes controversy over knowledge.[279]

Paul, the student of Hillel and disciple of Christ, is perhaps the most important example of a Christian who, within the church, practised theological training of leaders in church and missions.[280] His main objective was not simply to transmit a spiritual heritage to a limited number of leading persons in the apostolic church. Rather, it was to train every person belonging to the church. Leaders in the church were helped to continually improve in their God-given gifts and tasks, and regional leaders were prepared to serve the church and its overall mission. The New Testament underlines the importance and significance of the task of theological education, and warns of the inherent dangers of faulty application of this mandate.

Holistic theological education

Theological education in and for the mission of the church must be holistic. Whether or not the church and its mission remain active or fail to do so, depends on the theological training provided to its members. It is, therefore, absolutely necessary that theological training is offered and that it is provided in the spirit of God's mission. The concept of holistic education applies both to the educational programme as well as to the various levels of training within the church, i.e. all church members must receive appropriate training. Holistic education targets everyone at every level in the church. The Apostle Paul and his mission team modelled and taught this principle. On the basic level, they taught the fundamentals of Scripture to all members of the church and, at other

---

[279] P.F. Penner, 'Novosavetny Knishnik' (the New Testament Scribe)', *Chronograph* 4 (1999).

[280] D.J. Bosch, *Transforming Mission: Paradigm Shifts in Theology of Mission* (Maryknoll: Orbis Books, 1992), 131-33. Cf. G. Eichholz, *Die Theologie Des Paulus Im Umriss*, 2 ed. (Neukirchen: Neukirchener Verlag, 1977), especially the second chapter 'Der Apostelauftrag im Selbstverständnis des Paulus'.

levels, equipped leaders for the responsibility of training local congregations and promoting theological training regionally.[281]

On the one hand, this requires instruction in the local church (e.g. a church Bible school). On the other hand, it requires additional intensive regional and national training for leaders who are gifted; this training should enable them to train others (2 Tim. 2:2).

Diverse approaches are needed

The principle of holistic education is also related to the variety and diversity of gifts and tasks within the church. Gifts and tasks in the church belong together. The variety of gifts mirrors the diversity of God's mission. Thus, preparation for ministry must also utilize a variety of approaches, levels and emphases. In the latter part of the twentieth century, theological education by extension (TEE) was viewed as having the potential to meet the needs for theological education in many areas.[282] However, a critical analysis shows that this type of educational approach cannot be propagated as an absolute solution because it has its own shortcomings. Nevertheless, it is quite useful in training the church in its manifold mission.

The biblical reorientation that resulted from the development of TEE has been productive for TEE itself, as well as for the classical educational institutions, and has led to the formulation of alternative concepts. It is important that theological education is provided to the entire church, with all its diverse gifts and tasks, in order that the church might reach its maximum potential in fulfilling its mission. This requires that close attention be paid to the *context* the church finds itself in, the constant changes in its environment, as well as the *influences* from past and present that may affect mission and theological training.

Theological education in the FSU profits greatly by integrating the past and the present. In other words, orthodox and evangelical developments in theological education have to be evaluated for their potential usefulness for the present and future

The Spiritual Heritage of the FSU

A local perspective requires that evangelicals in the present FSU be aware that they have a rich spiritual heritage. This includes not only the more than one thousand years of church history in this part of the world, but also its history of theological education. There have been many attempts at various times and under various historical conditions to conduct theological education. The

---

281 W.-H. Ollrog, *Paulus und seine Mitarbeiter. Untersuchung zu Theorie und Praxis paulinischer Mission*, vol. 50 (Neukirchen-Vluyn: Neukirchener Verlag, 1979).

282 S.G. Snook, *Developing Leaders through Theological Education by Extension. Case Studies from Africa* (Wheaton, Ill: Wheaton College, Billy Graham Center, 1992).

Russian Orthodox Church looks back to 300 years of theological education. Evangelicals also have made several attempts at establishing schools; most of them were tragically persecuted and finally closed down.[283] All of these attempts were more or less culturally adapted and were marked by positive as well as negative aspects, enough so that many lessons can be learned from them. However, an awareness of this heritage and its lessons is largely absent not only among western missionaries, but also among many young Christians in the FSU. Often, the period of Perestroika is considered the starting point of theological education.

In actual fact, there is a rich experience to draw from, with many tested educational models, national and/or nationalized materials, as well as some training literature with which to start, whenever young evangelical theological educational institutions are called into being. If the evangelicals fail to connect with the elements of this national church history, it is possible, that there will be no future for the church or its theological educational institutions once the western missionaries withdraw. Those who do not start with the context, and who ignore the past, will probably both miss the current needs and develop faulty guidelines in the area of quality theological education. They will likely pursue an irrelevant mission, and will remain inauthentic within the environment they intend to serve.[284]

A local perspective also requires that the unique character of the development of the Russian evangelical movement also has to be taken into account. The evangelicals in the FSU are not a more or less contextualized continuation of western culture and history. They are a reform movement that grew out of the Russian Orthodox Church.[285] That origin, and its specific developments up to the present time, is the foundation upon which the evangelical movement in the FSU exists today. On this basis, it is impossible to that ideas for an educational construct can be drawn exclusively from the West. For example, the curriculum cannot be dominated by the theological thinking of the West, which circles around discussions between Lutheran, Reformed, Catholic, evangelical, western fundamentalist, and other theologies. At the same time, neither can it exclude these understandings, because our present world has become a 'global village' and many of the questions and inquiries in

---

[283] W. Sawatsky, *Soviet Evangelicals since World War II* (Scottdale, Pa: Herald Press, 1981).

[284] W. Sawatsky, 'Visions in Conflict: Starting Anew through the Prism of Leadership Training Effortss) ', in *Religion after Communism in Eastern Europe*, ed. N. Nielsen (Boulder, CO: Westview Press, 1994); A. Bodrov, *Pravoslavnoye Obrasovaniye V Rossii: K Voprosu O Prioritetakh (Orthodox Education in Russia: The Question of Priorities* (Moscow: 1994).

[285] M.S. Karetnikova, 'Russkoye Bogoiskatelstvo: Natsionalnye Korni Evangelsko-Baptistskogo Dvisheniya (the Russian Search for God: National Roots of the Evangelical-Baptist Movement) ', in *Almanakh Po Istorii Russkogo Baptisma* (St. Petersburg: Bibliya dlya Vsekh, 1997).

the East are similar. However, the theological, philosophical and practical questions of the 'Russian Soul' and of Russian history must be incorporated into the educational ethos. Consequently, questions of curriculum development, spirituality and spiritual formation need to receive answers from this perspective, and not merely copy western models.

How does one develop a contextually coherent course in church history? Will it be developed like in the West with its classical components: apostolic church, church fathers, Middle Ages, Reformation, etc.? Or is it more important to study church history that is relevant to the places and peoples of the area where the curriculum is being applied? Does one define the concept of spirituality from the perspective of the western church and tradition, or in terms of the uniquely Eastern spirituality? These differences in spirituality become evident, for example, in the alternative views and celebrations of Easter and the resurrection in the western and the eastern churches. Another significant aspect of the local heritage is the persecution and suffering of the evangelical movement throughout most of its history. This element formed and continues to shape its identity and cannot be overlooked. It must be reflected in the definition of quality of education, in the mission statement of the school and in all other contextual orientations.[286]

In addition to being sensitive to local contextual perspectives (e.g. the Orthodox background of the evangelical movement), we also must take a global perspective, which includes evaluating western influences. The identity and, therefore, the mission of the Russian evangelicals is unique: it is not Russian Orthodox in nature, nor is it western, nor is it a certain combination of the two. The historical and cultural environment that contributed to the identity of evangelicals also contains European and Asiatic elements. However, important western influences in the development of the evangelical movement cannot be overlooked or denied. For example, the thinking, the culture and the theology of the West influenced a number of leading Russian evangelicals in their formative years. In addition, the varied and consistent attempts of the western church to help Russian Christians, during the long years of communist rule and after its demise, have certainly left their mark. All of these aspects have a decisive place in the development of a theological education that is relevant for the FSU, one which grows out of its past, while utilizing the numerous current changes.

For the establishment of new and healthy theological schools, there must be a critical evaluation of the present strengths and shortcomings of evangelical theological education. This evaluation will focus not only on FSU and western schools, but also on worldwide developments

[286] P.F. Penner, 'Evangelskoye teologicheskoye obrasovaniye v techeniye poslednikh 10 let' (Evangelical Theological Education During the Last 10 Years)', *Chronograf* 1 (1997).

Evaluating Models

Due to the obvious western influence in the development of theological education in the FSU, the educational criteria of western schools play a significant role and, thus, need to be closely analysed. Such an analysis can lead to positive impulses for the formulation of theological education in the FSU (in a similar way as, for example, the Euro-Asian Accrediting Association [EAAA] attempted to suggest directions for further development).[287] However, they should not simply reproduce western models; the latter must be adapted and transformed in such a way that they are fully applicable to the unique situation of the schools in the FSU. For example, the Association of Theological Schools (ATS) followed such a process in three developmental phases: an emphasis in the area of quality, of defining the mission of the school, and of an orientation along the context.[288]

Further, criteria for thorough evaluation must not be limited to the criteria implemented in North American and European schools. The scope of the study of theological education (including the mistakes made by western mission organizations) must be expanded to include the global context. Lessons learned in various countries and cultures must be thoroughly reviewed within the cultures of the FSU. Wholesale borrowing from the West or from the two-thirds world of otherwise functional concepts will have fatal consequences.[289] TEE can serve as an illustration. A given concept that shows considerable promise in a given arena or region, and which predominantly western missionaries adhere to, should not automatically be assumed to be the only workable direction for theological education in the FSU. In fact, outside programmes of education are often greeted with distrust as to their quality and respectability; they rarely reach the more educated strata of society, in part because of their incompatibility with Russia's highly developed, globally recognized educational system and culture. They also often fail to take into account its impressive church history and church traditions, which have been in existence for more than one thousand years. When they analyse western education, FSU theological schools recognize the variety of programmes and the individualization of education which characterize the school systems of the West. They also are confronted with the extensive application of technological advances in the field of education.

These are important areas with which every school, in particular the EAAA, should seriously concern itself, because they offer enormous possibilities for

---

[287] S.V. Sannikov, 'Podkhody I Printsipy Sosdaniya Evro-Asiatskoy Akkerditatsionnoy Associacii (EAAA) (the Approaches and Principles of the Creation of the Euro-Asian Accrediting Association). Paper Read at the Conference Theological Education-2', (Kiev: 1996).

[288] J.H.Jr. Evans and J.I. Smith, 'What Is the Character of the Institutional Resources Needed for the Good Theological School', *Theological Education* 30:Spring (1994), 48.

[289] Elliot, 'Theological Education'.

the development of a higher quality of education in each school. Most of the residential schools are not compatible with each other, nor are they in a position to incorporate alternative programmes into their existing programmes. But exactly here lies the opportunity to provide holistic theological education in Christ's church on numerous levels. western schools, especially the Anglo-American ones, did this for their own programmes during the advance of the philosophy of individualization in society. In the FSU, an integration of alternative programmes into local schools, and compatibility among schools, will certainly lead to an increase in the quality and quantity of theological education programmes.

Theological Education and Secular Education

Young theological schools can draw a great wealth of experience not only from past Orthodox and evangelical theological training endeavours, but also from the world renowned state universities with their secular education. Here they will find some valuable directions for standards in the educational process. To acknowledge this and to evaluate these factors for the purpose of developing our own schools is very important. This is particularly necessary so that evangelical education can gain respectability and recognition in society, and perhaps even gain state accreditation. Orientation along the concepts of state education will enhance the process of contextualization.

For example, if the Ministry of Education requires more subjects in general education, this probably is due to the fact that they regard the level of education provided by secondary public schools as insufficient for entry into higher educational institutions (universities). An orientation along state university standards, along with an improvement of quality, could lead in the long run to recognition of theological educational institutions within the context of independent college education, offering them a position similar to state universities. Recent developments in the society and resulting regulations on education, as well as the reputation enjoyed at present by a number of independent (private) colleges, could make this possible. However, this means that evangelical theological schools cannot allow inferior standards, but must pursue strict quality control. They must consider this pursuit as part of their mission in society and culture, or as some of the schools have articulated it, as part of their mission statement. An appropriate utilization of the current possibilities for co-operation with state universities – taking advantage of the framework provided by law – will lead to greater stability and long term results. It may transform existing options and concepts that otherwise appear to limit theological education. Taking advantage of existing possibilities means, for example, designing agreements with state universities for sharing library resources and professors from humanities faculties, whether for instruction in biblical languages or foreign languages like English or German, or in history, philology, philosophy and logic.

Theological education and the state university

The absolute separation of state and evangelical education can be bridged at the point of common interests in the development of the humanities. This is possible not only in the sharing of resources, but also in the design of programmes. The latter would incorporate evangelical concepts of theological education and at the same time provide ways for students to receive a degree accredited by the state. These attempts can take direction from the following examples:

The British model: A private theological educational institution builds a relationship with a state university and works toward validation from it in an area of common interest. The Tübingen model: This model presupposes that a student studies at a state university in an accredited course, while being part of a community that provides spiritual formation and care, consultation, and a discussion forum for the integration of secular education and a Christian worldview. The Odessa model: The model describes an interrelationship between independent theological and state education whereby students study at both institutions while each accepts subjects of the other institution for its programme, so that in the end a student receives two degrees, one that is important for their ministry in the church and the other that is recognized by the state. Extension campus model or distance education: In this model, a validated course with a tested curriculum is contextualized and offered in a different context (country). This means that the programme is applicable to the latter context and yet, due to international validation, graduates of the programme receive a degree with which they can continue studies or work at an international level. This is the approach chosen by St. Petersburg Christian University in an effort to provide education that is relevant both locally and globally.

Summary

The objective of part one was to develop principles for new initiatives in theological education in the FSU by looking at several interrelated areas of concern. We noted that the biblical material of the Old and New Testaments provides foundational concepts for theological education, as well as its legitimation and direction. The influence of western and other educational concepts on FSU theological education cannot be underestimated and must be taken into account. The latter concepts provide valuable impulses, important warnings and possibilities for comparisons in the search for appropriate new efforts in the FSU. An exploration into the historical and cultural background of theological education in the FSU reveals that there is a great wealth of tradition and experience available in orthodox and evangelical educational circles. The future of today's theological schools will depend significantly on an appropriate regard for and integration of elements from these contexts. Part one provides the foundation and the starting point for an understanding of plans for the future development of St. Petersburg Christian University (SPCU). These general observations about theological education in the FSU received specific attention during a collaborative effort by SPCU and OCMS to develop a Masters course suited to the FSU context. The programme described in part two of this paper is based on excerpts from the documents submitted to a British university proposing the validation of a MTh in Biblical Studies.

Part two: The Masters Course at St. Petersburg Christian University

General History, Rationale and Justification of the Programme

St Petersburg Christian University (SPCU) had its origins in the early 1980s. Since it had not been possible to provide theological training to Christian leaders in the Former Soviet Union (FSU) for several decades, there was a great pressure to make a modest beginning when opportunities for theological education became available during the period of glasnost and perestroika. For a number of years, TEE programmes were run in several cities. In 1990 a residential Bible school was established in Southern Russia with 45 students. In 1992 the institution was transferred to St Petersburg, the location of the first evangelical Bible school in the 1920s. The programme of studies was extended to three, then to four years; students and faculty received access to excellent libraries of the Orthodox Academy and the St. Petersburg State University, and a number of renowned professors visited SPCU as guest lecturers. In 1993 the name was changed to St Petersburg Christian University. The mission of SPCU is to provide recognized theological education at university level in the conservative, evangelical, Free Church tradition.

The university is an institution with a multidenominational, international and multi-cultural faculty and student body. It attempts to meet the contemporary needs of the church and society in the post-soviet world from a Christian perspective. SPCU is also seeking ways to develop and coordinate quality theological education with other schools in the FSU and Eastern Europe and thus expand its availability. Therefore, SPCU has become one of the founding members of the Euro-Asian Accrediting Association (EAAA) and the Eastern European Schools of Theology (EEST). The development of a programme for postgraduate studies has been a vital issue at SPCU since 1993 when, together with the Odessa Baptist Seminary, a mutual project in Masters studies was designed and conducted as a pilot project from 1994-1996. Other avenues for preparing national faculty were used such as sending capable men and women abroad for studies. There is a great need, though, to provide indigenous Christians with high quality education such as is available in western Europe, albeit in their own culture, tradition and country, in order to avoid problems inherent to international studies. SPCU's efforts are, therefore, directed to the design of an in-country postgraduate studies programme, in order to train capable prospective faculty for SPCU and for other theological educational institutions in their own cultural and theological context and language, while exposing them to various theological trends. With the September 1997 law on freedom of conscience and religious organizations, the Russian government has closed the door to all religious groups in Russia, including the Protestant groups, providing education in programmes validated by the Russian government. For denominational theological schools, such as institutions of the Russian Orthodox Church and other denominations, this does not present a great problem, because they train ministers for their denominations and do not pursue governmental validation. SPCU is an interdenominational school that trains persons from different backgrounds, people groups and denominations.

Not all SPCU students necessarily have the goal in mind to work in a church pastoral ministry upon graduation. State social institutions, secondary schools, institutions of higher learning and other institutions where SPCU graduates apply, require an education that the state and state universities accept. In its postgraduate programme, SPCU is seeking this kind of degree for its students. The goals of the programme are to prepare MTh candidates for becoming Biblical Studies lecturers at Bible colleges, seminaries, and Christian institutions throughout Russia and the FSU; and to prepare evangelical theologians and apologists who are equipped to write and encourage the community of believers in Russia, the FSU and abroad. With a high quality programme accepted by the State, and with its already established leading role in theological education in Russia and the FSU, SPCU could offer various denominations and their theological educational institutions capable leaders. It also could, regionally and nationally, influence church and society positively in the area of religious life and morals, and support more effectively the ongoing changes in church and society.

General Educational Aims and Objectives

The programme is set in the context of the broad educational ethos of the UK University sector. At the under-graduate level, students are introduced to a corpus of knowledge and are expected to learn this knowledge and the basic skills to handle it. At the post-graduate level, students are required to learn a range of skills with which they can handle new corpuses of knowledge which they may encounter, after graduation, in their chosen field. Therefore, this programme is designed to impart advanced skills in handling knowledge in the biblical studies discipline in practical situations, some samples of which knowledge they will be introduced to in the programme. It is anticipated that these skills will also be suitable, in general, for use by the graduate in their encounters with other disciplines, thus building their skills for life. The general educational philosophy underpinning the programme is based on open education and field based learning. It is open education in that it gives important attention to the experience with which participants come to the programme, and seeks to make available to them the resources of an educational programme that will enable them to reflect on, question and evaluate that experience and relate it to a wide range of issues.

Relating general educational objectives more specifically to the programme in Biblical Studies it is anticipated that graduates will be equipped to function as biblically informed thinkers, scholars and communicators with critical and interpretational skills, who can interact from a biblical position with church and society. They will: develop a deeper understanding of the significance of God in the light of human history; develop skills in the use of various tools of biblical criticism; demonstrate skills in literary and theological analysis; work from exegetical study of OT/NT texts to themes in OT/NT theology, respectively; work from exegetical study to develop material for educational purposes by using different tools and educational methods; develop writing skills for the composition of articles and other biblical-theological literature from exegetical study and/or biblical theology.

In regards to various areas of their functioning, graduates will be able to demonstrate and apply the following range of competencies: *Professional:* be able to identify the ways in which Scripture has been interpreted throughout history; be able to analyse and evaluate them and make legitimate use of them; be able to interact from a biblical position with church and society; be able to communicate biblical insights to various groups. *Theological:* be able to deploy the skills appropriate to biblical scholarship, in the original language, in discussing key biblical concepts and themes; be able to think critically about issues of biblical interpretation; be able to describe the significance of Christ and the church in the world with reference to contemporary challenges in society; be able to relate missiologically to the wider context of the church's engagement with the aims of the state. *Theoretical:* be able to analyse and critique current approaches to biblical interpretation; be able to develop existing skills of communication; be able to give a perspective of ways of resolving ethical dilemmas in society. *Personal:* be able to demonstrate an integrated and holistic approach to society that embraces personal life, intellectual development and social involvement.

Evaluation and Future Perspectives

Evangelical theological education in the FSU has a relatively short history. Due to developments in their history, evangelicals had a limited opportunity for theological reflection about their own faith.[290] First they were persecuted by the Russian Orthodox Church and the Czarist regime, then persecution came from the side of the Soviet communist ideology. Due to the continuing experience of suffering and resistance, they developed a Bible oriented theology which

[290] A.I. Negrov and M. Charter, 'Why Is There No Russian "Protestant" Theology in Russia? A Personal Outcry', *Religion in Eastern Europe* XVII (1997).

helped them to survive as a movement, but which is not explicitly formulated. Cultural and historical elements have caused the Bible to become the foundation of all theological thinking for the evangelicals in the FSU, while the hermeneutic key for the interpretation of Scripture is their experience and the specific context.

The SPCU Masters course in Biblical Studies – placed in the context of global resources on the one side, and on the other side, the local Russian Orthodox cultural context and the heritage of evangelical churches in the FSU – will enhance the development of a theological identity of evangelicals in the FSU. Using global and local resources, churches in the FSU, who have gone through a difficult period during these last years of break-up and crisis, can find their place and identity and be able to continue their mission in the FSU and in the 'global village'. It is remarkable to note the many points of interaction between a programme validated in Great Britain and offered in this northern capitol of Russia. St. Petersburg is sometimes called 'the window to Europe' or 'the bridge-building city between East and West'.

The uniqueness of the resources in St. Petersburg is already evident from its rich historical, Orthodox theological, cultural and spiritual heritage. Here one can walk the streets of Dostoyevski and reflect about God in the Russian Christian tradition. Here, due to the preaching of a British nobleman, Lord Redstock, the evangelical movement began. Here the first efforts in evangelical theological education in Russia were undertaken. Here, during difficult times of war and revolution, the director of this Bible school, Ivan Prokhanov, received training from British Christians. This is a city that holds in its archives codices and other invaluable early manuscripts of the Holy Scriptures of the Old and New Testament. This city will host a school and a programme that may contribute tremendously to the moulding of various discrete strands of heritage and identity into one new evangelical identity and mission in the FSU. This mixture of cultures, of diverse spiritual heritages and of broad horizons of knowledge, is what makes the SPCU Course in Biblical Studies meaningful both from the global and from the local perspective.

Theological Education among Post-Soviet Protestants: The Masters of Arts in Contextual Theology

Darrell Cosden and Donald Fairbairn

Darrell Cosden is currently Lecturer in Christian Doctrine and Ethics at International Christian College in Glasgow.

Don Fairbairn is currently Lecturer in Church History and Missions at Erskine Theological Seminary (South Carolina, USA).

Introduction

It is commonly recognized among Christian thinkers today that all theology is contextual. That is to say, every expression of theology has been significantly and necessarily, although not exclusively, influenced by the context in which it is done. The way a given group of Christians looks at Scripture, the world, Christian tradition, doctrine and dogma, and Christian life is profoundly influenced by the historical and cultural factors which have shaped their development as a people. In many cases, however, this influence is unexamined and unacknowledged. As a result, a group of Christians may believe that it understands and expresses the truth of the Christian faith in exactly the same way as the New Testament writers did. When this happens, not only will that Christian group possess a very immature understanding of its own theological and contextual heritage, but that group will also have great difficulty interacting with other groups of Christians, whose different historical and cultural contexts have led them to view Scripture and express Christian life in somewhat different ways.

Such problems of interaction between different groups of Christians are especially evident in the relations between western conservative Protestants and post-Soviet Protestants in the 1990s. Both groups of Christians have lived in relative isolation from the broader currents of the Christian thought world. (In the case of post-Soviet Protestants, the isolation was forced; in the case of western conservative Protestants – especially in North America – the isolation was largely voluntarily imposed.) Both have a firm commitment to Scripture, to personal faith in Christ, to the importance of proclaiming the gospel through word and action, etc. However, in spite of these great similarities, the relation between the two groups has been an uneasy one. Part of the reason has been that on the whole, neither conservative western Protestantism nor post-Soviet Protestantism has been aware of the importance of context in the shaping of its theology.

Both groups have tended to see their own theology as absolute and universal in a greater sense than it actually is. The clash of theologies which have been inappropriately (and unconsciously) absolutized has left both western missionaries and Slavic Protestants bewildered and sometimes embittered. Perhaps a brief explanation of some factors which have influenced each of these groups will help to clarify this point.

Theology as Poetry or Prose?

A prominent Ukrainian protestant Christian leader recently commented on the difference between western conservative Protestantism and Slavic Protestantism by saying, 'The problem is that our pastors write poetry; theirs write systematic theologies'. By 'systematic theologies', this Ukrainian Christian meant the sort of theological manuals that regard Scripture as a book of universal propositions which must be uncovered (through scientifically devised principles of exegesis) and which see the task of theology as uncovering these propositions and arranging them in an orderly form (usually according to a pre-conceived organizing hook such as the idea of the 'covenant' or of the 'dispensations of God's grace').

Such a method for writing systematic theology grows out of the rationalistic atmosphere of medieval Roman Catholic and post-Reformation protestant scholasticism, in which the task of theology (as distinct from other aspects of Christian life) was seen as that of organizing and systematizing the 'facts', the propositions derived from reason and revelation. The rationalistic character of this enterprise received an added boost through the Enlightenment, which bequeathed to western Christianity a concern for universal truths accessible to reason. Finally, the fundamentalist-modernist controversy in North America led conservative Protestants to adopt unconsciously the 'weapons' of modernity (such as the longing for objective universals and an overly propositional understanding of language) in order to fight the liberals. The result was a theology which was extremely cognitive in orientation, which was fuelled by the belief in objectively verifiable truth lying behind the pages of Scripture, and which claimed an universality that belied the contextual nature of its formation.

On the other hand, when the Ukrainian Christian leader quoted above said that Slavic pastors write 'poetry', he was referring to a substantially different way of knowing, of viewing reality, and of understanding Christian faith. Rather than thinking in straight lines of reasoning from a premise to a conclusion (as intellectually trained westerners generally do), Slavs think in a more Asian way, which could be described as resembling a corkscrew spiralling and narrowing toward a conclusion or group of conclusions. To Slavs, thinking and knowing involve much more than logic, and Slavs understand reality in a way which is more complex than straight-forward propositional terms can indicate.

Given this pattern of thinking, the best and deepest thought is expressed not in propositional assertions, but in narrative or poetic literature (e.g. Pushkin or Dostoevsky). The influence of the Slavic way of thinking and knowing on the construction of theology is evident from the tendency for post-Soviet pastors to express themselves in poetry, testimony, sermon or song, rather than in a more propositional form of theology. This dramatic difference between the western (especially North American) and Slavic ways of approaching Christian truth makes it easy to see why tensions have developed in the relations between the two groups during the last decade.

A Crisis of the Soul

What is not so clear, however, is why Slavic protestants accept conservative western protestant theologies at all. Once again, the statement by the Ukrainian Christian leader cited above provides a clue. He refers to the tendency of post-Soviet pastors to write poetry as a *problem*, and even as '*the* problem'. He looks wistfully at the West, longing for his own people to be able to think and write in the linear, propositional way that conservative western Christians do. This comment is indicative of post-Soviet Protestantism's lack of an identity, its lack of confidence in its own theological thinking, and its consequent desire to imitate its elder sibling, western Protestantism. The clash between a desire to be like the West and an intuitive rejection of the West's ways of thinking and expressing truth helps to account for the current crisis in the post-Soviet protestant soul.

In brief, then, the problem is not that Slavic protestants write poetry rather than propositional theological manuals. Rather, the greater problem is that Slavic protestants have intuitively absolutized their own unexamined expressions of theology, while at the same looking with uncritical admiration at the theological productions of a foreign culture, even as they sense these productions to be ill suited for a Slavic context. The solution, we believe, is for post-Soviet Protestant theology to move from being a theology which is unconsciously influenced by its context to being a genuinely contextual theology.

By the term 'contextual theology', we mean a theology which self-consciously recognizes, examines, and critiques the historical and cultural factors which have influenced the expression of Christian life among a given group of people. Contextual theology does not seek to be the universal expression of Christian truth for all people in all times and places, for it insists that no theological expression of the faith can be the best expression for all people. Rather, contextual theology seeks to express the truth of Christianity in a way which is suited to the thought patterns and cultural inheritance of a particular audience.

How an MA Programme Can Help

In order to facilitate the development of a consciously contextual post-Soviet protestant theology, our Masters of Arts programme seeks to expose students to the cultural and religious heritages (traditions) which have dramatically shaped Slavic Protestantism, but about which many Slavic protestants are ill-informed. (These include eastern orthodox mystical theology and the heritage of Russian philosophical and literary thought as well as western protestant theology.) Furthermore, we seek to demonstrate to students the influence of historical and cultural context on any expression of Christianity. In doing so, we hope to impress upon the each student the need to evaluate critically the factors which have influenced one's own theology and expression of Christian life. Finally, we seek to acquaint students with other self-consciously contextual approaches to theology, so as to give them tools and ideas with which to work in developing their own genuinely contextual theology. (Other contextual theologies to be examined include post-liberal narrative theology and liberation theology.) At this point, one might well ask why the enterprise of equipping students to develop contextual theologies for post-Soviet Protestantism requires the use of a western pedagogical tool (namely, the structure of a British MA programme).

There are several reasons why we believe that such a tool is appropriate and necessary for our purpose. 1. The educational system in the former Soviet Union is still dominated by Soviet methodologies which are singularly inappropriate for the task we are undertaking. (In fact, it has been said that the entire Soviet educational system was a travesty of contextualization.) The system focuses on the dispensing of universal truth by an authoritative teacher, and the task of the student is to accept and memorize this truth/information. The system does not build skills in evaluating and critiquing various influences on one's thought, skills which are essential to the development of contextual theologies. Therefore, it will generally not be helpful for our purposes for students to pursue advanced degrees in former-Soviet institutions. 2. The isolation of Soviet Protestantism during the Communist regime has left most Slavic protestants unaware of (and thus unable to evaluate) the contextual influences on their own expression of Christian life. Simply stated, they have been unaware of the way Christianity was being expressed in other contexts, and therefore have been unable to see the influences of their own context. In order to remedy this lack, it will be necessary to expose students to Christian thinking from other parts of the world, and a western tool such as a British MA programme will be helpful in doing this. 3. British MA programmes are specifically skills-based, rather than being content-based (as are North American MA programmes, for example). As a result, we believe that a British programme provides the best possible environment for developing the capacity to understand, evaluate, and utilize historical and cultural influences in the construction of contextual theology.

Key Elements of the Programme

Criteria for Success

Student success in the MA was defined according to the following criteria: 1. Evidence that the student recognizes the influence of historical and cultural context on all expressions of Christian theology 2. Evidence that the student recognizes the need for Christian faith to be expressed in ways which are culturally sensitive and appropriate to the context in which a given group of Christians will live and work. 3. Evidence that the student is able to identify in general the major contextual factors which have influenced the way eastern and western Christians typically express their theology and Christian practice. 4. Evidence that the student is able to identify in particular the major contextual factors which have influenced the way post-Soviet Christians (orthodox, catholic and protestant) typically express their theology and Christian practice. 5. Evidence that the student is able to evaluate contextual theological constructs in terms of their relatedness to the Christian tradition and their appropriateness to the context in which a given group of Christians will live and work. 6. Evidence that the student is able to express a significant aspect of the Christian message in a way which is both rigorously biblical and appropriate for a specific post- Soviet context. 7. Evidence that the student is able to conduct high-level academic research in a particular field (biblical studies, systematic theology, historical theology, etc.) and to relate this research to the demands of expressing the Christian faith in a contextually appropriate way.

Module Titles

1. Hermeneutical and contextual case studies in Scripture 2. Community and mission: A Christian imperative for post-Soviet contexts 3. Context and soteriology: The absolutizing of emphases in East and West 4. Selected contemporary theologies in context 5. Narrative theology and great Russian thinkers 6. Orthodox theology: Tradition and mysticism in context 7. Post-Soviet protestant ecclesiastical practices 8. Dissertation module

Overall Programme Objectives

1. Compare and critique various constructs of theology in their cultural contexts and posit other relevant theological constructs for the post-Soviet (and particularly Slavic) cultures. 2. Describe, analyse, appropriate, and apply to the development of contextual theologies selected relevant cultural heritages within the post-Soviet era. 3. Describe, analyse, appropriate, and apply to the development of contextual theologies selected relevant church heritages within the post-Soviet era, as he or she seeks to be sympathetic with the church's practices and beliefs. 4. Describe, analyse, appropriate, and apply to the

development of contextual theologies for the post-Soviet era selected relevant scholarly perspectives. 5. Employ proficiently various methods to carry out high-calibre research in selected academic and professional areas of study. 6. Present selected results of their research through appropriate-level publication in peer-review journals, scholarly works, or other media suitable to the professional context. 7. Organize and construct appropriate strategies for enabling others to participate in the process of both developing and applying contextualized theologies in either academic or professional settings. 8. Aid the learning of others through relevant forms of training that will impart vision to them and empower them in their chosen fields. 9. Work proficiently in both Russian and English in fulfilling the above objectives and, if appropriate, demonstrate suitable skills in the English language sufficient for advanced research.

Conclusion

The MA Programme in Contextual Theology has been developed to address one of the critical needs of post-Soviet Protestantism. We hope is that programmes of this type will serve to help the church to move beyond a theology either unconsciously influenced by its context or imitative of the West. Our goal is to equip the church to construct more intentionally a unique understanding of the Christian faith suited to its local setting, a genuinely contextual theology.

On Theologizing Theology within the Secular University

Gavin D'Costa

Dr. Gavin D'Costa is Reader at the Department of Theology and Religious Studies, Bristol University

Theology should be theologized. I will argue that theology needs to be prized free of its subservience to the enlightenment model of the university. Theologians are in Babylonian captivity. One way of noticing this Babylonian captivity is in the arguments that are conducted in the modern university about the role of theology. The view expressed by some scientific atheists (Richard Dawkins for example) is that theology has no place in the modern university. It is a vestige of a religious world and society which has long since crumbled and been discredited. It is a disservice to a modern research university to include such a subject in the curriculum. A similar voice is heard from some who teach in departments of Religious Studies, believing that a scientific, objective, rational study of 'religion', without any privilege being granted to any one religion, is the only intellectually respectable practice in the modern university. Donald Weibe is one such academic. Both Dawkins and Weibe have one presupposition in common, which I shall be calling into question: that there is such a thing as neutral objectivity in any mode of research, either science, Dawkins' own area, or religious studies, Weibe's own specialism.

However, in another sense I agree with Dawkins and Weibe's conclusions, but for very different reasons. What are these reasons? The first is that theology is indeed out of place within the modern liberal university, but this should not make theology defensive, but rather push theologians into arguing for a different type of university that would both support the proper way of studying theology (shorn of many Enlightenment assumptions about historical positivism, neutral studies, the unity of the faculties, rather than the current fragmentation). The second, is that religious studies, in such a revisioning of theology, would be integrated into theology, just as theology utilizes textual analysis from English, or historical critical methods from history, or feminist philosophies from France, or Marxist analysis in Latin America and now the world over.

Hence, I would be saying to Weibe that he is right; theology cannot be accommodated within his view of academic study, but that the *telos* of his academic discipline falls short of truth, as theology might understand the matter. Or to put it in another way, religious studies, from the point of view of theology, requires to be theologized for the fullness of its orientation to come into view.

In advance I apologise to all those who I am bound to offend, and ask them to consider that I am being pushed to summarise for the sake of brevity. So let me take you through a brief tour of theology, to highlight some points – first to show why, in fact, most theology in the universities is indeed religious studies, and that my clarion call in the title is not an act of aggression against religious studies, but more widely a criticism of the modern research university – Bristol included.

In what follows I want to show two things. First, the roots of the process of secularism are very complex and may have sources in pre-Christian philosophy as well as Christian intellectual history. Secularism is a natural outgrowth of trajectories within Christianity, whereby a false reality has been generated: an autonomous secular realm. Second, in so much as this process transformed the medieval university into the modern Enlightenment university, embodied in Berlin, with the Reformation intervening between, modernity has dictated the methods whereby theology has been studied. From queen of the sciences, integrating and harmonizing the different disciplines, theology has become a marginalized and contested discipline within liberal arts programmes.

To the first aim: For most of western European history the study and practice of theology was an ecclesial practice, and the university, as such, does not enter the narrative until around the twelfth century. After surveying the patristic period, Aidan Nichols writes that 'in the ancient Church there were almost no theological academies dedicated to the systematic study of the subject'. This does not mean that theology was in any way stifled. On the contrary, practicing bishops and monks, often educated in pagan academies, like Augustine, produced brilliant and important works, adopting a variety of genres that mark one of the high points of Christian theological development. In the early middle ages, the two major institutional locations for theology were the monasteries and convents, and the cathedral schools, the latter usually, but not always, open only to those desiring a religious life.

This site of production had a number of strengths and weaknesses. Its greatest strength was the unity of theology with prayer and practice. While some monastic theologians were little interested in life outside the monastery and the liberal arts of the classical world, many of its best theologians, such as Aelred, William of Auberive and Geoffrey of Auxerre utilized the disciplines and traditions of the pagan world, Christianizing them through this process. Jean Leclercq argues that this monastic setting allowed such theologians to more quickly discern the abuses in the employment of dialectics in *university* theological reflection, an employment that was soon to be a hallmark of university scholasticism. Leclerq goes so far as to say that scholastic university theology, being wedded to the form of disputation and dialectics, eventually 'lost contact with the life of prayer'.[1] This loss would eventually lead to the

[1] J. Leclercq, *The Love of Learning and the Desire for God: A Study of Monastic Culture*, Reprint ed. (Fordham University Press, 1982).

slow divorce between 'knowledge and love, science and contemplation, intellectual life and spiritual life' and it would then become necessary to invent mystical or spiritual theology, the worse for its separation from dogmatic theology. Furthermore, the monastic site of theology allowed a limited theological education to women in some of the convents, whereas the creation of the university established an exclusion of women from the institutions of theological learning.[2]

It has been noted that the convents were a 'refuge for female intellectuals, as the monastery was for the male. Although the majority of nuns were at best literate, most of the learned women of the Middle Ages – the literary, artistic, scientific, and philosophical stars were nuns'.[3] Such stars, bringing together many branches of learning in theological wisdom, were women like Roswitha of Gandersheim, Hildegard of Bingen and Herrad of Landsberg, all trained within mixed convents. Of course, whether women were admitted to the sacred discipline or not, it was nevertheless a *clerical* monopoly. The twelfth century saw theology moving out of the monastery and cathedral school into the university faculties of theology. By the thirteenth century, the University of Paris was ecclesiastically established, with what is often called the Magna Carta of the university, Gregory XI's bull *Parens Scientiarum* (1231). Soon, the new *studium generales*, the places of study open to all, for all things, took root across Europe, and through that, eventually into the new world.

Particularly significant about the scholastic theology that developed in the university, although neo-Augustinians and Scotists also flourished, were three characteristics. First, the disputation was the primary form of learning, dependent on dialectics. Hence, the questioning mode was privileged, although Leclercq's emphasis on disputation alone in his criticism of scholasticism conceals this massively confessional enterprise of Thomism. MacIntryre has insisted that Thomism was both confessional and dialectical.[4] Second, because it was assumed that nature perfects grace, and analogically nature reflects the creator, intellectual interest in the natural world was institutionally enshrined. This would both create the possibilities of the heights of Christian Humanism as well as lay the seeds for the carving out of the secular, an autonomous realm claiming freedom from religious intervention. Whether these theological categories are indeed responsible for secularism is a matter I shall touch on

---

[2] See C.W. Bynum, ***Holy Feast and Holy Fast: The Religious Significance of Food to Medieval Women*** (Berkeley and Los Angeles: University of California Press, 1987); C.W. Bynum, ***Docere Verbo Et Exemplo: An Aspect of Twelfth-Century Spirituality. Harvard Theological Monographs*** (Missoula, Montana: Scholars Press, 1979); C.W. Bynum, ***Jesus as Mother: Studies in the Spirituality of the High Middle Ages*** (Berkeley and Los Angeles: University of California Press, 1982).

[3] F. Gies and J. Gies, *Women in the Middle Ages* (New York: Thomas Y. Crowell, 1978), 65.

[4] A. MacIntyre, *Three Rival Versions of Moral Enquiry: Encyclopedia, Genealogy and Tradition* (Notre Dame, IN: University of Notre Dame Press, 1991), 201.

below. Third, the division of the faculties in the University of Paris generated complex cross-currents.

The Faculties were structured into the 'inferior': arts (made up of the *trivium*, where three roads meet, grammar, rhetoric, and logic; and the *quadrivium*, made up of arithmetic, music, geometry and astronomy), followed by the 'superior': canon law, medicine, and theology. The benefit of such division was the assumption that all the disciplines were founded on a common unifying principle: that creation was from God, ordered, for the good of man, and to be used as such. Hence all the disciplines were subject to theological unification, and sometimes theological correction. The latter asymmetry was not always fruitful, and sometimes misused. However, in the fragmentation of faculties also lay the seeds for the fragmentation of knowledge. Nevertheless, at the beginnings of the European university both those who taught and those who learnt in the university believed their task was in service to God, church, and society. They were not bound to academic accreditation by secular authorities. In thirteenth century Paris, intellectual theology was integrally a sociopolitical-religious affair. To speak of the sacred and secular in this context would obviously be anachronistic.[5]

Despite all these complex crosscurrents set in motion with the creation of the university, there are three important positive elements that followed from thirteenth century Paris. First, the university would be a place of considered disputation, a location for rational argument, embedded within a tradition, to flourish and develop in engagement with rival traditions. The latter is exemplified in the debate between the Augustinians and Thomists. A distorted fragment of this tradition is developed in the modern secular university, a place of rational discussion, without adequate attention to tradition specific forms of enquiry within which rational discussion ensues. Second, even though university theology was the preserve of male clerics, the location of theology in the university meant that eventually in the Enlightenment University, lay theological education could develop, which would also be gender inclusive. Third, theology was given a prime place in harmonizing and integrating the four faculties of Arts, Medicine and Law.

That this disciplinary unity was unilaterally established by the theologians, the other faculties being banned from speaking of God, was decidedly counterproductive in the long term, but at least the vision of a proper relation between the disciplines had become institutionally embedded. The Reformation was to shake the structures of university theology in two distinct ways. First, theology faculties, as universities, were now divided according to Protestant (with its increasing variations) and Catholic lines. Hence, ancient universities

---

5 H. Radshall, *The Universities in the Middle Ages*, New ed., 3 vols. (Oxford: Clarendonesp., 1963); S.C. Ferruolo, *The Origins of the University* (Stanford: Stanford University Press, 1985); A. B. Cobban, *The Medieval English Universities: Oxford and Cambridge to C.1500* (Aldershot: Scholar Press, 1988), 209-38.

such as Oxford and Cambridge, from their Catholic foundations, came to explicitly exclude Catholics, just as Catholic institutions excluded Protestants. When such exclusions were eventually repealed at Oxford and Cambridge, with exceptions for the Faculties of Divinity, it reflected the structural implementation of secularism, not an ecumenical renewal with an open Christian university. There were both advantages and problems with this Reformation divide. One such advantage, noted by MacIntyre, is that such 'exclusions' provided some of the necessary preconditions for the Thomistic revival and thereby for the reappropriation of Aquinas' dialectical enterprise.[6]

These exclusions allowed for both flowerings of the distinct Protestant and Roman Catholic theological traditions, even if the early Calvinist tradition remained essentially scholastic following Calvin's own Catholic tradition. It was Luther who was to steer the Reformation into a very different mould, with Catholicism only initially reacting defensively, and only in the modern period taking on and developing some of Luther's positive themes (theology as salvation, theology of the cross), while robustly rejecting the anti-metaphysical tradition generated from Luther. If these denominational universities had very mixed blessings, they both began to have something in common, which takes me to the second point. Nichols writes that 'perhaps the most lasting result of the period from 1500 to 1700 was the rise of theological specialization'.[7] This was a result of many factors: rapidly expanding knowledge, discoveries (by Europeans) of new worlds, the accelerated emergence of the natural sciences, and eventually, with the emergence of the middle classes in the nineteenth century, the growth of professionalism within the universities.[8]

But specialisms would have a huge effect on the internal disintegration of theology, mirroring the greater fragmentation of knowledge reflected (negatively) in the divisions of the faculties. At the beginning of the nineteenth century the University of Berlin was designed to reflect the 'research university' along the lines of the Enlightenment vision of education.[9] In this respect, it intentionally defined itself against the earlier model of *paideia* that had characterized earlier ecclesial forms of education (and pre-Christian Greek education as at Athens) and instead emphasized a critical, orderly, and disciplined science of research. That is, no texts or ways of reading them were to be seen as authoritative, either because of spiritual authority or traditions deeming them so. Rather, all texts were to be critically scrutinized, using methods that were accessible to all rational men, and methods that could allow the repeating of tests to authenticate of establish results. In this sense, theology,

---

[6] MacIntyre, *Three Rival*, 224.

[7] A. Nichols, *The Shape of Catholic Theology: An Introduction to Its Sources, Principles* (Collegeville: The Order of St. Benedict, Inc., 1991), 318.

[8] B.J. Bledstein, *The Culture of Professionalism. The Middle Class and the Development of Higher Education in America* (New York: W. W. Norton, 1976).

[9] D. Fallon, *The German University* (Boulder: Colorado Assoc. University Press, 1980).

whose authority rested on revelation, was an obvious problem for the University of Berlin and there was considerable controversy about its inclusion into the new research university. It was only through the genius of Schleiermacher that theology made it into the university, and on the grounds that it was important for professional training. Just as medicine and law were included into the university, the historical and philosophical study of theology were also justified, for they provided the materials for a theological training that was required for ministers of the church.

However, there were strong criticisms of theology from the very disciplines that it sought to ally itself to: history and philosophy. Kant, like Fichte after him, could only tolerate theology as the practical working out of the truths available in philosophy via universal reason in a transcendental mode (Kant), then via an idealist philosophy (Fichte). Later this would be replaced by a positivist historicist mode (Harnack and Strauss) and later still, by various other developments in philosophy (Marxism, feminism, postmodernism). The Enlightenment university began the process of translating theology into its own philosophical, natural scientific, or social analysis modalities. The Enlightenment *Wissenchaft* dictated to theology the preconditions and limits of its enquiry and also regulated its agenda. Both Kant and Fichte reserved pride of place for philosophy, not theology. The genealogical picture is extremely complicated, but there are two main points I wish to emphasise as an outcome of the above. First, the secularization of theology was a process that reached its culmination in the nineteenth century, and we now live in the shadow of the 'great reversal' embodied in the history of the Enlightenment, such that institutional university theology bears many of the marks of this secularized process.

The ascendancy of historical positivism also explains the inevitable rise of the history of religions school transferring its hermeneutical strategies designed for reading ancient texts to now interpret living traditional texts, the New Testament, but without reference to its traditional form of exegesis (the multiple senses of scripture), which also invoked the aid of the Holy Spirit for proper exegesis. In part, the historical positivist reading of theology would result in the emergence of 'religious studies'. Second, while various intellectuals within the university have constantly alerted theologians to this situation, the significance of this crisis in requiring a new type of university has been less fully explored. This is in part due to very pragmatic pressures: university culture in England and the United States is in deep recession, with funding ever tighter even in the Ivy League institutions. Departments of theology have been a major casualty, such that for theologians to argue for alternative universities might almost seem tragi-comedy, or better, farce. Without minimizing these pressures, it must be said that one of the reasons for this crisis in funding and support of university education is precisely because large numbers of the general public and the intelligentsia schooled in such institutions, can see very little use for the universities.

Apart from professional training (law, medicine, engineering and so on) and scientific research where results are tangible, produce revenue, and finance themselves, the Arts are seen increasingly as a luxury. This year, Charles Clark publicly said that the study of medieval texts was a luxury that could hardly be justified from public funding. This is hardly surprising, for when the university becomes part of the instrumentalist culture of modernity and the fragmentation of the disciplines is so complete, their importance and interrelation is not even debated by the education minister. Hence, to draw this story to a provisional conclusion, we have seen how theology started as part of the ecclesial practice within small communities of practice, then engaged with the great currents of Hellenistic philosophy, although not from any organized institutional base, but in an ad hoc manner. Later, in the monasteries and cathedral schools it was wedded to prayer and the practice of contemplation and love, and later it became established as the 'Queen of the sciences' in thirteenth century Paris, even if this synthesis was not always achieved well and the university emphasis on dialectics sometimes lost its ecclesial moorings.

The Reformation saw denominational flowerings, although perpetuated the scandal of disunity among Christians. However, in an increasingly secularised culture, theology was finally symbolically toppled (even if it had lost its power within the university much earlier) at the University of Berlin, so that it would eventually, if lucky, be part of the liberal arts, not a faculty on its own, or be eclipsed by religious studies. In a sentence: from Queen of the Sciences to the laughing stock of the Arts Faculty, nicely portrayed in the contemporary Catholic novelist, David Lodge's, modern city of Rummage.[10] And now, I am in a position to move to my suggestion regarding religious studies. But this also requires a narrative account of it in England and its problematic status, at least in my view. My contention is that Religious Studies in England adapted secular methodologies (positivist history and neutral enquirers) as key to the study of religion, contesting that it, not theology, was the proper subject to be embedded in the emerging modern university.

Clearly, while the contexts are very different, some of the points here will be applicable more widely. The Oedipal configuration of 'bed-fellow' and 'successor' is not random, for at one level religious studies explicitly claims to cohabit the academic territory with theology, but if taken seriously, implicitly (and sometimes explicitly) seeks its destruction for it must rightly and properly claim Christianity as its object of investigation, in the same manner as it claims Buddhism or Islam as its objects. Hence, at best, religious studies subconsciously desires to seize and control the academic territory regarding the 'divine' from theology. At worse, it explicitly seeks to destroy the albatross that drags it down, as a prominent religious studies supporter notes, the 'theological establishment is therefore, a problem in that it is a kind of conceptual albatross

[10] D. Lodge, *How Far Can You Go?* (Harmondsworth: Penguin, 1981); D. Lodge, *Paradise News* (London: Secker & Warburg, 1991).

around the neck of religious studies'. The increasing secularity of theology, both institutionally and methodologically, produced a situation where many felt that actually what existed in the practice of theology was the study of religion. Historical accidents meant that the religion so selected was Christianity. Furthermore, in the context of both England's multireligious nature, its colonial conquests, and the growth of Indology and Orientalism, many argued that religions other than Christianity should be taught. If the study of religion was an academic specialty, it seemed right and obvious that to limit the menu to Christianity was parochial to say the least. This trajectory was predictable in the Enlightenment's resistance to the particularity of Christian revelation.

Furthermore, in the period of the introduction of religious studies to the universities in the late sixties, students were increasingly from secularized backgrounds. The attraction of Buddhism and Hinduism to these consumers, aligned to the Romantic European idealization of these traditions, meant that the market was just right for Religious Studies. The final factor worth mentioning, and perhaps the most significant in the English context, was the introduction of an allegedly scientific, objective and academic method appropriate to the study of religion: phenomenology. It is no accident that the supporter of such a method in this country was also the founder of the first Department of Religious Studies in England, in Lancaster in 1967, and the author of the albatross statement quoted above. Smart proposed a method which definitely and distinctively should not and could not involve faith as its starting point. Faith as a starting point was unscientific and unscholarly, according to the canons then acceptable to the secular academy and the cultured despisers of theology.

Hence, the phenomenological method started with epoché or bracketing. Epoché meant the suspension of one's own beliefs, attitudes, and values, in order to avoid contaminating objective description with personal prejudice such as one's own personal religious commitments. It was allegedly only in this fashion that the enquirer could really get at the object of enquiry and understand it correctly, be it Hinduism, Buddhism or Christianity. However, the very notion of different 'religions' related to each other as species of common genus, was itself a seventeenth century invention, as Peter Harrison has so persuasively argued.[11] The construction of such a field ('religion') is a project that is partly located in the Enlightenment's refusal to acknowledge the particularity of Christian revelation. Consequently, there followed the creation of a single secular history whereby different religions were organized within the Enlightenment's own overarching narrative, rather than taking seriously the different organizations of time, space and history within the various religions.

---

[11] P. Harrison, *'Religion' and the Religions in the English Enlightenment* (Cambridge: Cambridge University Press, 1990), 417; W.C. Smith, *The Meaning and End of Religion* (New York: Macmillan, 1962); G. D'Costa, 'A Christian Reflection on Some Problems with Discerning "God" In the World Religions', *Dialogue and Alliance* 5:1 (1991).

Such taxonomy also failed to attend to the epistemological prerequisites required for comprehension specified by some of the religions under examination.

John Milbank makes an interesting connection between the growth of comparative religion in the discipline of religious studies and the assumption that all religions are equal paths to the one divine. He suggests this connection because in the very creation of the field of 'religion' there is an in-built assumption of different species of a common genus, and with this assumption, the idea that the common genus is our 'own' religion of which others are various manifestations. Milbank writes: The usual construals of religion as a genus, therefore, embody covert Christianizations, and in fact no attempt to define such a genus (or even, perhaps, delineation of an analogical field of 'family resemblances') will succeed, because no proposed common features can be found, whether in terms of belief or practice (gods, the supernatural, worship, a sacred community, sacred/secular division, etc.) that are without exceptions. The most viable, because most general definitions ('What binds a society together', and so forth) turn out to be so all-encompassing as to coincide with the definition of culture as such.[12] It is no chance coincidence that Smart's phenomenological methodology bears striking resemblance to Descartes' and Locke's stripping-down process to get to the foundations of knowledge; nor is its similarity to Hume's positivism insignificant. In one sense the new scientific methodology of religious studies that was emulated by theology in its attempt to remain within the academy was clearly a child of the Enlightenment.

Admittedly there has been much debate about Smart's model by practitioners of religious studies in England, but the point I wish to make is this. While the methodology and subject matter of religious studies in its institutional setting was increasingly successful (there are now a number of Religious Studies Departments, while prior to 1967 there were none), intellectually the presuppositions of Smart's approach are deeply problematic. Its problematic nature lies in its Enlightenment marriage to objectivity and scientific neutrality. Hence, and I must make this clear, my argument is in no way directed against the study of Buddhism and Hinduism and other religious traditions in the academic curriculum (far from it), and all the many skills required for such a study, but rather the assumptions about how such subjects are studied and how they are related to theology within the curriculum. In short, the manner in which they are often currently studied serves modernity's agenda, whereas if religious studies were fully theologized, we would have two important outcomes. First, the proper horizons of theology would be embraced: that is all creation. Second, the question of the meaning and purpose of these religions, both from their own internal organic viewpoint and from the

---

[12] J. Milbank, 'The End of Dialogue', in *Christian Uniqueness Reconsidered*, ed. Gavin D'Costa (New York: Orbis, 1990).

Christian viewpoint, could be properly pursued. This would also mean that Christianity's public voice could be thoughtfully sharpened. There are important objections against epoché as a method and subsequently all that follows from it.[13]

As mentioned above, the success of the phenomenological method was in part due to the social episteme which looked favourably upon such an enterprise. Such consensus, though certainly not unanimous, is coming to an end, and the episteme is shifting in our times, in a period that is often described as 'postmodern'. The natural and social sciences have tended to move away from the positivist assumptions they both shared at the turn of the century – and which were imitated by Smart's religious studies. Both the former disciplines have tended to eschew objectivity and neutrality, and increasingly acknowledge that the role of the investigator and her sociopolitical location is crucial to the production of knowledge. One need only look at the work of Thomas Kuhn in science, Alasdair MacIntyre in philosophy, Bernard McGrane in anthropology, to see that this model is deeply flawed. But the flaw needs to be better focused upon, as it is also one of the great achievements of modernity that it has noted this flaw.

To examine this a little more, I turn to MacIntyre's work. Alasdair MacIntyre has argued persuasively against the possibility of neutral enquiry or a universal rationality, and has tried to show the tradition-specific nature of all moral and philosophical intellectual enquiry. John Horton and Susan Mendus provide a lucid summary of MacIntyre's project in its critical stance: The Enlightenment project which has dominated philosophy during the past three hundred years promised a conception of rationality independent of historical and social context, and independent of any specific understanding of man's nature or purpose. But not only has that promise in fact been unfulfilled, the project is itself fundamentally flawed and the promise could never be fulfilled. In consequence, modern moral and political thought are in a state of disarray from which they can be rescued only if we revert to an Aristotelian paradigm, with its essential commitment to teleology, and construct an account of practical reason premised on that commitment.[14]

MacIntyre's first book had many failings, the major one, in my opinion, being that its Aristotelianism required fuller explication and grounding in a community of practice (as opposed to an idealized past, based on heroic violence, as Gillian Rose so pertinently points out), from which it might create an alternative society of virtue.[15] This was slightly remedied in his second work,

---

[13] A.B. da Silva, *The Phenomenology of Religion as a Philosophical Problem* (Lund: Gleerup, 1982).

[14] J. Horton and S. Mendus, eds., *After MacIntyre: Critical Perspectives on the Work of Alasdair MacIntyre* (Oxford: Polity Press, 1994), 3.

[15] G. Stout, *Ethics after Babel: The Languages of Morals and Their Discontents* (Cambridge: James Clarke, 1988), 191-220.

Whose Justice? Which Rationality? (1988), but would have to await *Three Rival Versions* (1990) to be most fully explicated. This grounding drove him into Roman Catholic Thomism, as the only intelligible intellectual moral position on offer. *Three Rival Versions* finally takes more seriously the social political context which nourishes such practices: the church. *Three Rival Versions* continues MacIntyre's project and his final chapter addresses the question of the university specifically. MacIntyre argues that western European society is confronted by three rival versions of moral enquiry, each with its own epistemological, ontological, ethical and methodological assumptions. While they may seem incommensurable, MacIntyre also seeks to show that there may be the possibility of a historically narrated rational debate between them, such that one might emerge the superior. What are the three rival versions?

There is of course the Enlightenment project, which MacIntyre here calls the 'Encyclopaedic', for he characterises it in its embodiment in the ninth edition of the *Encyclopaedia Britannica*. The second tradition, which has always been on the horizon of MacIntyre's project, is that of the 'Genealogical', or the postmodern, typified by Nietzsche's *Genealogy of Morals*. The postmodern is parasitic upon the Enlightenment. Nietzsche was inevitable, given the irresolvable lacunae within the Enlightenment project which replaced the *telos* of the common good with the formal requirements of human freedom. Nietzsche saw that there could be no real foundation for ethics in this stance and consequently celebrated the will to power, which was always the repressed truth within the Enlightenment matrix. For MacIntyre's own argument to work, he develops a further critique of the postmodern or Nietzschean Genealogical 'tradition' which focuses on its internal contradictions regarding the continuities of a narrative self.[16] In the final chapter, MacIntyre calls for a post-liberal university. He notes three characteristics vital to the pre-modern university, essential to healthy intellectual enquiry. First, the emergence of agreement upon standards of rational justification through the work of enquiry itself, not only in the explicit discussion of the philosophers but also through the intellectual practice of professors of mathematics and history and law and theology.[17]

MacIntyre recognizes that such agreements are never static, but some shared consensus is important. Second, were 'enforced exclusions from the universities and colleges of points of view too much at odds with the consensus underpinning both enquiry and education'.[18] Of course, this system led to losses, and even grave injustices. MacIntyre bemoans the systematic injustice spawned, most notably towards Jews. Nevertheless, such exclusion was also the precondition of great success in building traditions of enquiry, and as

---

[16] J. Milbank, *Theology and Social Theory: Beyond Secular Reason* (Oxford: Blackwell Publishing, 1990), 278-326.

[17] MacIntyre, *Three Rival*, 223.

[18] MacIntyre, *Three Rival*, 223.

MacIntyre wryly notes, the natural sciences have always best succeeded with 'quiet, informal, characteristically unstated policies of enforced exclusion, unacknowledged and unnoticed except by sociologists of science'.[19] Third, a counterpart to such exclusions was 'the use of preferments and promotions to ensure that upholders of the consensus, including those who extended, corrected, and otherwise improved the standards of rational justification embodied in it, occupied the relevant professorial chairs'.[20] Again, he is fully aware of 'error and abuse', but notes that this sort of abuse is present in every system.

MacIntyre concludes, echoing my earlier arguments:

> For those who require sufficient resolution of fundamental disagreements in morality and theology in order that rational enquire in those areas may proceed, the liberal university can provide no remedy. And by providing no remedy it has successfully excluded substantive moral and theological enquiry from its domain.... the dethronement of moral philosophy, like the dethronement of theology in an earlier period, would in any case have deprived the curriculum of any but pragmatic principles of ordering.[21]

In one sense moral philosophy had already lost the plot with the dethronement of theology, a point that takes MacIntyre's three volumes to reach, but the significance of this loss of ordering, vision, and orientation is all important. It is precisely why there is no ability to argue for the 'flourishing of the whole', and a Charles Clark can actually represent 'education'. MacIntyre finally makes clear the implication of his proposals in seeing the real plurality, apparently sought after by liberal moderns, might best be promoted by 'rival universities':

> each modelled on, but improving upon, its own best predecessors, the Thomist perhaps upon Paris in 1272, the genealogist upon Vincennes in 1968 [and one might add, the modern, upon Berlin in 1810]. And thus the wider society would be confronted with the claims of rival universities, each advancing its own enquiries in its own terms and each securing the type of agreement necessary to ensure the progress and flourishing of its enquiries by its own set of exclusions and prohibitions, formal and informal. But then also required [sic] would be a set of institutionalized forums in which the debate between rival types of enquiry was afforded rhetorical expression.[22]

This conclusion, and MacIntyre's reasons for arriving at it, account for my extended attention to his work. There are two particular intersections between MacIntyre's and my own argument that I would like to highlight. First, religious studies, as I have been charting it above, is part of the Encyclopaedic

[19] MacIntyre, *Three Rival*, 225.
[20] MacIntyre, *Three Rival*, 224.
[21] MacIntyre, *Three Rival*, 227.
[22] MacIntyre, *Three Rival*, 234.

tradition and is properly located within that mode of enquiry. In this sense its murderous Oedipal desire towards theology can now be located within a wider picture. Theology must rightly contest religious studies' autonomous existence and its claim to objective production, although any sensible theologian would also recognize that there are invaluable skills, tools, methods and insights present within the phenomenological approach of Smart's religious studies. The only point I am contesting is Smart's epistemological claims for religious studies. It is not an objective and dispassionate methodology by which to approach 'religions', but a highly biased and historically and philosophically situated enterprise. Second, MacIntyre's material account lacks attention to the intellectual traditions of enquiry within other religions. Rather than MacIntyre's isolation of three traditions of enquiry (liberal modernity, parasitic genealogical criticism, and neo-Thomism), each requiring their own institutions of learning as their conceptions of education vary so profoundly (even if genealogy can only exist parasitically on the other two and in this sense, could not exist on its own), there are good reasons to consider further traditions for institutional developments within the formal, rather than material, terms of MacIntyre's discussion. Indeed, this very point has been made by a sympathetic Muslim critic of MacIntyre's, Muhammad Legenhausen. He notes Islam's relationship to the Aristotelian tradition upon which MacIntyre is so dependent, and therefore criticizes MacIntyre's inexplicable omission of Islam in the debate.

Furthermore Legenhausen, writing in Iran, also suggests that Islam can account for the aporia within MacIntyre's argument in *After Virtue*, whereby MacIntyre's espousal of the necessity of small sectarian communities to counter barbarianism, after the order of St. Benedict, fails entirely to engage with the problem of nation states that MacIntyre identifies as one of the roots of the malaise. Susan Mendus and John Horton make the same point: 'Moreover, given the importance which MacIntyre attaches to the social embeddedness of thought and enquiry, his largely negative view of modernity continually threatens to undermine any attempt to root his positive proposals in the contemporary world of advanced industrial societies'. According to Legenhausen, Islam, on the other hand, is able to offer a theocratic solution, allegedly avoiding both 'nationalism and liberalism', an alternative that is 'not taken seriously by Western theorists'.[23] Hence, Legenhausen takes up MacIntyre's critique of modernity, but points to the same weakness located by Horton and Mendus within MacIntyre's alternative, and at that point thereby commends Islam. In institutional terms, given MacIntyre's premises, this would amount to an argument for an Islamic university.

I have strayed from the theologizing of religious studies to the theologizing of the university, but I have intentionally strayed to make clear the context of

[23] M. Legenhausen, 'Book Review of Whose Justice? Which Rationality?', *Al-Tawhid* 14:2 (1997), 169. See also H.H. Bilgrami and S.A. Ashraf, *The Concept of an Islamic University* (Cambridge: Hodder & Stoughton/The Islamic Academy, 1985), 163-69.

my overall argument. I should register a couple of points before concluding. First, I am well aware that in England the Smart model has come under considerable criticisms from academics who classify themselves as doing Religious Studies. Second, Religious Studies as practiced, incorporates many methodologies and strategies, often stemming from postmodern currents that are not afraid of declaring themselves: semiotic, political liberative and feminist strategies are popular. Third, I have not had time to engage with this huge plurality within religious studies in what I have presented here, but venture to suggest (which I try to unpack in one of my books) that these different strategies can be located within modernity's and postmodernity's grand narratives, and in this sense alone, I still argue for a theologized form of religious studies.

Let me recall the second step of my argument. Religious studies was born into English universities: partly because of the anachronism of theology being located within the secular academy; partly due to the search for scientific and objective ways of carrying out research in religions to avoid theological sectarianism (but nevertheless creating another form); and to gain the approval of the secular academy (which has, in many other disciplines, moved on). Put together with part one of my argument, the cumulative case will require, if it is accepted, at least one of three possible responses, only the third of which I support. One would be to abolish both theology and religious studies departments altogether and integrate them into history, literature, politics and so on. On secular grounds, this seems to be logical and possibly inevitable. Second, one could rename theology and religious studies the historical critical study of religion and carry on with what went on previously. On secular grounds this option is attractive for two reasons. First, no hermeneutical privilege is given to any one religion in the study of 'religions'. Second, the world is full of religions and therefore justifies a field related to this social reality. Clearly, both these options are not attractive to theology as presented here. Or thirdly, one might allow specific starting points to flourish, label them clearly, and allow them to interact. Within this third option, many different models are possible.

My own specific theological option would be to argue for a Roman Catholic University or in England, a Christian university within a pluralist academy on the lines advanced by Alastair MacIntyre.

Is Missiology an Academic Discipline?

Jan A.B. Jongeneel

Dr. Jan A.B. Jongeneel is Professor of Missiology at the University of Utrecht, in the Netherlands.

Introduction

The subject-matter of this contribution – whether missiology can be regarded as an academic discipline – is a serious question: both in Europe, the U.S.A., and elsewhere. Before I outline this question, I deal with the general problem of the relation between 'theological studies' and 'religious studies' which since the nineteen-sixties has already been discussed by many scholars; because, in my view, the special problem of missiology as an academic discipline cannot be separated from the general problem of whether both Christian theology and religious studies are academic disciplines. Therefore, I include a reflection on the question of whether missiology as a discipline belongs to theological studies, to religious studies, or to both.

However, the main question of this paper is still: does missiology qualify itself as an academic discipline? I start with a terminological observation: what is the meaning and background of the terms 'mission' and 'missiology'? Then, I refer to the contemporary debate on the relation between 'theological studies' and 'religious studies'. Thereafter, I sketch briefly the history of the position which missiology as a discipline has received in western universities in the past and recent past. In addition, I discuss both the division of missiology into sections, or parts, and the question of whether each of these sections of missiology can be treated as 'academic' in the proper sense of the word. Finally, a conclusion will be drawn. This conclusion will make clear whether all sections of missiology as a discipline and missiology as such, can, or must, be regarded as 'academic'.

Terminology

Missiology is the discipline which deals with 'mission' as its subject-matter. The term 'mission' – as a technical term – was coined by the Jesuits. Ignatius of Loyola (1491-1556), the founder of the *Societas Jesu*, stated that all members of the Society must be willing to be sent to their special fields, i.e. to their 'divisions' or 'missions'. He interpreted the term 'missions' as both the 'destinations' and the 'territories' to which the Jesuits are, or will be, sent. Thereafter, this term is also used to convey in language both 'going' to the territories involved and the 'tasks' to be performed at the places of destination.

Other Roman Catholics and, thereafter, most Protestants have adopted this terminology, replacing older terms.[1]

Today, every missiologist uses the term 'mission'. However, scholars differ in their definitions of 'mission'. Here, I only quote the broad definition of the Lutheran missiologist James A. Scherer in the U.S.A.: 'the total activity of the church in preaching, teaching, healing, nurturing Christian communities, and witnessing to the kingdom, including advocacy of justice and service to humanity'.[2] The term 'missiology' is rather new. It was coined by the Dutch Jesuit Ludwig J. van Rijckevorsel in 1915.[3] Thereafter, it was frequently used by Roman Catholic scholars. In the beginning, Protestants vehemently criticized this term. The Frenchman Raoul S.P. Allier, for instance, declared in his review of the Report of the Sixth Missiological Week at Louvain (1928): 'I cannot approve of the word *missiology*, which, being half Latin and half Greek, has a barbarous appearance. Its structure is as bad as that of *sociology*, and has the same defects. This unnatural marriage of Latin and Greek hurts one's ears'.[4] After the Second World War, however, Protestants developed a more positive attitude.

Today, both Roman Catholic and protestant scholars accept the term 'missiology' as the best one to describe their discipline, replacing older terms such as 'the theory of mission' (Ger.: *Missionstheorie*), 'the science of mission' (Ger.: *Missionswissenschaft*), 'evangelistic theology' (Ger.: *Evangelistik*), etc. However, they disagree in their definitions of this discipline. Here, I only offer my own definition: Missiology is the academic discipline which – from a philosophical, empirical, and theological point of view – reflects upon the history, theory and practice of (Christian) world mission as a means for both preaching the gospel, healing the sick and casting out 'evil spirits' (active in idolatry and immorality), for the glory of God and the well-being of all human beings.[5]

Theological and Religious Studies

Since the establishment of theological faculties in some European state universities and private universities, Old Testament, New Testament and Church History are taught as academic disciplines. After the Second World

---

[1] J.A.B. Jongeneel, *Philosophy, Science, and Theology of Mission in the 19th and 20th Centuries: A Missiological Encyclopedia* (I. Frankfurt am Main etc.: 1995), 58-61.

[2] J.A. Scherer, *Gospel, Church, and Kingdom: Comparative Studies in World Mission Theology* (Minneapolis: Augsburg Publishing House, 1987), 244.

[3] L.J. van Rijckevorsel, *Missie en missieactie* (Nijmegen: 1917).

[4] R.S.P. Allier, 'Book Review Of: L'âme Des Peuples À Évangéliser: Compte-Rendu De La Sixième Semaine De Missiologie De Louvain (1928) ', *International Review of Missions* XVIII (1929), 282.

[5] Jongeneel, *Philosophy*, 64.

War, this situation has changed. Here and there, departments of religious studies have been established: either in the faculties of theology or in the faculties of arts. Today, we can observe that some faculties of theology have been transformed into departments of religious studies. This new trend must be connected with the process of secularization, on the one hand, and the emancipation of the non-Christian religions in the western world, on the other. Christian faith is no longer normative in western universities, their faculties of theology included.

In Canada and the U.S.A., Arvind Sharma has thoroughly discussed the relationship between theological and religious studies. He constructed the difference between both fields as follows: Theology starts by accepting the *beliefs as true per se* and then proceeds to wherever the subsequent discussion might lead. Religious studies start by accepting the beliefs as true or meaningful in the eyes of the believer *a*nd then proceeds to wherever the subsequent investigation might lead.[6] I differ from Sharma (Faculty of Religious Studies, McGill University, Montreal, Canada) about the nature of this subject matter. In my view, the difference does not lie in the *acceptance* of the truth of belief systems: 'true per se' or 'true in the eyes of the believer'; it lies in the *role* which a scholar plays: personal commitment or engagement, or not. Therefore, I define theological and religious studies as follows: Theology is methodological commitment or '*engagement*' (of the theologian as 'believer') in the object of study. Religious studies are methodological distance to the object of study. Sharma thinks in terms of institutions (faculties of theology versus departments of religious studies); whereas I start from the position of the individual scholar. I take into account that, on the one hand, scholars of Old Testament, New Testament, and church history in theological faculties can reflect and act as the scholars in the departments of religious studies do; and, on the other hand, scholars in the department of religious studies can be, outside their departments, committed theologians.

For instance, the great phenomenologist of religion, Gerardus van der Leeuw (1890-1950), was a great theologian as well. I can illustrate my own view by referring to the world of football: the (Christian) theologian can be compared with a football player who writes his own report on the match for his own club; whereas a practitioner of religious studies can be compared with the reporter who does not play in the match. According to me, we need both the view of the committed football-player and the view of the so-called 'neutral' observer who distantly looks at the match, i.e. who does not personally take part in the match. As a missiologist, I go one step further than Sharma: religious studies are fundamentally one, but theological studies are fundamentally plural. There is Christian theology; and there is, at the same time, a large variety of non-Christian theologies. The story of each football-match is threefold: it is (1) the

[6] A. Sharma, 'On the Distinction between Religious Studies and Theological Studies', *The Council of Societies for the Study of Religion Bulletin* XXVI:3 (1997), 50-51.

story of the outsider who is not a member of one of the two teams involved in the match; and (2) the conflicting stories of (2a) the winner and (2b) the loser (assuming that there is a winner and a loser).

Comparably, we have the following positions in theological and religious studies: 1. the story of the distant scholar(s) of religious studies; 2a. the story of the committed Christian theologian(s), the committed Christian missiologist(s) included; and 2b. the story of the committed non-Christian theologian(s) who contest Christian theology in general and Christian missiology in particular. In conclusion: 'religious studies' are studies done by scholars who deal 'at distance' with religious phenomena; whereas 'theological studies' are studies done by scholars who are 'committed' to i.e. 'engaged' in the religious phenomena which they are teaching and researching. The sources of this commitment, or 'engagement', differ from one theologian to the other: some start from a Christian point of view, and others from non-Christian viewpoints. Theological studies do not exclude religious studies; and the other way around. A (good) practitioner of theological studies can also be a (good) scholar in religious studies.

Missiology as a Discipline in the University: Historical Observations

Missiology is mainly taught in theological colleges and seminaries which are affiliated to churches, and not affiliated to universities. However, there are exceptions to this rule. These exceptions – mainly in Europe – are very important because they largely determine the academic nature of missiology. In universities, missiology is a relatively new discipline. As an independent 'academic' discipline, it originates from the second half of the nineteenth century. Before that time, some professors used to teach mission in the framework of other disciplines. For instance, Gisbertus Voetius (1589-1676), the founder of Utrecht University, taught mission as a part of the so-called *theologia elenctica*, i.e. the theology which refutes the arguments of the infidels (i.e. the adherents of non-Christian religions), the heretics, and the schismatics. The first full-time chair of missiology was established in Edinburgh (1867).

Alexander Duff (1806-1878),[7] 'the pioneer of missionary education',[8] became the first professor in this chair, known as the chair of 'evangelistic theology'. The first chair of missiology in Germany was established in Halle (1896). Gustav Warneck (1834-1910) was appointed as the first holder of this chair. He became the first full-time professor of 'the science of missions' (Ger.: *Missionswissenschaft*) in Germany. He never served as a missionary abroad but he had a son who, from 1892 to 1906, worked as a missionary in Indonesia: Johannes Warneck (1867-1944). The real 'founder' of missiology as an

[7] A. Duff, 'Evangelistic Theology: An Inaugural Address Delivered in the Common Hall of the New College, Edinburgh, on Thursday, 7th November 1867', (Edinburgh: 1868).
[8] W. Paton, *Alexander Duff: Pioneer of Missionary Education* (London: 1923).

academic discipline was not Alexander Duff, who for a long time served in India, but the theorist Gustav Warneck, who never worked outside Europe.[9] Warneck wrote the famous handbook *Evangelische Missionslehre*[10] which was instrumental in shaping not only protestant missiology but also Roman Catholic missiology.[11]

Here, I cannot tell the whole story of the acceptance of missiology in European universities as a discipline in its own right. In order to know this history, one can read the two volumes concerned with the Norwegian scholar, Olav G. Mykelbust:[12] His story, nation by nation, is, as far as Protestantism until 1950 is concerned, rather extensive. He makes it very clear that missiology, in the course of one century, became an accepted discipline in many universities. However, since the nineteen-sixties (decolonization, growing secularization, immigration of both Muslims and the adherents of other non-Christian religions), serious questions have been raised as to whether missiology is really 'academic'; and whether this discipline has links with religious studies. Many experts in the field are inclined to connect missiology with theological studies alone. But I regard their view as very questionable. My personal view of this subject is related to my concept of missiology as a many-sided discipline.

Therefore, I raise and discuss the question of whether all sections, or parts, of missiology as a discipline belong to theological studies, to religious studies, or to both; and whether they can all be strictly treated as 'academic'.

The Three Sections of Missiology as a Discipline

In his inaugural address at Edinburgh (1868), Alexander Duff dealt with the name, nature, and task of 'evangelistic theology'. However, he did not offer a division of this discipline into two or more sections. Gustav Warneck started his voluminous missiological handbook (1892-1903) with an introductory chapter; thereafter, he divided it into three parts: 1. the basis (*begründung*) of mission; 2. The agencies (*organe*) of mission; and 3. the enterprise (*betrieb*) of mission. This division, however, is not a tripartite division of missiology as a discipline but a tripartite division of its subject-matter. Warneck not only offered the above-mentioned division of the subject-matter but also made a

[9] D. Becker and A. Feldtkeller, eds., *Es begann in Halle…: Missionswissenschaft von Gustav Warneck bis heute* (Erlangen, 1997).

[10] G. Warneck, *Evangelische Missionslehre: Ein Missionstheoretischer Versuch*, 3 vols. (Gotha, 1892-1903).

[11] J. Schmidlin, *Einführung in die Missionswissenschaft* (zweite Aufl. Münster in Westfale: 1925).

[12] O.G. Myklebust, *The Study of Missions in Theological Education: An Historical Inquiry into the Place of World Evangelisation in Western Protestant Ministerial Training with Particular Reference to Alexander Duff's Chair of Evangelistic Theology* (I. Oslo: 1955), 158-242.

formal division. In his own missiological journal, *Allgemeine Missions-Zeitschrift*,[13] he presented the following tripartite structure of missiology as a discipline: 1. mission history (*missionsgeschichte*); 2. Mission theory (*missionstheorie*); and 3. Mission apologetics (*missionsapologetik*). The Dutch missiologist François E. Daubanton (1853-1920) is one of the main supporters and critics of Warneck.

On the other hand, he agreed with Warneck that missiology has 'mission history' and 'mission theory' as sections. On the other hand, he disagreed with Warneck because he did not treat mission apologetics as part of missiology; but, rather, as a part of apologetics.[14] Daubanton did not use subject-matters – the basis, the agencies, and the enterprise of mission (cf. Warneck) – as a criterion to divide the chapters of his handbook. After two introductory chapters, he wrote six chapters on 'the science of mission' (Dutch: *zendingswetenschap*) in which the following six academic subjects are dealt with: 1. the structure of the science of mission; 2. the name of the science of mission; 3. the history of the science of mission; 4. the place of the science of mission in the theological curriculum; 5. the science of mission and the so-called 'auxiliary sciences' (ethnology, linguistics, and religious studies); and 6. the methodology of the science of mission. In other words: Daubanton did not concentrate on the who, what, when, and how of Christian mission (cf. Warneck's handbook), but on the who, what, when, and how of mission studies. In line with my predecessor Daubanton, I adopt a formal way of doing mission studies. As I honour Warneck as the founder of material mission studies, so I honour Daubanton as the father of formal mission studies. Thomas Ohm,[15] Johannes Verkuyl,[16] and many other authors of missiological handbooks follow Warneck in doing mission studies with a concentration on the subject-matter; but Schmidlin, Hilko W. Schomerus,[17] André V. Seumois,[18] Walter Holsten,[19] Angel Santos Hernandez,[20] and Alphonsus J.M. Mulders[21] follow Daubanton in doing these studies with a concentration on the 'form', or 'structure', of the discipline.

---

[13] G. Warneck, 'Zur apologetischen Bedeutung der Heidenmission', *Allgemeine Missions-Zeitschrift* XVII; XXXIV (1890 & 1907).

[14] F.E. Daubanton, *Prolegomena van protestantsche zendingswetenschap* (Utrecht: 1911), 218-23.

[15] Th. Ohm, *Machet zu Jüngern alle Völker: Theorie der Mission* (Freiburg im Breisgau: 1962).

[16] J. Verkuyl, *Contemporary Missiology: An Introduction* (Grand Rapids: 1978).

[17] H.W. Schomerus, *Missionswissenschaft* (Leipzig: 1935).

[18] A.V. Seumois, *Introduction À La Missiologie* (Schöneck- Beckenried: 1952).

[19] W. Holsten, *Das Kerygma und der Mensch: Einführung in die Religions- und Missionswissenschaft* (München: 1953).

[20] A.S. Hernandez, *Misionologia: problemas introductorios y ciencias auxiliares.* (Santander: 1961).

[21] A.J.M. Mulders, *Missiologisch bestek: inleiding tot de katholieke missiewetenschap* (Hilversum-Antwerpen: 1962).

Neither the handbook of Warneck nor that of one of the above-mentioned scholars who did mission studies formally has been translated into English. In addition, it must be stated that no American, British, or South African missiologist (David J. Bosch included) produced a formal missiological handbook. I disagree with the tripartite division of missiology which is offered by Warneck. In my view, the apologetics of mission, or missionary apologetics, is certainly not the third section of mission studies; it is – to use Warneck's terms – a part of 'the theory of mission'. In addition: the terms 'mission history' and 'mission theory', which are used by both Warneck and Daubanton, are too narrow; they must be replaced by the terms 'the science of mission' and 'the theology of mission' respectively.

My division of missiology into three sections is the result of a thorough dialogue with the following disciplines: 1. The philosophy of religion (*religionsphilosophie*); 2. Religious studies, or the science of religion (*religionswissenschaft*); and 3. The theology of religion (*theologia religionum*; *religionstheologie*). Therefore, I divide missiology into the following three sections: 1. The philosophy of mission (*missionsphilosophie*); 2. The science of mission (*missionswissenschaft*), or empirical mission studies; and 3. The theology of mission (*missionstheologie*). In my view, the discipline 'mission history' (Warneck and Daubanton) is a section of 'the science of mission'; whereas 'the theory of mission' (Warneck and Daubanton) can be equated with 'the theology of mission'. So far, there is still some kind of similarity to the views of Warneck and Daubanton. For the rest, however, the difference prevails. The section 'the philosophy of mission' is wanting in the handbooks of Warneck and Daubanton. But this section is fundamental for mission studies as an academic discipline. I explain each of these three sections separately. I start with the 'the philosophy of mission(s)' (*missionsphilosophie*). This discipline belongs to both missiology and the philosophy of religion (*religionsphilosophie*). Its history started in 1828, when William Orme in the U.S.A. coined this term.[22]

Thereafter, most Anglo- Saxon scholars equated it with 'the theory of mission'. For instance, Donald A. McGavran[23] offered the following definition: 'An arrangement of convictions or theories about "what mission correctly is" we call a philosophy of missions'. Fundamental objections must be made to his use of this term. The words 'of mission(s)' in the term 'the philosophy of mission(s)' must not be understood as a subjective genitive, but as an objective genitive. Therefore, the philosophy of mission is not at all a philosophy developed by mission boards and missiologists (cf. McGavran), but a philosophy which reflects upon the nature of mission as a religious phenomenon. The philosophy of mission, defined as 'the logical study of missionary and missiological concepts, arguments and language', is not at all

---

[22] Myklebust, *The Study*, 358.

[23] D.A. McGavran, *How Churches Grow* (New York: New York: Friendship, 1959), 67.

identical with 'the theory of mission' (cf. McGavran), or 'the theology of mission'. It just has the task to reflect reasonably, that is critically, upon mission, and upon its theory as well. As the philosophy of religion reflects critically upon the nature of religion, so the philosophy of mission reflects rationally upon the nature of mission: both the nature of the Christian mission and the nature of the mission of non-Christian religions, ideologies, and worldviews (*weltanschauungen*). Secondly, I regard 'the science of mission(s)' (*missionswissenschaft*) as that discipline which belongs to both missiology and the science of religion (*religionswissenschaft*). In 1832, this term was coined by the German encyclopaedist Johann T.L. Danz. Thereafter, it became very popular. Many scholars – especially in Germany, Scandinavia, and the Netherlands – have used it as the over-arching term. In the nineteen-sixties, however, it was replaced by the term 'missiology'. Then, many scholars began to equate 'the science of mission' with 'missiology'. But the term 'missiology' is broader than the term 'the science of mission'.

'Science of mission' must be set aside for the empirical part of mission studies, or missiology. As the philosophy of mission is not limited to a critical reflection on the nature of the Christian mission – over against the nature of the mission of the non-Christian religions, ideologies, and worldviews – so the science of mission includes the empirical study of both the Christian mission and the Muslim mission, the Buddhist mission, Communist propaganda, etc. Finally, I consider 'the theology of mission(s)' (*missionstheologie*) as that discipline which belongs to both missiology and the theology of religion (*religionstheologie* or in Latin, *theologia religionum*). Gustav Warneck (1877) was the first scholar to advocate this term. Thereafter, Anglo-Saxons followed: George Smith,[24] *et al.* However, this term only became popular in the twentieth century: especially after the Second World War. In fact, it replaces the older term 'the theory of mission(s)' which was introduced in 1830 into the theological curriculum by the German encyclopaedist Friedrich E.D. Schleiermacher (1768-1834). Protestant missiologists were more inclined to adopt this new term than Roman Catholic missiologists.

In the end, however, most Roman Catholic missiologists also used it. Some scholars who developed 'a theology of mission' emphasize the biblical side (cf. biblical theology of mission), others the ecclesiastical side (cf. ecclesiastical theology of mission), the corporate side (cf. theology of mission related to mission agencies), or the individual side (cf. individual theology of mission). In essence, the theology of mission is not an empirical but a normative discipline. As the theology of religion deals normatively with all religions – from a Christian perspective – so the theology of mission deals normatively with all missions: both the Christian mission and the non-Christian missions – from a Christian point of view. The theology of religion and, therefore, the theology of

[24] G. Smith, *Short History of Christian Missions from Abraham and Paul to Carey, Livingstone, and Duff* (Edinburgh: 1884), 4-6.

mission is an integral part of Christian (systematic and practical) theology. I observe that many scholars – both in the West and in the non-western world – have reduced missiology to the theology of mission. They have the support of such great theologians and missiologists as Karl Barth (1886-1968) and Hendrik Kraemer (1888-1965). On the one hand, their concentration on what really matters in mission and mission studies are very helpful. On the other hand, their narrowing of the scope of mission studies is frustrating.

Although both Barth and Kraemer taught at European state universities, they support willy nilly the view of all those people who regard missiology as a discipline which must be taught only in theological colleges and seminaries. The ultimate significance of the theology of mission must be acknowledged but not at the cost of the philosophy of mission and/or the science of mission. Each of the three sections of missiology has its own rights and its own responsibilities.

The Academic Nature of the Three Sections of Missiology

I start the discussion of the academic nature of missiology as a discipline with a reflection on its three sections one by one. Thereafter, missiology as a whole is dealt with. Every university does philosophy. Many universities regard the philosophy of religion (*religionsphilosophie*) as an integral part of philosophy in general. However, they are not aware of the philosophy of mission (Ger.: *Missionsphilosophie*) which, in turn, is an essential part of the philosophy of religion. The key problem is that many philosophers of religion as well as many missiologists do not interact. On the one hand, many philosophers of religion are so static in their philosophical reflections that they ignore the dynamics of mission as an integral part of religion – at least of Hinduism, Buddhism, Christianity, and Islam as world religions. On the other hand, many missiologists find it difficult to read philosophical studies.

Now it is time to start a serious dialogue: philosophers must take the missionary side of religions seriously and missiologists must delve into philosophy and develop an epistemology, phenomenology, ontology, and axiology of mission. Both disciplines can benefit from this exchange. Philosophers can widen their horizon if they take into account the dynamics of the world religions. And missiologists can learn from the careful reflection practised by philosophers. The philosophers will take the missiologists more seriously if the missiologists proceed to use arguments. And they will regard missiology as an academic discipline if it reflects critically upon its subject-matters. No scholar will deny the academic nature of philosophy in general and the academic nature of the philosophy of religion. Why should the academic nature of missiology be doubted if missiologists reflect philosophically upon mission: both the Christian mission and the mission of non-Christian religions? Can the philosophy of mission be developed by a consortium of missiologists and philosophers of religion in such a way that nobody will doubt its academic nature? The philosophy of mission must become a mature discipline; after having reached maturity, it can claim full academic recognition. Secondly, every university does empirical studies. The curriculum of many universities includes the science of religion (*religionswissenschaft*) as an integral part of science (*wissenschaft*) in general. The science of mission (*missionswissenschaft*), in turn, is an integral part of the science of religion.

There is much more communication between the scientists of religion and the scientists of mission than between the philosophers of religion and the philosophers of mission. This is especially the case in Germany where chairs of *Missions- und Religionswissenschaft* have been established, dealing not only with the history of mission (cf. Warneck and Daubanton) but also with the language of mission, the geography of mission, the statistics of mission, etc. Contacts between both disciplines can, and should be intensified. Many departments of religious studies are not willing to appoint missiologists and many missiologists avoid contact with the secular scientists of religion. The missionary nature of the world religions must be studied by both. The Edinburgh scholar Frank Whaling,[25] for instance, paved the way by making an interesting comparative study of the missionary expansion in early Buddhism, Christianity, and Islam. Nobody is questioning the academic nature of the science of religion: why should the academic nature of the science of mission be doubted? The science of mission is a part of the science of religion and, therefore, essentially as academic as the science of religion and science in general. At least, it ought to be as academic as religious studies and science in general.

Finally, universities will not deny the reality and relevance of the world religions; for the simple reason that they are forces which shape the lives of millions of people. At the same time, they will not identify themselves with one particular world religion. They will regard both the past idea of a *corpus christianum* in the western world and the present idea of a *corpus islamicum* in the Arab world as contrary to reason. In other words: universities will take the middle road between the support of one religion (versus the others), on the one hand, and the denial of the relevance of religious involvements and manifestations, on the other. This middle road opens the possibility of cooperation 'at distance' between universities and religions. Whereas universities have no right to forbid the teaching of the philosophy of mission in the general framework of the philosophy of religion and the teaching of empirical mission studies as a part of religious studies, they have the right to say 'no' to including (systematic and practical) Christian theology – and by consequence the Christian theology of religions and the Christian theology of mission – in their curricula. In Europe, a long tradition of cooperation between

---

[25] F. Whaling, 'A Comparative Religious Study of Missionary Transplantation in Buddhism, Christianity, and Islam', *International Review of Missions* LXX (1981), 314-33.

universities and Christian theologians exists. However, there is no guarantee that this link will be continued ad infinitum. As far as the theology of mission, or missionary theology (missionary dogmatics, missionary ethics, missionary liturgics, etc.), is concerned, missiology as a discipline is now vulnerable. Here, the academic nature of missiology as such is at stake.

The foregoing makes clear that it is wise to distinguish between the three sections of missiology. A neglect of the tripartite character of missiology can quickly lead to the claim that missiology as such is not at all 'academic'. The complex nature of this discipline illustrates that missiology is largely academic and it may be only for a small part not 'academic' in the proper sense of the word. I am inclined to say to those scholars who quickly deny the academic nature of missiology as a whole because of the theology of mission: 'Be careful! If you deny the academic nature of missiology because of the theology of mission, then you also must deny the academic nature of all other disciplines which are shaped by worldviews and/or ideologies in one way or another'. One 'academic' challenge is the (missionary) 'witnessing' of committed Christian theologians in the universities; another 'academic' challenge is the (missionary) 'witnessing' of the committed 'disciples' of Charles Darwin, Karl Marx, Sigmund Freud, *et al.*

Conclusion

Missiology as a whole can and must be taught and researched in theological colleges and seminaries all over the world. At the same time, the philosophy of mission and the science of mission can and must be taught and researched in universities: both in faculties of theology and in departments of religious studies. In addition, faculties of theology can and must engage themselves in doing (systematic and practical) theology in an explicitly missionary way. A Christian theology of mission can only be developed and taught by Christian believers; however, the philosophy of mission and the science of mission can 'at distance' be taught and researched by both Christians and non-Christians. To be more specific: there are Hindu scholars such as K. Madhu Panikkar[26] who have engaged themselves in studying Christian missions; like the humanists, they can write a history of Christian mission, if they like to do so. In theory, the philosophy of mission and the science of mission are as academic as the philosophy of religion and the science of religion. In practice, however, the situation is quite different: because so far many missiologists have neglected the philosophy of mission and have often prioritized the theology of mission over against empirical mission studies. The philosophy of mission and the science of mission are not at all inferior to the theology of mission because they guarantee the academic nature of missiology as a discipline. Nothing is wrong

[26] K.M. Panikkar, *Asia and Western Dominance: A Survey of the Vasco Da Gama Epoch of Asian History (1498-1945)* (London: 1967).

with Christian theology, Christian theology of religion, and Christian theology of mission done by committed scholars. The departments of religious studies will become more or less 'museums' if religion is not anymore alive in society. As the football-player is more essential in a match than the reporter, so the committed believer is more essential in shaping contemporary religious life.

Therefore, the religious 'engagement' of scholars must not be excluded from the universities. The theologian of mission is called to be one of the most committed scholars in the faculties of theology. Academic standards are not only related to the problem of teaching and research by scholars who are committed or not; but also related to the widening of the horizon and the opening of new perspectives. In general: missiology as an academic discipline must not limit itself to the study of Christian mission; it must widen its horizon and also include the study of the non-Christian missions which belong to the context of Christian mission. In particular: Christian missiologists must initiate the study of new subject-matters such as the violation of religious freedom all over the world (persecution of Christians, *et al.*), the new religious movements (both new Christian and non-Christian movements), the religious life of the non-western ethnic minorities in western societies (e.g. new independent churches), etc. In universities, theological and missiological commitment does not at all endanger academic standards. We need both commitment and distance. It must always be clear whether we are committed or working at distance. The one attitude does not exclude the other, not even in one and the same person. I recapitulate the question of this paper: is missiology an academic discipline? My answer is: yes; because it involves both methodological distance to – Christian and non-Christian – mission (cf. the philosophy of mission and the science of mission) and methodological commitment or 'engagement' to – Christian – mission (cf. the theology of mission, missionary theology).

Private Universities, Christian Mission and Transformational Development

Michael Schultheis

Professor Michael J. Schultheis S.J. is the President of the Catholic University College of Ghana.

Introduction

One of the main priorities when we began the Catholic University in 1996 in Beira, Mozambique, was to set up a research and documentation centre (CIDDI) that could focus on policy issues in natural resources and the environment, good governance and institutions of political participation, health issues and HIV/AIDS. The proposal for the Centre went to Austria and the University of Salzburg. After some negotiation, the Austrian Government agreed to fund a Geographic Information System (GIS) at the University. The unit had just become operational when the floods of 2000 inundated river basin communities in southern and central Mozambique. Our GIS team prepared maps with coordinates of affected communities along the Save and Buzi Rivers. Pilots flying emergency relief missions used these maps and I am told the maps continue to be used to this day. Somewhat later the university undertook a project that employed satellite imagery to mark the extent of the flood waters and engaged students to study the impact of the floods on river basin communities. One day, a visitor to the university asked how we justified high tech GIS in a poor country. My reply was simple, 'We have our head in the clouds and our feet in the mud'. This phrase might serve as a parable for this workshop.

My reflections here address the role of private universities in the integration of Christian Mission and Transformational Development. I begin by limiting this topic in two respects.

The first is institutional and focuses on private universities with a Christian orientation and a vision of community that accord with the basic principles of the Gospel. As Christians, we may agree that the Christian Mission is sharing the good news of the Gospel and seeking to live by it. People of faith recognize that this implies building community. But what sort of community? The vision of community that is articulated by the World Council of Churches and Catholic social teaching is close to a community of life, for it embodies social and ethical principles that: recognize the dignity of each person; seek the good that is common to the community and beyond the good of any individual; protect the rights of individuals and groups, especially the weaker and more vulnerable; respect the integrity of the earth as the heritage of present as well as future generations; act in global solidarity across national, racial, economic and ideological differences.

The second limitation is geographic and focuses on institutions of higher learning in Africa. At the risk of widening the scope of this paper too much, let me add another dimension here, namely globalization and the challenge it presents to all our institutions, including higher education, as they seek to integrate Christian Mission and Transformational Development. In developing these reflections, I first consider the general characteristics of globalization and its impact on higher education. I then go on to examine the crisis in higher education in Africa and the growth of the private universities, and explore the role of Christian universities. Finally, I conclude in considering some ways forward.

Globalization: The Impact of the Knowledge Based Economy on Education

The Google search on 'globalization' lists a large number of references. While scrolling through them one finds articles and organizations taking both a pro- and anti-globalization stance. With so many references, how do we understand globalization? More useful than *Google* is the recent working document of the International Federation of Catholic Universities (IFUC), which suggests that to understand globalization we would do well to consider it as both a phenomenon and a process. It presents many faces, multiple voices and different interpretations with diverse and often dramatic impacts on persons, cultures and societies. Some observers reduce it to the economics of growing interdependence, and to international agreements in an exclusively market-oriented and competitive environment.

A better understanding emerges from viewing and analyzing it as a multidimensional phenomenon that involves diverse domains of activity and interaction across borders and across continents, including economic, political, socio-cultural, technological, ethical, environmental and personal domains. This multidimensional nature of globalization would indicate that it embodies a number of complex processes that have created a web of networks of capital, technology and information that affect almost all aspects of human life, and significantly redefine the manner in which individuals, communities and institutions perform their functions and define their roles. From these processes, global integration has created an environment that compels productive sectors to achieve greater competition, efficiency, and increased output, while at the same time it displaces workers and causes heavy adjustment costs for sectors that are not ready or able to compete.

The forces driving globalization include technological developments and innovation, especially in the fields of information and communication technologies. On the positive side, these technologies significantly reduce the cost of transmitting information and enable populations worldwide to access information at light speed. On the negative side, they widen the information divide and exclude individuals, sectors and countries that lack the resources and the capacity to be connected with the information networks. The consequences of globalization reach far beyond the productive sectors of the economy and affect the environment, health, education and society as a whole. It also touches all our institutions – governments, churches, NGOs, local communities – and the manner in which they carry out their work and interact with one another.

This is part of the context in which we work and has many practical implications for our discussions on 'The Integration of Christian Mission and Transformational Development'. Institutions of higher education have always had an international dimension. Think of the great universities of Europe in the middle ages – Bologna, Coimbra, Cologne, Louvain, Paris, as well as Oxford and Cambridge. The University of Paris was a magnet attracting students from all over Europe. In later periods, colonisation became the dominant avenue for the internationalisation of higher education and most universities in Africa trace their origins to Europe. Today, globalization is having a far-reaching impact on every feature of higher education. Driven by new technologies of communication, globalization is characterised by the transformation of economies into information and knowledge societies. It is forcing fundamental changes in educational institutions everywhere, and causes particular stress in poorer countries and weaker societies. It challenges the future of the university, questions its core objective of serving the common good, and puts traditional academic values under pressure in an emerging global education market.

Universities train the people required for this emerging economy and help to create the new knowledge that drives economic growth. In a knowledge-based economy, universities have an active role in defining the distribution of the fruits of this new economy. Universities in the richer countries that reap the benefits of globalization are those with the resources to be connected with the information networks and to be centres of the research creating new knowledge. Other universities, including many in the richer countries, benefit from this interconnection, but mainly as consumers of new knowledge. Their competitive edge will be in training human resources for the knowledge based economy. In poorer countries, universities will maintain instruction as the key activity of their academic pursuit, but become excluded from the creation of knowledge and the training of people who meet the demands of a competitive global economy. This intensifies and widens the education divide between the rich and the poor, between the central and the peripheral institutions.

To some extent, institutions of higher education everywhere face the same difficulties: provision of services valued in the market, often with inadequate funding; more precise accountability in the use of funds; increased competition for students; far reaching changes in the global economy that are driven by the new technologies of communication. How are institutions of higher education responding to this challenge? Propelled by changes in the global economy, institutions of higher education seem to be immersed in the search for financial resources to acquire the technology required to train people for a more knowledge based economy. Let us look as some aspects of this in Africa.

The Crisis of Higher Education in Africa and the Growth of Private Universities

While the specific elements of the crisis differ from country to country, and continue to change, the difficulties generated by globalization can be generally applied to most African nations. In September 2004, the World Bank and the Association of African Universities sponsored conference on Higher Education in Africa. Representatives of public universities from across Africa met in Accra to assess changes that are underway and to reflect on the theme, 'Things that Work'. Over the past decade, the four major foundations – Ford, Rockefeller, McArthur and Carnegie – have committed some US $100 million to assist African universities in addressing the main problems they confront, and to make the changes required to meet the educational needs of their countries. The Bank was and is interested in identifying positive features that have resulted from efforts to reshape and revitalize the universities in Africa. The world is different now from what it was in the 1970s, when African governments and intellectuals looked to the universities as agents of nation building and development. In the 1980s and 1990s, the external environment began to shift towards a neo-liberal ideology that was pro-market and anti-state. This was marked by changes in the global economy, the declining importance of manufacturing and primary commodity production, and the shift to an information and service economy.

These changes carried enormous social costs to local communities and countries in Africa. At the same time African universities faced the new challenges associated with rapidly rising enrolment and the effort to maintain quality of education without a corresponding increase in revenue. Some problems facing higher education in Africa today are associated with population growth and the increased demand for education at the tertiary level. Although statistics vary somewhat, the World Bank notes that in 1960 the number of universities or university colleges in Sub Sahara Africa (SSA) was 52 (45 public, 7 private); these were present in 18 of the 48 countries of SSA. In 1975 the total enrolment was 181,000. By 1980 tertiary institutions had increased in number to 143 institutions (130 public; 13 private), with an enrolment of some 600,000. By 1995 enrolment had increased to 1,750,000 students; in 2000, the number of tertiary institutions was 316 (245 public; 71 private).

The problems facing higher education in Africa can be linked to several factors: the origins of higher education immediately before and after independence; the few universities at the apex of the educational pyramid in most SSA countries: 15 per cent have none; 41 per cent, one or two; 13 per cent, three-to-five; and 13 per cent, more than five universities; the rapid increase in enrolment together with unmet demand; with low national and average incomes, higher education is a heavy charge on most countries; low levels of literacy and pervasive poverty make it difficult to sustain higher education at levels of access and quality appropriate to current needs; poor infrastructure for teaching and research; weak links to the global knowledge system.

Associated with these problems are new demands. Governments in Africa look to universities to support national efforts to meet basic human needs in a sustainable manner and to strengthen the capacity of the nation and of enterprises to compete globally through the development of science, technology and other forms of knowledge. Universities are expected to provide access to larger numbers of students and to address issues of social equity such as gender and regional representation, while maintaining the quality and relevance of instruction, updating their curricula and pedagogical approaches, and expanding their facilities. In this they must somehow strike a balance between the desirable and possible in teaching and research, all with limited resources. The changes forced by globalization are beginning to affect the governance of the universities. It could be argued that the main academic centres – the Harvards, MITs and Oxfords – are forcing an homogenization of disciplines and fields that affects universities in all nations, imposing standards for the academic world, and widening the educational divide between the 'centres' and periphery.

Ghana has one of the strongest education systems in Africa, with a fairly well developed system in every sector, primary, secondary and tertiary. Ghana has five public universities with a total enrolment of more than 50,000. The University of Ghana/Legon, the parent university, has already celebrated its 50th anniversary. Yet the universities have many problems. Buildings are old and need repair, classrooms are crowded, instructors are aging and the training of qualified replacements is lagging. The situation in Ghana is not unique in Africa. In the past five years several meetings have addressed these problems. With international assistance they are beginning to address these as well as the new problems they face: the demands of information technology, the mass production of higher education and the growing needs for highly educated manpower. One result is that the core values and attitudes in the general education curriculum are being replaced by skills and competencies in professional training courses, often by private service providers. A recent phenomenon in the higher education scene in Africa is the emergence of private universities. In part this has occurred because governments recognize that public universities cannot cope with the increased demand. It also reflects the growing openness of governments.

In South Africa, private universities increased in number from seven (7) in 1960 (45 public), to 13 in 1980 (130 public), 27 in 1990 (199 public), 71 in 2000 (245 public) and 84 in 2002 (247 public). In Ghana the first private university began in 1988. In 2002, 21 private universities were registered with the National Accreditation Board of the Ministry of Education. What are the general characteristics of the private universities? In general their enrolment is small but growing. They offer programmes that are limited and market oriented (except for theological institutes). Students pay fees, even if nominal and below the actual costs. They tend to rely on part-time instructors, many of whom are drawn from public universities. Many have a church foundation and mission statements that proclaim a Christian vision that seeks to provide an education that is holistic, gives a sound formation to individuals and that contributes to the development of communities. All but one or two have a religious foundation; some are affiliated to churches abroad and are assisted with external funding. Of those with a religious foundation, most are associated with mainline Christian churches (one has ties to the Christian fundamentalist Oral Roberts University in Tulsa Oklahoma; one is the Islamic University).

How would they score in an evaluation of their efforts to integrate Christian Mission and Transformational Development? It is too early for a general evaluation, but in most instances they are dedicated to the general goals of providing a sound education and serving the community. Africa University in Zimbabwe with a Methodist foundation, and Valley View University in Ghana with a Seventh Day Adventist foundation, already are success stories.

Higher Education and the Christian Churches in Africa

Across SSA, Christian Missions were responsible for the establishment of formal education with the construction of a network of primary and later, secondary schools. Until perhaps a decade ago when Government began to erect secondary schools in many communities, about 40 percent of secondary schools had Catholic foundations and another 40-50 percent were secondary schools which had other Christian foundations. Most national leaders today are graduates of those schools. When talking of Higher Education, it is helpful to distinguish between tertiary institutions that the churches own and operate and others that the churches support in some manner.

Clearly the contribution of the Christian churches to higher education in SSA goes beyond an institutional presence. The churches and church-personnel helped to establish and continue to be actively engaged in national institutions of Higher Education. Public university professors and top administrators include many deeply committed Christian laypersons, as well as priests/ministers and religious men and women. Many students are products of church secondary schools, and chaplains and chaplaincies are an important presence on many campuses. It would be instructive to chronicle the number and type of private religious universities in Africa. However, it might be all but impossible.

For my part, I can only speak about the Catholic universities and, in Africa today, they are limited in number and scope. In late June 2003, the International Federation of Catholic Universities (IFCU) met in Uganda to reflect on the theme of the New Technologies and the Shaping of University Education.

Among the nearly 200 member universities of IFCU were representatives of the Association of Catholic Universities and Higher Institutes of Africa and Madagascar (ACUHIAM). This Association was formed in 1989 with five founding members; today it numbers 13 members, of which six are French speaking and five English speaking (including the Catholic University of West Africa in Port Harcourt, Nigeria, and the Catholic University of East Africa in Nairobi, Kenya), and two Portuguese speaking (Universidade Catholic de Angola and the Universidade Catolica de Mozambique) [see the IFCU web page: www.fiuc.org/ and http://www.fiuc.org/asunicam/]. The Catholic University of Ghana became a member of IFCU in March 2004. Most of these universities are new and still in their formative years. Most offer only undergraduate programmes and some have grown out of theological institutes. Most are under-funded and under-staffed. Yet Bishops' Conferences in most sub-Saharan African countries that do not yet have a Catholic university have plans to establish one.

The Catholic University of Ghana

The Catholic University College of Ghana (CUCG) is among the late arrivals. In 1998, the Catholic Bishops Conference announced their decision to establish a Catholic University. In their vision statement the Catholic Bishops gave these reasons for their decision: To provide a complete and full Catholic education for all who wish to avail themselves of the opportunity at the highest levels; To advance higher culture as well as form men and women truly outstanding in learning, ready to shoulder society's burdens and witness the faith to the world; To offer students the opportunity to study in an environment that stresses the acquisition of high skills as well as a sound ethical and spiritual formation; and To supplement existing facilities and provide greater access to university education, in view of the limited intake each year in public universities.

Subsequently planning committees were formed to address the issues involved. The Ministry of Education through the National Accreditation Board granted accreditation to the Catholic University of Ghana (CUG) in December 2002. The Catholic University opened its doors to fifty students for the first academic year on 3 March 2003. The baby has been born! The second academic year began in early November 2003 and the third began with the arrival of new students for a week of orientation on 23rd August 2004. The academic calendar now coincides with that of the public universities in Ghana. Presently CUG offers four-year Bachelor degrees in three Faculties: Economics and Business Administration, Information and Communication Sciences, and Technology, and Religious Studies (Philosophy, Theology and Adult Education). The priorities have been are twofold: firstly, consolidate the present programme with the addition of a fourth year. Secondly, construct permanent facilities adequate to both accommodate a projected enrolment of 500 students and enable further expansion in student numbers.

The Catholic University of Mozambique (Universidade Católica de Moçambique)

The Catholic Bishops of Mozambique began the Universidade Católica de Moçambique (UCM) in 1996 with the Faculty of Economics and Business Administration in Beira and the Faculty of Law in Nampula. Today UCM has seven faculties in four sites: added are Religious Studies, Medicine, Education, Agriculture and Hotel Management. Of the first entrants in 1996, some 50 received Bachelors' degrees; six were helped to continue studies in Zimbabwe and Botswana and have returned to UCM as instructors or in administration as fulltime members of staff. In the academic year 2001/02, the Faculty of Economics and Management enrolled about 650 students. Of the teaching staff of 39, ten were expatriates; of the nationals, only four were full time. Due to the shortage of nationals who were qualified lecturers, in August 2001 UCM began the first MA degree programme in Mozambique. Two years later, on 27 September 2003, the first group of 12 students received their MBA. Four of the graduates remained with UCM as faculty in the undergraduate programme. In its first year, UCM initiated a Research and Documentation Centre.

By means of the Centre, UCM has international links and a reputation for its studies on governance and decentralization, refugee and resettlement issues, natural resources, urban living conditions, and HIV/AIDS. In 1999, UCM established a Geographical Information System with assistance from the University of Salzburg and funding from the Austrian Government, with practical research output as described above. UCM also conducted the first empirical study on HIV/AIDS among the general population, with a focus on awareness and sexual behaviour patterns of households in Beira. This was followed by a programme to involve UCM students in working with other groups of young people, informing them about HIV/AIDS and helping them develop constructive alternatives to what are often exploitative social relationships.

What does 'Catholic University' mean and what is its potential contribution to Africa? An anecdote from Mozambique is illustrative: at the beginning of each semester, senior members of the Universidade Católica gather for a day of reflection. One year, our discussions focused on the theme: 'What does it mean to be a Catholic University and in Mozambique at the beginning of the third millennium?' The discussions were engaging, sometimes provocative, even if inconclusive. Engaging and provocative surely, because these are critical issues; inconclusive perhaps, because education and the education mission of the church present dynamic questions and suggest an open-ended process. However, a consensus emerged that, in addition to its teaching function, the Catholic University should be a locus and forum that would encourage the serious discussion of socio-economic problems and public policy issues. Some urged that it should go much further, by becoming actively engaged in these policy debates to attempt to bring about a transformation of society.

Directions for the Future: Is There a Way Forward?

In this time of rapid change in the structures and technologies and values associated with the term globalization, what are the concerns and questions about its impact on Christian institutions and values? What is the role of institutions of higher education with a Christian foundation? Is it possible to keep values at the centre of the academic mission and to avoid being drawn completely into the commercialization that characterizes much of contemporary higher education in this age of globalization? It is clear that the impact of the process of globalization on the knowledge environment is far-reaching and has special implications for Church-related institutions. They have a special mission that is both global and spiritual in nature and is at the same time at odds with many of the market forces that are integrally linked with globalization.

This is seen in the following characteristics of globalization: increased linkage of education and economic prosperity; shift from intrinsically valuable wisdom to instrumentally valuable or codifiable information; emphasis on technical and professional training over education of the whole person; replacement of the role of cultivating the person with the cult of information; reducing the social responsiveness of higher education to market responsiveness; mutation of the university into a technology based multiversity that is based on cost-benefit principles and treats students as consumers. In the face of this onslaught of globalization, what is the way forward for Christian universities? For many, the only option is to follow the standards set by academic centres and become dependent on them in terms of content, pedagogy, analysis and discourse of various disciplines. Yet their response should neither be a denial nor an uncritical embrace of the reality, but a tempered view that manages to balance the risks and opportunities of globalization.

There are opportunities for co-operation in the development of international linkages between universities – the exchange of faculty and students, physically and electronically. Yet there are dangers in this exchange, for the best academic centres of learning and research tend to reap the benefits of setting the standards in curriculum, research topics and methodologies, which in turn make scholars dependent on them. What might be an appropriate response to these trends, based on the strengths of Christian Universities? A collaborative effort would seem to be in order, with the stated objectives of undertaking the following: reflect on globalization in order to discern how it can be put to the authentic good for human society and the total development of individuals and peoples; give a central place to the formation of the human person and the promotion of human development that is beyond the perspective that education is an investment in human capital with emphasis on productivity and efficiency; develop creative governance structures that are flexible, decentralized and efficient.

Contribution to the Integration of Christian Mission and Transformational Development

Let me offer some final reflections on the potential contribution of Christian universities to the discussion of globalization. These can be grouped in three areas: 1) *Social Issues*: The primary mission of the church is to proclaim the Gospel and human salvation in such a way that a relationship between faith and life is established in each person and in the socio-cultural context in which individuals live, act and communicate with one another. The Holistic Gospel urges attention to those excluded from society on account of poverty, illness, hunger and homelessness. 2) *The Nature of the University*: The ethos of the Christian university is marked by service to church and to society.

The means are research and teaching that study contemporary problems of society. Research and action programmes can address issues such as the preservation of indigenous cultures, protection of the environment, and the impact of policies on the poor and vulnerable groups. Service to the university community may take the form of encouraging professors to improve their competence and to set their teaching and research within the framework of a coherent world vision. It must always try to create an environment that is conducive to the intellectual, moral, spiritual and social formation of students, leading them to a commitment to shaping a more humane global community. 3) *Forms of pedagogy:* An appropriate pedagogy for the Christian university will promote concern for wider social and humanitarian norms of justice, hope, peace, equity and social inclusion. It will incorporate an ethos of participation and be based on the personal life experience of each person, integrating love of learning and inquiry with the recognition that spirituality is at the heart of learning and thinking. How do we keep values at the centre of the academic mission? How do we avoid being drawn completely into the commercialization that characterizes much of contemporary higher education in this age of globalization? How do we keep our heads in the clouds and our feet in the mud?

In my view there are three priority-domains for action: *1) Formation of Integral Human Development:* promote Christian higher education as a dynamic learning process where the community is served and the spiritual dimension of various cultures is recognized; provide sound pedagogical tools and encourage exchanges for the formation of citizens with a critical attitude in dealing with the challenges of the reality of globalization. *2) Transmission of Knowledge and Search for Truth:* reinforce Christian values in education of the truth by integrating faith and life with professional competence, and focus on human rights, poverty reduction, good governance, peace and conflict resolution and thereby, address the current challenges of globalization to society; stimulate the exchange of teachers and researchers from different countries and disciplines with the aim of promoting sound formation and a critical analysis of globalization based on human values and principles. *3)*

Serving Community within and outside Christian Universities: encourage the academic community in the analysis of the process of globalization and of alternatives for serving community from within; create a culture of communication and dialogue, inter-religious and inter-cultural, as a vehicle for the understanding of shared values and the attainment of the common good.

Given the costs in terms of personnel and finances, are Christian universities likely to make a significant contribution to a country and its development and to the church's mission to evangelize? Given the theme of this conference, the following rephrasing of this question might be appropriate: are Christian universities in Africa likely to succeed in the integration of Christian Mission and Transformational Development? This remains an open question, but I suggest that already the results are promising and the limited contribution to date of Christian universities to the societies in which they find themselves is positive.

PART 5

Methodologies for Theological Studies

Pentecostal Theological Method and Intercultural Theology

Mark J. Cartledge

Dr. Mark J. Cartledge is Senior Lecturer in Pentecostal and Charismatic Theology, University of Birmingham.

Introduction

It could be argued that Pentecostal theology has come of age. It now has its own academic societies, journals, monograph series and biblical commentaries. However, there is still some debate regarding its place within the academy and its global and multicultural approach to theology has not always been appreciated. It has even been suggested that 'Pentecostal theology' is in fact an oxymoron – as if Pentecostals actually did theology! Of course, times have changed and now there is such a great diversity of approaches in the contemporary academy that different perspectives are accepted to a limited extent even if they might not be fully valued. But if we were to articulate a Pentecostal approach to theology what might it look like? Is there a distinctive method or approach to help us to understand its nature? In this essay, I address these questions by bringing together two distinct but historically related areas in the field: theological method and intercultural theology. I intend to explore recent Pentecostal scholarship in its attempt to articulate a Pentecostal theological method. In order to appreciate the roots of the academic study of Pentecostalism more broadly I connect this material to the field of intercultural theology as expressed by Walter J. Hollenweger. I have chosen Hollenweger because he has led the way in the academic study of Pentecostalism, allowing it to be appreciated as an important field of study. As a missiologist, his work has always been open to horizons beyond his own and his approach to theology has both affirmed western theology and critiqued it through his appreciation of oral cultures and non-western Christianity. I shall place these approaches side by side in an attempt to appreciate how they can illuminate each other and offer insights.

The term 'Pentecostal' is a designation that has been used in a variety of ways to classify particular Christian groups and denominations in the twentieth century. For many it denotes those groups who have used *glossolalia* and has its origins with Charles Parham and William J. Seymour, especially in the Azusa Street revival. For others Pentecostalism has multiple and global origins that cannot be reduced to 'made in America' and includes not just 'speaking in tongues' but the manifestation of all of the *charismata*.[1] My own view is that the terms Pentecostal, Neo-Pentecostal and Charismatic will continue to be applied unevenly in the literature and that it is always important to distinguish the kind of Pentecostalism that is in view. For me there is something that I have called the 'charismatic tradition', which has transcended particularities across time and place in the history of the church. It has manifested itself differently across the centuries, but established itself uniquely at the beginning of the twentieth century through various global expressions.[2] From the early alignment of this tradition with the Wesleyan and Holiness traditions in the West and forms of Evangelical Christianity elsewhere there emerged different forms of Pentecostalisms. What I normally refer to as Pentecostalism is the expression of this spirituality as it became institutionalized in what is usually called classical Pentecostalism. This expression of Christianity is associated with particular denominations that have codified beliefs through statements of faith and specific doctrines, usually 'subsequence' and 'initial evidence'.[3] Charismatic Christianity in general is more fluid and aligns itself with other Christian traditions more readily, such as forms of Protestantism and Roman Catholicism because it usually stresses the experience of the *charismata* rather than particular doctrines associated with them. In this essay, I am focusing on one form of American classical Pentecostalism, namely the Church of God (Cleveland, Tennessee) and theologians associated with it.[4]

The phrase 'intercultural theology' is one that is associated with mission studies and inter-religious dialogue. It was coined in the 1970s and was usually associated with a liberal and pluralistic approach to theology. It is normally taken to mean that theology should pay attention to the cultural embeddedness of all language, thought and practice and by doing so achieve greater openness and dialogue because of the relativity that such recognition obtains. With the development of local theologies,[5] it refers to the dialogues that these local theologies have one with another and as a comparative approach it stimulates critical and creative thinking.[6] It has recently been revived in British scholarship by George Newlands who argues for a progressive orthodoxy in the liberal tradition.[7] However, his position, while acknowledging something of its

---

[1] Allan Anderson, *An Introduction to Pentecostalism: Global Charismatic Christianity* (Cambridge: Cambridge University Press, 2004), 166.

[2] M. Cartledge, *Encountering the Spirit: The Charismatic Tradition* (London/and Maryknoll, NY: Darton, Longman & Todd/Orbis Books 2006/2007).

[3] Anderson, *An Introduction*, 190-92.

[4] W.J. Hollenweger, *The Pentecostals: The Charismatic Movement in the Churches* (London: SCM, 1972), 517.

[5] R.J. Schreiter, *Constructing Local Theologies* (London: SCM, 1985).

[6] F. Wijsen, 'Intercultural Theology and the Mission of the Church', www.sedos.org/english/wijsen.htm.

[7] G. Newlands, *The Transformative Imagination: Rethinking Intercultural Theology* (Aldershot: Ashgate, 2004).

heritage, fails to appreciate the nature of intercultural Christianity as western and non-western perspectives dialogue. Instead he assumes that the 'cross-cultural' and the 'intercultural' in relation to the non-western usually mean the inter-religious. He thus domesticates the term to an exclusively western conceptualization by construing 'culture' largely in terms of western subcultures and interdisciplinary dialogue. Whilst this may be necessary for a western liberal theology to find its place, it simply does not connect to other forms of Christianity, especially Pentecostalism. Therefore, I shall use the term in its broadest cultural sense as defined by Hollenweger (see below).

Pentecostal Theological Method

I want to suggest that Pentecostal theological method in recent scholarship can be best understood by focusing on the Church of God (Cleveland, Tennessee) theologians who have pioneered the reflection on the subject. This is not to suggest that other Pentecostals have not been active in the field,[8] but that it is useful to identify a particular tradition of thought within Pentecostalism for our purposes. Therefore I have chosen the work of John Christopher Thomas and Kenneth J. Archer as representative of this constituency. As an illustration of how this kind of method is being applied I have summarised the vision for a Pentecostal Bible commentaries series.

Spirit-Text-Community

These American Church of God (Cleveland, Tennessee) theologians have argued for a method of doing theology that works with a triad of sources: the text of Scripture, the community of the church and the person of the Holy Spirit. All three sources are expected to work together in order to generate theological reflection and inform ecclesial decisions in relation to missiological praxis. The key illustration of how this method works has been articulated by John Christopher Thomas in relation to Acts 15 and the decision by the Jerusalem Council to include the Gentiles in the household of faith. First, attention is given to what had already taken place among the Gentiles: they had heard the gospel, believed, received the gift of the Holy Spirit, had their hearts purified by faith and experienced signs and wonders (vv. 7-9). Second, attention is given to Scripture and James' choice of Amos 9.11-12 to argue that there is continuity between David and Jesus as David's fallen tent is both rebuilt and expanded to include the Gentiles. In other words the experience of the Spirit and the response to the gospel can be explained by this text. Third, in the light of these two aspects the whole group makes a decision together to include the Gentiles without requiring that they pass through Judaism (vv. 24-

[8] A. Yong, *Spirit-Word-Community: Theological Hermeneutics in Trinitarian Perspective* (Aldershot: Ashgate, 2002).

26). Testimony is given and received and this enables a group decision to be discerned. In the context of Acts 15, the Gentiles are allowed into the fellowship of the church provided that table fellowship is maintained and in order to do this they are required to adopt specific attitudes towards Jewish food laws and sexual codes. The Holy Spirit is seen as acting through the text of Scripture, experiences such as signs and wonders and the testimonies in the group.[9]

Kenneth J. Archer has built upon this proposal in his work on Pentecostal hermeneutics. He agrees with Thomas' reading of Acts 15 that there must be a dialogical and dialectical relationship between 'the Scripture, Spirit and reader/readers'.[10] He argues for a contemporary Pentecostal hermeneutical strategy that embraces a triadic negotiation for meaning, borrowing from semiotics and reader-response criticism. He integrates these insights within the Bible reading method of the early Pentecostals in the context of the community. The voice of the Holy Spirit is heard through the community and Scripture, and permeates the hermeneutical process.[11] Archer has recently extended his argument from biblical hermeneutics to theological method, to which we turn more fully.

Method and Manner

Archer contends that there is such a thing as a Pentecostal way of doing theology.[12] This approach takes the 'world of Pentecostalism' as its starting point and appropriates insights from other traditions. This means that orthodoxy cannot be separated from orthopraxy and orthopathy. Instead of seeing Pentecostalism as a form of Evangelicalism, it is understood as a distinct and authentic Christian tradition and its theological manner and method is equally distinct. Commending the insights of Hollenweger, he notes how early Pentecostal sources suggest that theology is done via testimonies, songs, trances, sermons and dances. This builds on the work of Deborah McCauley, who has shown how oral communication and narrative are the primary modes of expression for the American Christians of the 'Mountain Region'. These Christians are largely Pentecostal, marginalized and are predominantly oral/aural learners. Similarly Frank Macchia refers to the 'nonacademic'

---

[9] J.C. Thomas, 'Reading the Bible from within Our Traditions: A Pentecostal Hermeneutic as a Test Case', in *Between Two Horizons: Spanning New Testament and Systematic Theology*, ed. J.B. Green and M. Turner (Grand Rapids: Eerdmans, 2000), 41-56; J.C. Thomas, 'Women, Pentecostals and the Bible: An Experiment in Pentecostal Hermeneutics', *Journal of Pentecostal Theology* 5 (1994).

[10] K.J. Archer, *A Pentecostal Hermeneutic for the Twenty-First Century: Spirit, Scripture and Community* (London: T & T Clark International, 2004), 145-47, 47.

[11] Archer, *A Pentecostal Hermeneutic*, 156-91.

[12] K.J. Archer, 'A Pentecostal Way of Doing Theology: Method and Manner', *International Journal of Systematic Theology* 9:1 (2007).

theology of Pentecostals through prayers, commentaries, devotional writings and disputations. However, Archer wonders whether Macchia has given too much away by using the language of 'non-academic', suggesting inadvertently that such theology lacks academic credence.[13] Therefore the word 'pietistic', Archer suggests, might be a better adjective for Pentecostal theology. Whatever, we call it, the Pentecostal tradition requires that the affective and experiential aspects be included, which he suggests come primarily through worship.

The method that Archer advocates is 'integrative', by which he specifically means the integration of orthopraxis and orthopistis with orthopathos. Praxis embraces the idea that theology and practice are inseparable and mutually informing as theory arises from a reflection on praxis and returns to inform further praxis. But praxis needs to be supplemented in order to nurture Pentecostal theologian and it does this by attending to orthopathos, that is an identification by the theology with the suffering community allowing a 'firsthand, direct existential engagement' among the marginalized.[14] Both personal and communal experience is affirmed and cognitive doctrine is never detached from the pathos of God. This 'conjunctive methodology' 'takes seriously orthopathos as the integrative centre for our Pentecostal theology without setting aside either praxis or dogma'.[15]

For Archer, the manner of this Pentecostal theology is narrative. It proceeds by understanding Scripture as the grand meta-narrative with the Gospels and Acts as the centre of the story. The social doctrine of the Trinity is the central character with Jesus Christ at the very heart, thereby emphasizing the gospel of Christ as its significance for the church and the world: the hub around which other theological themes revolve. Pentecostals have articulated this gospel in terms of the 'full gospel', or 'five-fold' gospel: Jesus as saviour, sanctifier, Spirit baptiser, healer and coming king, giving what Archer calls central narrative convictions. These convictions flow out of the doxological community bestowing identity and affording guidance in the Christian life. Therefore, if this gospel is the hub, the Pentecostal doctrines, beliefs and practices are the wheel connected to the centre: Jesus Christ. Each dimension of the gospel is linked to the others and provide a way of reflecting on other themes such as ecclesiology and eschatology, being 'held together around our missional story of the Social Trinity'.[16]

---

[13] F.D. Macchia, 'African Enacting Theology: A Rediscovery of an Ancient Tradition?', *Pneuma: The Journal of the Society for Pentecostal Studies* 24:2 (2002).

[14] Archer, *A Pentecostal Hermeneutic*, 10.

[15] Archer, *A Pentecostal Hermeneutic*, 11.

[16] Archer, *A Pentecostal Hermeneutic*, 13.

Pentecostal Bible Commentaries

In 2004 a new Bible Commentary series was launched by T & T Clark and edited by the New Testament scholar, John Christopher Thomas. The first two commentaries appeared in that year by the editor on the Johannine epistles and by Rebecca Skaggs on the epistles of Peter and Jude.[17] These commentaries provide an interesting insight into how the Pentecostal theological method noted above has been used in a creative way to provide resources for pastors, lay people and students available through popular, non-technical language. In the Editor's Preface to the series the nature of the commentary and the process of writing is outlined. A number of points are worth noting.

First, Thomas points out that contrary to those who understand Pentecostalism as either fundamentalist Christianity with Spirit Baptism and *charismata* or an experience capable of fitting with any spirituality or theological system, it is a distinct theological tradition. At the heart of the tradition is a message of the five-fold gospel: Jesus as saviour, sanctifier, Holy Spirit baptiser, healer and coming king. This message reveals the heart of the tradition and displays aspects which are similar and dissimilar to other Christian traditions. Writers of the commentaries should therefore be people who do not just speak in tongues but who represent this tradition's ethos. The writers should represent the diversity of the constituency coming from different continents, races and communities.

Second, the writing process has been designed in order to represent this tradition. Each contributor is 'urged' to include a number of spiritual disciplines in his or her work. They are encouraged to pray for the project both individually and as members of Pentecostal communities, asking specifically for the guidance of the Holy Spirit and for the leadership of the Spirit in interpretation. It is expected that there will be specific times of prayer when the community intercedes on behalf of the writer and seeks to hear from the Lord through prophetic words. As part of this engagement with their church community it is expected that commentators will explore ways in which their scholarship might be contextualized within their own local setting, thus strengthening the interaction between the Spirit, the body of Christ and the Word of God. As part of this contextualisation, writers are encouraged to covenant with their churches regarding spiritual support and where possible lead a group Bible study on the book that they are writing about. Writers are also encouraged to seek the advice and critique of a gifted colleague, so that their work would not be done in isolation.

Third, the physical format of the commentary is designed to reflect the dialogical manner in which the tradition approaches the text. Each commentary begins with a set of questions aiming to draw attention to the corporate and individual issues addressed in the book. The reader is invited to interpret his or

---

[17] J.C. Thomas, *The Pentecostal Commentary on 1 John 2 John 3 John* (London: T & T Clark, 2004).

her context in a 'confessional-critical' manner. This means that the commentary is contextualized within the life of the church from the beginning. From this initial section the introduction to the commentary proper informs the reader regarding the composition of the book, but avoids unnecessary and irrelevant questions. It includes topics of interest to Pentecostals as well as discussing genre, structure and organisation of the book. A section on the book's teaching on the Holy Spirit is included. The commentary proper provides a running exposition of the text, interacts with major interpretive options, and provided periodic opportunities for reflection on the text with the use of questions and a section guiding personal responses to issues arising, with possible concrete responses being offered. This is regarded as the literary equivalent to an altar call.

Therefore, it is through this approach that these Bible commentaries give expression to the Pentecostal theological method in a tangible form. I now turn to the subject of Intercultural theology by way of a comparison.

Intercultural Theology

The father of the academic study of Pentecostalism and the former Professor of Mission at the University of Birmingham, Walter J. Hollenweger, began to argue from the late 1970s for what he called 'intercultural theology'.[18] By this he meant the appropriation of 'cultural media' outside the theologian's own tradition that can serve as raw material and tools for doing theology, in particular missiology. Intercultural theology does not jumble together languages and cultures but rather chooses a cultural framework and sticks to it without assuming that the theologian's cultural background is universal. It searches for 'a body of Christ', contributing to the body without assuming that it is the most important or the most academic. It is a way of doing theology that escapes the western religious and academic ghetto and places it in the world in which we live.[19]

He offers five main points in order to define his approach. First, intercultural theology operates within a given culture but without absolutizing this particular culture. It reflects or mirrors the sacramental body of Christ, open to the universal and sacramental dimension of the Christian faith. Second, the methods by which this is achieved are chosen on the basis of their suitability. No one tradition should be ruled out nor taken for granted as the only or most important. 'In this "body of Christ"-approach, theology has to hold its ground against all pagan and sectarian schools of learning (and in the churches!). It cannot conform to the *stoicheia tou kosmou*'.[20] Third, it is suggested that

[18] W.J. Hollenweger, 'Intercultural Theology', *Theological Renewal* 10 (1978).

[19] L. Price, *Theology out of Place: A Theological Biography of Walter J. Hollenweger*, JPTSup 23 (Sheffield: Sheffield Academic Press, 2002), 64.

[20] Hollenweger, 'Intercultural Theology', 12.

narrative theology is one of the possible approaches towards a theology of one culture which is open to other cultures. Fourth, experiments in intercultural theology can be tested for their suitability and thereby build bridges of communication which is lacking in normal western academic theology. Fifth, intercultural theology is not a form of 'pop-theology' and makes the task of theology more difficult not easier. Critical scholarship continues but it is also applied to the process of communication not just the content. Doing theology interculturally within the body of Christ pays attention not just to what is 'broadcast' but equally what is 'received' thereby 'demonstrating theology's place in the world in which we live'.[21]

By the mid 1980s Hollenweger's ideas about intercultural theology had become clearer and he was able to articulate seven presuppositions: (1) all theologies are contextually conditioned; (2) there is nothing wrong with theology being contextually conditioned; (3) it may take others to show us how conditioned, parochial, or ideologically captive our own theology is; (4) even if once we could ignore such voices, now we can no longer do so; (5) the point of contact between our traditions and the new theologies of the Third World is Scripture; (6) only in creative tension with the widest possible perspective can we develop theologies appropriate to our own particular situations; and (7) since within the church the ultimate loyalty is not simply to nation, class, culture, the universal church is uniquely suited to provide the context in which the task of creative theologizing can take place.[22]

At the time of writing, Hollenweger explains that he is involved in training theological teachers for the Third World and that in their research work he looks for three things: (1) originality, (2) work that is relevant to *their* context, country, culture and society; and (3) familiarity with the research conventions of a European university.[23] Quite often there is a clash between (2) and (3). So he offers a plea for an intercultural theology that uses both the tools of classical western theology as well as attending to the oral spiritualities of Third World religious communities and the narrative structure of their theology, so akin to the first generation of Christians.[24] Therefore, we need to combine story *and* analysis, dream *and* critical interpretations in our theological articulation. However, it is through the basic category of narrative that theology has the possibility of becoming universal.[25]

Lynne Price, in her theological biography of Hollenweger, notes how he engages in all three 'publics' of theology: academy, church and society by experiential, dialogical and reflective modes but always paying attending to

---

[21] Hollenweger, 'Intercultural Theology', 13.

[22] W.J. Hollenweger, 'Intercultural Theology', *Theology Today* 43:1 (1986), 28.

[23] Hollenweger, 'Intercultural Theology', 34.

[24] W.J. Hollenweger, *Pentecostalism: Origins and Developments Worldwide* (Peabody MA: Hendrickson, 1997), 81-82.

[25] Hollenweger, *Pentecostalism*, 131.

context.[26] His theology is both global and ecumenical and relies significantly on the narratives set within particular cultural settings.[27] His use of 'narrative exegesis' allows him to share the fruits of critical scholarship with non-academic and cross-cultural audiences, as he playfully re-scripts biblical stories to elucidate their messages for different settings.[28] Price observes that while Hollenweger defends the use of critical scholarship, he did not support its claim to objectivity or neutrality. As she says: For him, the Bible remains foundational – not as a source of proof texts to support particular dogmatic positions, but in a much more complex way a truly universal collection of inspired writings whose meanings become clear only as succeeding and diverse communities engage with them in the midst of present realities and share their insights with each other. In answer to the question: 'Who interprets Scripture correctly?' his reply is: 'no one person interprets Scripture correctly on his [sic] own. It is only in conflict, debate, and agreement with the whole people of God, and also with non-Christian readers that we can get a glimpse of what Scripture means'.[29]

It is this desire for an ecumenical and multi-cultural conversation that drives Hollenweger's model of intercultural theology. Indigenous non-western theology should be developed in dialogue with European church history in order to advance ecumenism.[30] However, such a theology is, according to Hollenweger, necessarily pluralistic, partial and transitional with truth emerging from out of different times and places. Thus the oral and narrative categories of non-western cultures are given priority in Hollenweger's theological method because these forms allow 'the "ruling language" to be brought into intercultural dialogue as one possible language next to other possible languages'.[31] The non-western 'other' is necessary for both insight and correction and should not be domesticated or over-ruled by the western academy, church or culture. In his intercultural theology Hollenweger mediated between the western academy and the non-western world: to the West he argued for diversity and oral/narrative modes of theological discourse, to the non-West he promoted analysis, reflection and the need to relate to the wider history of the church. To all 'he stressed the need for sensitive, appropriate and critical Christian response to the concrete realities of local and global, historical and contemporary, contexts'.[32]

---

[26] Price, *Theology Out*, 26-28.
[27] Price, *Theology Out*, 36.
[28] Price, *Theology Out*, 42-63.
[29] Price, *Theology Out*, 63.
[30] Price, *Theology Out*, 74.
[31] Price, *Theology Out*, 79.
[32] Price, *Theology Out*, 90-91.

Theological and Methodological Reflection

The juxtaposition of Pentecostal theological method and intercultural theology outlined above raises a number of interesting and important points for the broader discussion of how we do our theology. There are similarities and differences between the two approaches. I make four main points by way of a theological and methodological comparison.

First, both approaches stress the nature of theology in terms of narrative and this is a category that is now being fully recognized as important, but it will always need to be supplemented by dogmatic statements, metaphors and models that assist in the explication of theology. Of course these metaphors and models may vary across time and place but will certainly need to be constructed for the communication of the gospel. This is exactly what Archer does in terms of his five-fold gospel, which provides a Christological centre, and his appeal to the social doctrine of the Trinity, which provides an overarching 'theological framework', even if he does not call it that. It is not entirely clear from the work of Hollenweger what the role of a dogmatic core plays in Intercultural theology. He has in the past criticized Pentecostals for a western Calvinist view of the Trinity that subordinates pneumatology to Christology, which he traces to the filioque clause.[33] His answer is to use the Barthian language of *seinsweise* (modes of being) in order to overcome this problem. But a social doctrine of the Trinity would, theoretically at least, remove such subordinationism, even if it has other problems and, after all, many Pentecostal theologians are influenced by Moltmann rather than Barth (the most notable exception is Frank Macchia). The critical question that the Pentecostal theological method offers the Intercultural theology of Hollenweger is in relation to the role that Christian doctrine plays in relation to narrative theology. On this point they appear to diverge considerably.

Second, both approaches wish to give priority to local voices, although it is expressed differently. The Pentecostal method offers this through community testimony and group prayer meetings, while the Intercultural method uses indigenous categories to critique and challenge western categories.[34] In this attention to the local, both approaches, it could be argued, are forms of postmodern theology, although expressed differently. The Pentecostal method uses an 'in front of the text' reading while nevertheless seeing the Bible as the judge of contemporary praxis. Hollenweger's method uses the insights of 'behind the text' historical-critical scholarship and assumptions about plurality and conflict in the canon, which are then used to engage with contemporary forms of conflict and plurality through rescripted narrative and drama. In this

---

[33] Hollenweger, *The Pentecostals*, 218-22; M. Cartledge, 'Trinitarian Theology and Spirituality: An Empirical Study of Charismatic Christians', *Journal of Empirical Theology* 17:1 (2004), 76-84.

[34] R.S. Sugirtharajah, *Vernacular Hermeneutics* (Sheffield: Sheffield Academic Press, 1999).

sense both approaches resolve the issue of universality versus particularity but in different ways. Both align experience with the text but again in very different ways. Ultimately, for the Pentecostal theological method the Bible is the norming norm, around which experience is tested and interpreted, even as it used to interpret the Bible: it is the final form of the text in the hands of the community that inspires. For Hollenweger, the assumptions of modern critical scholarship are not challenged but simply communicated via a narrative medium. It is not the final form that is important but the perceived issues and processes in the texts that inspire a rereading in new contexts. Although apparently similar, these approaches could not be so different.

Third, both approaches are interested in the church but ecclesiology appears to be understood very differently by them. The Pentecostal method never really defines the community. One is bound to ask: Which community? Whose community? One suspects the community is a fairly small one that believes in an American version of the five-fold gospel! Global Charismatic Christianity in all its diversity is apparently excluded by a narrow definition of Pentecostalism and Pentecostal tradition. By contrast, Intercultural theology is ecumenically open, although this perhaps reflects the period in which Hollenweger was involved in the World Council of Churches. In this ecumenical winter the possibilities of ecumenical theology look somewhat different. Nevertheless the openness of such an approach is certainly more appealing to someone standing outside of classical Pentecostalism. In this regard a number of the key presuppositions of Intercultural theology are pertinent. Given that all theology is contextual, listening to others outside of our tradition is necessary in order to highlight the 'blind spots'. It is in creative tension with the widest possible perspectives that theologians can best understand their own context and this is best achieved ecumenically as global Christianity engages in dialogue.

Fourth, both are interested in spirituality but only one puts it at the heart of the process of doing theology, the other puts it as the object for research. This may be a crucial difference between the seminary model of the Pentecostals and the university model of Intercultural theology. But in an age in which different perspectives are accepted and even a Tübingen Professor can argue for the epistemological advantage of contemplation and 'spiritual gaze' for theology,[35] it seems an unnecessary and unfortunate divide. This difference may well relate to the question of who does theology. Both see theology as conducted by the professional and by the ordinary person in the church. But it is not entirely clear how these different roles are to be worked out and where the balance of power lies despite the support for the marginalized and powerless. The university theologian may well be asked to put matters of 'faith' to one side for the sake of academic credibility but increasingly it is accepted that spirituality and worldview issues cannot be divorced from intellectual

---

[35] J. Moltmann, *The Spirit of Life: A Universal Affirmation* (London: SCM, 1992), 202-08.

pursuits. The integrated Pentecostal theological method is one that has the capacity to travel. Yet it is not without its difficulties. Theologians are not always comfortable people to be around because they often raise the hard and difficult questions, however committed they are to the faith once received by the saints. A communitarian approach to theology can also domesticate insights that are new and different because the power of the reading tradition and the pressure of spiritual enactment stifle creativity whilst ironically claiming to promote it.

Conclusion

It has been interesting and useful to consider afresh two very different approaches to theology, both of which have engaged with the Pentecostal tradition. On balance I suspect that most Pentecostal theologians will gravitate towards the Pentecostal theological method outlined above, and with some good reason. However, Intercultural theology has much to offer, not least a wider appreciation of issues of cultural and global Christianity which overcomes the label 'made in America'. As a practical theologian I can see advantages and disadvantages with both approaches. However, neither appears to engage in a multi/inter-disciplinary approach to theology, which is surely an important aspect of twenty-first century theology;[36] and neither explains the processes by which oral and local data is identified, gathered and analysed. My answer is to integrate Pentecostal-charismatic spirituality, as per the insights of Pentecostal theological method, within the process of practical theology as an intercultural and comparative empirical discipline, thus addressing the weaknesses noted above.[37] In this way the three publics of church, academy and society may be mutually informed for the benefit of all.

---

[36] A. Yong, *The Spirit Poured out on All Flesh: Pentecostalism and the Possibility of Global Theology* (Grand Rapids: Baker Academic, 2005), 27-30.

[37] M. Cartledge, *Practical Theology: Charismatic and Empirical Perspectives* (Carlisle: Paternoster, 2003).

'Can We Now Bypass That Truth?' – Interrogating the Methodology of Dalit Theology[1]

J. Jayakiran Sebastian

Dr. J. Jayakiran Sebastian is Professor in the Department of Theology and Ethics at the United Theological College, Bangalore, India, and is currently H. George Anderson Professor of Mission and Cultures at the Lutheran Theological Seminary at Philadelphia, PA, USA.

Back from the Bypass

Dalit studies, once relegated to squiggles on the margins and faint traces on the fringes of academia, has now emerged as one of the most productive and creative correctives to dominant ways of interpreting history, understanding economics, probing sociology, studying culture, investigating globalization, exposing racism, unlocking accepted anthropological 'truths' and indeed reconfiguring the whole gamut of social sciences.

The field of Christian theology has not lagged far behind, thanks to the pioneering efforts of people like Arvind P. Nirmal, who in a range of evocative and iconoclastic writings firmly placed Dalit theology and Dalit hermeneutics not as another 'branch' in the study of theology, but as a discipline, which while developing its own methods of inquiry, massively impacted the whole theological enterprise and the life of the church.[2] No longer could Dalit issues be confined to the bypasses and byways of dominant ways of progressing on the theological highway, but either grudgingly or enthusiastically, such issues and themes have become part of the exploratory process, without which the whole process is doomed to irrelevance, or worse, insignificance.

To give just two from a range of possible recent examples – Jeffrey Cox investigates the interlink between Christianity and imperialism in Punjab in a major work[3] that carefully reconstructs the role of the Indians themselves in

---

[1] Originally presented at the Seminar on 'Revisiting and Resignifying the Methodology of Dalit Theology' organized by the Department of Theology and Ethics, United Theological College, Bangalore, Centre for Dalit/Subaltern Studies, New Delhi and Christian Institute for the Study of Culture and Society, Bangalore. The seminar took place at the Ecumenical Resource Centre, UTC, Bangalore from 13th–14th July 2007

[2] A. P. Nirmal, 'Towards a Christian Dalit Theology', in *Frontiers in Asian Christian Theology: Emerging Trends*, ed. R.S. Sugirtharajah (Maryknoll, NY: Orbis, 1994), 44-52.

[3] J. Cox, *Imperial Fault Lines: Christianity and Colonial Power in India, 1818-1940* (Stanford, CA: Stanford University Press, 2002).

trying to build up 'an Indian Church for the Indian People', takes seriously the indigenous initiatives, and looks for motives not just in the 'official' records, but also in the songs written and sung by new converts. This work is also important in that it looks at another neglected group and investigates female agency in the mission work. Cox writes:

The itinerant villager Ditt initiated the surprising and initially unwelcome mass conversions to Christianity in central Punjab. In the 1880s and 1890s, unmarried European and Indian women missionaries turned the missionary movement into a predominantly female cause, and Indian women doctors raised issues of racial prejudice in the mission. After the turn of the century the Indian national movement reminded missionaries of what they had always claimed to believe, that the 'illusion of permanence' of British rule reflected in Kipling was theologically unacceptable.[4] Cox notes the importance of the contributions of John Webster and James Massey, several decades after independence to come to terms with, interpret, and interrogate the history of 'Dalit Christians'.[5]

The recent analysis by Sharmila Rege on Dalit women's 'testimonios' posits significant methodological comments that cannot be brushed aside. She points out that:

> [a] dalit feminist standpoint acknowledges the significance of the experience of oppression and resistance among dalit women acquiring a perspective against an unjust order but it does not celebrate oppressive traditions merely because they are practiced by the oppressed. By directing attention to the cultural and material dimensions of the interface between gender and caste, the focus of a dalit feminist standpoint is squarely placed on social relations, which convert difference into oppression.... 'Translating' dalit women's historical experience, in writing caste/writing gender, underscores the inseparability of caste and gender identities and the material and symbolic gains of complicity for upper caste women and undifferentiated community for dalit men.[6]

Locating herself as a 'non-dalit woman', Rege asks what such a project meant for her and for feminism as such, and writes that this:

> meant addressing my own ignorance about their histories, struggles, preferred social relations and utopias. It means challenging the normative epistemological status of unmarked feminism, recognizing its social situation to be a scientifically and epistemologically disadvantaged one for generating knowledge.... Adopting a dalit feminist standpoint means sometimes losing, sometimes revisioning, the 'voice' that we had as unmarked feminists.[7]

---

[4] Cox, *Imperial Fault Lines*, 28, 118-19.
[5] Cox, *Imperial Fault Lines*, 269, n.70, 327.
[6] S. Rege, *Writing Caste/ Writing Gender: Narrating Dalit Women's Testimonios* (New Delhi: Zubaan, 2006), 74.
[7] Rege, *Writing*, 387-88.

This observation is not something that is peculiar to the project that Rege undertook, but directly addresses the wider issue of the construction of ways of knowing, ways of interpreting, and ways of behaving that are a part of the ways of being. Dalit studies are now firmly established as an important and indispensable aspect of all attempts to understand and analyse the complexities of Indian society. For far too long, there seemed to be an almost embarrassed silence when it came to fleshing out the harsh experiences of Dalit communities in independent India. Should one speak of an 'embarrassed silence' or of a 'conspiracy of silence' when it comes such matters? The resurgence of Dalit pride and the increasing recognition of the vital role played by Dalit communities in the political landscape of India have resulted in the flourishing of studies dealing with the variety and range of the Dalit experience. To the growing literature interrogating various aspects of the Dalit experience and the Dalit realities in India must be added two more books.

A major book edited by S.M. Michael (1999) contains a number of very important essays and articles investigating various issues in depth. Thus, we have articles looking back at how Indian society, in coming to terms with stratification, worked out a theory of untouchability (Shrirama). John C.B. Webster carefully responds to the question regarding 'Who is a Dalit' in a nuanced essay, which reflects his years of research and writing on this topic. Historical realities are fleshed out in essays dealing with the interaction and critique of Brahmin power by Phule (Mahesh Gavaskar) and an analysis of Ambedkar's understanding of religion and the role played by Buddhism in the Dalit movement (Timothy Fitzgerald). The expectations of the Dalits and their legitimate demands are specified in an essay regarding how society can be re-ordered in India, in terms of a Dalit vision (S.M. Michael) and the contribution and interrogation of mainstream sociology by the Dalit movement (Gopal Guru). The importance of a revamp of present sociological discourse in India is also indicated (S. Selvan). There are fascinating and stimulating studies in delineating the realities of marginalized communities in various contexts – the Adivasis in South Gujarat and the attempts of Hinduization (Arjun Patel); Mahar women in Ahmednagar district (Traude Pillai-Vetschera); a comparative study of Black American and Dalit liberation (K.P. Singh); an examination of the phenomenon of demon possession in Catholic communities (Robert Deliege); and an examination of the widespread reality of *Asprashyeekaran* (Dalitization) (Shyam Lal). The collection also includes major articles on various aspects of Dalit realities within the framework of the Indian economic realities, including an analysis of Ambedkar to economic policy and its impact on the Dalits (Gail Omvedt); how the new economic policy forces the Dalits to bear the brunt of liberalisation (B.L. Mungekar); an analysis of the development paradigm in relation to Dalit employment (S.P. Punalekar); and how employment functions as a vehicle of social mobility (R. Pais).

The reason why I have given this overview of the contents of the book is to show the broad array of the issues under consideration. This also serves to specify the magnitude of the task of addressing and problematizing centuries of deliberate injustice and sanctioned marginalization of the Dalit communities in India. The sub-title of the book, 'Vision and Values', indicates that despite all that the Dalit communities have had to experience, and in spite of the travails they had to undergo, and notwithstanding the tragedies that have become part of their lived reality, nevertheless there remains an optimism that change is possible and that far from allowing the oppressive forces to silence Dalit aspirations and hopes, such oppression has only steeled the resolve of the Dalit communities to proactively agitate, protest and work toward the realization of the vision of a truly free and democratic nation, where values are upheld and not paid lip-service to.

This collection raises several issues that demand urgent attention and response and I can only point to some of these. In the Introduction, Michael has done a commendable job of highlighting the background on which the essays are built and also offers a historical overview of the ideology of the terminological considerations. Terminology is constantly in a process of being interrogated and refined and one must continue to be aware of this. Interrogating terminology prevents words and concepts, as well as real people with real emotions, from being frozen in time and space, and constantly alerts us to the power of the politics of representation.

One must also take into consideration the fact that so-called foundational texts and their interpretation have a power and reach far beyond that envisaged or even anticipated. One must recognize this and be prepared to perceive how meanings have been generated and values reinforced. This of course raises the question of the role of Sanskrit and the Sanskrit texts as being primary agents in reinforcing the ideology of Dalit enslavement. One cannot wish these texts away. The texts are there to be read and re-read. It is when one understands the processes that created a context where enslavement was legitimised that the movement towards liberation is possible.

The emergence of Ambedkar as an icon of Dalit suffering and hope has led to a spurt in interest in his immense and wide-ranging contribution not only to the Dalit cause, but also to his role in the emergence of the Indian nation-state. The immensity and the magnitude of his achievements still have much to offer the committed researcher. Aspects of such contributions, which are indicated in various places in the essays, offer extremely valuable analysis and also point to directions in which Ambedkaran studies could profitably go. Provocative theses have also been advanced – most notably by Gail Omvedt – who speculates that Ambedkar would have welcomed aspects of globalization if it would help in the process of Dalit emancipation and would promote the process of moving towards equality. Such ways of thinking cannot be dismissed out of hand, but need to be investigated, using Ambedkaran categories of understanding the mechanism of state intervention in promoting social and economic justice.

The book edited by H. Kotani (1997), Professor of History at the Tokyo Metropolitan University, is an outstanding and splendid example of cross-cultural historical investigation, where those coming from a particular location and from a specific situation – in this case, specialists in South Asian studies at various universities in Japan, offer an invigorating and fertile analysis of historical and contextual studies of Dalit life.

Here again, I would like to give a rapid indication of the assortment of essays collected and the topics covered: In the section on 'Untouchability in History' there are essays on tracing the reality of social discrimination from ancient India to the medieval period, indicating how the ruling classes benefited from the transfer of discriminatory discourse to actual social practice (Gen'ichi Tamazaki); an analysis of references to the untouchables in Tamil inscriptions and historical sources in Tamil Nadu, exploring neglected yet indispensable sources (Noboru Karashima); a comprehensive survey of the social and economic decline of the Chamar community in Rajasthan from the middle of the seventeenth to the beginning of the nineteenth centuries (Masanori Sato); and a survey of the Ati Sudra castes in the Medieval Deccan, clearly pointing out the deep ambivalence that lay at the heart of their interaction with other castes and amongst themselves (Hiroyuki Kotani). Kotani also offers a fine overview of the legal status of the depressed castes under the British colonial rule to start the next section, which deals with the theme of the position and positioning of the depressed castes during the colonial period. The nomenclature is faithful to the period represented and the period is enfleshed through the description of the economic change in a south Indian village and its impact on the untouchables in a context when there was a great water scarcity (Tsukasa Mizushima); in addition there is the description of conflict and controversy among the Mahars in Bombay Presidency over hereditary patrimony (Hiroyuki Kotani again). The concluding section on the liberation movements has five essays: an introductory overview and analysis of movements among the depressed castes seeking liberation (Masao Naito); a case study, rich in statistical data, of the Tiyya community in British Malabar, showing the connections and inter-connections with other social and ideological movements of that time (Toshie Awaya); the rhetoric of anti-untouchability and the anti-untouchability movements in the Maharashtra of the late nineteenth century and early twentieth century, including studies of a wide spectrum of influential leaders, (Masao Naito); an essay demonstrating the significant contribution of Jogendranath Mandal, within the framework of the movement toward Partition (Masayuki Usuda); and a final essay on how elections at the Gram Panchayat level in West Bengal in 1993 led to debates on the politics of naming and the policies of social and economic benefits (Masahiko Togawa).

These essays, which are painstakingly written and meticulously researched, offer us a large mass of data which needs to enter into and interact with the wider discourse on Dalit realities and Dalit liberation in India today. While it is easy to speak in generalities and engage in over-simplifications, the importance of this book lies in the display of thorough and detailed analysis, which forms the seedbed on which scholarship on Dalit issues can continue to expand.

What strikes one is the scrupulous attention to detail that characterises each contribution. This is evident in the scope of information provided and the richness of the literature quoted and used. Ongoing scholarship on the caste system and its discontents is well served by these contributions. There is no over-simplistic problematizing of caste realities that are then addressed with prescriptive formulae. Rather it is in the laying out and enfleshing of the complexities of human interaction that are generated by the caste system, and in the indication of the various levels of desire that the caste system produces, including the desire produced in those who are the victims of this system, that the book succeeds in demonstrating how pioneering and dedicated academic work can serve as an instrument of Dalit liberation.[8]

All this leads me to my first methodological point: Dalit theology, which at one stage was accused of being a narrow theological 'ism', of relevance only to those who had the 'pathos' experience, or were in empathetic or sympathetic agreement with it, draws its strength from the rich and complex inter-connections with the methodological possibilities thrown up by epistemological inquiry in the spectrum of fields of knowledge. In other words, the strength of Dalit theology lies precisely in the possibility of its inter-disciplinarity, something that needs to be acknowledged and fostered.

Representation and Identity: Some Questions

In his contribution to a colloquium on Christian identity and cultural nationalism, Satish Deshpande, who is Professor of Sociology at Delhi University, in an extremely interesting and thoroughly documented study of 'Caste Inequalities among Indian Christians: A Statistical Note',[9] makes certain observation that need a thorough analysis. Using data from the National Sample Survey Organisation (NSSO) 55th Round national survey conducted in 1999-2000 he indicates, with detailed statistical tables, a very comprehensive and at times quite startling interpretation of the social and economic realities of Indian Christians. One of the most attention-grabbing and controversial figures that are presented relates to Caste and Religion in both Rural and Urban India. Noting that 'all NSSO data on caste and community are self-reported data; they are not matched with official lists as is done in the Census', the figures reveal that as far as Caste composition of Indian Christians are concerned, in the rural areas

---

[8] J.J. Sebastian, 'Review of Kotani, H. Ed., 1997 'Caste System, Untouchability and the Depressed,' Japanese Studies on South Asia No. 1 (New Delhi: Manohar)', *Religion and Society* 48:1, March (2003).

[9] E.C. John and S. Prabhakar, eds., *Christian Identity and Cultural Nationalism: Challenges and Opportunities* (Bangalore: BTESSC/SATHRI for Ecumenical Christian Academy, 2006), 50-77.

the reported figures are Scheduled Tribes – 36.9%, Scheduled Castes – 12.5%, Other Backward Castes – 18.1%, and 'Upper' Castes, where this category 'is a residual one – it includes all those who do not fall into any of the other caste categories' – 32.6%.[10] For Urban India the figures are Scheduled Tribes – 17.9%, Scheduled Castes – 8.4%, Other Backward Castes – 26.4%, and 'Upper' Castes – 47.4%. These are indeed disquieting figures. Deshpande notes that the 'word "upper" is put in quotes to indicate that it a claimed rather than legally sanctioned data'. If this is so, given the assertion of the Dalit scholar and writer Chirakarodu in the same book[11] that 50 – 60% of Christians in India come from the Dalit background, then the figures here of 12.5% (rural) and 8.4% (urban) is indeed astounding.

This raises several questions – in terms of 'self-reporting' there seems to be a huge tendency among Christians of Dalit origin to claim a different status, and scholars and researches would do well to investigate this phenomenon. Also, this calls into question the methodology adopted by those who were involved in the survey – were they attuned to how people responded to issues regarding caste? Did they try to probe beneath what was 'self-reported'? Deshpande also offers several other tables which offer much food for thought, not to say anything about matter for analysis, including comparing caste inequality across religious communities, consumption patterns, figures regarding those living below the poverty line by caste and religion, and also regional variations in intra-Christian caste inequality, the last including tables regarding the regional distribution of Christian population by caste and region in rural and urban India. In conclusion he points out two areas of concern: 'the wide gap between the Scheduled Tribes of the North East and those in the rest of India; and the question of Dalit Christians in all regions, who continue to suffer from the disadvantages of their caste status and lag far behind upper caste Christians'. Given the statistical figures quoted, the further question is, if this is the case regarding those who have claimed the Dalit status for themselves, then there seems to be a correlation between economic mobility and the denial or rejection of certain caste identities. This is another matter that requires investigation by sociologists and theologians who are concerned about the question regarding identity and self-assertion.[12]

The Princeton philosopher Kwame Anthony Appiah writes:

---

[10] Scheduled Tribes, Scheduled Castes and Backward Castes are recognized by the Constitution of India as special population groupings that have traditionally been on the margins of Indian society generally led in most periods of Indian history by the Higher Castes.

[11] P. Chirakarodu, 'Dalit Christians: A Case of Social Plight', in *Christian Identity and Cultural Nationalism: Challenges and Opportunities*, ed. E.C. John and S. Prabhakar (Bangalore: BTESSC/SATHRI for Ecumenical Christian Academy 2006), 30-36.

[12] J.J. Sebastian, 'Review', *Bangalore Theological Forum* XXXIX:1, June (2007).

> [It] may be helpful to consider two rival pictures of what is involved in shaping one's individuality. One, a picture that comes from romanticism, is the idea of finding one's self – of discovering, by means of reflection or a careful attention to the world, a meaning for one's life that is already there, waiting to be found. This is the vision we can call *authenticity*: it is a matter of being true to who you already really are, or would be if it weren't for distorting influences.... The other picture, the *existentialist* picture, let's call it, is one in which, as the doctrine goes, existence precedes essence: that is, you exist first and then have to decide what to exist as, who to be, afterward....
>
> But neither of these pictures is right. The authenticity picture is wrong because it suggests that there is no role for creativity in making a self that the self is already and in its totality fixed by our natures....
>
> By the same token, the existentialist picture is wrong because it suggests that there is *only* creativity, that there is nothing for us to respond to, nothing out of which to do the construction.... The reasonable middle view is that constructing an identity is a good thing (if self-authorship is a good thing) but that the identity must make some kind of sense. And for it to make sense, it must be an identity constructed in response to facts outside oneself, things that are beyond one's own choices.[13]

This leads to my next methodological point: Dalit theology is a theology that is in constant quest of defining, refining, interrogating, forming and re-forming/reforming the identity question. Rather than merely affirming simplistic and essentialist myths of origin, Dalit theology constantly searches for that existential yet elusive element, identity, which offers a fertile possibility of understanding the self, leading in turn to the interrogation of those forms of self-understanding that, very often, have been constructed or imposed.

Popular Dalit Religion, the Bible, and Questions Regarding Baptism

Given the numbers, it is surprising that Indian Christian theology too had ignored Dalit hopes, fears, aspirations and modes of theologizing for so long. The emergence of Dalit theology and the growing literature on various phenomenological aspects of the Christian Dalit experience is a welcome corrective to traditional modes of discourse.[14]

---

[13] K.A. Appiah, *The Ethics of Identity* (Princeton: Princeton University Press, 2007), 17-18.

[14] Nirmal, 'Towards', 27-40; S. Clarke, *Dalits and Christianity: Subaltern Religion and Liberation Theology in India* (Delhi: Oxford University Press, 1998); J. Webster, *Religion and Dalit Liberation: An Examination of Perspectives*, 2 ed. (New Delhi: Manohar, 2002); J. Massey and S. Prabhakar, eds., *Frontiers in Dalit Hermeneutics* (Bangalore/Delhi: BTESSC/SATHRI/CDSS, 2005); J. Massey et al., eds., *Breaking Theoretical Grounds for Dalit Studies* (New Delhi: Centre for Dalit/Subaltern Studies, 2006).

Homi Bhabha, in his programmatic essay 'Signs Taken for Wonders', has offered us a very interesting reading of a particular incident regarding missionaries, Indian Christians, and the Bible, where he comments that 'the words of the master become the site of hybridity – the warlike, subaltern sign of the native – then we may not only read between the lines but even seek to change the often coercive reality that they so lucidly contain', and goes on to conclude by quoting a 'much-tried missionary' who wonders angrily as to why the 'natives' would want to receive a Bible and exclaims that it may be for curiosity value, to sell for a pittance, as an object for barter, or to 'use it for waste paper'.[15] Such questions and attitudes recur with telling familiarity two hundred years later.

I want to offer four examples from my pastoral ministry, the first three coming from my time as a pastor in the rural, predominantly Dalit, Gauribidanur congregation of the Karnataka Central Diocese of the Church of South India. During my many pastoral visits, I rarely took my own Bible with me, but after the usual preliminaries, asked for their Bible, so that I could read a passage before prayer. In one case, the family proudly pulled out a steel trunk which was under the rolled-up mattresses in the small house, took out several layers of folded clothing, took out a clean white towel in which a pristine Bible, with many of its pages uncut, lay wrapped; in another, the family pointed to the open Bible which had been placed on a small shelf on the wall, decorated with coloured flashing lights, but when I gingerly took it off the shelf, discovered not only a thick layer of dust, but the remains of a number of flying insects; and in a third case, was given the Bible from among a pile of magazines, only to discover on opening it, that it was serving as a store for the cut-out pictures of film actors and actresses, preserved amongst its pages. The fourth example comes from the time when I was a pastor in the urban Hudson Memorial Kannada congregation in Bangalore, where (among many other things) I had to bless unusual objects, including in this case a machine which converted old paper into pulp and then into egg-trays. The owner told me that he employed a number of 'rag-pickers' to bring him paper of suitable quality for this purpose, and discovered that there were a large number of New Testaments and Bibles (most probably those distributed gratis by organizations like the Gideons) in what had been brought in. He told me that at first he had tried to 'rescue' the Bibles from the pile, but then when he realized how many there were, just let them continue the journey of reincarnation into egg-trays.

The question of the 'fetishization' of objects is an old issue in religious studies and the interaction between religious objects precious to one tradition in

---

[15] H. K. Bhabba, 'Signs Taken for Wonders: Questions of Ambivalence and Authority under a Tree Outside Delhi, May 1817', in *The Location of Culture* (London: Routledge, 1994), 102-22, 21-22.

the encounter and acceptance of another is also an important area of research.[16] The question that we need to ask now is whether 'fetishization' describes this reverence to the object and not the 'Word'? Is there something that we have not tried to understand while trying to use such explanations as fetishization? What is interesting and intriguing in the examples is the complex nature of the inter-link between the reality of commitment to a faith-praxis and the instrumentalization of the orienting symbols of that faith. The Bible, in these cases, has variously been seen as something so precious that it needs to be carefully stored away and although out of sight, is unlikely to be out of mind; as something to be illuminated externally, while the 'lamp to our feet' idea, in terms of 'containing' something illumining, is switched off; as something adding value and providing security to that which offers enrichment to one's life; as something whose worth would not be erased, even when the 'black marks on white paper' were no longer legible. These are just some of the ways in which the incidents can be interpreted and there is certainly a wide assortment of interpretations that they can generate. Hence we need to investigate the relationship between the way in which the local has interacted with what was sought to be a given. Clarke in his analysis of the religion of the Paraiyar community, where he looks at the use of the drum in countering a word-centred religion, talks about subaltern religion making use of 'all and sundry in its religious construction. Bits and pieces are collected from various sources through numerous ways: some religious resources are discarded as irrelevant, many others are useful pieces annexed conveniently from the dominant communities' framework, while some are discovered from years of their own collective life experience'.[17]

In recent years the work of the Mylapore Institute for Indigenous Studies, in Chennai, has moved in the direction of identifying, exploring and researching the growth of indigenous forms of Christianity in India. This kind of work also involves, directly and indirectly, analysing the phenomenon of 'unbaptized believers'[18] and one of the most important pieces of research on this area is the work by Herbert E. Hoefer, originally published in 1991 and recently reprinted.[19] Some of the questions that can be raised in relation to baptism when one examines Dalit religious practices, the growth of indigenous Christ-oriented communities, and attitudes to the Bible include questions regarding

---

[16] T.F. Mathews, *The Clash of Gods: A Reinterpretation of Early Christian Art* (Princeton, NJ: Princeton University Press, 1993).

[17] Clarke, *Dalits and Christianity*, 127-28.

[18] R.E. Hedlund, ed., *Christianity Is Indian: The Emergence of an Indigenous Community* (Mylapore/Delhi: MIIS/ISPCK, 2000); R.E. Hedlund, ed., *Quest for Identity: India's Churches of Indigenous Origins, the 'Little Tradition' in Indian Christianity* (Mylapore/Delhi: MIIS/ISPCK, 2000); O.L. Snaitang, ed., *Churches of Indigenous Origins in North East India* (Mylapore/Delhi: MIIS/ISPCK), 2000).

[19] H.E. Hoefer, *Churchless Christianity* (Pasadena: William Carey Library, 2001).

how baptism is understood as a 'physical' phenomenon – is the water seen as something that 'physically' functions to 'achieve' something during the baptismal sacrament? Is water understood metaphorically? How is the water used during baptism seen in relation to water in daily life, especially in a context where Dalit communities are marked by boundaries of purity and pollution and denied access to common wells and sources of water by those so-called 'upper caste' people? If, as Bradshaw notes '[i]n our fallenness, brokenness and confusion there is no place for rejection and lack of care for those intending discipleship... the baptismal imperative challenges all cold judgmentalism',[20] then what about those who have been judged and denied access to possibilities of a fuller life for no fault of their own? If it is a fact that many of the 'unbaptized believers' come from a Dalit background, how can there be growth and nurture of such people in a context where they decide to remain where they are and not openly identify with a Christian church?[21]

One must also note that the role of the Bible and Christian practices have come under increasing scrutiny in recent years, especially by those who have benefited from the challenges set forth by postcolonial thinking. R.S. Sugirtharajah, in a series of writings,[22] has challenged the way in which the Bible was used to create and foster 'colonizing monotheistic tendencies' and reminded us of the need to recollect 'the many-layered polytheistic context out of which it emerged'.[23] For him the recollecting is not a passive activity, but something that has to be done with a sense of urgency, given the explosive way in which adherents of different religious strands deal with each other. Focusing on the exponentially burgeoning strategies being used to 'market' the Bible to all kinds of interest groups in the West, and the transformation of the Bible into a kind of 'indulgence', he wryly notes that:

> [T]he Bible is introduced into various sub-cultures and a niche carved out for it. The Bible which was hailed as a universal word, transferable to all cultures irrespective of time and space without contaminating the purity of its message, is now being marketed tarnished with traces of the very cultures it once abhorred.

---

[20] T. Bradshaw, 'Baptism and Inclusivity in the Church', in *Baptism, the New Testament and the Church: Historical and Contemporary Studies in Honour of R.E.O. White, Journal for the Study of the New Testament, Supplement Series 171* ed. Stanley E. Porter and Anthony R. Cross (Sheffield: Sheffield Academic Press, 1999), 466.

[21] B. Heymes, 'The Moral Miracle of Faith', in *Dimensions of Baptism: Biblical and Theological Studies, Journal for the Study of the New Testament*, ed. S.E. Porter and A.R. Cross, *Supplement Series 234* (Sheffield: Sheffield Academic Press, 2002), 332.

[22] R.S. Sugirtharajah, *The Bible and the Third World: Precolonial, Colonial and Postcolonial Encounters* (Cambridge: Cambridge University Press, 2001).

[23] R.S. Sugirtharajah, 'Scripture, Scholarship, Empire: Putting the Discipline in Its Place', *The Expository Times* 117:1, October (2005), 3.

> Now it is presented as an easily consumable commercial object – a postmodern fate for an artefact which emerged as a shining example of modernity.[24]

Although his primary examples are drawn from marketing strategies and the identification of niche groups in the West, nevertheless, in completely different contexts, issues and themes emerge which are of interest to those who want to learn from religious practices of Dalit communities. This brings me to my next methodological point: the traditional understanding/s of religion, religious practices, the 'why' of conversion, religious 'objects', the instrumentality of worship and the liturgy, the importance given to the mediation of priests and those believed to have access to the numinous, have to be investigated using methodological tools that recognize that so-called academic 'respectable' modes of inquiry not only have serious in-built shortcomings and overt and covert 'prejudices', but that such modes of inquiry are deliberately skewed against the knowledge-praxis of the modes of inquiry of those marginalized communities, whose very marginalization was actively promoted by such 'scholarship'.

Conclusion: Bypassing the Bypass

Diverting one from the undoubted gains is something that can easily be done. Dominant forms of discourse have the disconcerting habit of raising questions like 'relevance' and 'viability' which forces people to enter into the bypass once again. Questions raising issues like 'reality' and 'representation', often lead to internecine conflicts that help no one but the dominant. Contemporary globalization discourse has also thrown up a number of such 'issues' which, for various reasons, become fashionable, gain an audience, and demand all one's time and energy, and a lot of effort is expended in trying to fit ones own concerns into this dominant frame of discourse. One perceptive commentator notes:

> Neoliberal capitalism, in its triumphant phase, offers no ideological alternative to laissez-faire; nothing else – no other political-economic system – seems even plausible, save as an embodiment of primitive or 'fundamentalist' unreason. The primary question left to public policy is how to succeed in the new world order. Why? Because this new world order hides its ideological scaffolding in the dictates of economic efficiency and capital growth, in the fetishism of the free market, in the exigencies of science and technology.... Under its hegemony there

---

[24] Sugirtharajah, 'Scripture, Scholarship, Empire', 11; R.S. Sugirtharajah, *The Bible and Empire: Postcolonial Explorations* (Cambridge: Cambridge University Press, 2005).

> exists no such thing as society; the social is dissolved into the natural, the biological, the transactional, or the mythic chimera of community.[25]

Although so much has been achieved, including major interventions in the field of Biblical studies and hermeneutics and the rediscovery of Dalit literature, there is much that still needs to be done in the field of Dalit theology. This brings me to my final methodological point: in so far as Dalit theology has systematically questioned all attempts at theological reductionism, the ongoing challenge is that of continuing to fearlessly speak the 'truth' to power, without succumbing to the dictates of mere fashion, without simplistic mimesis, without pandering to the desires of the dominant, and without overlooking the intra-Dalit dynamics. Apart from this via negativa, Dalit theology should affirm what it has always been – a way of living, of praying, of relating, of questioning, a way that is not a bypass, but a way that is itself the way of truth.

Let the last words of this presentation come in the form of a challenge from Namdeo Dhasal:

> The naked infant of our existence in the Kali Yuga
> Pisses in your direction,
> O devil among devils!
> Do shower some kindness on it.
> We slaved away for generations
> We were worn-out and died
> While we hoped for good luck and happiness.
> O beguiling spy! O grand illusion of gravitation!
> Bond with our family;
> Become our kin.
> From now on, live for us; die for us.
> And if that does not happen,
> As of now, you're nobody to us.
> O brazenfaced one!
> I slay the seven horses of your chariot
> And break its wheel.[26]

---

[25] J. Comaroff, 'The End of History, Again? Pursuing the Past in the Postcolony', in *Postcolonial Studies and Beyond*, ed. Ania Loomba and Suvir Kaul et. al. (Delhi: Permanent Black, 2006), 125-44, 32.

[26] D. Chitre, 'I Slew the Seven Horses of the Chariots of the Sun', in *Namdeo Dhasal: Poet of the Underworld - Poems 1972- 2006* (Chennai: Navayana, 2007), 120-26.

Who Does Theology?

D.P. Davies

D.P. Davies was John James professor of theology at the Department of Theology and Religious Studies, University of Wales, Lampeter, UK.

Introduction

Anselm saw theology as *fides quaerens intellectum*, faith searching for understanding. Theology concerns itself with human awareness of something that transcends humanity. It starts where we are and involves a given-ness which forms its fundamental basis. Human experience or awareness of God is interpreted from within this agreed framework. Theology is a way of experiencing and interpreting life but it is also dynamic body of knowledge. Within the Christian tradition, this can be seen in the theologies from the so-called 'margins'. The study of such a dynamic body of knowledge has been the concern of theology and religious studies degree programmes in modern Universities. Theology is however, not the preserve of the elite professionals. The professional theologians need to stand alongside ordinary people and learning from their experiences as much as theirs.

I

There have been many attempts at defining theology, not least in Anselm's famous dictum *fides quaerens intellectum* – faith in search of understanding. Anselm's use of the word intellectus is significant and reminds us that theology is, to some extent at least, an intellectual activity, though I want to suggest it is much more than that. Anselm was working within the community of faith. Faith was assumed, faith in the sense of the content of what was believed rather than as an attitude of heart and mind in relation to God. I want to amplify and extend the scope of Anselm's definition and say that theology concerns itself with human awareness of something that transcends the human; it tries to interpret it and to articulate it. In other words, theology tries to make sense of a dimension of human existence experienced at some time or other by almost all human beings; it is awareness that there is something above and beyond the human and the material, what we might call the divine, for want of a better word. Others would use the word 'God', but for the moment let us adopt a wider definition. I need hardly say that when I speak of human awareness of the divine I am including the awareness of humans of every age and of all cultures, through time and across space. Theology literally means study of God, of course, which might suggest that we should start by defining God, but my firm conviction is that as human beings we should start where we are, so our contemplation of the divine begins with such awareness of the divine as we humans think we experience or have experienced.

I have used the word 'experience' and spoken of 'human awareness'. Others would say that this experience is triggered by something outside the human world; in other words, that what humans experience is an act of divine self-disclosure, a self-revelation. I have no wish to rule this out of order, nor do I wish to deny that this may not be the origin of what we experience; I simply want to start where we are and therefore to postpone, for the moment, any discussion of the explanation of what it is we experience and why.

If the task of theology then is to concern itself with human awareness of the divine, and with interpreting and articulating that experience, where do we start? As I suggested earlier, many theologians have insisted on starting from a given definition of the divine. Where theology is understood as passing on the faith delivered to the saints, there is obviously a given-ness which forms the fundamental basis of theology, such as a traditional Christian understanding of God – for example, that God is the Creator and Sustainer of the universe, that God is the Father of our Lord Jesus Christ, that God is a Trinity of persons, Father, Son and Holy Spirit. Human awareness of God is then interpreted from within this agreed framework. As someone nurtured in the Christian tradition it would not be difficult for me to accept the parameters of a Christian framework as my basic terms of reference, but that is not what I see as the role of theology in the modern University, even if individual teachers and students accept that it is an appropriate framework for formulating their own individual beliefs, as I do myself. Limiting ourselves to such a framework leads to exclusivism and blinds us to the insights and experiences of other civilisations and other cultures in a way that is unforgivable in any academic discipline, and especially in theology, which claims ultimately to be concerned with the universal, the eternal and the infinite.

So where do we start? I repeat the question, since I am persuaded that getting the method right is more important for our understanding of theology than establishing what the subject matter of theology is. Theology is not, in my view, a body of knowledge so much as a way of experiencing and interpreting life. I want therefore to suggest that there are three stages in doing theology, though I recognize that there is no clear-cut division into stages in practice. Many, probably the vast majority, never move beyond the first stage, and to a large extent this is because the professionals, whether the hierarchy of the church, particularly in earlier generations, or professional academic theologians today, have established a kind of closed shop, which now needs to be smashed, and indeed is being smashed in many parts of the contemporary world.

My three stages are these: first, there is human experience (what I earlier described as 'human awareness of something that transcends the human'); this may be at an individual level, i.e. it may be a private, personal experience, though I want to emphasize that I am not just thinking of what are popularly called 'religious experiences', or it may be and more often is a corporate experience: for example, the experience of being part of a particular community or a particular culture or of being heir to a particular tradition. Of its very nature such experience is local, not universal; it is experienced in a particular time and place. So even if the divine is universal, eternal and infinite, our awareness of it is mediated in and through our particular, temporal and finite experience.

Now this experience can be and almost invariably is highly subjective; it is often highly personal and idiosyncratic. It needs to be balanced, and this brings us to stage two, which is that we need to read our experience in the light of the common inheritance of faith – in terms of the Christian tradition, of which I am part, this would mean Scripture (the Bible) along with the inherited tradition of the church's life, history and teaching from the earliest times down to the present day; in other words, I see tradition as a living, dynamic force rather than as a static collection of creedal statements and ethical maxims.

The professional study of theology has concentrated almost exclusively on stage two, and in so doing has made an enormous contribution to human understanding of the divine. Nevertheless, stage three is where the professional theologian's role becomes vitally important, even if we have largely neglected to fulfil it, since this is the stage of critical reflection on experience read in the light of the common inheritance of faith. I want to emphasize the adjective 'critical'. We are to reflect critically on our experience and the accumulated wisdom of the ages; in other words, we are to apply reason, our rational faculties, to this part of our task. And that is the justification of theology as an academic discipline in a University, a place where the whole range of human experience comes under critical scrutiny. I shall return to this point at the end, but for the moment I want to elaborate on the three stages and to ask who then does theology, if doing theology involves all three kinds of activity.

II

I suggested earlier that almost all human beings throughout time have or have had experiences, which can arouse in them an awareness that there is a dimension to existence that transcends the human and the material. Sometimes these are religious experiences, the kinds of visions and auditions experienced by the Hebrew prophets or Joan of Arc, but such experiences are not common and I want to concentrate more on experiences that are the common lot of ordinary mortals. For example, almost all religions have as a standard feature of their practice so-called *rites de passage* (rites of passage), rites which mark birth, puberty, marriage and death. And our experience is that there are times when we are invariably brought to see the limits of human existence and to ask what, if anything, lies beyond, above or below our mortal, finite existence. Few can witness the birth of a child or keep vigil at a deathbed without being conscious of the wonder and mystery of life alongside its apparent futility and incompleteness. Similarly, the common phenomenon of strong feelings of attraction, not to say devotion, between a man and a woman that is commonly called love and which frequently leads to bonding in marriage and the procreation of children raises huge questions about the purpose of existence, about the created order of which we are part, and gives rise to an awareness that there seems to be some power, the power of love perhaps, that transcends it all.

So there are special religious experiences as well as common experiences marked by religious observance, such as funerals to mark the end of human life, which are almost universally religious. Furthermore, these kinds of experiences, which lead us to wonder about human existence and its apparent finitude, to marvel at the creation of which we are part and to speculate about its nature and origin, are not confined to mature adults or persons of high intelligence. Anyone who has had the privilege of bringing up a child knows that the most profound, and often unanswerable, theological questions come from the mouths of babes and sucklings. It was always a matter of some amusement to me that my daughter at the tender age of four could tie my father, an experienced parish priest, in theological knots with these kinds of questions – not that I would claim to have offered any more convincing answers myself!

Or again we can think of what we often call the inspiration of poets, writers, artists, sculptors, composers and the like, and of how they are themselves aware and help us to be aware of dimensions of human existence that transcend the merely human. If this is inspiration, then we are bound to ask what it is that inspires. I once had the stimulating and exciting experience of working with an artist in producing a series of TV programmes, which were meditations on biblical themes read in the light of the world around us, and was left quite flabbergasted at the way he interpreted my commentary in ways of which I had myself been totally unaware before seeing his pictorial and symbolic representation of my ideas.

All these are positive experiences. We are on a high when we hear music that moves us to tears of joy or sorrow, or when we fall in love or see a new-born baby. And certainly those who have mystical experiences are on a high, not unlike the high induced by drugs. But most of our experience is not of this order; indeed, just as we can reach the heights, so we can plumb the depths. There are experiences which far from making us aware of the divine induce in us an overwhelming sense of the absence of the divine. Despair is as much a part of the human condition as hope. We are just as prone to pessimism as to optimism. Human beings can and do sink into such depths of depression that life becomes unbearable. Whether or not suicide is the consequence, questions are raised about claims that there is a power above and beyond the human, for what sort of power is it that fails us when we most need support? Here we are beginning to confront one of the most profound and intractable theological problems posed by human existence, the problem of suffering, especially where the suffering seems to be totally undeserved and inexplicable. All the theological expertise in the world is humbled before a stricken mother whose child has been killed in a road accident or the husband whose young wife has died of leukaemia.

And when we move from our own personal, individual experience of human existence to look at the corporate dimension of human life, it is the dark side of life that hits us more than the opposite. I have no reason to believe that life today is any worse than in previous ages, and in many ways it is certainly more comfortable and enjoyable for many of us, but we know only too well that we live in a world characterized by extremes of wealth and poverty that leave millions of our fellow humans struggling simply to stay alive and often failing in the struggle. We know only too well of wars and rumours of wars, many of them, let us admit it, caused or at least fuelled by religious differences, with their devastating effects on innocent bystanders. We know all about oppression and exploitation, of man's inhumanity to man. And yet in the face of all this several of the major faiths of the world assert that theirs is a God who works in history. Think, for example, of the Jewish faith and its claim that the hand of God can be seen in the history of Israel, both in ancient and in modern times, and consider this claim alongside all we now know about the horrors of the holocaust. Another feature of the Jewish faith, as of Christianity and Islam, is belief in the ultimate justice of God. In the aftermath of the mass murders of the gas chambers and of Hiroshima, enormous theological questions about the so-called divine dimension of human history are bound to be posed for such a faith. I am not, however, for the moment concerned with finding answers to these questions, since all I am trying to show is that all areas of human experience produce the raw material of theology; in undergoing such experiences, individually or collectively, we are aware that there is more to life than what we see on the surface, and for those nurtured in a community of faith these kinds of experiences point them not only to an awareness of the presence of God but also, paradoxically, to a sense of God's absence.

Ironically, within the Christian tradition in recent times it is those whose earthly existence is one of unrelenting suffering who seem most aware of the divine dimension of their experience. Within the Roman Catholic Church, for example, we have seen the development of a new way of doing theology in some of the poorest and most oppressed communities in the world, especially in Latin America. We have seen the Roman Catholic Church, and indeed the World Council of Churches following their lead, adopt what is called the preferential option for the poor, and we have heard theologians claim that the God of love is incarnated in the poor and the God of justice at work in liberation movements. For such theologians the task of theology is not simply to interpret the world, but to transform it. Consequently, we now have black theology, feminist theology, liberation theology, gay theology and so on being done by those who are engaged in the struggle to liberate blacks or women or the poor or gays or whatever from exploitation and oppression. And in this struggle they claim to find God. Once again I am not concerned with the validity of such claims; I wish only to show that these claims raise questions about the nature of human society and human existence which suggest that there is more to it than first meets the eye.

The phenomenon of religion has rarely excited such wide public interest as it does in today's world, even if religious commitment is not as widespread in western European countries as it has been in previous generations. In this country popular books on theology and religion attract a wide readership. Furthermore, religious broadcasting, both on TV and radio, is a growth industry. Theology also has a high profile in current affairs programmes.

What I am suggesting is that our experience of being human, whether as individuals or in society, suggests that there is more to it than merely being human. At times, this awareness comes from a leap of imagination, a kind of leap in the dark; at other times, it seems to spring from a kind of intuition or instinct. Most of us are aware of it. Ours, however, is not the first generation of humans to feel this way nor is ours the only culture to experience such an awareness. The next step in our theological task is therefore to measure our experience against the touchstone of the wisdom and experience of earlier generations and other cultures; this is a particular obligation on those of us who are heirs to a religious tradition which to a very large extent accounts for us being what we are. I hope, however, that I have already established that theology is not in the first place an activity confined to a professional elite; it is done by all. It is an activity undertaken by the people and for the people.

III

I suggested earlier that my three stages were not necessarily a clear-cut sequence. There is considerable potential overlap between them. Indeed, for those nurtured in the community of a particular faith, knowledge of the Scriptures of that faith and of its traditions invariably precedes the kind of experience I have been describing. Be that as it may, at some stage or other we all need the input of tradition; we also need to understand that tradition is not something static, not something given once-for-all and passed on unaltered to future generations. Tradition is a dynamic force. This, I think, is true of all faiths, even of a faith like Judaism which gives the impression of having a fixed tradition or the kind of Christianity found in the Eastern Orthodox Churches which appears to claim that tradition was fixed for good and all more than a thousand years ago.

What I am saying is that a proper interpretation of our human awareness that there is a dimension to existence beyond the merely human and material requires us to look at the wisdom of the ages and the experience of cultures other than our own. This by and large has been the concern of theology and religious studies degree programmes in modern Universities. For Christians this involves detailed study of the Bible, courses in Church history and the history of Christian doctrine, study of ethics and liturgy as well as the philosophy of religion. More recently, we have come to see the need for the study of religion as a phenomenon and of religions, and this has become a distinct discipline in its own right alongside theology. We have also become conscious of the need to study particular religions, such as Christianity or Islam, in the context of the society of which they are part, and this has led to a more inter-disciplinary approach to the study of religion. All this is a respectable programme of academic study, which rightly finds it place in the modern secular University. What I have tried to do is to give it a proper context, one which will give greater meaning and purpose to what we can do than is the case when we see it simply as academic study pursued for its own sake.

The further challenge is to give the people, ordinary people, knowledge of their Scriptures and the traditions of their faith, or in the case of those who have no faith a knowledge of the common wealth of the world's religions, to enable them the more easily to interpret their experience and to test the validity of those intuitions of the divine presence they receive. For over twenty years I have been heavily involved in extension education in theology, work which is intended to meet such a need. I am much encouraged by what has been done so far, though we are still a long way from achieving the kind of appeal to the masses enjoyed by the Theological Education by Extension movement in Latin America. Nor have we, internally or externally, really got to grips with what is, in my view, the real task of theology, what I have called my third stage, namely critical reflection on experience read in the light of the common inheritance of the faith. This is the real challenge to theology today, and to a discussion of that I finally turn.

IV

May I once again emphasize the word 'critical'. We are to reflect *critically* on our experience in the light of the common inheritance of the faith. The exercise of our critical faculties, our reason, is important because our experience is inevitably personal and consequently partial. It is confined to a particular place and a particular time in history; it comes to us in the context of a particular culture. In these circumstances there is always a danger that we shall be tempted to absolutize our particular way of seeing things, our ideology, our set of beliefs and customs, or to generalize on the basis of our partial apprehension of truth in such a way as to overlook or worse still to reject the insights of peoples of other times and other cultures.

It is at this point that a proper dialogue between our inheritance from the past and our present experience becomes essential, but not simply to provide a corrective, as if our present understanding is being judged against some absolute standard handed down to us. It is just as wrong to absolutize tradition or to generalize on the basis of the experience of our ancestors as it is to absolutize our own ideologies or beliefs. We must avoid every kind of fundamentalism both in our attitude to Scriptures or traditions and indeed in our interpretation of our own experience, whether this is derived from reason or intuition or emotion. Our only fundamentalism is a recognition of the need to return to the fundamentals to achieve a better understanding of ourselves, our world and our destiny.

Adopting such a critical stance will almost certainly bring the theologian into conflict with authority, both within the community of faith and outside. It is not unknown for theologians to clash with Church hierarchies, and today we hardly need to look far for examples of theologians in conflict with the political powers that be. And that is as it should be. All education, or in this specific case doing theology, poses a challenge to those with a vested interest in preserving the status quo.

What all this tells us about God, the subject and the object of all theological activity, I am not entirely sure, but we have learned a good deal about the way or ways we apprehend God. God has traditionally been conceived of in absolute, universal terms. God is thought to be transcendent and eternal. God is above nature (supernatural) and beyond the physical (metaphysical). In essence God is infinite. I do not for a moment wish to deny that any or all of these things may not be true of God, but what I have been saying leads me to conclude that, though God may be all these things, our apprehension of God is relative and particular rather than absolute and universal. We experience God as immanent and temporal, not as transcendent and eternal. We encounter God in our natural and physical existence; indeed, we encounter God in the natural and the physical, not as supernatural and metaphysical. In other words, it is the accidence not the essence of God that we apprehend in our finite existence and with our finite minds. For us the infinite is quite literally mind-boggling, and I am inclined to think that we should not waste too much time worrying about it.

And so what have we learned about doing theology? I have stressed, by now I imagine *ad nauseam*, that theology is a combination of action and reflection. Though the reflection may involve analysis and interpretation and be primarily an intellectual activity, what I have said has, I hope, indicated that this is secondary to the primary activity of experiencing God, which is open to all. Theology is an activity for all, without distinction. Who then does theology? Why everyone!

What then is left for the professional theologian? What is the proper role of a professor of theology, for example? My submission is that the professional theologian is first and foremost a resource person, though not in the manner of an armchair pundit who sits on the sidelines and avoids committing himself to the action. The professional theologian must rather be alongside people, learning from their insights. He must be humble and self-critical before the experience of others. The professional theologian needs to empathize with people, ordinary people; he must help them put into words what they experience, and give them confidence to think theologically, not to be afraid of talking about God or seeing the presence of God in their world and in their lives. There will also be times when the theologian will need to correct and even to be critical, especially in the context of the household of faith.

Anselm saw theology as *fides quaerens intellectum*, faith searching for understanding. Yes, the theologian needs to have faith, not in the sense of blind adherence to a set of propositions of varying degrees of credibility, but in the sense of humility and openness to that which ultimately transcends our partial, finite, human existence and our all too feeble attempts to interpret and to understand it.

Researching Christian Action[1]

David Adams and Bernard Farr

Mr. David Adams was Tutor in Professional Studies and Dr. Bernard Farr is Senior Residentiary Fellow at the Oxford Centre for Mission Studies, UK.

Faith and Advanced Practice

The church is growing rapidly in many parts of the world, creating an increasing demand for competent leadership in many fields of Christian action. There is also the continuing and pressing need for that leadership to be able to articulate the relationship between Christian faith and Christian action. The calling to 'ministry', and the associated training for ministry, is increasingly located in the world of work rather than in the church. Christians working in the professions are demanding to understand how their professional practice can be understood in relation to their faith. They want to work on the fundamental issues which arise from a Christian understanding of the nature of their profession, as against just being Christians working within a profession which explains and justifies itself in wholly or mainly secular terms. They also want to reflect on their personal calling to this form of Christian ministry and gain an integrated understanding of their own professional practice and their own Christian faith.

Once established in their field many practitioners are keen to update themselves professionally but most find that conventional post-graduate study may not be compatible with the realities of their professional practice. Programme content may not be relevant to their professional experience, or the delivery structure required by the educational institution may not fit their busy lives, or the modes of assessment may not be adequate to their need. The traditional academic PhD is awarded in recognition of an original contribution to knowledge. Practical knowledge, however, is not fully known in or entirely expressible in propositional terms since it is embedded, in and formative of, and not detachable from action. To that extent it is not amenable to propositional formulation in any simple way. Specifically here we have in mind the actions of those Christians who are achieving major organisational change and/or excellence in professional life. Professional learning therefore must be designed to integrate closely with each participant's current work, to enable them to add quality and value to their professional practice.

---

[1] This is a revised and updated version of the paper originally published in *Transformation*.

At the same time, global factors of economy, ecology, population, migration, communication, religion, politics and technology are contributing to rapid and radical change, presenting the leadership of the emerging church and faith-based organisations with new and challenging problems and opportunities for compassionate and transformative action in society and culture and particularly within all forms of professional practice. The range and complexity of such issues facing Christian professionals globally is thus widening and deepening, and demanding ever higher levels of competence.

On OCMS entering its 25th year in 2008, it re-visited the question of how a response can effectively be made to these needs and the challenges they bring. How might OCMS continue best to fulfil its calling to increase human capacity for Christian action in society and culture, particularly in the non-western world?

Responding to Need

This question has occasioned a fundamental review by OCMS of its activities. The review looked not simply to find new ways of doing old things but to commit OCMS to new ways of doing new things.

This paper describes one important strand of this review and of the nature of the 'new things' and the 'new ways" which it envisioned. The thought was that the best of previous practice would be kept and so the traditional MPhil/PhD programme validated by the University of Wales would continue as before. To this would be added a new programme which had a different epistemological, theological and methodological basis for equipping Christian leaders exercising their profession calling as a Christian calling. The new initiative would draw on best practice in work-based learning and reflective practice, privileging the practical knowledge and experience of the practitioner and facilitating a process of critical inquiry and transformative action in their context.

The new initiative would be designed therefore to enable transformative leadership in professional life in the most significant fields of Christian involvement – in, for example, community care, the media, education, development, business – and to do so by taking the various forms of professional practice as themselves the object of study and research. It would also arbitrate between those things which are situation-specific and those which form a common core to any form of professional practice. Participants would for this reason work collaboratively as well as individually and this will be a distinctive feature of their research experience.

The programme would be for Christian activists who want to make a difference in their world and enables them to make this difference through and throughout their research in an iterative manner. Activists are interventionists do not want to study practice at a distance of time or space. They want to study the processes of transformation from the inside and to understand their own engagement in that transformation and the ways in which they themselves are also thereby transformed. This opportunity for senior practitioners from around the world to engage for themselves, and together, in rigorous research-based inquiry into professional practice, leading to the award of a PhD in Professional Practice from a leading UK University would be in these ways be unique. Some market research around these ideas occasioned considerable excitement and the idea was extended to envisage cohorts of students being formed in various locations around the world.

This new programme would aim, then, to develop a mature and critical awareness of the relationship between the practitioners' personal faith and values, organisational setting and professional practice, by interaction with relevant disciplines of study, using a multi-dimensional grid of reflective practice and research.

Christian Scholarship

While increasingly evident in higher education in general, the considerations just articulated are consistent with a Christian understanding of the human person and the natural world and are therefore integral to an understanding of the Christian vocation. For this reason, both implicitly and explicitly, this programme enables participants to think and act theologically and ethically in their practice. It is assumed that the participant in the programme is sympathetic to this worldview and is committed to critical, creative and compassionate thought and action in society and culture. Thinking and acting theologically and ethically is a 'disposition', an 'active mindfulness' of a particular kind which is brought to bear on whatever issue arises in professional practice or life. It is not the application of a learned theological or ethical content and skill in applying it but the ability to respond to a situation from within one's being as a person for whom 'theological thinking' has become a skill, a trait, a way of seeing, a way of thinking, a way of acting. To use an analogy, it is akin to 'musicality' as a condition of being musical rather just regarding a musician as one who can achieve some level of musical performance.

The programme would therefore attend to students as themselves in a process of personal transformation through their research, and provides the opportunity for each participant to evaluate and improve themselves in their practice in the light of this vision of personal, social, cultural, ethical and theological transformation. It was expected that during and after the programme the 'reflective' practitioner would write up their work for wider circulation in professional journals and other contexts and in ways which exhibit this Christian disposition or active mindfulness.

Professional Relevance and Location

Gardner, Csikszentmihalyi and Damon[2] describe good work as occurring 'when excellence and ethics meet'. This new programme is located at this juncture of quality and integrity in professional practice, providing the opportunity to enhance competence and skills at the same time as deepening personal values and sense of vocation. While providing exposure to the intellectual traditions and developing trends in the participant's professional field, the programme also probes the personal characteristics necessary for improvement in individual performance. This is presented as not merely an academic exercise but one that can only be done in practice.

Practice-based Learning

Practice-based learning is learning grounded in action – learning in and through action in the community or workplace. It is not the same as learning for work (e.g. a work placement) or at work (e.g. a training course related to work) but learning through work in the regular course of work. The programme focuses on the challenges and choices faced in professional life; and it also recognizes these as a participative and social process. It contributes to the development of communities of practice through personal and collaborative inquiry and stimulates the pursuit of excellence and innovation in practice. The programme draws on best practice in work-based learning and reflective practice, privileging the practical knowledge and experience of the practitioner and facilitating a process of critical inquiry and transformative action in their context.

Research-based Reflective Practice

The envisaged programme was designed to support the development of research-minded practitioners who take an attitude of inquiry into all aspects of their work, generating an understanding of their practice as 'living theory'[3] or 'personal theory'[4] in a continuous cycle of reflection and action that develops into a scholarship of practice.

At the heart of this process lie the skills of research-based reflective practice – in its simplest form a conscious cycle of reflection and action which, as it deepens, develops the ability to establish critical distance from action (a critical subjectivity), regarding the sphere of action as micro-experiments from which to learn. The choices involved in this process are sharpened by the development of a critical awareness of the assumptions (beliefs, conventions and causal

---

[2] H. Gardner et al., *Good Work* (New York: Basic Book, 2001).

[3] J. Whitehead, *Action Research, Living Theory* (Thousand Oaks, CA: Sage, 2006).

[4] P. Jarvis, *The Practitioner-Researcher* (San Francisco: Jossey-Bass, 1999).

influences) that shape the 'habitus'[5] of practice. The mature research-based reflective practitioner is simultaneously aware of these tacit influences on practice, reflecting in and on action in both the personal and social domain.

Research-based Reflective Mission Practice

Mission practice is committed to change in personal and community life. It is impossible to understand this process without attending to the values and convictions that inspire such action. Yet traditional research approaches seek ways of knowing that are value free. What can be known about mission practice, however, if the values and convictions that inspire it are ignored? Or, to express the question more hopefully, how can a practitioner inquire into the processes involved in translating values and convictions into practice? By attending to the processes of transformation the practitioner-researcher will seek to understand the motives and intentions of their action in the world and reflect upon the alignment between their values and their action. The practitioner is prepared for his or her claims to be judged, not only by the external criteria of originality, significance and rigour, but also in terms of the meanings of their own lives that are evident in their practice.

OCMS had in mind that this programme would seek to equip practitioners through their research to fulfil the biblical mandate to bring freedom to prisoners, recovery to the blind, release to the oppressed – all through action which proclaims the year of the Lord's favour (Luke 4:18-19). The pursuit of transformation (theologically this may perhaps be stated as God's preference for the poor, the coming of the Kingdom, shalom, etc.) of course implies that there is an oppression, a marginalization, a disempowerment which needs addressing and transforming. There is, thus, a perhaps surprising contiguity, or even a continuity and a shared commitment, between a research programme which has transformation as a goal and the activist concerns of critical theory. *Both* 'thinking and acting theologically with the intent to transform' *and* 'critical theory' envisage that research fundamentally addresses issues of power, and both see research as inevitably and inescapably authored by a raced, gendered, and politically oriented individual. They both also interestingly construct the goals of research as embracing the marginalized and giving voice to the oppressed. The theologically informed practitioner-researcher is active therefore through sustained critique, and strategic thinking, and engaged practice so as to make a difference, effect radical change, enable advocacy and action, bring emancipation, provoke transformation in their own context (or 'own town' [Luke 4:23]).[6]

---

[5] P. Bourdieu, *Outline of a Theory of Practice* (Cambridge: Cambridge University Press, 1977).

[6] C. Marshall and G.B. Rossman, *Designing Qualitative Research* (London: Sage Publications, 2006).

The traditional dichotomy between theory and practice (the Cartesian legacy) usually gives precedent to theory. Even when empirically based, this approach to theory takes it away from the specificity of the empirical world. It moves from the empirical world towards the generalization and non-specificity of universal propositions. The role of practitioners then becomes secondary to that of theorists, and essentially derivative from such theoretical knowledge, and of lower esteem. The practitioner is left with the lesser task of bringing abstract theory back to the empirical world so as to apply theory developed away from context into his or her particular context. What is sometimes overlooked is the subtle way in which, as such theory bumps into reality, there is a resistance from that reality which affects that knowledge and changes it. When that happens what emerges is rarely investigated or articulated. Not being investigated, the 'knowledge' becomes tacit and its links to propositional theory get forgotten and broken.

In practitioner research such considerations have particular relevance as they raise the question of the way in which the place and function of theory may be (re)conceived. The practitioner lives with change and is aware of the provisional nature of any claim to knowledge. Life presents the professional with contradictions and choices that need to be reflected in the way he or she conceptualizes 'the way things are'. One way in which this can be done is to recognize practice as expressing 'living theory' and explore ways of representing this dynamic form of theory in appropriate ways. In this way practitioners are able to ground their claims in the living reality of their own practice offering their practice as evidence of good scholarship.

Some General Principles of the PhD in Professional Practice

A few general principles consequently shape the envisaged programme's approach to practitioner research thus understood:

i) It would be about developing awareness in the moment of action, enabling the practitioner to reflect in and on our practice with the intention of bringing about change.

ii) It would be about attending to the practitioner's purposes in action with the intention of achieving congruity between our espoused values and action.

iii) It would be about the practitioner living out values in practice, by inquiring into his or her concerns for love, freedom, truth, justice and wisdom in daily life and relationships.

iv) It would be about appreciating that the practitioner understands and communicates about the world in many different ways – intuitively, practically, emotionally and spiritually as well as intellectually. This would mean not letting any of these ways of understanding dominate the others, but choosing ways of knowing that fit the circumstances, and finding appropriate ways to communicate what the practitioner learns with others.

v) It would be about the practitioner noticing that he or she lives in complex, inter-connected worlds, making it impossible to separate issues from their context, without diminishing the practitioner understandings and ability to act with wisdom.

vi) It is about creating inquiring relationships with others, as the practitioner seeks understanding in all these aspects of his or her professional and personal life, often in organisational environments in which these values are denied or contradicted.

vii) It would be about remembering that we cannot be perfect, that we often struggle to reconcile our beliefs and action; our personal needs and those of the wider community; our aspirations for transformation and awareness of the shadow side of our experience; and that these contradictions are a valuable source of knowledge.

From Swampy Lowlands to Higher Ground

In keeping with the commitment to enable the participant to become 'the author of their own practice', and current views on effective learning, the practitioner in the programme would be expected to manage his or her own research programme, guided and facilitated by the course team. Practitioners work in the 'swampy lowlands'[7] where 'messy, confusing problems defy technical solution'. The programme would be designed to recognize this as the reality of practice and to help the practitioner and his/her colleagues apprehend, in the moment of action, the complexities faced and to respond as a whole person. Since participants need support close to their field of activity, the delivery of the programme ensures that both local personnel and the latest resources in internet technology and distance learning pedagogy are deployed to support the participant in the swamp (so to speak!).

The assessment of the student's research would also be configured to allow presentation of the research undertaken in appropriate ways. The final PhD portfolio would be that the participants demonstrate that he or she has risen above the swampy lowlands of daily practice to the higher ground of transformed practice – and not just to the higher ground from which practice in the lowlands may be viewed from the distance of abstract theory. The write-up of the students' research could comprise one substantial piece of practice-based inquiry up to 90,000 words; or two equivalent separate projects of practice-based inquiry involving either one smaller and one larger project; or two medium scale projects; or other equivalent arrangements agreed by the external examiner.

---

[7] D. Schon, *Educating the Reflective Practitioner* (San Francisco: Jossey-Bass, 1987).

Benefits to Employers and Organisations

The envisaged PhD in Professional Practice would thus not only be significant for the individual student but be designed to be of considerable benefit to their employing organization where its mission includes the intention to make a difference. It would offer a development programme for senior staff that can be fully integrated into the organisation. The programme would increase an organisation's intellectual capital through the creation of knowledge of direct value to the organisation – and staff skilled in research methods appropriate to its organisational goals. The programme would enable the participant to create new knowledge for professional use through project development and practitioner research. In more specific terms an employer could expect the programme to benefit their staff by giving the participant increased knowledge, understanding and skill in their chosen field, resulting in greater professional confidence, and requiring the participant to design work-based projects directly related to their organizational responsibilities through a three way partnership between employer, participant and programme. The employer would not have to wait for the student to learn and then apply what they have learned some years later. The programme would help the participant diffuse new ideas and skills amongst colleagues at work.

Organizational culture and individual style would influence how this occurs but the programme would be designed to provide different opportunities for the learning experience to impact individual performance in the organization. This would include enhanced ability to think and act strategically and implement strategic projects, improved inter-personal and communication skills, ability to lead and to support others in leadership roles, appreciation for different leadership styles and ability to match style to context, richer understanding of the missiological justification for strategic action and ability to motivate others, confidence to ask difficult questions and suggest innovative answers.

Making the PhD in Professional Practice Happen

A new-style PhD in Professional Practice has been delineated therefore in response to the perceived growing need for practice-focused study at the highest level. As a result of market research a notable feature of the initiative would also be to explore the viability of offering candidates with a Doctor of Ministry degree to be allowed an element of advanced standing as a means of proceeding to a full PhD that is recognized universally and not just in the church.

To provide a distinctive institutional framework for such a different PhD the Institute for Professional Excellence (i4Pe) was formed at OCMS and it was intended that the i4Pe would also offer a Masters in Professional Practice at some point. A leading UK University was identified that shared the same vision and which had also pioneered work-based learning and had extensive experience in accrediting learning in the workplace and community, namely City University, London.

At the joint launch of the PhD the City University delegation met with a number of students who formed the first cohort on the programme. Professor Mary Watts, who was then Pro-Vice Chancellor of City University London and Head of the School of Community and Health Sciences, turned to the pioneer students in her closing remarks, 'This is about what you will be doing and the difference your work will make to the wider world'. Reflecting on the partnership between City University and OCMS she noted that from the beginning of the relationship it was clear that the two institutions were aspiring towards something very similar. 'City has much to learn from you – this is a partnership of equals. I don't know where it will lead but I feel very excited by what this partnership can mean to us'.

Wonsuk Ma, Executive Director of OCMS, responded by recalling the personal responsibility he took in supporting the development of this programme when he first arrived as the newly appointed Executive Director of OCMS in September 2006. 'We are learning as we go' he said, recalling his own journey as a missionary and as a theologian. 'What has become clear in the past 12 months is that this programme has the potential to meet a huge need for reflective, research-based practice in Christian action around the world'.

Postscript

Some months into the running of the programme major changes in personnel, policy, management and budgetary environment at City led the University to withdraw from facilitating the programme. Much of the grand vision described above, which to the authors of this paper still remains cogent and powerful and awaiting full implementation at another time in another place, had to be accommodated within the quite different structures of the modular PhD which OCMS already offered through the University of Wales. A distinctive practitioner research strand was developed since OCMS remains committed to a firm emphasis on enabling practitioner research geared to making a difference in the actual lives of people and institutions in their specific contexts. This strand retains some but not all of what was envisioned in the PhD in Professional Practice but most the more radical parts of the initiative (for example, cohort entry, group supervision, joint delivery with a University, common and collaborative core of professional practice research) had to be sacrificed. In this lies a caution and an encouragement. The encouragement is to continue to have dreams and pursue visions that challenge the *status quo* of educational and professional practice and that prioritise the needs of students over against received practices. The caution is that the world is not always ready or able to fully instantiate those dreams and visions.

[illegible]

Postscript

[illegible]

PART 6

Personal Reflections

Religious Experience: Learning and Meaning

Peter Jarvis

Peter Jarvis is Professor of Continuing Education at the University of Surrey, Guildford.

Introduction

In 1999, Jossey-Bass published a book of mine *The Practitioner Researcher* and two of my then MSc students (both nuns working in Zambia) asked me if I would go out to Zambia and conduct workshops on this study with community doctors and community nurses – they asked me what my fee would be and I replied, 'You cannot afford my fee, and so it will be nothing – Just get me there!' Towards the end of the week, they asked me what they could do to repay me and I, not knowing the geography of Zambia very well, said 'I would love to see Victoria Falls'. Well on my next to final day, my first free one, they packed me into a small car and drove hundreds of kilometres across Zambia to Victoria Falls – and we stood there as the sun-set and watched the wondrous scene of the sun through the haze of the Falls and over the beauty of the Zambezi river. Again, early the following morning, I, amongst only about six people, stood there and watched the sun rise over the river and the Falls.

Words could not describe my feelings. As we travelled back to the airport, I said to them that no fee could have paid for those experiences. What I experienced was awe-inspiring. It was a feeling of creature-consciousness that Otto[1] called the numinous. Otto describes this as 'the emotion of a creature, submerged, and overwhelmed by its own nothingness in contrast to that which is supreme above all creatures'.[2] Significantly, once I describe this non-rational, emotional experience it ceases to be that experience and my description can only be transmitted in words which are non-emotional and rational. Any explication does this to sense experience and in order to understand it we need to understand something of the nature of experience, which we will do in the first part of this presentation. The second part will look at learning from experience and, finally, we will examine meaning and learning.

Experiencing

The experience I described was something that could not be put into words – it was, in this sense, pre-linguistic. However, it was also pre-cognitive but it was

[1] R. Otto, *The Idea of the Holy* (Harmondsworth: Penguin, 1917/1959).

[2] Otto, *The Idea*, 24.

something very conscious. It was a sense experience but, in order to understand this within a wider context it is necessary to understand the nature of the person, the one who experiences. The person comprises body and mind and the relationship between them is contested, with there being a number of dominant theories about it. Now is clearly not the time to deal with these in any detail. I have done this elsewhere[3] and so let me summarise these here. Maslin[4] suggests five main theories:

Dualism: The mind and the body are separate entities and there was certainly a dualism in the experience that I described above although the extent to which mind and body are totally separate is very debateable.

Mind/Brain Identity: This is a monist theory that claims that only physical substances exist and that human beings are just part of the material world; therefore, mental states are identical with physical ones. This raises fundamental problems about the nature of culture and meaning, including the experience that we have described above. But, we know, for instance, that when we think brain scans reveal increased neuron activity; Greenfield writes: '[T]here is no magic ingredient for consciousness… the issue is a quantitative one, depending on the degree of recruitment of neurons: the extent of recruitment will determine your consciousness at any one time….'[5]

This is a very popular reductionist theory which, in my view is over-simple because it cannot explain the meaning of the type of experience that I have described above. Indeed, Bruner[6] rightly, in my view, suggests that it is culture rather than biology that shapes human life, although I would not claim that biology has no influence at all.

Analytical Behaviourism: Maslin summarises the behaviourist position thus: 'behaviourism maintains that statements about the mind and mental states turn out, after analysis, to be statements that describe a person's actual and potential public behaviour',[7] which again fails to deal with such ideas as contemplation. In this sense, it almost denies the existence of a separate mind and is, I think, very weak.

Functionalism: This approach regards the mind as a function of the brain, so that if we can understand all the inputs and outputs and also the state of operating mechanism, we account for our understanding of mental states. In other words, the brain is seen as a complex computer – a picture that has become rather common in recent years. But we are not computers – we do not

---

[3] P. Jarvis, *Towards a Comprehensive Theory of Human Learning* (London: Routledge 2006).

[4] K.T. Maslin, *An Introduction to the Philosophy of Mind* (Cambridge: Polity, 2001).

[5] S. Greenfield, 'Soul, Brain and Mind', in *From Soul to Self*, ed. J. Crabbe (London: Routledge, 1999), 124.

[6] J. Bruner, *Acts of Meaning* (Cambridge Mass: Harvard University Press, 1990), 34.

[7] Maslin, *An Introduction*, 106.

think or function like one – but information processing theories in learning suggest that we do. This also is a weak theory.

Non-reductive Monism: This theory is also dualistic in terms of properties but not substances. Maslin describes it thus: It is non-reductive because it does not insist that mental properties are nothing over and above physical properties. On the contrary, it is willing to allow that mental properties are different in kind from physical properties, and not ontologically reducible to them. It is clusters and series of these mental properties which constitute our psychological lives… property dualism dispenses with the dualism of substances and physical events, hence it is a form of monism. But these physical substances and events possess two very different kinds of property, namely physical properties and, in addition, non-physical, mental properties.[8]

While none of the theories are totally compelling, the last one seems to come closest to being able to explain my experience – the person is a mind and a body which are inextricably intertwined. But experience itself is a major problem although at the very least, when we say that we have had an experience we can be sure that something happened to us! At this point I do not wish to enter the Cartesian debate.

However, what I have described is a sense experience – it was something I saw, I felt emotionally although I could not explain the sensations I felt while it was perfectly possible to describe the material factors, the angle of the sun, the speed of the water flow, etc. etc. This experience was fundamentally primary – it was experienced through my bodily organs without words or information being transmitted to me. There are clearly other forms of primary experience in which we actually do things and learn in the doing – but this is not the place to extend this analysis in that direction. But when I described my experience to you – I was providing for you a secondary experience – but if the description was merely factual I was giving you information and not information having intrinsic meaning. This is an experience that may have meaning imputed into it and it is this meaning and not in the sound of the words that becomes the focus of our attention. In this sense, all theory, all theology – all transmitted and mediated meaning – is secondary. It is mediated to us by another – usually through language and through that mediation we may learn. However, at the heart of these two types of experience that we are discussing here – my experience and my explication of that experience to you – are different forms of learning in relation to meaning itself. But before we can explore these, we need to explore the whole idea of learning from experience.

Learning from Experience

My own work on learning from experience began over twenty years ago when I conducted nine workshops in UK and USA in which adults examined how they

---

[8] Maslin, *An Introduction*, 163.

learned. I gathered all the data and wrote an initial book describing the results.[9] Since then I have conducted similar workshops on enumerable occasions and as a result of each I have refined my understanding of the processes of learning. I have even modified the models that I included in my last book on learning.[10]

It is here that recognizing the nature of the person becomes important because we have experiences through our senses – primary ones – and those through our cognitions – secondary ones. Initially my experience was primary and through the senses. The process can be described in the following sequence: standing at the water's edge I took my world for granted, but then this equilibrium was destroyed by the wonder, beauty of the occasion. I could no longer take that world for granted: I was in a disjunctural situation and the experience was quite intense. I then had to give meaning to my experience and I will return to this below and, thereafter, I learned to live with the new meaning and eventually I was able to take my world for granted again. This process is one of learning: indeed, all learning begins with the sensations and so we may depict this form of learning by the following diagram.

Figure 1: The Transformation of the Senses: initial and non-reflective learning

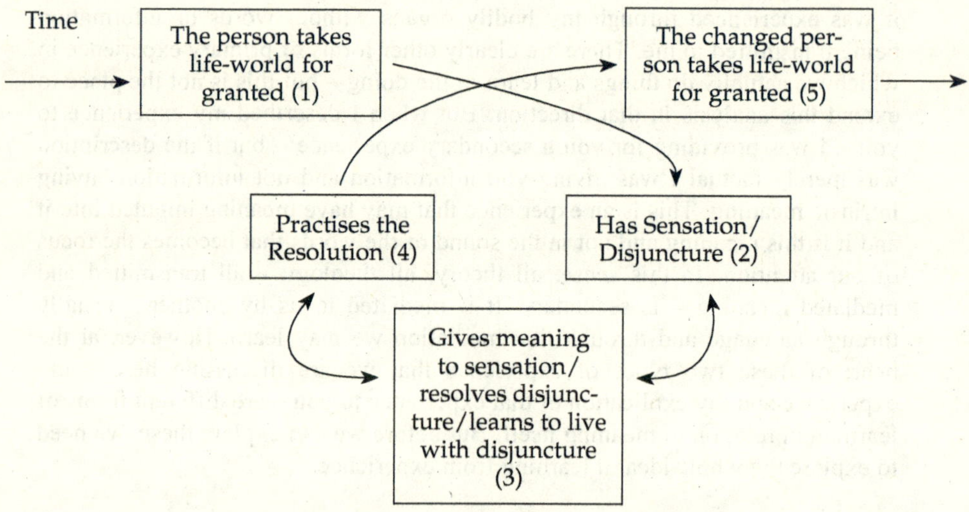

In order to understand this process, it would be possible to discuss the manner in which sensation is transmitted through the nervous system of the body as the

---

9 P. Jarvis, *Adult Learning in the Social Context* (London: Croom Helm, 1987).

10 Jarvis, *Towards*. Cf. P. Jarvis, *Democracy, Lifelong Learning and the Learning Society: Active Citizenship in a Late Modern Age* (London: Routledge, 2008).

monist would claim but then we are faced with a major problem – how do these sensations get translated into awe, wonder and experience of beauty? Herein we see the weakness of the theory.

Another way of describing this process has been undertaken by Ricoeur[11] which, I think, accurately describes both the process through which I went but also illustrates the way in which we learn from the senses in general. He makes five points and these are similar to the process I have described here:

i. The 'numinous' element of the sacred is not first of all something to do with language. ii. Following Eliade, this is hierophantic – that is, while we cannot describe the numinous element as such, we can at least describe how it manifests itself – this I have already done. iii. The sacred may also reveal itself in significant behaviour – although this is only one modality of the numinous and it may have been my intense concentration, my contemplative nature, and so on that could be described as behavioural. iv. The sacred is dramatic. v. Each of these elements point to a logic of meaning – to signify something other than itself.

These five points describe precisely what happens between box 1 and box 3 in the above diagram – what we have described is a phenomenology of manifestation in which he concludes by claiming that 'in the sacred universe the capacity for saying is founded on the capacity of the cosmos to signify something other than itself'.[12] In his study Ricoeur goes on to discuss a hermeneutic of proclamation but this takes us in a different direction to the one underlying this study.

It is, however, to the second point in Ricoeur's discussion to which we need to return – we cannot describe it, but we can describe how it manifests itself. But any description that I might give to this experience is already clothed in a language and a culture into which I have been socialized and this moves us on to Ricoeur's final point: each of these elements point to a logic of meaning and so the meaning that I might give the experience is almost certainly bound to reflect my own life-world and my previous experiences. But the process may be one of meaning-making, meaning-taking or meaning-transforming; we will return to this in the final section.

This is a function of language – but it is through language that my description of this event becomes a secondary experience for those who either hear me describing it or read the words of the paper. This is the nature of secondary experience and it is secondary experience from which we learn most things. Consequently, it is now important to look at the nature of learning itself – something in which we can already see has a number of different processes. We learn though both the body and the mind – it is the whole person who learns and who learns from the whole of the experience. In this sense learning is both an existential phenomenon and an experiential one – it relates to our

---

[11] P. Ricoeur, *Figuring the Sacred* (Minneapolis: Fortress Press, 1995), 48-55.

[12] Ricoeur, *Figuring*, 54.

existence and is lifelong long. In my own work I have depicted these complex processes in the following diagram:

Figure 2: The Transformation of the Person through Learning

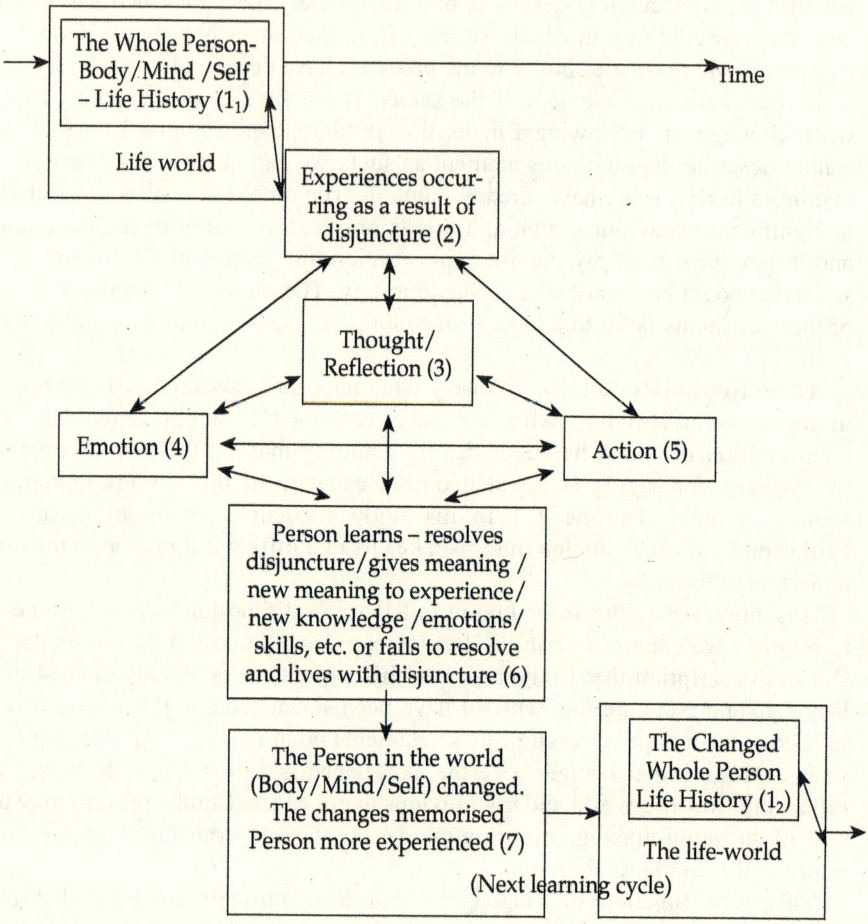

Box 1_1 depicts the situation of people in their life-worlds and we shall look at this in greater detail below but we would argue that learning stems from social experience but that experience is determined to some extent by the nature of both the body and the mind in relation to each other and the external world. However, we continue to live in a taken-for-granted situation until such time as a situation causes us to question this taken-for-grantedness. Hence the arrow from Box 1 pointing forwards in time that merely depicts the unquestioning process of much daily living. It is in the social situation that people are most likely to experience disjuncture (Box 1), although this state can occur when people are alone, reflect on previous events, or even when they have an experience in interacting with the natural world, so that not all disjunctural experiences occur as a result of language as we have seen. The state of disjuncture occurs when we can no longer presume upon our world and act upon it in an almost unthinking manner; it is at this point that we have an experience (Box 2) and it need not be contained within the bounds of language. Indeed, it can and does precede language in small children and in inexplicable situations.[13] Experience can be transformed by thought, emotion or action (Boxes 3-5), or any combination of them: the precise mechanisms of these transformations constitute considerable studies in their own right and these have not been undertaken here. Box 6 is a new addition to the diagram and it is included to underline the fact that the outcome of the transformation is that people actually learn or fail to resolve their disjuncture, but this process itself always results in a changed person, even when there is apparently no learning since the experience still affects the self of the learner (Box 7). When people fail to resolve their disjuncture they can either learn to live in ignorance or with an awareness that they need to learn in order to resolve their disjuncture or they can start the whole process off again. But even when they have learned the process of living is on-going and so, then, is the process of learning as Box 12 indicates.

This diagram shows that all learning is experiential but that we go through many different processes as we learn and that as a result of our learning we become changed persons: the significance of this when we relate it to the whole person is immense but we cannot pursue it here. Suffice to note, however, that learning itself is a difficult concept to grasp, as the following definition shows:

> [T]he combination of processes throughout a lifetime whereby the whole person – body (genetic, physical and biological) and mind (knowledge, skills, attitudes, values, emotions, beliefs and senses) – experiences social situations, the perceived content of which is then transformed cognitively, emotively or practically (or through any combination) and integrated into the individual person's biography resulting in a continually changing (or more experienced) person.[14]

Learning is, therefore, existential and through it we give meaning to experience.

[13] Jarvis, *Adult Learning*.
[14] Jarvis, *Towards*, 134.

Learning and Meaning

In order to understand the process that we have been describing we need to return to Box 1 in Figure 2: here, individuals always learn within the context of their life-world. This means that it would have been very difficult for me to give a meaning to my experience which did not in some way reflect my previous socialization – the alternative would have been to offer no meaning at all and just point to an inexplicable experience and in the light of a dominant scientific and materialistic world these experiences are relegated to insignificance. This we know often happens.

However, Ricoeur[15] in his discussion of proclamation since he points out that the whole of the Hebraic faith of the Old Testament is based around discourses not experiences of the numinous. This is also the logic of any form of communication since it is just not possible to communicate the numinous experience and so we are confined to language and, therefore, to the meaning that can provide secondary experience. The meanings need to gain acceptance in the community and they will be either those ascribed by the elite of the community of practice to their own numinous experiences or will reflect the meanings assumed and accepted by the community leaders. The logic of this is that gradually prevailing interpretations achieve an accepted status – orthodoxy, if you like, which reflects one's membership of the community of practice. Significantly, the orthodoxy is based upon secondary experience and, therefore, is learned from secondary experience rather than primary ones.

Additionally, new members of any faith community need not have had the numinous experience so long as they accept the meaning system that they are taught by the community and this system can change in dialogue with other systems of meaning without reference to any primary experience, and interestingly enough this is precisely what Mezirow regards as learning. He writes that: 'Learning may be understood as the process of using a prior interpretation to construe a new or a revised interpretation of the meaning of one's experience in order to guide a future action'.[16]

Consequently, we can see how transformative learning theory has emerged and how it deals with other the linguistic and cognitive level of learning.

There is, however, another scenario that we might paint at this time. Imagine that when I stood beside the Zambezi I had standing besides me a devout Muslim who also had a profound experience like mine and the Muslim when through precisely the same process as I did. Now the meaning that the Muslim placed upon that experience would reflect another life-world to mine and, almost certainly but not necessarily, a different language of thought. Consequently, a similar numinous experience might be described in a totally different language and within the context of a totally different theology. Both

---

[15] Ricoeur, *Figuring*, 56.

[16] J. Mezirow, *Transformative Dimensions of Adult Learning* (San Francisco: Jossey Bass 1991), 12.

make sense to the person who has the experience and both individually make sense to members of each faith community but they may appear totally different experiences because they are described differently. Indeed, this might now be taken one stage further since we can only describe how the numinous manifests itself rather than the experience itself, we do not know whether we experienced the same thing. Even if we assume it was, we are still faced with the problem of bridging the gap between different life-worlds and only through intensive dialogue between the two people who have these experiences are we in a position to reach agreement, which is precisely how Habermas understands communicative action.[17] At this point different faiths can join together and this lies at the heart of inter-faith dialogue.

Conclusion

The extent to which the fusion points to truth or whether it is just a further extension of Ricoeur's fifth point (the logic of meaning), suggests that faith is based upon a logic of meaning. Once we have reached this stage we can return to the initial discussion of learning from sense experience. The interpretations of future numinous experiences are more likely to be meaning-taking than meaning making, so that any system of meaning reinforces itself by incorporating subsequent interpretations of numinous experiences into itself. Thus, we remain at the point where we can recognize that the experiences themselves point to a logic of meaning. The meanings we place upon our numinous experiences are an expression of faith but the gap between meaning, faith and truth remains unbridgeable.

[17] J. Habermas, *The Theory of Communicative Action*, vol. 2 (Cambridge: Polity Press 1987).

Doing Theology in One's Own Language

D.P. Davies

Introduction

In this presentation, I want to explore the issue of language and some of the other challenges we face in the process of making educational resources and programmes truly accessible to all. From the perspective of our experience at the University of Wales, I will discuss some of the issues involved in validating external degree programmes, particularly questions related to the language of instruction and assessment, as well as quality and standards, course delivery, instructional resources; and the externality of the examination process.

These remarks may be influenced, in part, by reflections on my own personal background and experience. In addition to having a Welsh name, I was born in Wales; I received my primary and secondary education in Wales, and both my parents and their parents were Welsh. Going back as far as I can trace, all my ancestry is not only Welsh in name, but Welsh in the cultural and linguistic sense as well as in the ethnic and geographical sense. This meant that the language that I first spoke, that I learned 'on my mother's knee', was not English, but Welsh. So in this presentation, I am speaking in my second language – the same reality faced by most distance education students around the world today.

The Language of Assessment

In Wales, about one in five or 20 per cent of the people speak Welsh, but almost all of them speak English as well. Very few people are monoglot Welsh. So we are used to being bilingual. On the other hand, we are very much aware of what could be called (and I have to choose my words carefully, since it is an emotive term) cultural imperialism. Thus, I understand when people ask, 'Why should we pursue our studies, why should we follow university degree courses, why should any form of public acknowledgement by the academic community, be through the medium of another language', as in my case, the increasingly international language of English? Now I have nothing at all against the English language.

I followed my own education in its entirety through the medium of the English language. It enables me to communicate easily in many situations without having to have an interpreter alongside me to translate sentence by sentence. On the other hand, I am well aware of the need to avoid insisting that English is the only language of academic communication, and of the ideological reasons which sometimes lie behind such an assertion. From a study of the Roman Empire one can see a dynamic that has been repeated in imperial systems throughout known history, namely, the attempt to assimilate people into a particular imperial system by imposing a language on them. The language in that case was Latin, but a similar situation prevailed in South America, where Spanish and Portuguese were imposed upon people, even as English was imposed in the British Empire. An international language of communication is a very good thing.

But at the same time, we have to safeguard other so-called 'minority' languages and cultures, because, in fact, we in the West are not the great majority. It is very important that we recognize and preserve these cultures and what is valid and valuable in them. This suggests that we also must recognize the basic human right of a person to have their academic work assessed in the way that is fairest for that individual. Judging from the many students I have taught over the years and whose research I have supervised, there is a sense in which persons are disadvantaged if they have to work through the medium of a second language which for them is not as good as their first language. I feel sorry for people who are put into an examination room and presented with a paper and told to answer three questions in three hours – and the questions are in English, and the answers must be written in English.

The whole process is not fair to such students and they face great difficulties, because they constantly have to translate when they are writing. Granted, if you want to pursue, say, research in astrophysics through the medium of Welsh, you would immediately run into the problem of finding adequate resources. Obviously, those of us who belong to a culture such as Welsh have to work through the medium of an international language, alongside our own language. My daughter, for example, went to a Welsh medium school, but ended up reading philosophy in an English university. She made the switch without any real difficulty, because all along the line, she had the choice of writing an essay or taking an oral exam in Welsh or English. The point is, the choice was there. In many cases, students do not have the same choice as you or I have.

The Welsh Experience

When I first entered university teaching in Wales over thirty years ago, Welsh speakers began a campaign to be allowed to submit work for assessment through the medium of Welsh. Up to that point, the University of Wales had assumed that students should be assessed in English. This was true even in the case of Welsh. For example, my mother (who did a degree in Welsh) was in the first generation where some of the Welsh lecturers taught Welsh to Welsh people through the medium of Welsh – not English. That was revolutionary at that time (the late 1920s), because within academic circles it was thought that teaching in English was more respectable. By the late 1960s when I became a university teacher in Wales, students doing degrees in subjects other than

Welsh (e.g. history, theology, education, sociology) were beginning to say, 'I wish to be assessed through the medium of my own language'. They were saying, 'I have this basic human right to be assessed in my own language – to submit essays for assessment, to sit examinations, through the medium of Welsh'. However, it was some time before that battle was won. Nevertheless, it is interesting to note that the same counter-arguments were brought up then as are being brought up now by quality assurance agencies, for example, the dangers of allowing people to be assessed through the medium of a language other than the international language of the examiners or of the teachers.

The Validation of External Programmes

The University of Wales is a national university. Until 1993, it had a monopoly on higher education in Wales. We now have 70,000 students in eight different institutions that make up that university, with campuses in Newport, Cardiff, Swansea, Lampeter, Aberystwyth and Bangor. Though we have been in existence for just over 100 years, the University of Wales, like many British universities, has seen an enormous growth over the last quarter of the twentieth century. Over the last decade, growth has been particularly dramatic – 250 per cent to 300 per cent between 1990 and 2000. But alongside this, we 'validate' degree courses, and thus have students, outside Wales.

In brief, the validation approach enables students, wherever they may be located, to follow degree courses leading to a University of Wales degree outside the main campus of the University of Wales itself. OCMS, for example, is one of the institutions where the University Wales validates degree courses. Validation schemes developed following the demise of the Council for National Academic Awards (CNAA) in the UK. A number of British universities then decided that they would get involved in validating degree courses that would be taken by students in other places, usually in a particular external institution. This added a new dimension to the validating we did previously within Wales itself. We began by validating some courses in English institutions, and gradually expanded. Now we are involved in about twenty-two different countries around the world, including England, Ireland and Scotland in the UK; Spain, Germany, Switzerland, Italy and elsewhere within Europe; Israel and Saudi Arabia in the Middle East; Hong Kong, Singapore, China, Taiwan, South Africa; and elsewhere.

There are now close to 8,000 students involved in these various educational schemes around the world. What is the university's motivation for validating programmes outside of its normal geographical and educational sphere? Practically and pragmatically, we do not go and look for this work. Usually we are reactive rather than proactive. We are responding to a demand. For example, the Spanish higher education system is simply not able to cope with the demand from the potential students. As a result, a number of private institutions have sprung up in Spain. They are offering courses that they want validated. The

Spanish universities will not validate these programmes, in part, because they are afraid of the competition. Consequently, private institutions look for help from universities in other countries. That is why we are there, because when we were approached, we responded. Similarly, we were asked to validate the degree in Social Science at the Gregorian University. Why? Because the State of Italy was refusing to acknowledge the validity of Social Science degrees taken at the Gregorian University by Italians who then wanted to go into the Italian Civil Service or work for the Italian state. The Gregorian University was forced to address this problem because Italians were not enrolling in the Gregorian simply because their degrees would not be recognized by the state. When such degrees were validated at the University of Wales, the Italian state was forced to recognize their degrees, because of agreements within the European Union. It was a pragmatic arrangement; they came to us, not us to them.

At the base level, you could say we make money out of it. But we are increasingly being required to show that we deliver what we promise for the fee that we require. And increasingly, we are finding that there is less and less 'profit'. Some universities are coming to the point where they see there is no profit at all in validation schemes, and are pulling out altogether. That may be a commentary in itself. The University of Wales certainly does not make a vast profit out of it. Nevertheless, we are committed to this approach.

Assessment in Languages Other than English

One of the unusual principles that we adopt when we agree to validate a course is that we accept that *students may follow the course, and be assessed in the course, in languages other than English and Welsh,* which are the two official languages of the University of Wales. And so in Spain there are a large number of students who are following the courses through the medium of Spanish. In China there are students following courses in the medium of Mandarin or Cantonese. In Israel there are students following courses through the medium of Hebrew. We accept this principle because, as a national University, we had already accepted the principle that we would allow our own people to be assessed through the medium of their own language – namely, Welsh.

So our assessment policy is an extension of that principle. If one of the reasons for being involved in validation is to enhance student opportunities wherever they may be, then it is proper that we affirm that a student can often have those opportunities enhanced most effectively through the medium of the language that they normally think in, the language that represents the culture, country or society of which they are part. Now, in the context of doing theology this principle is even more important. Speaking as a theologian and not as a representative of a validating body, I would argue that it is vital that we accept that the principle of contextualization demands that we deliver courses which are most appropriate to a particular context *through the medium of whatever language may be most appropriate to that context.*

The Debate over Quality and Standards

As chairman of the validation board of the whole of the University of Wales, I frequently come across this issue of teaching and assessing degree courses through the medium of languages other than English or Welsh, and the alleged problems it causes. One of the reasons why this topic is particularly important within the UK context is because the British Government has become increasingly concerned about safeguarding the good name of British higher education, which it thinks has been tarnished by malpractice or poor practice on the part of certain British universities and other institutions of higher education in the UK and in overseas countries. It is also concerned about the maintenance of quality and standards in the UK itself. Some of these concerns can be traced to the fact that a large number of new universities were created overnight in the UK in the 1990s when a number of polytechnics became universities. But to some extent, the debate is also a response to what has been happening in higher education in certain parts of the world. Therefore, there is now an increasing emphasis within the UK on maintaining quality and standards.

One of the issues is whether the higher education system should police itself, or whether it should have a policeman imposed on it from the outside, e.g. by government. The good British compromise initially involved the establishment of a Higher Education Quality Council – this was very largely an attempt to police the thing ourselves. But this has been transformed into what is called the Quality Assurance Agency (QAA), which involves a certain amount of policing being imposed upon the system (although in actuality, the people who are in the QAA tend to be academics who are themselves part of the system). There is now more external involvement, and certainly much more government interest in this issue of quality and standards, even down to committees of the House of Commons summoning representatives of universities and making them answer for what they see as malpractice in certain parts of the world. This brings us back to the issue of language: The chief executive of the QAA has gone on record repeatedly over the last couple of years in saying that he does not feel confident that the quality and standards of British degrees can be guaranteed if they are offered through the medium of languages other than English. And that causes considerable difficulties for us in a Welsh context. Now, of course, he hastens to add that he recognizes that in Wales they can do things differently, and they can, if they so wish, deliver courses and assess them through the medium of Welsh.

But Wales is considered an exception – 'The natives can do what they like in their little patch now and again, and we won't worry too much about that. But if we are talking about the delivery of courses in other countries outside the UK, then it's a different matter'. This has led to extensive discussions with the QAA as part of a larger debate. I hope this debate will go on, and I hope we resolve it in the right way. Specifically, I hope it will be recognized that not only is it right for students to be given the opportunity to follow courses and be assessed through the medium of their own languages, but that this approach does not constitute a serious threat to the quality and standards of the degree course which is being offered.

Defining 'Quality'

Certainly, there are problems involved in running external degree programmes in languages other than English. Many other British universities will not get involved in the validating of courses through the medium of languages other than English because they think that is the only way to safeguard the standard of their degree. At the University of Wales, we seek instead to address and resolve these problems, doing so in a way that safeguards the quality and standards of the University of Wales degree. What do I mean by 'quality'? Quality is one of those trendy 'in' words at the moment; everybody seems to be saying, 'Yes, yes, quality is hugely important'.

However, before 1990, no one ever spoke about quality. Instead, one talked about 'good teaching' or 'successful results' or whatever. The word quality came in from the business world. The word is appropriate inasmuch as students increasingly see themselves as customers. They are the ones who are paying for what they do. Thus, it is very important that we can demonstrate that what we do is of quality. Those who teach in higher education cannot get away with things in the way they might have been able to at one time. An easy way of thinking about quality, perhaps, is to talk about it as *suitability for purpose*. We have a purpose, and so what we are trying to guarantee is that what we do is suitable for that purpose. This applies to several elements of the degree programme.

Content and Method

For example, the *content* of a course must be suitable for the purpose. So if, for example, you are talking about a particular MA programme in, say, contextual theology or developmental management, what you offer in that degree course, the content, must be suitable for the purpose for which it is intended and which is identified in the title of the degree. Related to this is the *method* involved. How the course is delivered, not just what is being delivered, must also be suitable for the purpose. Sometimes it might be delivered in a lecture, at other times with a power-point presentation or with resource packages that are sent to people. It may be that people will interact through the internet. It may involve small group teaching, or people working on their own, and so on. There are scores of different ways in which something can be made available.

However, the manner by which content is delivered needs to be suitable to the purpose. For example, for about thirteen or fourteen years I have been involved in an extension education programme in theology. This came about because I was once in a conference where we were talking about contextual theology. We talked about doing theology and about how theology really belonged to the people. It was not something that could be imposed on people by so-called theologians and experts; it was not a top-down thing; it was a bottom-up thing. Then somebody said to me, 'Well, yes, okay. That sounds fine. But what do you actually do about it? Because if you look at your practice, at what you actually do, you get into a lecture room and you top-down it to the people in front of you. Moreover, they, too, are an elite, because they have come through an elite system. What about this theology that belongs to the people, the whole people of God?' So I felt we had to respond to that challenge.

Therefore, we devised a whole programme whose most important characteristic was the way it was done – not what was done, but the way it was done. What we said was, 'Everybody doing it has to be part of a group'. We would not allow individuals to study on their own; it was not to be a home-based study or correspondence course. It had to be something where people would interact with a group. There was not a lecturer, but simply an enabler in the group, a resource person; they were not to give lectures; everything was to come out in the group. The point of this illustration is that how we did it was part of the quality, the suitability for purpose; the how was as important as what we did. So whatever people were studying, whether a book of the Bible, or the creeds, or a period of church history, or the philosophy of religion, or theology in literature, the experiential learning process which they had together was part of that quality.

Teachers

Further, quality relates to the *people* who do the delivering, the teachers. I am not sure I like the word teachers, because when we are teaching, we are all learning at the same time, but I have to make that distinction in this context. If we are validating a programme, we look at the content, we look at the means that will be used for delivery, and we look also at those who will be responsible for the delivery. Who does the teaching? Are they competent? Do they have the necessary knowledge? Do they have the skills which are necessary? Do they know what they are talking about? Do they do it in an effective way, and so on? All of these are things that reflect on quality. Because if you get poor teachers, the result is poor courses, and the quality is thereby impaired by what you do.

Resources

Another element in assessing quality is the *resources* that are available. If it is a course that requires a good deal of personal research on the part of individuals, or where students require a good deal of support in the form of written material, is that available? For example, would the library resources support the kind of course that you are talking about? Recently, I was in Singapore looking at business studies and information studies. There (as in South Africa and other countries) they are saying, 'We have moved on ahead of you. We do not necessarily want those big dusty libraries. We can access all the data that we need through the internet'. Now, if people say that by getting into the right databases they can get access to journals and other material, then we have to test it. We want them to demonstrate that they actually can get that information in that way. We also need to test whether the students have access to it, e.g. are there enough computers for them? Do they have the right skills? Have they been trained to use the software, etc.? You have to be sure that all of that is being done. If so, then you can say that the quality is guaranteed. If it were not being done, you would say that the quality is shaky. Further, what teaching rooms are available, or what facilities are there for private study? If the course is distance based, where the individual is working on his/her own, what sort of support is there? Can they telephone or contact a tutor if they are in trouble? All of these considerations and more have a bearing on the quality of what we do. Thus, we need to know the resources that are available.

Language

If quality, as I define it, is suitability for purpose, then I would maintain that offering a course through the medium of a language other than English does not necessarily impair any of that quality. Now sometimes it might be difficult because there is not enough material available in whatever language you are talking about, but I don't see that that necessarily is going to be an obstacle. You can always translate material, or you can say, yes, the course is basically available for somebody in their own language, but we do recognize, as we do in Wales, that people speak another language. They can read English, or they can read another international language, and they can get material in that form. You build that into your assumption about what resources are available to people.

Thus, when you can deliver a course you can say what the content of the course is and what resources are available. But none of these things necessarily is impaired if you deliver a course through the medium of a language other than English, although in some cases, it will be a help if the students can understand, at least to the point of being able to read, one of the international languages. There was a big debate recently involving a Korean student that I was supervising, who was presenting his thesis for a PhD. It was in a biblical subject and one of the issues that came up was whether that student should have shown some familiarity with the literature in German. Normally in the field of biblical studies, you would say 'Yes, that must be the case'. But if you are talking about somebody who is already working in English, i.e. through a second language, you begin to ask, 'Well, is it absolutely, utterly necessary? Is there not, by now, enough information available to people through the medium of English as to what has been written in German?' Therefore, I would argue that we can say in principle, quality can be guaranteed even if the language that is the medium of the delivery is not English.

Standards

Now, what about standards? A standard is what you are assessing at the end. A good way of thinking about it is to say, 'what are the outcomes?' Can you define what the outcomes are? Can you then assess whether these outcomes have been achieved? What I think we are saying in a British context is that the outcomes, in so far as they can be measured, can be measured in the case of students who follow a course through the medium of their own language. But are these outcomes comparable with the standard that would be expected of those who are following a similar or identical course here in the UK through the medium of English?

In other words, do you have that comparability of standards? Now that does not mean that everything is identical. That would defeat the object of the exercise. But it does mean that it is *comparable*. In other words, and this is very important for the students themselves, when they say 'I have obtained an MA of The University of Wales, but actually I studied in Indonesia', or wherever it might be, anybody hearing that will know that they are making the same sort of claim as can be made by somebody saying, 'I have obtained an MA of The University of Wales, but I studied in Cardiff'. The standard is the same. You have the same exchange rate, as it were; it has the same value, whether it is obtained by internal study in one of the campuses of the University of Wales, or whether it is obtained through a validated scheme, whether in India or Indonesia or South Africa, or wherever it might be. We need to be able to say the standard is the same.

Assuring Quality and Standards

How, then, do we set about assuring anybody – whether it is the British government, colleagues in our own university, the students themselves, or partners with whom we are involved in collaborative activity – that we can guarantee that the standard is comparable? This is where, I think, we have to set in place certain safeguards. Because what we are about in this is not only the control of quality and standards, but also the *assurance* of quality and standards. And that is where we come in. We as an university, the validating body, the body whose degrees they are, need to be able to say, 'We can give the assurance that the controls are in place, whether they are being exercised by the partner, or being exercised by ourselves in partnership with each other. We can assure you that these controls are in place, therefore, we can assure anybody that the standard is comparable'. This is something we put before the senior staff of the Quality Assurance Agency. As a result of that meeting, he said that they were reasonably assured that what we were about was all right. We argued the case as strongly as we could, but at the same time, we said candidly, 'You've got to remember that there are big dangers and risks in this'. The university has to be sure that it has control of the situation in such a way that it is not putting itself at risk.

The Requirement of Externality

Fortunately, within the British system there is always a requirement of *externality*. So, if somebody is doing a university degree in Swansea, that person will be assessed, not only by the staff at Swansea, but by an external person. Inasmuch as externality is part of the British system, we in Wales are not peculiar in that respect. There is also a lot of interchange of external examiners between different British universities. This externality helps to maintain standards across the system. Not all countries insist on externality, and we have had some interesting debates in some countries where it is not the practice to have external examiners. I remember a very furious debate with distinguished German professors, who do not see why they should have an external examiner tell them whether their mark is right or wrong. We had a similar experience in Italy.

For example, as I have said, we validate a programme at the Gregorian University in Rome. We had a humorous experience there recently. We have a proforma, which people have to fill in before we determine if there is a prima facie case for validation. One of the questions on this form concerns the destination of graduates. People have to fill this in, in order that we may have some evidence in relation to the 'suitability of purpose' argument. This answer came back: 'Fifteen of our graduates have become popes'. There is simply no answer to that! That is the best answer I have seen! Nevertheless, it is difficult to go there and impose externalities on this very distinguished university, which has been in existence for hundreds of years longer than the University of Wales. It has superb library facilities, and teaches in about ten different languages. We asked them, 'What language do you teach in?' The answer was, 'Well, it depends on the class'. There was a very interesting man who was a professor there, so I said to him, 'Well, in theory, how many languages could the class be conducted in?' And he said, 'Well, eight or nine'. I then asked, 'Does that mean you would teach in eight or nine languages?' And he said, 'Yes, yes, there's German and there's French and there's Spanish and there's English and so on'. And he was conversant in all these languages! It was as if you took a vote in the class and asked, 'Will you have it in German today, or will you have it in Portuguese, or what have you?' So there was not a great deal of worry about the quality there.

But I do remember there being great debates about externality: 'No, we have been doing this for hundreds of years. Why do you want to bring somebody in from the outside? Don't you trust us to do our own assessment?' The point is that it has been difficult in certain circumstances to insist, as we do insist, on externality in the assessment process. In any case, externality is part of the British system. Now, when somebody is doing a degree course through, say, the medium of Mandarin, we have to be sure that the externality can cope with it. We also want to be sure that the externality understands what British standards are. So there is a double requirement. First of all, the external examiner needs to be competent enough to understand what he or she is reading. Secondly, the external examiner needs to be familiar enough with the British system to be able to guarantee that comparability of standard. What we have decided at the University of Wales is that we will have one British based external examiner who, therefore, knows what the system is; (he/she may or may not be familiar with Mandarin, because it is not always easy to find somebody who is both fluent in Mandarin and an expert in the subject).

On the other side, we will have another examiner from the other country who is a native speaker of that language, someone who is a distinguished academic and external to the institution where the student is studying. Between them we hope they will guarantee these two things – being able to understand what is going on, and at the same time, being able to guarantee the comparability of standards across the board. That is one process we have set in place – double externals – so that we are covering all the requirements set by the university.

Sample Translation into English

In addition to double external examiners, we also require *a certain proportion of the work to be translated into English*. We do this in order that, if there is an external who cannot understand whichever language it happens to be, he or she can nonetheless sample the work of students. At the moment our target is 10 per cent of the whole amount translated into English. Some people think the percentage should be put much higher; there has been talk in some academic circles of pushing the percentage up to about 25 per cent. But at the moment we insist on only 10 per cent. This percentage is more an aspiration than a reality with us, for up until now we have accepted percentages which are lower than that.

Nevertheless, we have that this is our aim in the next two or three years. We must achieve our target because we have to be able to say that the external from the UK is able look at and assess the proper amount of material. At the same time, you have to make sure that the translation you get is accurate, and that it properly reflects the work of the student. In other words, that somebody who is sympathetic to the student is not improving the work of the student in the course of translation. Thus, another requirement that must be built into the assessment process is independent verification of the translation. You could achieve that in one fell swoop by saying that it has to be independently translated. But we do not actually ourselves say that. Instead, we allow people to arrange for their own translation of the material, but where that happens, we insist that it be independently verified, to ensure that it is a reasonably faithful reflection of what was written by the student. While we accept that certain things may be lost in translation, what may actually be lost in translation are the students' weaknesses as well as his/her strengths.

Thus, we require not only translation of a sample, but also independent verification that that sample has been properly translated. In addition, we are exploring *how that sample will be determined.* Again, one can imagine situations where a particular institution – for good or less than good reasons – might say, 'Yes, we will get certain things translated – and that will cover up everyone else's poor work'. Thus, we will have to set down very clear rules as to how that sample of work is to be chosen. The sample must reflect the wide range of abilities of the whole cohort of students who are following the course at the time. These are some of the ways we are attempting to deal with the issue of standards. With these considerations and guarantees in view, including the availability of an external examiner and translation facilities in that language, we are happy to provide the means for students to follow courses – in their own language – leading to degrees of the University of Wales.

First and Second (Masters) Degree Programmes

Finally, this extension programme is available currently at the first [undergraduate, Bachelors] degree level (comprising three-year full-time study for UK programmes), as well as at the 'taught' Masters Degree level. We have not yet allowed students to write the whole of a research thesis for a MPhil or a PhD in the medium of a language other than English or Welsh; this level represents the next stage of the debate. We have yet to resolve publicly whether there is a distinction between the level of the 'taught' Masters, and the 'research' Masters. In most people's eyes there is a distinction, since most people seem to see the 'research' Masters as being on a higher level than the 'taught' Masters. But that's not publicly acknowledged in any quality document. The same is true for the upper level of the Doctorate, the PhD in the UK. This is a pure research degree. However, increasingly universities are introducing professional doctorates with a taught element along with a dissertation or a thesis, and such programmes would not run as long as the full research PhD.

Conclusion

What I have been talking about is the need for a student to be able to follow a course, particularly an undergraduate or 'taught' Masters course, and if he/she so wishes, to offer work for assessment through the medium of his/her own language. I think it is important that we recognize that the choice is the choice of the individual, and not a choice forced on the individual, since that is no choice at all. Granted, in some cases, the resources are not there for study in their own language. Nevertheless, I would suggest that we explore ways to combine the use of an international language with the means for people to conceptualize and articulate what they think in their own language. A bilingual, trilingual or quadrilingual student often can translate in his/her head what is read, and articulate it in another language. Switching from one language to another is part of the process of expression and communication. It can be made a part of the learning process.

Putting Heart and Soul into Research: An Inquiry into Becoming 'Scholar-Practitioner-Saint'

David Adams

David Adams is a Consultant in Higher Education and Director of transformlearning.net. He was formerly a Tutor in Professional Studies at the Oxford Centre for Mission Studies (OCMS), Oxford, UK.

Introduction

In this paper I want to explore a personal question that may find an echo with others. What is the relationship between my research and my own personal development? Like many involved in doctoral research I have used the metaphor of a journey to describe the experience. Four years ago, when my PhD studies began, I saw the task in practical terms. I had been involved in developing an MA in Communication Practice with the Oxford Centre for Mission Studies (OCMS) and wanted to explore ways of improving the programme. I turned to Action Research[1] as a way of addressing the challenge. I expected to discover some new educational tricks that would enhance the quality of my teaching and programme management. Today I have come to recognize and appreciate the intellectual and spiritual as well as the practical demands of research, and the way in which it can become a life changing experience.

Let me share a story with you. A short time ago, I was in Cyprus, working on a consultancy contract with the executive staff of an international media organisation. I had been locked up in the beachside hotel for several days and it was late afternoon when I finally ventured out of the hotel to walk along the beach. After walking for perhaps fifteen or twenty minutes I noticed that the sand beneath my feet had given way to pebbles and as I looked down I found myself surrounded by small white stones. I reached down and picked one up, fingering it in the palm of my hand. I was immediately reminded of Charles Handy's[2] reference, taken from the book of Revelation, to the white stone. 'To the one who prevails, the Spirit says, I will give a white stone… on which is written a name, which shall be known only to the one who receives it'. (Rev 2:17)

---

1 There are as many definitions of Action Research as there are practitioners of the craft but for a general introduction to the territory the reader is invited to consult Reason, P., Bradbury, H. (Eds) *The Sage Handbook of Action Research: Participative Inquiry and Practice* (2nd edition 2008).

2 C. Handy, *The Hungry Spirit* (London: Hutchinson, 1997).

I saw several things in this idea. The 'name' to be revealed suggests the unveiling of my identity. When the Spirit gives me my stone I will then know who I am. This suggests that my life is a search for my true identity. Who I am is who I am becoming. This is, of course, a different idea to James Hillman's notion of the acorn in each of us that contains the seeds of our destiny, the Greek *daemon*, or the Roman *genius.* My identity is not foreordained. Otherwise I could receive the stone at the beginning of my life. It suggests a deeply relational notion of identity shaped by my interactions with others, like the stones knocking against each other in the waves. I will only receive the stone after struggle, 'to the one who prevails…'. This gives tremendous value and importance to life, and is an enormous incentive to 'living life as inquiry'.[3]

As I stood and gave attention to the stone I began to realize that the name on the white stone, given by the Spirit, will not be engraved on it. Perhaps, like Michelangelo with his statues, it will emerge from deep inside, its truth revealed by the battering of life. I am on a journey towards wholeness where identity and daily living meet. Martin Buber reminds us of the words of Rabbi Zusya, a short while before his death: 'In the world to come I shall not be asked, "Why were you not Moses?" I shall be asked, "Why were you not Zusya?"'[4]

So I have a sense of something drawing me forward, inviting me into the future. Life is a vocation. My earlier Christian upbringing put a lot of emphasis on this, stressing the importance of discerning my life calling. Looking back, I realize that it lacked a teleological dimension – the notion that God was calling me to become all that I could be. Over time it is too easy to be influenced by a culture that sees no purpose to life beyond satisfying one's personal needs. Kathleen Norris suggests that this might explain our mania for credentials as a way of distinguishing ourselves from others. 'A call, on the other hand, is pure process; it cannot be measured, quantified, or controlled by institutions'.[5] This sense of purpose, of calling, has been renewed through my research journey and I want to explore some of its dimensions in this paper and draw out its possible implications.

Background

The Oxford Centre for Mission Studies (OCMS) was born out of the missiological commitments of the emerging leadership of the two-thirds world church in the last quarter of the twentieth century. This generation created a global platform for what emerged as a coherent and comprehensive call for

---

[3] J. Marshall, 'Living Life as Inquiry', in *Handbook of Action Research*, ed. H. Bradbury and P. Reason (Thousand Oaks: Sage 2001).

[4] M. Buber, 'Heart Searching and the Particular Way', in *Modern Spirituality*, ed. J. Garvey (London: Darton, Longman and Todd, 1985).

[5] K. Norris, *The Cloister Walk* (New York: Riverhead Books, 1987), 41.

rigorous and fresh engagement with the Bible and culture, and a commitment to holistic mission practice. Living, in most cases, as members of minority religious communities and amongst the world's poor, they articulated a strong conviction in the power of the gospel to transform human life, culture and society, often expressed in terms of the kingdom of God and in programmes of social transformation. This was the womb in which OCMS was conceived and it clearly defined its mandate.

OCMS is a centre for 'mission studies'. For me, the term 'mission' can be misunderstood and creates problems in professional contexts and hostile environments (why should an employer hire a journalist if he studied his practice in a centre for mission studies, for example?) We mean by the term critical, creative and compassionate action in society and culture. In reality, OCMS is a centre for the study of Christian action. In a thoughtful article on 'Christian Scholarship in Africa in the Twenty-First Century' Andrew Walls points out that 'Christian scholarship follows Christian mission and derives from Christian mission'.[6] This is perhaps the most significant insight we can offer the academy (and the world of professional practice), scholarship as the fruit of Christian action. Whenever the church has rolled up its sleeves and committed itself to compassionate and creative involvement with its surroundings it has yielded fresh insight into reality.

Early missionary work in Africa or Asia began with the assumption that the challenge was mainly one of language, and many missionaries did exemplary work in providing spoken languages with a written script and then an indigenous literature. But 'it was not long before it became plain that language is only the outer skin of the consciousness we now call culture'.[7] 'The missionary movement, out of its essential concern to communicate the gospel, was forced into innovative scholarship.... New disciplines or fields of study were invented or made possible: in the languages and literatures of the world beyond Europe, in comparative linguistics, in anthropology, comparative religion and tropical medicine. The western academy in its present secular phase has forgotten where these things came from. They arose, or were made possible, by the desire that Christ should be known in other cultures'.[8]

Although there was substantial success, the challenges of achieving 'deep translation, the appropriation of the Christian gospel in terms of that culture, down to the very roots of identity' exposed the gaps and inadequacies of western scholarship. 'Deep translation is necessary to deep mission. So periods of active mission need to be periods of active scholarship. The converse is also true; when the sense of mission is dulled or diverted, the death knell sounds for

---

[6] A. Walls, 'Christian Scholarship in Africa in the Twenty-First Century', *Journal of African Christian Thought* 2:2 (2001), 44.
[7] A. Walls, 'Christian Scholarship', 45.
[8] A. Walls, 'Christian Scholarship', 46.

Christian scholarship'.[9] Scholarship has developed on the cutting edges of Christian action.

At the beginning of the twentieth century, eighty percent of Christians lived in Europe and North America. Today, well over half the world's Christians live in Africa, Asia, Latin America and the Pacific. These facts are well known to us. Although demographically the composition of the church has shifted southwards, its thought processes and cultural understanding remain western. western theological dominance has become an incongruity. We must now look to scholars from the non-western world to shape the future of Christian scholarship and the quality of their work will be shaped on the anvil of mission practice. Theology (Christian scholarship) 'is about making Christian decisions in critical situations, and it is in the southern continents that those decisions will be most pressing, and the key theological developments are accordingly to be looked for'.[10]

Walls goes on to describe the process by which western Christianity has been deeply shaped by the Enlightenment, a process that made it quite unsuited to its encounter with non-Christian cultures. The Enlightenment view established a clear demarcation between the empirical world (what we could see and touch) and the world of the spirit. While the Christian worldview shaped by the Enlightenment recognizes the existence of crossing places (e.g. revelation, the incarnation, resurrection and prayer) these are limited when contrasted with the African experience where the frontier between the empirical and spiritual is crossed every day in both directions.

If Africa, Asia and Latin America have become 'the leading theatres of mission' in the twenty-first century then they must also become centres of scholarship and learning. As a community of people from these very different contexts, the OCMS community has chosen to work in a western academic environment. This suggests the need for epistemological vigilance as context, culture and faith give direction to research. To put the question in the more personal terms I began with, in what ways are the epistemological assumptions of the academy influencing what am I becoming through my inquiry? Some will find the taken-for-granted worldview intimidating and easily succumb to what Donald Schon calls its 'technical rationality'.[11] None of us are immune to its subtle inoculation into particular ways of framing reality.

I would like to suggest a way of exploring these questions through a simple threefold typology of what we aspire to become. I am proposing that we see our personal development in three dimensions, intellectual, practical and spiritual. I am personalizing them by speaking of 'scholar, practitioner and saint'.

[9] A. Walls, 'Christian Scholarship', 46.

[10] A. Walls, 'Christian Scholarship', 47.

[11] D.A. Schon, 'Knowing-in-Action: The New Scholarship Requires a New Epistemology', *Change*:November/December (1995).

Inevitably ideal types[12] are more abstract than the reality they suggest, but they can serve as heuristic devices to facilitate discussion. I am not attempting to define reality, and the types are not mutually exclusive. Perhaps the best known use of this approach in a field familiar to the OCMS community is the work by H. R. Neibuhr[13] on the relationship between the church and culture. He proposed a fivefold typology to describe the different ways in which the relationship has been understood and practised (opposition, agreement, synthesis, duality and transformation). He was not suggesting them as distinct categories but as a helpful way of distinguishing different approaches to the relationship. In the same way, I offer the following threefold typology.

The Model

The typology can be represented by a simple diagram of overlapping circles representing scholar, practitioner and saint. The model suggests an ecology of human being, a balance of personal development involving intellect, action and spirit, or mental, physical and spiritual health, or, as an OCMS partner describes it, 'head, hand and heart'. The academy has often separated these spheres of human life although this is not healthy or necessary. Exaggerated growth in one dimension without the others has consequences. Non-western cultures are holistic and there is growing acceptance of reflective practice in professional development (at its best a holistic discipline) and of action research (a holistic research paradigm) in the academy.

However the hegemony of the Enlightenment remains. It is easy to postpone attention to experience by honouring theory over practice. 'The epistemology of the empirical tradition is that theory determines practice'.[14] It is equally possible to relegate spiritual formation to the personal and private realm. One can imagine the model with the circles separating in various ways. The practitioner-scholar without saint, or the scholar-saint without attention to practice. In the worst case, all three could separate. Clearly the more convergent these three domains are, the stronger and more integrated is the individual. This requires constant vigilance, even pro-active design, in our educational policies and research practice if our aim is to see greater convergence, coherence and integrity.

At the same time each pair can be analysed individually with the intention of creating stronger and deeper relationships. So, for example, the scholar-practitioner could be strengthened if our research is conducted with regular, intentional attempts to address the 'so what?' question, reflecting on the

---

[12] M. Weber, *Economy and Society: An Outline of Interpretative Sociology*, ed. G. Roth and C. Wittich (Berkeley, CA: University of California Press, 1978).

[13] H. R. Niebuhr, *Christ and Culture* (New York: Harper & Row, 1951).

[14] J. McNiff, *Action Research: Principles and Practice*, Second ed. (London: Routledge/Falmer, 2002).

application of knowledge in process, not just at the end of the research. For an institution committed to holistic transformation, research interventions can be seen as actions intended, in themselves, to make a difference in the world. 'The unique and uncertain situation comes to be understood through the attempt to change it, and changed through the attempt to understand it'.[15]

In a similar way the scholar-saint could be strengthened by more rigorous attention to theological reflection whatever the field of research, and the practitioner-saint could be developed by attention to the spiritual disciplines essential to vital Christian formation. The challenge is to hold these dimensions together and to manage the tension they inevitably bring to our research and teaching. It would be worthwhile to define the qualities of a graduate in the light of these commitments and to explore the epistemological implications of these dimensions to leadership development, an epistemology that is theologically grounded, practice focused and spiritually oriented.

Scholar

Let me briefly consider each type separately. Bentz and Shapiro[16] observe that 'as our society has moved increasingly toward being a knowledge-based society, structured inquiry of a scholarly kind has come to shape knowledge in every field'. What distinguishes such activity 'from more informal, everyday, intuitive inquiry is primarily the existence of rationally grounded procedures of creating knowledge that is accepted as reliable and valid within scholarly discourse'. The highest form of scholarship is what Boyer calls the 'scholarship of discovery', making a contribution to human knowledge.[17] Although I do not intend to confuse scholarship with obtaining a PhD, it is possible to see scholarship in similar terms to the expected standard of doctoral work which the UK Quality Assurance Agency for Higher Education (QAA) describes in these terms:

> Doctorates are awarded for the creation and interpretation of knowledge, which extends the forefront of a discipline, usually through original research. Holders of doctorates will be able to conceptualise, design and implement projects for the generation of significant new knowledge and/or understanding. (QAA 2001)

So the notion of scholarship is not just about knowing the subject matter of a discipline, but is equally about competence in the specific methods of scholarly inquiry in the field. Although there are disagreements about what constitutes reliable knowledge, there are appropriate procedures for generating such

---

[15] D. Schon, *The Reflective Practitioner: How Professionals Think in Action* (Aldershot: Ashgate 1983), 132.

[16] V.M. Bentz and J.J. Shapiro, *Mindful Inquiry in Social Research* (Thousand Oaks: Sage 1998).

[17] Schon, 'Knowing-in-Action'.

knowledge. It is therefore possible to identify the broad traditions and intellectual foundations that define what knowledge in a discipline looks like and how it is created.

If I reflect on my own development as a scholar I am aware of being involved in a process in which I am constructing a map of the intellectual traditions in which I work: the major thinkers, key theories, landmark findings and appropriate methods of research in the field, and gaining experience in this way of exploring reality. In the process I am experiencing a gradual shift in the way I read and think. In the past I read in order to find answers, to access knowledge created by others. At the beginning of my research my supervisor pointed out how my use of copious quotations sometimes smothered my own voice. I let others do the talking. Slowly I gained confidence to think critically about what I read and I became more competent at translating their ideas into my own language. From time to time I would make a claim about something that I did not read in a book. I felt invigorated and alive as if, in a small way, I was contributing to the pool of human knowledge. Occasionally, amongst the greater minds in my field I sometimes feel like a peer and not just a student. Although I may never know as much as they know, I know some of what they know, and I know some things they do not know.

My interaction with the community of scholars in my field is a process of socialisation, an induction into ways of thinking and talking about ideas, an entry into a discourse and a particular canon of methods, evidence and argument suited to the field that gives me a sense that I belong. Bentz and Shapiro (1998) have summarised the conditions which apply to membership in a particular academic community as:

> The first characteristic of the academic context which an outsider will notice is its specialized language. A second is the high value placed on theories rooted in traditional disciplines or established fields of academic study. A third is the obligation to place one's ideas in close relationship to those of other writers by profuse citation. A fourth is the authority structure whereby the epistemological authority upheld by institutional norms and practices is reinforced by the positional authority of assessment. These characteristics limit the ways in which knowledge can be used in academic contexts with important consequences for knowledge acquisition.[18]

This already hints at the limits of scholarship but there are others too. The so called 'scientific method' of observation, hypothesis and verification remains the dominant paradigm of the western academy. Empirical, atomised data (observable and discrete) is the raw material and human reason the means by which its reliability is asserted. Such knowledge is self-justifying and lies beyond ethical control. Its influence has extended far beyond the scientific

---

[18] Bentz and Shapiro, *Mindful Inquiry*.

community to impose its 'technical rationality',[19] what Jacques Ellul[20] calls 'la technique', on the social, bureaucratic and cultural world.

Its most pernicious characteristic, and of particular relevance to my purpose, is its self-justification. It assumes that there is a basis for knowledge (in observable phenomena and human reason) that does not need to be questioned. However the reluctance to reflect on the philosophical and social conditioning of knowledge limits its scope and value.[21] Outside its empirical framework the researcher is forced to become his own philosopher. 'To be an inquirer in the human and social sciences, you now have to become something of an epistemologist, a theorist of knowledge'.[22] This is a highly significant issue for Christian researchers, and I will return to this later.

The criteria for membership in a community of scholars, essential to the recognition of my work, can have a negative effect upon the other communities in which I live. As my vocabulary changes I can begin to sound correspondingly strange to my former colleagues and friends. As I deepen my understanding of my specialist knowledge I can lose touch with other realities and begin to sound theoretical or abstract to those who are outside the community of scholars I have joined. In a March 2003 lecture at OCMS, Vinay Samuel, its founding director, said: 'People who have been doing research here have never been able to communicate adequately their research to the local churches. OCMS should be in the business of producing "the best of scholarship at the service of mission". We have been given the responsibility as scholars to make our research "church friendly". The challenge from our research should be to the discipleship of those churches. The issue is the question of obedience. So we must be stewards of knowledge, not mere researchers'.

An academic institution, like OCMS, is rightly concerned with the creation of knowledge, but this cannot be separated from the one who creates the knowledge or the nature of the knowledge created. This brings us back to the roots of the vision, in an emerging and flourishing church in the non-western world, rich in the experience of mission and energised by the Spirit. The students who enrol in the programmes of OCMS come from these critical edges of mission practice. Their churches expect them to return to their context with greater knowledge, and with renewed energy and passion for mission.

However in the hegemonic atmosphere of the western academy there is a danger of emphasizing the intellectual development of students at the expense of other aspects. It is easy to succumb to the traditional understanding of education as the transmission of knowledge and of research as the creation of knowledge without seeing this as a fundamental compromise of our vocation. If

[19] Schon, *The Reflective Practitioner*.
[20] J. Ellul, *The Technological Society* (New York: Vintage Books, 1964).
[21] J. Habermas, *Knowledge and Human Interests* (London: Heinemann, 1972).
[22] Bentz and Shapiro, *Mindful Inquiry*, 31.

the expectation of OCMS is transformed leaders able to transform, it raises two immediate questions: what is meant by 'leaders' and what is involved in 'transforming'? Rarely do we explore the dimensions of this goal, or the curriculum and pedagogy required to achieve it.

Practitioner

When I reflect on my own identity I am more comfortable describing myself as a practitioner than a scholar. I have spent most of my life in the media, reporting, producing and managing the production, broadcasting or publishing process. I understand the stress of daily experience, meeting the conflicting demands of quality and punctuality, success and failure. Most research students join the OCMS community as activists who are leaders of their Christian community, development workers, pastors, journalists or educators. They arrive with practical concerns and a desire to address these concerns through research.

It is legitimate to ask of the scholar, what his or her efforts are all for. I am reminded of the story of the sultan who asked his vizier to find someone who could do what nobody else could do. After a long search the vizier brought him a man who could throw a thread through the eye of a needle at a distance. He accomplished this marvellous feat several times, at greater and greater distances. The admiring sultan then said to his vizier: 'Give the man 100 gold pieces and 100 lashes with a stick'. The performer was delighted with the gold but astonished by the beating. The sultan then said to him: 'The 100 gold pieces are for accomplishing this extraordinary feat, and the 100 lashes are to punish you for wasting your time on something so futile'.[23]

Under the heading 'rigor or relevance' Donald Schon[24] offers the image of high ground overlooking a swamp. 'On the high ground, manageable problems lend themselves to solution through the use of research-based theory and technique. In the swampy lowlands, problems are messy and confusing and incapable of technical solution. The irony of this situation is that the problems of the high ground tend to be relatively unimportant to individuals or to society at large, however great their technical interest may be, while in the swamp lie the problems of greatest human concern'.[25]

Seeing as an observer is not the same as seeing as a participant. A practitioner sees from *within* the action, not from outside it. 'We should think about practice as a setting not only for the application of knowledge but for its generation. We should ask not only how practitioners can better apply the results of academic research, but what kinds of knowing are already embedded in competent practice'.[26] Practitioners are inevitably actors, agents of change in

[23] K. Erguner, *Journeys of a Sufi Musician* (London: Saqi, 2005).
[24] Schon, *Educating*; Schon, 'Knowing-in-Action'.
[25] Schon, 'Knowing-in-Action'.
[26] Schon, 'Knowing-in-Action'.

their environment. They live and work in the situations they try to understand. Their continuous interaction with their environment helps them come to see and act in new ways. The detached posture of the social scientist is impossible, and the knowledge created through critical engagement with practice cannot be contained in propositional form.

Practitioners live with complexity and uncertainty and, through experience, develop a sophisticated insight into the particulars of their practice. They are interested, not just in 'knowing about', or even 'knowing how', although these are important contributing insights. Practitioner aspire to a *praxis* that is informed by what Aristotle called *phronesis*, 'the ability to think and act in relation to values, to deliberate about "things that are good or bad for humans"'.[27] We recognize this in those we call professional, a quality of 'in-the-moment' discernment, deliberation or judgement. It is what might be summarised by the term, 'practical wisdom'. This is a challenge to an educational system that has often eliminated values from public scrutiny and is premised on Aristotle's other ways of knowing: *episteme*, scientific or analytical knowledge, and *techne,* technical knowledge. Yet *phronesis* was, for Aristotle, the most important of the intellectual virtues.

Since practitioners live in a doing not just a knowing environment, the knowledge they seek will be judged by how well it works, in the sense of enabling them to do something they want to do. This suggests an important distinction between the social scientist and the practitioner. They espouse different criteria for validity. 'The normal social-science model of causal inference aims at generalizability: it employs general cause and effect variables and calls for observation of multiple instances in which those variables take on different values. The practitioner's model of causality is situation-specific'.[28]

I find myself in the middle of this uneasy relationship between the academy and professional practice. Whether I admit it or not, I have spent many years in awe of the special expertise emanating from the research community and a ready recipient of what Schon describes as 'the Veblenian bargain'.[29] Just look at my bookshelves, bulging with big ideas. Thorsten Veblen objected to the decision by the board of trustees of the University of Chicago to establish a business school in the early years of the twentieth century. As a compromise, it was resolved that a gulf would divide the 'schools of higher learning' whose proper business is the kind of scholarship based on science and the 'lower schools' whose business was to prepare individuals for professional practice. 'From the practitioners, their problems; from the researchers, the expert

---

[27] B. Flyvbjerg, 'Phronetic Organizational Research', in *Sage Dictionary of Qualitative Management Research* (Thousand Oaks: Sage, 2007).

[28] C. Argyris and D.A. Schon, *Organizational Learning II: Theory, Method and Practice* (Indianapolis: Addison-Wesley, 1996).

[29] Schon, *The Reflective Practitioner*; Schon, 'Knowing-in-Action'.

knowledge whose application to those problems enables practitioners to solve them in a distinctively professional way'.[30]

However the bargain has not worked well for either side. As Argyris and Schon explain, there are two possible outcomes. Practitioners will either question the fit between the theories of the researcher and the practice situation and reject the knowledge generated by research, or they will become 'little social scientists', depended upon the expert's esoteric knowledge, using 'fragments of theories as ritual clichés, floating, without palpable connection to the ways in which work is actually done'.[31] I am not suggesting that the sphere of professional practice is a closed system, impervious to scholarship. What is involved, however, is something similar to the process when seed is sown in the ground. Knowledge is not first acquired and then used. New concepts or ideas introduced to the practice situation change in the process of being used. Learning takes place in the process. As Eraut says, 'the transformation of knowledge into a situationally appropriate form means that it is no longer the same knowledge as it was prior to it first being used'.[32] To be fruitful, theory must, like a seed, first die in the soil of daily practice.

I am not unconcerned about the difficulties of validating practical knowledge. *Phronetic* knowledge is situation specific and cannot be generalized. Because it cannot be explained in propositional terms, we often resort to a different language to describe its nature. Polanyi used the term 'tacit knowledge'[33] to describe that which we know but cannot tell. It is often conveyed in stories and conversations. We recognize professional judgment and 'practical wisdom' acquired through experience and developed in conversation with peers. It is situated and current, and particularly valued in contexts of uncertainty and complexity. This does not invalidate what is known but requires different criteria for assessment. Its value, to the practitioner, lies in its utility and in its ability to explain and generate experimentation in other situations. *Phronetic* knowledge is often represented in narrative form and its quality measured in its ability to generate 'reflective transfer'[34] into other practice contexts.

Scholar-Practitioner

The discussion of the scholar and practitioner has already indicated their separate importance. It is time to bring them together. The Melbourne Institute of Technology has coined a new phrase to describe the graduates of their DBA

---

[30] Argyris and Schon, *Organizational Learning II*.

[31] Argyris and Schon, *Organizational Learning II*.

[32] M. Eraut, *Developing Professional Knowledge and Competence* (London: Routledge/Falmer, 1994), 20.

[33] M. Polanyi, *The Tacit Dimension* (New York: Doubleday, 1966).

[34] Argyris and Schon, *Organizational Learning II*.

programme as 'executive scholars'. While we may regret the further encroachment of management-speak into the academy we should not, in my opinion, miss the intended meaning of this phrase. It suggests a combination of academic rigor and professional excellence, an aspiration of significance to our development. It certainly hints at the potential value of bringing together the contribution of the scholar and practitioner, promising significant gains in our knowledge of the world and improvements to our interventions in it. Each role has its contribution and limitation. The scholar brings the theoretical tools for analysis and critical reflection, while the practitioner brings their experience and access to multiple layers of practical knowledge inaccessible to the outsider. 'As a member of both cultures the practitioner-scholar is able to translate and create meaning between the two cultures. The scholar-practitioner has an appreciation of the norms, appropriate behaviour and values embodied in both'.[35]

Once we begin to acknowledge, and indeed embrace and privilege experience and context, we move on to a new set of epistemological questions. Several authors have called for 'a new scholarship'.[36] While confirming the continued importance of what he calls 'the scholarship of discovery', Boyer suggests three new forms of scholarship. The *scholarship of integration* makes connections between the disciplines, and places isolated facts in their wider context. The *scholarship of application* explores the wider relevance and usefulness of knowledge. The *scholarship of teaching* (or we might call it a *scholarship of practice)* gives attention to the transformation of knowledge that occurs when the practitioner experiences the 'backtalk' of the specific situation.[37]

This is a reminder of Habermas's caution,[38] that once we move beyond the limits of the empirical world we must give attention to our epistemological foundations. In each of these forms of scholarship, what counts as knowledge and how is it validated? What are the appropriate methods required to capture data that might be considered as evidence?

Saint

I am more than just head and hand: my pursuit of knowledge is also shaped by and influences my development as a spiritual being. I am uneasy with the label 'saint' but have failed to find a better term. I am only willing to use it in the

---

[35] P. Sorensen, 'Managers' Learnings in Action: The Scholar-Practitioner, Organization Development and Action Research', in *Managers Learning in Action: Management Learning, Research and Education* ed. D. Coghlan, et al. (London: Routledge, 2004), 160.

[36] Schon, 'Knowing-in-Action'; Whitehead, *Action Research*.

[37] Schon, *The Reflective Practitioner*.

[38] Habermas, *Knowledge*.

sense of what I might be becoming. 'Scholar' and 'practitioner' point towards what I think and what I do. 'Saint' points towards the one who thinks and acts. I am not just a human *doing* but a human *being*.[39] This dimension of inquiry has caught me by surprise. When I started my research I knew I would face intellectual challenges and was committed to a form of inquiry that would produce change in the way I (and possibly we) do things. What I had not expected was the effect this would have on me and, even more, bring me to realize the significant contribution my own spiritual experience has had and will have on my knowing and doing.

In discussing the curriculum needed to support what he calls 'The African Renaissance', Kwame Bediako, a founder-member of the OCMS community, observes the danger that scholarship can remain external and that training may not 'equip *us* for meeting *our* own needs and problems, for dealing with the monster of sin and evil within *us* who are being trained. In other words, we are not asking the question whether the theological training we receive makes *us* holy people'.[40] Recalling the focus of the early Church, which he points out had African roots, 'one embarked on theological training not to receive information to pass on, not to acquire status through diplomas and degrees, not even to acquire skills for ministry, but to be changed inwardly'.[41]

Again, the influence of the Enlightenment is noted, 'The real harm that the Enlightenment has done, has been to separate knowledge from character, intellectual development from spiritual growth, and, therefore, to produce scholars and intellectuals, theologically trained people, who are left morally weak because they have not been taken through the disciplines of being changed. The theory of knowledge on which they have been brought up is not holistic and so does not produce integral development'.[42] This has an echo in the twelfth century writings of Bernard of Clairvaux: 'For there are some who desire to know only for the sake of knowing; and this is disgraceful curiosity. And there are some who desire to know, that they may become known themselves; and this is disgraceful vanity.... And there are also some who desire to know in order to sell their knowledge, as for money, or for degrees; and this is disgraceful commercialism. But there are also some who desire to know in order to edify; and this is love'.[43]

This more holistic scholarship encourages me to live out who I am becoming, to pursue knowledge in action that gives direction to my values.

[39] M. Lichtmann, *The Teachers Way: Teaching and the Contemplative Life* (New York: Paulist Press, 2005), 32.

[40] K. Bediako, 'The African Renaissance and Theological Reconstruction: The Challenge of the Twenty-First Century', *Journal of African Christian Thought* 2:2 (2001).

[41] Bediako, 'The African Renaissance'.

[42] Bediako, 'The African Renaissance'.

[43] Lichtmann, *The Teachers Way*, 10.

Thus the inquiring life becomes a way of living 'that helps you live in a way you feel is good. Helps you live out the things you believe in and give good reasons for every step of the way'.[44] This is a perspective echoed by Jay Wood.[45] 'Epistemological excellence', he argues, is found in 'the unfolding careers of knowers and the care they display in orienting themselves toward ends they deem valuable'. Spiritual formation lies at the heart of a holistic epistemology, shaping what kinds of persons we are and are becoming.

The exploration of the inner world brings great promise. Peter Senge (the author of the influential book on the Learning Organisation, *The Fifth Discipline*) quotes the economist Brian Arthur, 'Every profound innovation is based on an inward-bound journey, on going to a deeper place where knowing comes to the surface'.[46] Senge continues: 'This "inward-bound journey" lies at the heart of all creativity, whether in the arts, in business, or in science. Many scientists and inventors, like artists and entrepreneurs, live in a paradoxical state of great confidence and profound humility knowing that their choices and actions really matter and feeling guided by forces beyond their making. Their work is to "release the hand from the marble that holds it prisoner", as Michelangelo put it. While they know that their actions are vital to this accomplishment, they also know that the hand "wants to be released"'.

The core capacity for such intervention, according to Senge and his colleagues, is *presence*. This is not just a state of being fully conscious and aware but a 'deep listening, of being open beyond one's preconceptions and historical ways of making sense'. Senge observes similarities between this kind of shift in awareness and what has been recognized in different ways in the spiritual traditions for thousands of years. Angela Brew[47] observes that although the concept of inner knowing is strange within the western intellectual context it is widely recognized in all the mystical traditions. 'It is akin to the knowing of the Hebrew prophets. They had knowledge of the social and political conditions of their day which came not from an analysis of the situation but from an inner spiritual source'. This is different from knowledge that resides in the head (e.g. ideas, imaginings, explanations). It is not the same as 'tacit' knowledge. It is a knowing that is located somewhere in the centre of my being.

The question is, does this inner knowing have a place in our research? As Maria Lichtmann puts it, 'Reason has served us so well as a laser tool in

---

[44] McNiff, *Action Research*.

[45] J. Wood, *Epistemology: Becoming Intellectually Virtuous* (Downers Grove, IL: Apollos, Inter Varsity Press, 1998).

[46] P. Senge et al., 'Awakening Faith in an Alternative Future', *Reflections: The SoL Journal* 5:7 (2004), 7.

[47] A. Brew, 'Unlearning through Experience ', in *Using Experience for Learning*, ed. D. Boud, et al. (Maidenhead: The Society for Research into Higher Education & Open University Press, 1993).

overcoming prejudice, ignorance, and error, that we would be foolish to abandon it. Yet, a "shrunken rationality", to use philosopher Elizabeth Minnich's phrase, a rationality lacking emotion, embodiment, spirit, and intuition, deadens our spirits'.[48] Bernard of Clairvaux provides a clue. 'Love is the fountain of life, and the soul which does not drink from it cannot be called alive'. James Houston expands on this in his introduction to Clairvaux's writings. 'We shall then begin to find that love and reason give us bifocal vision on life; we are given depth to reality that is beyond mere intellectualism as love enlightens reason and reason instructs love. Without love, reason leads only to pride, while love without reason is passion. This bifocal view, then, provides wisdom. Indeed it is the love of God within us that is true wisdom, for wisdom is only another name for the enjoyment of God'.[49]

Blaise Pascal was a respected mathematician and physicist but he is probably best known for his 'apology' for the Christian faith that was published as a random collection of thoughts under the French title *Pensees*. Like the writer of Ecclesiastes he concluded that human knowledge is vain because we pursue it only for our own pride, not to help or educate others, but only to show off in front of them. He writes, 'curiosity is only vanity. Usually one only wants to know something in order to talk about it'.[50] 'Knowledge has two extremes which meet. The first is the pure, natural ignorance in which all people are born. The other extreme is reached by great souls who, having run through everything that humans can know, find that they know nothing, and they return to that same ignorance from which they departed; but it is a wise ignorance which knows itself'. Wise ignorance is a humbled and self-reflective knowledge. Here, according to Poffenroth, is Pascal's real contribution to our understanding: human reason can know and diagnose its own limitations. Reason knows when to step aside, 'the way the sense of smell is uninvolved when reading a book.... Like a telescope that cannot take us to the stars but that lets us know the stars are there and fans the flames of our desire to get there, reason points us to what lies beyond itself'.

Pascal talks about this human faculty in terms of the heart that 'feels' things, but it is more than this. It also 'knows' and 'understands'. Pascal says that people who understand through the heart are 'wise' and see with the eyes of the heart. 'Knowledge presupposes love. One will know the truth – really know it, in the most profound sense, with the passion of appropriation – to the extent that one is loving'. In knowing and loving, the heart also gives itself to what is known: 'Really to know something is to give oneself to it, follow its lead, let it

---

[48] Lichtmann, *The Teachers Way*.

[49] J.M. Houston, *The Love of God and Spiritual Friendship (Bernard of Clairvaux)* (Portland, Oregon: Multnomah Press, 1983).

[50] K. Poffenroth, *In Praise of Wisdom* (New York: Continuum, 2004).

shape and guide one's thought.... The heart... discerns and it loves, and in it knowledge and feeling... are mutually helpful'.[51]

All this gives help for the journey. My research has been pushing me towards the questions of the relationship between myself and my work. The more personal, inner, journey is not easy. Brew[52] talks about the way we deny who we are and so fail to access what we know. This is compounded by our education, the clutter and congestion that surrounds us, and the jumble of conflicting desires that we find inside. I am aware of my obsession with knowledge, the idea that I will find the key to everything in the next book I read, although my hunger is never satisfied. To my surprise my research journey has renewed my interest in the spiritual disciplines and personal practices that can help open the inner world.

I am encouraged in this process by the recent acknowledgement, in some parts of the academic community, of the spiritual dimension,[53] and in particular the tentative exploration of spiritual practices in research, for example in the contribution Coghlan sees of the Ignatian exercises, 'inquiring into action (practice) through the eyes of faith'.[54] I can agree too with Elena Pinto, another contributor to Senge's work on presence. 'I have learned that when I have to make a decision or want to know what to do in the future, I need to listen to myself. If I listen with my heart and my body, not just my mind – if I am fully *present* and not distracted from what my senses and intuitions tell me - I gain deeper understanding and arrive at better, more viable decisions'.[55]

Scholar-Practitioner-Saint

I return now to my opening question and the full model with which I began. What kind of person am I becoming through research? What kind of graduate are we producing? Is the answer to these questions coincidental or intentional? What might be involved in becoming what Jesus called 'a learner in the kingdom', able to work with the new and the old (Matthew 13:52)?

The notion of Christian Scholarship has been discussed elsewhere,[56] and this is not the place to add to that discussion. However, a couple of comments are in

---

[51] Poffenroth, *In Praise*.

[52] Brew, 'Unlearning'.

[53] D. Freshwater, 'The Philosophers Stone', in *Transforming Nursing through Reflective Practice*, ed. C. John and D. Freshwater (Oxford: Blackwell Science, Oxford, 1998); S. Wright, 'The Reflective Journey Begins a Spiritual Journey', in *Transforming Nursing through Reflective Practice*, ed. C. Johns and D. Freshwater (Oxford: Blackwell Science, 1998).

[54] D. Coghlan, 'Ignatian Spirituality as Transformational Social Science', *Action Research* 3:1 (2005).

[55] Senge et al., 'Awakening Faith', 14.

[56] G. Marsden, *The Outrageous Idea of Christian Scholarship* (Oxford: Oxford University Press, 1997); D. Jacobsen et al., *Scholarship and Christian Faith* (Oxford:

order in conclusion. While affirming the scholar-saint we must be careful not to exclude the practitioner. Most Christians are activists, seeking to make a difference in their world. If the Puritan Joseph Hall is right and 'God loveth adverbs',[57] then it is not enough for theology to be done from the neck up. We should not just study theology (as a subject) but learn to think and act theologically. We also need, I suggest, to avoid turning any other subject into a noun to be studied for its own sake. We must aspire to a scholarship of practice that is good for society as well as good social science.

The discovery of the social sciences in Practical Theology in recent years has undoubtedly enriched theological reflection. However, in thinking strategically about the role of faith in the academy it is myopic to think of faith-based inquiry as exclusively, or even primarily, the domain of the theology faculty. Thinking and acting theologically is the vocation of all Christians seeking to contribute to scholarship across the academy. We should not hide our light under the bushel of 'practical theology'. If faith is to contribute to human enquiry it should speak across all the disciplines with a voice that is respected throughout the academy.

This leads me to my final point. The contribution of faith to inquiry must not be at the expense of rigour. Like Daniel and his colleagues in exile, we should aspire to a scholarship that is judged exceptional by the standards of the prevailing culture. There is no hint, in the Old Testament text, that their immersion in the culture of Babylon was unwelcome. Indeed, as Michael Sadgrove points out, the book abandons Hebrew in the middle of chapter two and continues in Aramaic, the language of Babylon, for the next six chapters. This is a surprising switch, particularly when one recalls the distinctive contribution of language to Jewish identity.[58] It was Daniel's bi-cultural knowledge that enabled him to subsequently offer such practical wisdom to those in authority.

Conclusion

Together, Christian scholar-practitioner-saints form a unique but not exclusive community of inquirers, seeking holistic development in themselves and their context through research and action. It is my proposal that we recognize the challenges of our vocation and actively encourage and hold one another accountable on this journey. We are members of a global research community that is passionate about translating faith and knowledge into practical action in culture and society. While there will be differences in subject and discipline

---

Oxford University Press, 2006); T.A T.A. Howard, ed., *The Future of Christian Learning* (Grand Rapids, Michigan: Brazos Press, 2008).

[57] C. Taylor, *Sources of the Self: The Making of Modern Identity* (Cambridge: Cambridge University Press, 1989).

[58] M. Sadgrove, *Wisdom & Ministry: The Call to Leadership* (London: SPCK, 2008).

between us, we share a common view on the purpose of research and therefore have the possibility of developing an expansive culture of inquiry that can support us all. I am not suggesting a unified scientific method but an attempt to help one another validate different approaches to the creation of knowledge that will enrich and empower the church in mission, contributing to the flourishing of human life and a sustainable future for our world.

Bibliography

Minutes of the Regent's Park Chapel Church Meeting, 1891, 26 January.
Minutes of Pastors' Spurgeon's College Trustees, 1893, 2 November.
Minutes of the Spurgeon's College Council, 1958, 14 April.
Minutes of Spurgeon's College Council, 1968, 9 April.
Minutes, Executive Committee of Spurgeon's College, 29 September 1967.
Minutes of the College Students' Missionary Association, 1900, 18 September: Minute Book, 1886-1917.
M. Piper to A. Steen, 1964, 9 April at the Baptist Revival Fellowship Archive, Held in Spurgeon's College Heritage Room.
The Sword and the Trowel.
C.H. Spurgeon to W.Y. Fullerton, 1883, 1 October - Held in the Spurgeon's College Heritage Room in Spurgeon's College Minute Book, 1893-98, Box 14.
C.H. Spurgeon from Mentone, 1888, 14 December, Correspondence of Spurgeon, 1863-1886, Spurgeon's College Heritage Room.
Spurgeon College Magazine.
Spurgeon College Record, December, 1963, Pp. 17-19; 1967, Pp. 2-4; 968, Pp. 4-5; 1950, Pp. 22-3; 1982, Pp. 15-17; June 1967, Pp. 3-5; November 2000.
Spurgeon's College Council Executive Committee Minutes of 19 June 1985.
'Education Is Not Filling a Bucket, but Lighting a Fire'. *i202 Fall 2009*, http://courses.ischool.berkeley.edu/i202/f09/blog/education-not-filling-a-bucket-lighting-a-fire
'Playing before God: Theology and Play in Dialogue'. http://forum.llc.ed.ac.uk/si2/gabelman.pdf.
'Stanford Encyclopedia of Philosophy'. http://plato.stanford.edu/entries/feminist-religion/.
Outline of the Lord's Work by the Pastors' College, 1869. London: Passmore & Alabaster, 1870.
Annual Paper Concerning the Lord's Work in Connection with the Pastors' College. 1884-85.
East London Tabernacle. London: East London Tabernacle, 1956.
A Call to Commitment – Baptist Christians through the 1980s. London: Baptist Union, 1980.
Religion in Geschichte Und Gegenwart. Edited by K. Galling. Vol. IV. Tübingen: J.C.B. Mohr, 1986.
'Manifesto 1995, on the Renewal of Theological Education'. *Evangelical Review of Theology* 19: 3, July (1995), 307-13.

Eurostat Jahrbuch '95. Edited by Statistisches Amt der Europäischen Gemeinschaft. Luxemburg: European Union, 1995.

Religion and Society 49: 2 & 3, June & September, on 'Dalit Concerns' (2004).

'Religion' (2007), http://www.heinrich-pestalozzi.de/en/documentation/fundamental-ideas/religion/

A. Walls. 'Christian Scholarship in Africa in the Twenty-First Century'. *Journal of African Christian Thought* 2: 2 (2001).

Ackroyd, P.R., and C.F. Evans, eds. *The Cambridge History of the Bible*. Vol. 1. Cambridge: Cambridge University Press 1970.

Adams, D. 'Putting Heart and Soul into Research: An Inquiry into Becoming 'Scholar-Practitioner-Saint''. *Transformation* 25: 3, July-September-December (2008), 144-57.

Adams, D., and B.C. Farr. ' Researching Christian Action'. *Transformation* 25: 3, July-September-December (2008), 144-57.

Allen, D. *An Introduction to Pentecostalism: Global Charismatic Christianity*. Cambridge: Cambridge University Press, 1989.

———. *Christian Belief in a Modern World: The Full Wealth of Conviction* Louisville, KY: Westminster and John Knox, 1989.

Allier, R.S.P. 'Book Review Of: L'âme Des Peuples À Évangéliser: Compte-Rendu De La Sixième Semaine De Missiologie De Louvain (1928) '. *International Review of Missions* XVIII: (1929).

Althaus, P. *The Theology of Martin Luther*. Philadelphia: Fortress, 1966.

Anderson, Allan. *An Introduction to Pentecostalism: Global Charismatic Christianity*. Cambridge: Cambridge University Press, 2004.

Anderson, H. 'The Bible and Pastoral Care'. In *The Bible in Pastoral Practice: Readings in the Place and Function of Scripture in the Church*, edited by P. Ballard and S.R. Holmes. London: Darton, Longman and Todd, 2005.

Anderson, H., and E. Foley. *Mighty Stories, Dangerous Rituals: Weaving Together the Human and the Divine*. San Francisco: Jossey-Bass, 1998.

Appiah, K.A. *The Ethics of Identity*. Princeton: Princeton University Press, 2007.

Archer, K.J. *A Pentecostal Hermeneutic for the Twenty-First Century: Spirit, Scripture and Community* London: T & T Clark International, 2004.

———. 'A Pentecostal Way of Doing Theology: Method and Manner'. *International Journal of Systematic Theology* 9: 1 (2007), 1-14.

Argyris, C., and D.A. Schon. *Organizational Learning II: Theory, Method and Practice*. Indianapolis: Addison-Wesley, 1996.

Bacon, E.W. *Spurgeon: Heir of the Puritans*. London: George Allen & Unwin, 1967.

Baker, G.P., and P.M.S. Hacker. *Wittgenstein: Understanding and Meaning*. 2 ed. Oxford: Blackwell Publishing, 2005.

Ballard, P. 'The Bible as Pastor'. *A Dedicated Edition of Contact: Practical Theology and Pastoral Care* 150: (2006).

———. 'The Scriptures in Church and Pastoral Practice'. *Transformation* 24: 1 (2007), 34-42.

Ballard, P., and S.R. Holmes, eds. *The Bible in Pastoral Practice: Readings in the Place and Function of Scripture in the Church.* London: Darton, Longman and Todd, 2005.

Banks, R. *Reenvisioning Theological Education: Exploring a Missional Alternative to Current Models.* Eerdmans: Grand Rapids, Mich., 1999.

Barnes, D., J. Britton, and M. Torbein. *Language, the Learner, and the School*: Boynton/Cook, 1989.

Barr, J. *Holy Scripture, Canon, Authority and Criticism.* Oxford: Oxford University Press, 1983.

Bartholomew, C., C. Evans, M. Healy, and M. Rae, eds. *Behind the Text: History and Biblical Interpretation.* Carlisle: Paternoster, 2003.

Bartholomew, C., C. Greene, and K. Möller, eds. *Renewing Biblical Interpretation.* Carlisle: Paternoster, 2000.

———, eds. *After Pentecost: Language and Biblical Interpretation.* Carlisle: Paternoster, 2001.

Bartholomew, C., M. Healy, K. Möller, and R. Parry, eds. *Out of Egypt: Biblical Theology and Biblical Interpretation.* Milton Keynes: Paternoster, 2004.

Bartlotti, L.N. 'Open Access in Closed Societies: Theological Education in Muslim Contexts'. *Transformation* 18: 2, April-June (2001), 99-113.

Barton, J. *Studies in the Biblical Canon.* London: SPCK, 1997.

Beasley-Murray, P. *Fearless for Truth: A Personal Portrait of the Life of George Beasley-Murray.* Carlisle: Paternoster Press, 2002.

Beasley-Murray, P., and A. Wilkinson. *Turning the Tide.* London: The Bible Society, 1981.

Bebbington, D. *The Dominance of Evangelicalism.* Leicester: IVP, 2005.

Bebbington, D.W. *Evangelicalism in Modern Britain: A History from the 1730s to the 1980s.* London: Routledge, 1995.

———. 'Spurgeon and British Evangelical Theological Education'. In *Theological Education in the Evangelical Tradition*, edited by D.G. Hart and Jr. R.A. Mohler. Grand Rapids: Baker Books, 1996.

Becker, D., and A. Feldtkeller, eds. *Es begann in Halle: Missionswissenschaft von Gustav Warneck bis heute*: Erlangen, 1997.

Bediako, K. 'The African Renaissance and Theological Reconstruction: The Challenge of the Twenty-First Century'. *Journal of African Christian Thought* 2: 2 (2001).

Bennett, D. 'The Leader as Disciple'. *Transformation* 12: 4, September-December (1996), 13-15.

Bentz, V.M., and J.J. Shapiro. *Mindful Inquiry in Social Research.* Thousand Oaks: Sage 1998.

Bergquist, J.A., and P.K. Manickam. *The Crisis of Dependency in Third World Ministries. A Critique of Inherited Mission Forms in India*. Madras: Madras: Christian Literature Society, 1974.

Berkouwer, G.C. *Studies in Dogmatics: The Work of Christ*. Kampen: J.H. Kok N.V., 1965.

Berling, J.A. 'Hard-Earned Counsel for Assisting Post-Soviet Seminaries'. *East West Church and Ministry Report* 8: 4, Fall (2000).

Best, E. *Disciples and Discipleship: Studies in the Gospel According to Mark*. Edinburgh: T.&T. Clark, 1986.

Bhabba, H. K. 'Signs Taken for Wonders: Questions of Ambivalence and Authority under a Tree Outside Delhi, May 1817'. In *The Location of Culture*, 102-22. London: Routledge, 1994.

Bilgrami, H.H., and S.A. Ashraf. *The Concept of an Islamic University*. Cambridge: Hodder & Stoughton/The Islamic Academy, 1985.

Bledstein, B.J. *The Culture of Professionalism. The Middle Class and the Development of Higher Education in America*. New York: W. W. Norton, 1976.

Bloomfield, F. *The Book of Chinese Beliefs. A Journey in the Chinese Inner World*. London: Arrow, 1983.

Blue, L. *Hitching to Heaven: An Autobiography*: Hodder and Stoughton, 2004.

Bodrov, A. *Pravoslavnoye Obrasovaniye V Rossii: K Voprosu O Prioritetakh (Orthodox Education in Russia: The Question of Priorities*. Moscow, 1994.

Bonhoeffer, D. *Ethics*. London: SCM, 1955.

Bonino, J.M. *Doing Theology in a Revolutionary Situation*. Philadelphia: Fortress, 1975.

Bosch, D. 'Theological Education in Missionary Perspective'. *Missiology* 10: 1 (1982), 13-33.

Bosch, D.J. *Transforming Mission: Paradigm Shifts in Theology and Missions*. Maryknoll, NY: Orbis, 1991.

———. *Transforming Mission: Paradigm Shifts in Theology of Mission*. Maryknoll: Orbis Books, 1992.

Bourdieu, P. *Outline of a Theory of Practice*. Cambridge: Cambridge University Press, 1977.

Braaten, C.E., and R.W. Jensen, eds. *Reclaiming the Bible for the Church*. Edinburgh: T & T Clark, 1996.

Bradshaw, T. 'Baptism and Inclusivity in the Church'. In *Baptism, the New Testament and the Church: Historical and Contemporary Studies in Honour of R.E.O. White, Journal for the Study of the New Testament, Supplement Series 171* edited by Stanley E. Porter and Anthony R. Cross. Sheffield: Sheffield Academic Press, 1999.

Brew, A. 'Research as Learning'. University of Bath, 1988.

———. 'Unlearning through Experience '. In *Using Experience for Learning*, edited by D. Boud, R. Cohen and D. Walker. Maidenhead: The

Society for Research into Higher Education & Open University Press, 1993.

Bria, I., ed. *Go Forth in Peace: Orthodox Perspectives on Mission*. Geneva: World Council of Churches, 1986.

Brown, C., and W. Brown. 'Progress and Challenge in Theological Education in Central and Eastern Europe'. *Transformation* 20: 1 (2003), 1-12.

Brown, C.G. *The Death of Christian Britain*. London: Routledge, 2001.

Bruce, F.F. *The Books and the Parchments*. Aldershot: Marshall Pickering, 1981.

Brueggemann, W. *The Prophetic Imagination*. Philadelphia, PA: Fortress Press, 1978.

———. *The Book That Breathes New Life: Scripture, Authority and Biblical Theology*. Minneapolis: Fortress, 2004.

Bruner, J. *Acts of Meaning*. Cambridge Mass: Harvard University Press, 1990.

Brussat, F., and M.A. Brussat. 'Review of E. Hays Holy Fools & Mad Hatters:A Handbook for Hobbyhorse Holiness. (2009)', http://www.spiritualityandpractice.com/books/books.php?id=7089.

Buber, M. 'Heart Searching and the Particular Way'. In *Modern Spirituality*, edited by J. Garvey. London: Darton, Longman and Todd, 1985.

Buschart, D., K.G. Friebel, and R.L. Webb. 'Faith and Horizons: Biblical and Theological Studies in Non-Western Contexts. A Report to the Association of Theological Schools on a Faculty Team Project on the Globalization of Theological Education'. 1993.

Bynum, C.W. *Jesus as Mother: Studies in the Spirituality of the High Middle Ages*. Berkeley and Los Angeles: University of California Press, 1982.

———. *Holy Feast and Holy Fast: The Religious Significance of Food to Medieval Women*. Berkeley and Los Angeles: University of California Press, 1987.

C.W. Bynum. *Docere Verbo Et Exemplo: An Aspect of Twelfth-Century Spirituality. Harvard Theological Monographs*. Missoula, Montana: Scholars Press, 1979.

Cameron, S. 'The Practice of Attention: Simone Weil's Performance of Impersonality'. *Critical Inquiry*, no. 2, Winter (2003), http://www.journals.uchicago.edu/doi/abs/10.1086/374026.

Carlile, J.C. *C.H. Spurgeon: An Interpretative Biography*. London: The Kingsgate Press, 1933.

Carson, D.A.M. *The Expositor's Bible Commentary*. Edited by F.E. Gaebelein. Vol. 8. Grand Rapids: Zondervan, 1984.

Cartledge, M. *Practical Theology: Charismatic and Empirical Perspectives*. Carlisle: Paternoster, 2003.

———. 'Trinitarian Theology and Spirituality: An Empirical Study of Charismatic Christians'. *Journal of Empirical Theology* 17: 1 (2004), 76-84.

———. *Encountering the Spirit: The Charismatic Tradition.* London/and Maryknoll, NY: Darton, Longman & Todd/Orbis Books 2006/2007.

———. 'Pentecostal Theological Method and Intercultural Theology'. *Transformation* 25: 3, , July-September-December (2008), 92-102.

Charter, M.L. 'Theological Education for New Protestant Evangelical Churches in Russia: Indigenous Judgments of Appropriateness of Educational Models and Styles. A Dissertation Proposal'. 1994.

Cheesman, G. 'Competing Paradigms in Theological Education Today'. *Evangelical Review of Theology* 17: 4 (1993), 484-99.

Childs, B.S. *Biblical Theology of Old and New Testament Texts: Theological Reflection on the Christian Bible*. Minneapolis: Fortress, 1994.

Chirakarodu, P. 'Dalit Christians: A Case of Social Plight'. In *Christian Identity and Cultural Nationalism: Challenges and Opportunities*, edited by E.C. John and S. Prabhakar, 30-36. Bangalore: BTESSC/SATHRI for Ecumenical Christian Academy 2006.

Chitre, D. 'I Slew the Seven Horses of the Chariots of the Sun'. In *Namdeo Dhasal: Poet of the Underworld - Poems 1972- 2006*, 120-26. Chennai: Navayana, 2007.

Christine, S., and M. Robinson. *Planting Tomorrow's Churches Today: A Comprehensive Handbook.* Tunbridge Wells: Monarch, 1992.

Clarke, S. *Dalits and Christianity: Subaltern Religion and Liberation Theology in India.* Delhi: Oxford University Press, 1998.

Cobban, A. B. *The Medieval English Universities: Oxford and Cambridge to C.1500.* Aldershot: Scholar Press, 1988.

Coghlan, D. 'Ignatian Spirituality as Transformational Social Science'. *Action Research* 3: 1 (2005), 89-107.

———. 'Ignatian Spirituality as Transformational Social Science'. *Action Research* 3: 1 (2005), 89-107.

Comaroff, J. 'The End of History, Again? Pursuing the Past in the Postcolony'. In *Postcolonial Studies and Beyond*, edited by Ania Loomba and Suvir Kaul et. al., 125-44. Delhi: Permanent Black, 2006.

Comblin, J. *The Meaning of Mission: Jesus, Christians and the Wayfaring Church.* New York, 1977.

Condon, J.C., and F. Yousef. *An Introduction to Intercultural Communication.* New York/London: MacMillan/Collier MacMillan, 1975.

Cootsona, G.S. 'The Telos of Beauty: A Common Quest for Theologians and Scientists'. *The Global Spiral, an e-publication of Metanexus Institute* (2007), http://www.metanexus.net/Magazine/tabid/68/id/10032/Default.aspx

Cosden, D., and D. Fairbairn. 'Contextual Theology among Post-Soviet Protestants: The Masters of Arts in Contextual Theology at Donetsk Christian University: A Case Study'. *Transformation* 18: 2 (2001), 125-28.

Cox, J. *Imperial Fault Lines: Christianity and Colonial Power in India, 1818-1940*. Stanford, CA: Stanford University Press, 2002.

Crabbe, J., ed. *From Soul to Self*. London: Routledge, 1999.

Cracknell, K. 'A Response from Another Context'. In *Ministerial Formation in a Multi-Faith Milieu. Implications of Interfaith Dialogue for Theological Education*, edited by Sam Amirtham and S. Wesley Ariarajah, 36-47. Geneva: WCC, 1986.

D.P. Davies. 'Doing Theology in One's Own Language'. *Transformation* 8: 2, April-June (2001), 129-36.

D'Costa, G. 'A Christian Reflection on Some Problems with Discerning "God" In the World Religions'. *Dialogue and Alliance* 5: 1 (1991).

———. 'On Theologising Theology within the Secular University'. *Transformation* 22: 3, July - September (2005), 148-57.

D'Costa, G. 'A Christian Reflection on Some Problems with Discerning "God" in the World Religions'. *Dialogue and Alliance* 5: 1 (1991).

———. 'On Theologising Theology within the Secular University'. *Transformation* 22: 3, July-September (2005), 148-57.

da Silva, A.B. *The Phenomenology of Religion as a Philosophical Problem*. Lund: Gleerup, 1982.

Daubanton, F.E. *Prolegomena van protestantsche zendingswetenschap* Utrecht, 1911.

Davies, D.P. 'Who Does Theology?'. *Transformation* 25: 3, July-September-December (2008), 73-79.

Davies, P.R. *Whose Bible Is It Anyway?* Sheffield: Shefield Academic Press, 1995.

de Mello. 'Participation Is Everything'. *International Review of Missions* 60: April (1971).

Dearborn, T. 'Transforming Theological Education through Multi-Institutional Partnerships'. *Transformation* 12: 4 (1995), 7-12.

Dhavamony, M., ed. *Evangelization, Dialogue, and Development: Selected Papers of the International Conference, Nagpur (India)*. Roma, 1972.

Donahue, J.W. 'History of Education'. In *New Catholic Encyclopedia*. New York: McGraw Hill, 1967.

Drummond, I.S. 'The Spurgeon Legacy'. CNAA BA Dissertation, 1990.

Drummond, L.A. *Spurgeon: Prince of Preachers*. Grand Rapids, Mich.: Kregel, 1992.

Duff, A. 'Evangelistic Theology: An Inaugural Address Delivered in the Common Hall of the New College, Edinburgh, on Thursday, 7th November 1867'. Edinburgh, 1868.

Duraisingh, C. 'Ministerial Formation for Mission: Implications for Theological Education'. *International Review of Missions* LXXXI: 321 (1992).

Dykstra, C. *Vision and Character*. New York: Paulist Press, 1981.

Earhart, B.H. *Religions of Japan: Many Traditions within One Sacred Way*. New York: Harper Collins, 1984.

Ebeling, G. *The Study of Theology*. Philadelphia: Fortress, 1978.

Egelkraut, H. 'Theological Education in Europe'. *Evangelical Review of Theology* 14: 1 (1990), 30-35.

Eichholz, G. *Die Theologie Des Paulus Im Umriss*. 2 ed. Neukirchen: Neukirchener Verlag, 1977.

Elliot, M. 'Increasing Options for Theological Training in East Central Europe and Soviet Successor States'. *EWCMR* 1: 1, Winter (1993).

———. 'Theological Education after Communism: The Mixed Blessing of Western Assistance'. *EWCMR* 3: 1, Winter (1995).

Ellis, J. *The Russian Orthodox Church: A Contemporary History*. London/Indianapolis: Croom Helm/Indiana University Press, 1986.

Ellul, J. *The Technological Society*. New York: Vintage Books, 1964.

Eraut, M. *Developing Professional Knowledge and Competence*. London: Routledge/Falmer, 1994.

———. *Developing Professional Knowledge and Competence*. London: Routledge/Falmer, 1994.

Erguner, K. *Journeys of a Sufi Musician*. London: Saqi, 2005.

Esposito, J. 'Islam in Asia: An Introduction'. In *Islam in Asia: Religion, Politics and Society*, edited by J. Esposito. New York and Oxford: Oxford University Press, 1987.

Evans, J.H.Jr., and J.I. Smith. 'What Is the Character of the Institutional Resources Needed for the Good Theological School'. *Theological Education* 30: Spring (1994), 45-59.

Fallon, D. *The German University*. Boulder: Colorado Assoc. University Press, 1980.

Farley, E. *Theologia - the Fragmentation and Unity of Theological Education*. Philadelphia: Fortress, 1983.

———. *The Fragility of Knowledge*. Philadelphia, PA: Fortress Press, 1988.

Federov, V. 'Ecumenical Missionary Needs and Perspectives in Central and Eastern Europe Today: Theological Education with an Accent on Mission as a First Priority in Our Religious Rebirth'. *International Review of Missions* 92: (2003), 66-83.

Fergusson, D. *Community Liberalism and Christian Ethics*. Cambridge: Cambridge University Press, 1998.

Ferris, R.W. *Renewal in Theological Education: Strategies for Change*. Wheaton, IL: Billy Graham Center, Wheaton College, 1990.

———. 'The Future of Theological Education'. *Evangelical Review of Theology* 19: July (1995), 248- 67.

Ferris, R.W., and Ralph E. Enlow. *Reassessing Bible College Distinctives*. American Association of Bible Colleges: Unpublished manuscript, 1995.

Ferruolo, S.C. *The Origins of the University*. Stanford: Stanford University Press, 1985.

Fiedler, K. *The Story of Faith Missions from Hudson Taylor to Present Day Africa*. Oxford: Regnum, 1994.

Flyvbjerg, B. 'Phronetic Organizational Research'. In *Sage Dictionary of Qualitative Management Research*. Thousand Oaks: Sage, 2007.

Forrester, D. et. al. , ed. *Encounter with God*. Edinburgh: T&T Clark, 1983.

Fowl, S.E. *Engaging Scripture: A Model for Theological Interpretation*. Oxford: Blackwell, 1998.

Freire, P. *Pedagogy of the Oppressed*. New York: Herder & Herder, 1970.

———. *Erziehung Als Praxis Der Freiheit*. Stuttgart: Kreuz Verlag, 1974.

———. 'Education, Liberation and the Church'. *Religious Education* 79: Fall (1984), 524-45.

Freshwater, D. 'The Philosophers Stone'. In *Transforming Nursing through Reflective Practice*, edited by C. John and D. Freshwater. Oxford: Blackwell Science, Oxford, 1998.

Fullerton to Trustees. 11 November 1893.

———. 25 November 1893.

Fullerton, W.Y. *At the Sixtieth Milestone: Incidents of the Journey*. London: Marshalls, 1917.

———. *C.H. Spurgeon: A Biography*. London: Williams and Norgate, 1920.

Gangel, K.O., and W.S. Benson. *Christian Education: Its History and Philosophy*. Chicago: Moody Press, 1983.

Gardenfors, P. *Belief Revision*. Cambridge: Cambridge University Press, 1992.

Gardner, H., M. Csikszentmihalyi, and W. Damon. *Good Work*. New York: Basic Book, 2001.

Georgiou, G. *The Use of Scripture*. Swindon: Bible Society, 2000.

Gidoomal, R., and R. Thomson. *A Way of Life: Introducing Hinduism*. London: Hodder and Stoughton, 1997.

Gies, F., and J. Gies. *Women in the Middle Ages*. New York: Thomas Y. Crowell, 1978.

Green, G. *Theology, Hermeneutics and Imagination: The Crisis of Interpretation at the End of Modernity*. Cambridge: Cambridge University Press, 1999.

Greenfield, S. 'Soul, Brain and Mind'. In *From Soul to Self*, edited by J. Crabbe. London: Routledge, 1999.

Greenway, R. S. 'Evangelists: Recovering a Lost Gift'. In *Fullness of Life for All: Challenges for Mission in Early 21st Century* edited by I. Daneel, C. Van Engen and H. Vroom. Amsterdam: Rodopi, 2003.

Griffith, G. 'New Bible Institute Registered in Bulgaria'. *EWCMR* 8: 1, Winter (2000).

Griffiths, M. 'Contextualization of Overseas Theological Education'. *Evangelical Review of Theology* 19: 3, July (1995), 292-97.

Guder, D. L. 'From Mission and Theology to Missional Theology'. *The Princeton Seminary Bulletin* 24: 1, New Series (2003).

Guder, D.L., and L. Barrett, eds. *Missional Church*. Grand Rapids, Mich.: Eerdmans, 1998.

Habermas, J. *Knowledge and Human Interests*. London: Heinemann, 1972.

———. *The Theory of Communicative Action*. Vol. 2. Cambridge: Polity Press 1987.

Hafner, T. 'Versuche zur Reform des Theologiestudiums'. In *Studienreform – Kirchenreform*, edited by W. Bittner, 11-13. Luzern: Idea-Schweiz, 1993.

Handy, C. *The Hungry Spirit*. London: Hutchinson, 1997.

Harr, Gerrie ter. *The Healing Ministry of Archbishop Milingo of Zambia*. London: Hurst & Co., 1992.

Harrison, P. *'Religion' and the Religions in the English Enlightenment*. Cambridge: Cambridge University Press, 1990.

Harte, G.W. *Historical Tablets*. Southport: Thomas Seddon, 1951.

Hedlund, R.E., ed. *Christianity Is Indian: The Emergence of an Indigenous Community*. Mylapore/Delhi: MIIS/ISPCK, 2000.

———, ed. *Quest for Identity: India's Churches of Indigenous Origins, the 'Little Tradition' in Indian Christianity*. Mylapore/Delhi: MIIS/ISPCK, 2000.

Hempelmann, H. *Kritischer Rationalismus und Theologie als Wissenschaft: Zur Frage nach dem Wirklichkeitsbezug des christlichen Glaubens*. 2 ed. Wuppertal: Brockhaus, 1987.

Hernandez, A.S. *Misionologia: problemas introductorios y ciencias auxiliares*. Santander, 1961.

Heron, A.I.C. *A Century of Protestant Theology*. Guildford and London: Lutterworth, 1980.

Hesselgrave, D.J. *Communicating Christ Cross-Culturally: An Introduction to Missionary Communication*. Grand Rapid, MI: Zondervan, 1978.

Heymes, B. 'The Moral Miracle of Faith'. In *Dimensions of Baptism: Biblical and Theological Studies, Journal for the Study of the New Testament*, edited by S.E. Porter and A.R. Cross. Sheffield: Sheffield Academic Press, 2002.

Hiebert, P. *Missiological Implications of Epistemological Shifts: Affirming Truth in a Modern/Postmodern World*. Valley Forge: Trinity Press International, 1999.

Hiebert, P.G. 'The Flaw of the Excluded Middle'. *Missiology* 10: 1 (1982), 35-47.

Hoefer, H.E. *Churchless Christianity*. Pasadena: William Carey Library, 2001.

Hollenweger, W.J. 'The Social and Ecumenical Significance of Pentecostal Liturgy'. *Studia Liturgics* 8: (1971-1972).

———. *The Pentecostals: The Charismatic Movement in the Churches*. London: SCM, 1972.

———. 'Intercultural Theology'. *Theological Renewal* 10: (1978), 2-14.

———. 'Creator Spiritus'. *Theology* 81: (1978).

———. 'Intercultural Theology'. *Theology Today* 43: 1 (1986), 28-35.

———. 'After Twenty Years Research on Pentecostalism'. *International Review of Mission* 75: January (1986).

———. *Pentecostalism: Origins and Developments Worldwide*. Peabody MA: Hendrickson, 1997.

Holsten, W. *Das Kerygma und der Mensch: Einführung in die Religions- und Missionswissenschaft*. München, 1953.

Horton, J., and S. Mendus, eds. *After MacIntyre: Critical Perspectives on the Work of Alasdair MacIntyre*. Oxford: Polity Press, 1994.

Houston, J.M. *The Love of God and Spiritual Friendship (Bernard of Clairvaux)*. Portland, Oregon: Multnomah Press, 1983.

Houston, T. 'Theological Education through the Apostles'. *Transformation* 18: 1, January-March (2001), 15-30.

Hurding, R. *The Bible and Counselling*. London: London: Hodder and Stoughton, 1992.

Imasogie, O. *Guidelines for Christian Theology in Africa*. Ghana: African Christian Press, 1983.

Inwood, M. 'Thrownness and Facticity'. (1999), http://www.blackwellreference.com/public/tocnode?id=g9780631190950_chunk_g978063119095021_ss1-6.

Jacobsen, D., R.H. Jacobsen, and M. Marty. *Scholarship and Christian Faith*. Oxford: Oxford University Press, 2006.

Jarvis, P. *Adult Learning in the Social Context*. London: Croom Helm, 1987.

———. *The Practitioner-Researcher*. San Francisco: Jossey-Bass, 1999.

———. *Towards a Comprehensive Theory of Human Learning*. London: Routledge 2006.

———. *Democracy, Lifelong Learning and the Learning Society: Active Citizenship in a Late Modern Age*. London: Routledge, 2008.

———. 'Religious Experience: Learning and Meaning'. *Transformation* 25: 3, July-September-December (2008), 65-72.

Jaspers, K. *The Idea of the University*. London: Peter Owen, 1959.

John, E.C., and S. Prabhakar, eds. *Christian Identity and Cultural Nationalism: Challenges and Opportunities*. Bangalore: BTESSC/SATHRI for Ecumenical Christian Academy, 2006.

Johns, C.B. 'Yielding to the Spirit: A Pentecostal Approach to Group Bible Study'. *Journal of Pentecostal Theology* 1: October (1992), 109-34.

———. 'Pentecostals and the Praxis of Liberation: A Proposal for Subversive Theological Education'. *Transformation* 11: 1 (1994), 11-15.

Johnson, D. *Contending for the Faith*. Leicester: IVP, 1979.

Johnson, T.L. *Twenty-Eight Years a Slave, or the Story of My Life in Three Continents*. Bournemouth: W. Mate & Sons, 1909.

Jones, C. et. al., ed. *The Study of Liturgy*. London: SPCK, 1992.

Jongeneel, J.A.B. *Philosophy, Science, and Theology of Mission in the 19th and 20th Centuries: A Missiological Encyclopedia*. I. Frankfurt am Main etc., 1995.

———. 'Is Missiology an Academic Discipline?'. *Transformation* 15: 3 (1998), 27-32.

Kaplan, R.B. 'Cultural Thought Patterns in Intercultural Education'. *Language Learning* 16: 1-2 (1970), 1-20.

Karetnikova, M.S. 'Russkoye Bogoiskatelstvo: Natsionalnye Korni Evangelsko-Baptistskogo Dvisheniya (the Russian Search for God: National Roots of the Evangelical-Baptist Movement)'. In *Almanakh Po Istorii Russkogo Baptisma*. St. Petersburg: Bibliya dlya Vsekh, 1997.

Kearney, R., ed. *Paul Ricoeur: The Hermeneutics of Action*. London: Sage Publications Ltd., 1996.

Kelsey, D. 'Scripture, Doctrine Of'. In *A New Dictionary of Christian Theology (London: SCM)*, edited by Alan Richardson and John Bowden, 1983.

———. *To Understand God Truly*. Louisville, KY: Westminster John Knox Press, 1992.

King, F. 'Theological Education and Mission'. *Mission Studies* 19: 2 (2002), 82-3.

Kinsler, F.R. *The Extension Movement in Theological Education*. Pasadena, Ca: William Carey Library, 1981.

———, ed. *Ministry by the People: Theological Education by Extension*. Geneva/Maryknoll, NY: WCC/Orbis, 1983.

Kirk, A. *The Mission of Theology and the Theology of Mission*. Valley Forge: Trinity Press International, 1997.

Kraft, C. *Christianity with Power. Your Worldview and Your Experience of the Supernatural*. Ann Arbor, MI: Servant Publications, 1989.

Kruppa, P.S. *Charles Haddon Spurgeon: A Preacher's Progress*. New York: Garland Pub., 1982.

Lambourne, R.A. *Community, Church and Healing*. London: Darton, Longman and Todd, 1963.

Land, S.J. *Pentecostal Spirituality: A Passion for the Kingdom*. Sheffield: Sheffield Academic Press, 1993.

Lange, M., and K. Schmid. 'The Council of Students of Protestant Theology (Seth) on Theological Education in Germany'. *Ministerial Form* 76: (1997), 36-40.

Leclercq, J. *The Love of Learning and the Desire for God: A Study of Monastic Culture*. Reprint ed: Fordham University Press, 1982.

Legenhausen, M. 'Book Review of Whose Justice? Which Rationality?'. *Al-Tawhid* 14: 2 (1997), 158-76.

Lengrand, P. 'Lifelong Education: Growth of the Concept'. In *Lifelong Education for Adults: An International Handbook*, edited by C.J. Titmus. Oxford: Pergamon, 1989.

Lichtmann, M. *The Teachers Way: Teaching and the Contemplative Life*. New York: Paulist Press, 2005.

———. *The Teachers Way: Teaching and the Contemplative Life*. New York: Paulist Press, 2005.

Little, M., C.F.C. Jordens, and E-J. Sayers. 'Discourse Communities and the Discourse of Experience'. *Health* 7: 1 (2003), 73-86

Lodge, D. *How Far Can You Go?* Harmondsworth: Penguin, 1981.

———. *Paradise News*. London: Secker & Warburg, 1991.

Loewen, H. *Russische Freikirchen: Die Geschichte Der Evangeliumschristen Und Baptisten Bis 1944* Bonn: Bonn: Verlag für Kultur und Wissenschaft, 1995.

Macchia, F.D. 'Sighs Too Deep for Words: Towards a Theology of Glossolalia'. *Journal of Pentecostal Theology* 1: October (1992), 47-73.

———. 'African Enacting Theology: A Rediscovery of an Ancient Tradition?'. *Pneuma: The Journal of the Society for Pentecostal Studies* 24: 2 (2002), 105-09.

MacIntyre, A. *Three Rival Versions of Moral Enquiry: Encyclopedia, Genealogy and Tradition*. Notre Dame, IN: University of Notre Dame Press, 1991.

Maddox, R.L. 'John Wesley - Practical Theologian?'. *Wesley Theological Journal* 23: Spring-Fall (1988), 122-47.

Magee, J.H. *The Night of Affliction and Morning of Recovery: An Autobiography*. Miami, Florida: Mnemosyne Publ., 1969.

Magister, S. 'Pope: The Proof of God Is Beauty'. (2008), http://www.catholic.org/international/international_story.php?id=30760.

Marchant, C. *Signs in the City*. London: Hodder & Stoughton, 1985.

Marsden, G. *The Outrageous Idea of Christian Scholarship*. Oxford: Oxford University Press, 1997.

Marshall, C., and G.B. Rossman. *Designing Qualitative Research*. London: Sage Publications, 2006.

Marshall, J. 'Living Life as Inquiry'. In *Handbook of Action Research*, edited by H. Bradbury and P. Reason. Thousand Oaks: Sage 2001.

Martin, D. *Tongues of Fire: The Explosion of Protestantism in Latin America*. Oxford: Basil Blackwell, 1990.

Maslin, K.T. *An Introduction to the Philosophy of Mind*. Cambridge: Polity, 2001.

Massey, J., S. Lourdunathan, and I.J.M Razu, eds. *Breaking Theoretical Grounds for Dalit Studies*. New Delhi: Centre for Dalit/Subaltern Studies, 2006.

Massey, J., and S. Prabhakar, eds. *Frontiers in Dalit Hermeneutics*. Bangalore/Delhi: BTESSC/SATHRI/CDSS, 2005.

Mathews, T.F. *The Clash of Gods: A Reinterpretation of Early Christian Art*. Princeton, NJ: Princeton University Press, 1993.

McBain, D. *Fire over the Waters: Renewal among Baptists and Others from the 1960s to the 1990s*. London: DLT, 1997.

McFague, S. Te Salle. 'Between Athens and Jerusalem: The Seminary in Tension'. *The Christian Century* 93: 4 (1976), 89-93.

McGavran, D.A. *How Churches Grow*. New York: New York: Friendship, 1959.

McKim, D.K., ed. *John Calvin: A Companion*. Cambridge: Cambridge University Press, 2004.

McNiff, J. *Action Research: Principles and Practice*. Second ed. London: Routledge/Falmer, 2002.

———. *Action Research: Principles and Practice*. 2 ed. New York: Routledge/Falmer, 2002.

Mendus, J., and S. Horton, eds. *After MacIntyre: Critical Perspectives on the Work of Alasdair MacIntyre*. Notre Dame: University of Notre Dame Press, 1995.

Mezirow, J. *Transformative Dimensions of Adult Learning*. San Francisco: Jossey Bass 1991.

Mieo, C.S., ed. *Education for Service in the Christian Church in China*. New York: Nanking Theological Seminary, 1935.

Milbank, J. 'The End of Dialogue'. In *Christian Uniqueness Reconsidered*, edited by Gavin D'Costa, 174-91. New York: Orbis, 1990.

———. *Theology and Social Theory: Beyond Secular Reason*. Oxford: Blackwell Publishing, 1990.

Miller, R. C. 'The Language Gap and God: Religious Language and Christian Education'. Place Published, 2010.

Moffett, Samuel H. *A History of Christianity in Asia: Beginnings to 1500*. Vol. 1. New York: Harper San Francisco, 1992.

Mojzes, P. 'Religious Studies in Russia'. *Religion in Eastern Europe* XVI: 4, August (1996), 30-34.

Moltmann, J. *The Spirit of Life: A Universal Affirmation*. London: SCM, 1992.

Morris, L. *The Gospel According to Matthew*. Grand Rapids: Eerdmans, 1992.

Mulders, A.J.M. *Missiologisch bestek: inleiding tot de katholieke missiewetenschap*. Hilversum-Antwerpen, 1962.

Murphy, N. *Theology in the Age of Scientific Reasoning*. New York: Cornell University, 1990.

Murray, S. *Church Planting: Laying Foundations*. Carlisle: Paternoster Press, 1998.

Myklebust, O.G. *The Study of Missions in Theological Education: An Historical Inquiry into the Place of World Evangelisation in Western Protestant Ministerial Training with Particular Reference to Alexander Duff's Chair of Evangelistic Theology*. I. Oslo, 1955.

———. 'Mission in Contemporary Theological Education: A Factual Survey'. *Mission Studies* 7: 2 (1989), 87-107.

Neely, A. 'The Teaching of Missions'. In *Toward the Twenty-First Century in Christian Mission*, edited by J.M. Phillips and R.T. Coote, 269-83. Grand Rapids, Mich.: Eerdmans, 1993.

Negrov, A.I., and M. Charter. 'Why Is There No Russian "Protestant" Theology in Russia? A Personal Outcry'. *Religion in Eastern Europe* XVII: (1997), 30-41.

Newbigin, L. 'Theological Education in a World Perspective'. *Churchman* 2: 93 (1979), 105-15.

———. *The Gospel in a Pluralistic Society*. Grand Rapids/Geneva: Eerdmans/WCC, 1989.

Newlands, G. *The Transformative Imagination: Rethinking Intercultural Theology*. Aldershot: Ashgate, 2004.

Nicholls, M. *C.H. Spurgeon: The Pastor Evangelist*. Didcot: Baptist Historical Society, 1992.

———. *Lights to the World: A History of Spurgeon's College, 1856-1992*. Harpenden: Nuprint, 1994.

Nichols, A. *The Shape of Catholic Theology: An Introduction to Its Sources, Principles*. Collegeville: The Order of St. Benedict, Inc., 1991.

Nicole, J. 'Brief History of the So-Called "Classical Model" For Theological Education'. *Ministerial Form* 67: (1994), 33-34.

Niebuhr, H. R. *Christ and Culture*. New York: Harper & Row, 1951.

Nikolaev, S. 'The Problems of Euro-Asian Theology for the New Millennium: Address Given to the Euro-Asian Accrediting Association (EAAA)'. Kiev, Ukraine, 1999.

Nirmal, A. P. 'Towards a Christian Dalit Theology'. In *Frontiers in Asian Christian Theology: Emerging Trends*, edited by R.S. Sugirtharajah, 27-40. Maryknoll, NY: Orbis, 1994.

Norris, K. *The Cloister Walk*. New York: Riverhead Books, 1987.

———. *The Cloister Walk*. New York: Riverhead Books, 1987.

Northrop, F.S.C. *The Meeting of East and West: An Inquiry Concerning World Understanding*. London: Macmillan, 1950.

Nouwen, Henri. *Creative Ministry*. New York: Doubleday, 1971.

Ohm, Th. *Machet zu Jüngern alle Völker: Theorie der Mission*. Freiburg im Breisgau, 1962.

Oliver, G. *Holy Bible: Human Bible. Questions Pastoral Practice Must Ask*. London: Darton, Longman and Todd, 2006.

Ollrog, W.-H. *Paulus und seine Mitarbeiter. Untersuchung zu Theorie und Praxis paulinischer Mission*. Vol. 50. Neukirchen-Vluyn: Neukirchener Verlag, 1979.

Ott, B. 'Mission Orientated Theological Education'. *Transformation* 18: 2 (2001), 74-86.

———. 'Mission and Theological Education'. *Transformation* 18: 2 (2001), 87-98.

Otto, R. *The Idea of the Holy*. Harmondsworth: Penguin, 1917/1959.

Overmyer, D.L. *Religions of China: The World as a Living System*. New York: Harper Collins, 1986.

Panikkar, K.M. *Asia and Western Dominance: A Survey of the Vasco Da Gama Epoch of Asian History (1498-1945)*. London, 1967.

Paton, W. *Alexander Duff: Pioneer of Missionary Education*. London, 1923.

Pattison, S. *A Critique of Pastoral Care*. London: SCM, 2000.

Pearce, W.M. *Knight in Royal Service*. London: Pioneer Mission, 1962.

Penner, P. 'Contextual Theological Education among Post-Soviet Protestants: The Development of a Masters Degree at St Petersburg Christian University'. *Transformation* 18: 2, April-June (2001), 114-24.

Penner, P.F. 'Evangelskoye teologicheskoye obrasovaniye v techeniye poslednikh 10 let' (Evangelical Theological Education During the Last 10 Years)'. *Chronograf* 1: (1997), 212-69.

———. 'Theologische Ausbildung – eine verpflichtende Mission: Faktoren zur Bestimmung von Leitlinien für theologische Ausbildung in der GUS (Theological Education – an Engaging Mission: Factors for Defining Guidelines for Theological Education in the Cis). Submitted in Accordance with the Requirements for the Degree of Dth at the University of South Africa, Pretoria, South Africa, November 1997'. 1997.

———. 'Novosavetny Knishnik' (the New Testament Scribe)'. *Chronograph* 4: (1999), 3-14.

Perry, E. *The Gospel in Dispute: The Relation of Christian Faith to Other Missionary Religions*. New York: Doubleday and Co., 1958.

Pilli, T. 'Union of Evangelical Christians-Baptists of Estonia 1945-1989: Survival Techniques, Outreach Efforts, Search for Identity'. *Journal of European Baptist Studies* 1: 2, January (2001), 31-50.

Plueddemann, J.E. 'The Future of Evangelical Theological Education'. *Evangelical Review of Theology* 14: 1 (1990), 14-24

Poffenroth, K. *In Praise of Wisdom*. New York: Continuum, 2004.

Polanyi, M. *Personal Knowledge: Towards a Post-Critical Philosophy*. Chicago: University of Chicago Press, 1958.

———. *The Tacit Dimension*. New York: Doubleday, 1966.

———. *The Tacit Dimension*. New York: Doubleday, 1966.

Pospelovsky, D.V. 'Impressions of the Contemporary Russian Orthodox Church: Its Problems and Its Theological Education'. *Religion, State & Society* 23: 3 (1995), 249-62.

———. *Pravoslavnaya Tserkov V Istoriyi Rusi, Rossii I SSSR (the Orthodox Church in the History of Rus, Russia and the USSR)*. Moscow: The Institute of St. Andrews, 1996.

Price, L. *Theology out of Place: A Theological Biography of Walter J. Hollenweger*, JPTSup 23. Sheffield: Sheffield Academic Press, 2002.

Prokop, E., and K.A. Geissler. *Erwachsenenbildung. Modelle und Methoden*. Munich/Basel: Reinhardt, 1974.

Radshall, H. *The Universities in the Middle Ages*. New ed. 3 vols. Oxford: Clarendonesp., 1963.

Randall, I.M. 'Conservative Constructionist: The Early Influence of Billy Graham in Britain'. *The Evangelical Quarterly* 67: 4 (1995), 309-33.

———. *Evangelical Experiences: A Study in the Spirituality of English Evangelicalism, 1918-1939*. Carlisle: Paternoster, 1999.

———. *Spirituality and Social Change*. Carlisle: Paternoster Press, 2003.

———. *The English Baptists of the Twentieth Century*. Didcot: Baptist Historical Society, 2005.

———. *A School of the Prophets*. London: Spurgeon's College, 2005.

———. 'A Mode of Training': A Baptist Seminary's Missional Vision'. *Transformation* 24: 1 (2007), 2-13.

Ray, C. *The Life of Charles Haddon Spurgeon*. London: Passmore and Alabaster, 1903.

Reason, P., and H. Bradbury, eds. *The Sage Handbook of Action Research: Participative Inquiry and Practice*. Thousand Oaks: Sage, 2008.

Reason, P., and W.R. Torbert. 'The Action Turn: Toward a Transformational Social Science'. *Toward a Transformational Science: a further look at the scientific merits of action research. Concepts and Transformations* 6: 1 (2001), 1-37.

Rege, S. *Writing Caste/ Writing Gender: Narrating Dalit Women's Testimonios*. New Delhi: Zubaan, 2006.

Ricoeur, P. *The Symbolism of Evil*. New York: Harper Row, 1967.

———. *Figuring the Sacred*. Minneapolis: Fortress Press, 1995.

Rijckevorsel, L.J. van. *Missie en missieactie*. Nijmegen, 1917.

Rorty, R.M., ed. *The Linguistic Turn: Essays in Philosophical Method*. Chicago: The University of Chicago Press, 1992.

Runyon, T. 'Wesley and the Theologies of Liberation'. In *Sanctification and Liberation*, edited by T. Runyon. Nashville, TN: Abingdon Press, 1981.

Russell, H.O. 'The Ministry of the Presidency or Principalship with Special Reference to the Two-Thirds World'. *Transformation* 12: 4 (1995), 16-17.

Sadgrove, M. *Wisdom & Ministry: The Call to Leadership*. London: SPCK, 2008.

Samuel, V. 'Globalization and Theological Education'. *Transformation* 18: 2, April-June (2001), 68-74.

Sannikov, S.V. 'Podkhody I Printsipy Sosdaniya Evro-Asiatskoy Akkerditatsionnoy Associacii (EAAA) (the Approaches and Principles of the Creation of the Euro-Asian Accrediting Association). Paper Read at the Conference Theological Education-2'. Kiev, 1996.

Sawatsky, W. *Soviet Evangelicals since World War II*. Scottdale, Pa: Herald Press, 1981.

———. 'Visions in Conflict: Starting Anew through the Prism of Leadership Training Efforts) '. In *Religion after Communism in Eastern Europe*, edited by N. Nielsen. Boulder, CO: Westview Press, 1994.

———. 'Evangelical Schools in Fsu Now Accrediting'. www.georgefox.edu.

Scherer, J.A. *Gospel, Church, and Kingdom: Comparative Studies in World Mission Theology*. Minneapolis: Augsburg Publishing House, 1987.

Scherer, J. A., and S. Bevans. *New Directions in Mission and Evangelization: Basic Statement 1974-1991*. Vol. 1. Maryknoll, NY: Orbis, 1992.

Schipani, D. *Religious Education Encounters Liberation Theology*. Birmingham, AL: Religious Education Press, 1988.

Schipani, D.S. 'The Church and Its Theological Education: A Vision'. In *Theological Education on Five Continents: Anabaptist Perspectives*, edited by N.R. Heisey and D.S. Schipani, 5-35. Strasbourg: Mennonite World Conference, 1997.

Schmidlin, J. *Einführung in die Missionswissenschaft*. zweite Aufl. Münster in Westfale, 1925.

Schomerus, H.W. *Missionswissenschaft*. Leipzig, 1935.

Schon, D. *The Reflective Practitioner: How Professionals Think in Action*. Aldershot: Ashgate 1983.

———. *Educating the Reflective Practitioner*. San Francisco: Jossey-Bass, 1987.

Schon, D.A. 'Knowing-in-Action: The New Scholarship Requires a New Epistemology'. *Change*: November/December (1995).

Schreiter, R.J. *Constructing Local Theologies*. London: SCM, 1985.

Schultheis, M. 'Head in the Clouds and Feet in the Mud: The Role of Private Universities in the Integration of Christian Mission and Transformational Development'. *Transformation* 22: 2 (2005), 97-105.

Scobie, C.H.H. *The Ways of Our God: An Approach to Biblical Theology*. Grand Rapids: Eerdmans, 2003.

Sebastian, J.J. 'Creative Exploration: Arvind P. Nirmal's Ongoing Contribution to Christian Theology'. *Bangalore Theological Forum* XXXI: 2, December (1999), 44-52.

———. 'Review of Michael, S.M. Ed., 1999 Dalits in Modern India: Vision and Values, (New Delhi: Vistaar Publications)'. (2003).

———. 'Review of Kotani, H. Ed., 1997 'Caste System, Untouchability and the Depressed', Japanese Studies on South Asia No. 1 (New Delhi: Manohar)'. *Religion and Society* 48: 1, March (2003), 96-101.

———. 'Review'. *Bangalore Theological Forum* XXXIX: 1, June (2007), 209-12.

———. 'Can We Now Bypass That Truth? Interrogating the Methodology of Dalit Theology'. *Transformation* 25: 3, July-September-December (2008), 80-91.

Senge, P., C. Scharmer, J. Jaworski, and B. Flowers. 'Awakening Faith in an Alternative Future'. *Reflections: The SoL Journal* 5: 7 (2004).

Seumois, A.V. *Introduction À La Missiologie*. Schöneck- Beckenried, 1952.

Sharma, A. 'On the Distinction between Religious Studies and Theological Studies'. *The Council of Societies for the Study of Religion Bulletin* XXVI: 3 (1997), 50–51.

Shenderovsky, L.L. *Ivan Prokhano*. Toronto: Evangelical Faith Publishers, 1986.

Shindler, R. *From the Usher's Desk to the Tabernacle Pulpit*. London: Passmore and Alabaster, 1892.

Skaggs, Rebecca. *The Pentecostal Commentary on 1 Peter 2 Peter Jude*. London: T & T Clark, 2004.

Sklyarova, M. *Sosud Isbranny: Istoriya Rossiyskikh Dukhovnykh Shkol (Chosen Vessel: The History of Russian Spiritual Schools)*. St. Petersburg, 1994.

Smith, G. *Short History of Christian Missions from Abraham and Paul to Carey, Livingstone, and Duff*. Edinburgh, 1884.

Smith, W.C. *The Meaning and End of Religion*. New York: Macmillan, 1962.

Snaitang, O.L., ed. *Churches of Indigenous Origins in North East India*. Mylapore/Delhi: MIIS/ISPCK), 2000.

Snook, S.G. *Developing Leaders through Theological Education by Extension. Case Studies from Africa*. Wheaton, Ill: Wheaton College, Billy Graham Center, 1992.

Sobrino, J. *The True Church and the Poor*. Translated by M.J. O'Connell. Maryknoll, NY: Orbis Books, 1984.

———. *Jesus in Latin America*. Translated by R.R. Barr. Maryknoll, NY: Orbis Books, 1987.

Sorensen, P. 'Managers' Learnings in Action: The Scholar-Practitioner, Organization Development and Action Research'. In *Managers Learning in Action: Management Learning, Research and Education,* edited by D. Coghlan, T. Dromgoole, P. Joynt and P. Sorensen. London: Routledge, 2004.

SPAEF. 'A Review of the Adoption of Just in Time Method and Its Effect on Efficiency'. (2008), http://www.spaef.com/article.php?id=118.

Spurgeon, C.H. *Autobiography; Compiled from His Diary, Letters, and Records by His Wife and His Private Secretary*. 4 vols. Vol. 2. London: Passmore and Alabaster, 1899.

Stamoolis, J. 'Theological Education in the 21st Century: Emerging Critical Issues'. In *ICETE Conference*. Moorlands College, 1996.

Stanley, B. 'C.H. Spurgeon and the Baptist Missionary Society, 1863-1866'. *Baptist Quarterly* 28: 7 (1982), 320.

———. *The History of the Baptist Missionary Society, 1792-1992*. Edinburgh: T&T Clark, 1992.

Stewart, B.C. 'Tensions in North American Theological Education'. *Evangelical Review of Theology* 14: 1 (1990), 42-49.

Stewart, J.A. *A Man in a Hurry*. Asheville, NC: Russian Bible Society, n.d.

Stiver, D.R. *Theology after Ricoeur: New Directions in Hermeneutic Theology*. Louisville, Westminster: John Knox, 2001.

Stout, G. *Ethics after Babel: The Languages of Morals and Their Discontents*. Cambridge: James Clarke, 1988.

Street, B.V. 'The Mullah, the Shahnameh and the Madrasseh: Some Aspects of Literac in Iran'. *Asian Affairs* 62: (1975), 290-306.

Sugirtharajah, R.S. *Vernacular Hermeneutics*. Sheffield: Sheffield Academic Press, 1999.

———. *The Bible and the Third World: Precolonial, Colonial and Postcolonial Encounters*. Cambridge: Cambridge University Press, 2001.

———. *The Bible and Empire: Postcolonial Explorations*. Cambridge: Cambridge University Press, 2005.

———. 'Scripture, Scholarship, Empire: Putting the Discipline in Its Place'. *The Expository Times* 117: 1, October (2005).

T.A. Howard, T.A, ed. *The Future of Christian Learning*. Grand Rapids, Michigan: Brazos Press, 2008.

Tapp, N. 'Karma and Cosmology. Anthropology and Religion'. In *Asia's Cultural Mosaic: An Anthropological Introduction*, edited by Grant Evans, 287-306. New York: Prentice-Hall, 1993.

Taylor, C. *Sources of the Self: The Making of Modern Identity*. Cambridge: Cambridge University Press, 1989.

Thiselton, A. *New Horizons in Hermeneutics*. London: Harper Collins, 1992.

Thomas, J.C. 'Women, Pentecostals and the Bible: An Experiment in Pentecostal Hermeneutics'. *Journal of Pentecostal Theology* 5: (1994), 41-56.

———. 'Reading the Bible from within Our Traditions: A Pentecostal Hermeneutic as a Test Case'. In *Between Two Horizons: Spanning New Testament and Systematic Theology*, edited by J.B. Green and M. Turner. Grand Rapids: Eerdmans, 2000.

———. *The Pentecostal Commentary on 1 John 2 John 3 John*. London: T & T Clark, 2004.

Thompson, A. 'Ministerial Training from a London Perspective'. 20 May 1985.

Tracy, D. 'Theology as Public Discourse'. *The Christian Century*, (March 19) 1975, 280-84.

Trustees to W.Y. Fullerton. 1893.

Vanhoozer, K.V. *First Theology: Scripture and Hermeneutics*. Leicester: IVP, 2002.

Verkuyl, J. *Contemporary Missiology: An Introduction*. Grand Rapids, 1978.

von der Ruhr, M. *An Apprenticeship in Attention*, Outstanding Christian Thinkers: Continuum, 2007.

Warneck, G. 'Zur apologetischen Bedeutung der Heidenmission'. *Allgemeine Missions-Zeitschrift* XVII; XXXIV: (1890 & 1907).

———. *Evangelische Missionslehre: Ein Missionstheoretischer Versuch*. 3 vols: Gotha, 1892-1903.

Water, D.P. van der. 'Transforming Theological Education and Ministerial Formation'. *International Review of Missions* 94: 373 (2005).

Watson, F. *Text and Truth: Redefining Biblical Theology*. Edinburgh: T & T Clark, 1997.

Weber, M. *Economy and Society: An Outline of Interpretative Sociology*. Edited by G. Roth and C. Wittich. Berkeley, CA: University of California Press, 1978.

Webster, J. *Religion and Dalit Liberation: An Examination of Perspectives*. 2 ed. New Delhi: Manohar, 2002.

———. *Holy Scripture, a Dogmatic Sketch*. Cambridge: Cambridge University Press, 2003.

Werner, D. 'Theologie zum Leben bringen. Anforderungen an eine zukunftsorientierte Ausbildungb'. In *Emw-Informationen 105*. Hamburg: Evan- gelisches Missionswerk, 1995.

Westerhoff, J. 'Formation, Education and Instruction'. *Religious Education* 82: Fall (1987).

Whaling, F. 'A Comparative Religious Study of Missionary Transplantation in Buddhism, Christianity, and Islam'. *International Review of Missions* LXX: (1981), 314-33.

White, S. *Groundwork of Christian Worship* Peterborough: Epworth, 1997.

Whitehead, J. *Action Research, Living Theory*. Thousand Oaks, CA: Sage, 2006.

Wijsen, F. 'Intercultural Theology and the Mission of the Church'. www.sedos.org/english/wijsen.htm

Williams, R. 'CEFACS Lecture, Birmingham'. http://www.archbishopofcanterbury.org/1048.

Wilson, M. *A Coat of Many Colours*. London: Epworth, 1988.

Wimberly, E.P. *Using Scripture in Pastoral Counseling*. Nashville: Abingdon, 1994.

Wood, J. *Epistemology: Becoming Intellectually Virtuous*. Downers Grove, IL: Apollos, Inter Varsity Press, 1998.

———. *Born in the Fire*: privately published, 1998.

Worley, R. *Preaching and Teaching in the Earliest Church*, Philadelphia. Westminster, 1967.

Wright, S. 'The Reflective Journey Begins a Spiritual Journey'. In *Transforming Nursing through Reflective Practice*, edited by C. Johns and D. Freshwater. Oxford: Blackwell Science, 1998.

Yong, A. *Spirit-Word-Community: Theological Hermeneutics in Trinitarian Perspective*. Aldershot: Ashgate, 2002.

———. *The Spirit Poured out on All Flesh: Pentecostalism and the Possibility of Global Theology*. Grand Rapids: Baker Academic, 2005.

Yu, C.T. *Being and Relation: A Theological Critique of Western Dualism and Individualism*. Edinburgh: Scottish Academic Press, 1987.

Yung, Hwa. 'D.Miss. Dissertation'. Asbury Theological Seminary, 1994.

———. 'Critical Issues Facing Theological Education in Asia'. *Transformation* 12: 4 (1995), 1-6.

Zizioulas, J.D. *Being as Communion*. New York: St. Vladimir's Seminary Press, 1985.

———.. *Communion and Otherness: Further Studies in Personhood and the Church*

: T. & T. Clark Publishers, 2007.

Zumstein, J. 'Theologische Fakultäten an staatlichen Hochschulen'. In *Kirche Und Staat*, edited by A. Schindler. Zürich: TVZ, 1994.

Subject Index

REGNUM EDINBURGH 2010 SERIES
Series Listing

David A. Kerr, Kenneth R. Ross (Eds)
Mission Then and Now
2009 / 978-1-870345-73-6 / 343pp (paperback)
2009 / 978-1-870345-76-7 / 343pp (hardback)

No one can hope to fully understand the modern Christian missionary movement without engaging substantially with the World Missionary Conference, held at Edinburgh in 1910. This book is the first to systematically examine the eight Commissions which reported to Edinburgh 1910 and gave the conference much of its substance and enduring value. It will deepen and extend the reflection being stimulated by the upcoming centenary and will kindle the missionary imagination for 2010 and beyond.

Daryl M. Balia, Kirsteen Kim (Eds)
Witnessing to Christ Today
2010 / 978-1-870345-77-4 / 301pp

This volume, the second in the Edinburgh 2010 series, includes reports of the nine main study groups working on different themes for the celebration of the centenary of the World Missionary Conference, Edinburgh 1910. Their collaborative work brings together perspectives that are as inclusive as possible of contemporary world Christianity and helps readers to grasp what it means in different contexts to be 'witnessing to Christ today'.

Claudia Währisch-Oblau, Fidon Mwombeki (Eds)
Mission Continues
Global Impulses for the 21st Century
2010 / 978-1-870345-82-8 / 271pp

In May 2009, 35 theologians from Asia, Africa and Europe met in Wuppertal, Germany, for a consultation on mission theology organized by the United Evangelical Mission: Communion of 35 Churches in Three Continents. The aim was to participate in the 100th anniversary of the Edinburgh conference through a study process and reflect on the challenges for mission in the 21st century. This book brings together these papers written by experienced practitioners from around the world.

Brian Woolnough and Wonsuk Ma (Eds)
Holistic Mission
God's plan for God's people
2010 / 978-1-870345-85-9 / 277pp

Holistic mission, or integral mission, implies God is concerned with the whole person, the whole community, body, mind and spirit. This book discusses the meaning of the holistic gospel, how it has developed, and implications for the church. It takes a global, eclectic approach, with 19 writers, all of whom have much experience in, and commitment to, holistic mission. It addresses critically and honestly one of the most exciting, and challenging, issues facing the church today. To be part of God's plan for God's people, the church must take holistic mission to the world.

Kirsteen Kim and Andrew Anderson (Eds)
Mission Today and Tomorrow
2010 / 978-1-870345-91-0 / 450pp
There are moments in our lives when we come to realise that we are participating in the triune God's mission. If we believe the church to be as sign and symbol of the reign of God in the world, then we are called to witness to Christ today by sharing in God's mission of love through the transforming power of the Holy Spirit. We can all participate in God's transforming and reconciling mission of love to the whole creation.

Tormod Engelsviken, Erling Lundeby and Dagfinn Solheim (Eds)
The Church Going Glocal
Mission and Globalisation 2011 / 978-1-870345-93-4 / 262pp
The New Testament church is… universal and local at the same time. The universal, one and holy apostolic church appears in local manifestations. Missiologically speaking… the church can take courage as she faces the increasing impact of globalisation on local communities today. Being universal and concrete, the church is geared for the simultaneous challenges of the glocal and local.

Marina Ngurusangzeli Behera (Ed)
Interfaith Relations after One Hundred Years
Christian Mission among Other Faiths 2011 / 978-1-870345-96-5 / 334 pp
The essays of this book reflect not only the acceptance and celebration of pluralism within India but also by extension an acceptance as well as a need for unity among Indian Christians of different denominations. The essays were presented and studied at a preparatory consultation on Study Theme II: Christian Mission Among Other Faiths at the United Theological College, India July 2009.

Lalsangkima Pachuau and Knud Jørgensen (Eds)
Witnessing to Christ in a Pluralistic Age
Christian Mission among Other Faiths 2011 / 978-1-870345-95-8 / 277 pp
In a world where plurality of faiths is increasingly becoming a norm of life, insights on the theology of religious plurality are needed to strengthen our understanding of our own faith and the faith of others. Even though religious diversity is not new, we are seeing an upsurge in interest on the theologies of religion among all Christian confessional traditions. It can be claimed that no other issue in Christian mission is more important and more difficult than the theologies of religions.

Beth Snodderly and A Scott Moreau (Eds)
Evangelical Frontier Mission
Perspectives on the Global Progress of the Gospel
2011 / 978-1-870345-98-9 / 312pp
This important volume demonstrates that 100 years after the World Missionary Conference in Edinburgh, Evangelism has become truly global. Twenty-first-century Evangelism continues to focus on frontier mission, but significantly, and in the spirit of Edinburgh 1910, it also has re-engaged social action.

Rolv Olsen (Ed)
Mission and Postmodernities
2011 / 978-1-870345-97-2 / 279pp

This volume takes on meaning because its authors honestly struggle with and debate how we should relate to postmodernities. Should our response be accommodation, relativizing or counter-culture? How do we strike a balance between listening and understanding, and at the same time exploring how postmodernities influence the interpretation and application of the Bible as the normative story of God's mission in the world?

REGNUM STUDIES IN GLOBAL CHRISTIANITY
(Previously GLOBAL THEOLOGICAL VOICES series)
Series Listing

David Emmanuel Singh (Ed)
Jesus and the Cross
Reflections of Christians from Islamic Contexts
2008 / 978-1-870345-65-1 / 226pp

The Cross reminds us that the sins of the world are not borne through the exercise of power but through Jesus Christ's submission to the will of the Father. The papers in this volume are organised in three parts: scriptural, contextual and theological. The central question being addressed is: how do Christians living in contexts, where Islam is a majority or minority religion, experience, express or think of the Cross?

Sung-wook Hong
Naming God in Korea
The Case of Protestant Christianity
2008 / 978-1-870345-66-8 / 170pp

Since Christianity was introduced to Korea more than a century ago, one of the most controversial issues has been the Korean term for the Christian 'God'. This issue is not merely about naming the Christian God in Korean language, but it relates to the question of theological contextualization - the relationship between the gospel and culture - and the question of Korean Christian identity. This book demonstrates the nature of the gospel in relation to cultures, i.e., the universality of the gospel expressed in all human cultures.

Hubert van Beek (Ed)
Revisioning Christian Unity
The Global Christian Forum
2009 / 978-1-870345-74-3 / 288pp

This book contains the records of the Global Christian Forum gathering held in Limuru near Nairobi, Kenya, on 6 – 9 November 2007 as well as the papers presented at that historic event. Also included are a summary of the Global Christian Forum process from its inception until the 2007 gathering and the reports of the evaluation of the process that was carried out in 2008.

Young-hoon Lee
The Holy Spirit Movement in Korea
Its Historical and Theological Development
2009 / 978-1-870345-67-5 / 174pp

This book traces the historical and theological development of the Holy Spirit Movement in Korea through six successive periods (from 1900 to the present time). These periods are characterized by repentance and revival (1900-20), persecution and suffering under Japanese occupation (1920-40), confusion and division (1940-60), explosive revival in which the Pentecostal movement played a major role in the rapid growth of Korean churches (1960-80), the movement reaching out to all denominations (1980-2000), and the new context demanding the Holy Spirit movement to open new horizons in its mission engagement (2000-).

Paul Hang-Sik Cho

Eschatology and Ecology

Experiences of the Korean Church

2010 / 978-1-870345-75-0 / 260pp

This book raises the question of why Korean people, and Korean Protestant Christians in particular, pay so little attention to ecological issues. The author argues that there is an important connection (or elective affinity) between this lack of attention and the other-worldly eschatology that is so dominant within Korean Protestant Christianity.

Dietrich Werner, David Esterline, Namsoon Kang, Joshva Raja (Eds)

The Handbook of Theological Education in World Christianity

2010 / 978-1-870345-80-4 / 759pp

This major reference work is the first ever comprehensive study of Theological Education in Christianity of its kind. With contributions from over 90 international scholars and church leaders, it aims to be easily accessible across denominational, cultural, educational, and geographic boundaries. The Handbook will aid international dialogue and networking among theological educators, institutions, and agencies

David Emmanuel Singh & Bernard C Farr (Eds)

Christianity and Education

Shaping of Christian Context in Thinking

2010 / 978-1-870345-81-1 / 374pp

Christianity and Education is a collection of papers published in *Transformation: An International Journal of Holistic Mission Studies* over a period of 15 years. The articles represent a spectrum of Christian thinking addressing issues of institutional development for theological education, theological studies in the context of global mission, contextually aware/informed education, and academies which deliver such education, methodologies and personal reflections.

J.Andrew Kirk

Civilisations in Conflict?

Islam, the West and Christian Faith

2011 / 978-1-870345-87-3 / 205pp

Samuel Huntington's thesis, which argues that there appear to be aspects of Islam that could be on a collision course with the politics and values of Western societies, has provoked much controversy. This study is offers a particular response to Huntington's thesis by making a comparison between the origins of Islam and Christianity.

David Emmanuel Singh (Ed)

Jesus and the Incarnation

Reflections of Christians from Islamic Contexts

2011 / 978-1-870345-90-3 / 250pp

In the dialogues of Christians with Muslims nothing is more fundamental than the Cross, the Incarnation and the Resurrection of Jesus. Building on the *Jesus and the Cross*, this book contains voices of Christians living in various 'Islamic contexts' and reflecting on the Incarnation of Jesus. The aim and hope of these reflections is that the papers weaved around the notion of 'the Word' will not only promote dialogue among Christians on the roles of the Person and the Book but, also, create a positive environment for their conversations with Muslim neighbours.

REGNUM STUDIES IN MISSION
Series Listing

Kwame Bediako
Theology and Identity
The Impact of Culture upon Christian Thought in the Second Century and in Modern Africa
1992 / 978-1870345-80-2 / 508pp

The author examines the question of Christian identity in the context of the Graeco–Roman culture of the early Roman Empire. He then addresses the modern African predicament of quests for identity and integration.

Christopher Sugden
Seeking the Asian Face of Jesus
The Practice and Theology of Christian Social Witness in Indonesia and India 1974–1996
1997 / 1-870345-26-6 / 496pp

This study focuses on contemporary holistic mission with the poor in India and Indonesia combined with the call to transformation of all life in Christ with micro-credit enterprise schemes. 'The literature on contextual theology now has a new standard to rise to' – Lamin Sanneh (Yale University, USA).

Hwa Yung
Mangoes or Bananas?
The Quest for an Authentic Asian Christian Theology
1997 / 1-870345-25-5 / 274pp

Asian Christian thought remains largely captive to Greek dualism and Enlightenment rationalism because of the overwhelming dominance of Western culture. Authentic contextual Christian theologies will emerge within Asian Christianity with a dual recovery of confidence in culture and the gospel.

Keith E. Eitel
Paradigm Wars
The Southern Baptist International Mission Board Faces the Third Millennium
1999 / 1-870345-12-6 / 140pp

The International Mission Board of the Southern Baptist Convention is the largest denominational mission agency in North America. This volume chronicles the historic and contemporary forces that led to the IMB's recent extensive reorganization, providing the most comprehensive case study to date of a historic mission agency restructuring to continue its mission purpose into the twenty-first century more effectively.

Samuel Jayakumar

Dalit Consciousness and Christian Conversion

Historical Resources for a Contemporary Debate 1999 / 81-7214-497-0 / 434pp

(Published jointly with ISPCK)

The main focus of this historical study is social change and transformation among the Dalit Christian communities in India. Historiography tests the evidence in the light of the conclusions of the modern Dalit liberation theologians.

Vinay Samuel and Christopher Sugden (Eds)

Mission as Transformation

A Theology of the Whole Gospel

1999 / 978-18703455-13-2/ 522pp

This book brings together in one volume twenty five years of biblical reflection on mission practice with the poor from around the world. This volume helps anyone understand how evangelicals, struggling to unite evangelism and social action, found their way in the last twenty five years to the biblical view of mission in which God calls all human beings to love God and their neighbour; never creating a separation between the two.

Christopher Sugden

Gospel, Culture and Transformation

2000 / 1-870345-32-0 /152pp

A Reprint, with a New Introduction, of Part Two of Seeking the Asian Face of Jesus
Gospel, Culture and Transformation explores the practice of mission especially in relation to transforming cultures and communities. - 'Transformation is to enable God's vision of society to be actualised in all relationships: social, economic and spiritual, so that God's will may be reflected in human society and his love experienced by all communities, especially the poor.'

Bernhard Ott

Beyond Fragmentation: Integrating Mission and Theological Education

A Critical Assessment of some Recent Developments
in Evangelical Theological Education

2001 / 1-870345-14-2 / 382pp

Beyond Fragmentation is an enquiry into the development of Mission Studies in evangelical theological education in Germany and German-speaking Switzerland between 1960 and 1995. The author undertakes a detailed examination of the paradigm shifts which have taken place in recent years in both the theology of mission and the understanding of theological education.

Gideon Githiga

The Church as the Bulwark against Authoritarianism

Development of Church and State Relations in Kenya, with Particular Reference to the Years after Political Independence 1963-1992

2002 / 1-870345-38-x / 218pp

'All who care for love, peace and unity in Kenyan society will want to read this careful history by Bishop Githiga of how Kenyan Christians, drawing on the Bible, have sought to share the love of God, bring his peace and build up the unity of the nation, often in the face of great difficulties and opposition.' Canon Dr Chris Sugden, Oxford Centre for Mission Studies.

Myung Sung-Hoon, Hong Young-Gi (eds.)

Charis and Charisma

David Yonggi Cho and the Growth of Yoido Full Gospel Church

2003 / 978-1870345-45-3 / 218pp

This book discusses the factors responsible for the growth of the world's largest church. It expounds the role of the Holy Spirit, the leadership, prayer, preaching, cell groups and creativity in promoting church growth. It focuses on God's grace (charis) and inspiring leadership (charisma) as the two essential factors and the book's purpose is to present a model for church growth worldwide.

Samuel Jayakumar

Mission Reader

Historical Models for Wholistic Mission in the Indian Context

2003 / 1-870345-42-8 / 250pp

(Published jointly with ISPCK)

This book is written from an evangelical point of view revalidating and reaffirming the Christian commitment to wholistic mission. The roots of the 'wholistic mission' combining 'evangelism and social concerns' are to be located in the history and tradition of Christian evangelism in the past; and the civilizing purpose of evangelism is compatible with modernity as an instrument in nation building.

Bob Robinson

Christians Meeting Hindus

An Analysis and Theological Critique of the Hindu-Christian Encounter in India

2004 / 987-1870345-39-2 / 392pp

This book focuses on the Hindu-Christian encounter, especially the intentional meeting called dialogue, mainly during the last four decades of the twentieth century, and specifically in India itself.

Gene Early

Leadership Expectations

How Executive Expectations are Created and Used in a Non-Profit Setting

2005 / 1-870345-30-4 / 276pp

The author creates an Expectation Enactment Analysis to study the role of the Chancellor of the University of the Nations-Kona, Hawaii. This study is grounded in the field of managerial work, jobs, and behaviour and draws on symbolic interactionism, role theory, role identity theory and enactment theory. The result is a conceptual framework for developing an understanding of managerial roles.

Tharcisse Gatwa

The Churches and Ethnic Ideology in the Rwandan Crises 1900-1994

2005 / 978-1870345-24-8 / 300pp

(Reprinted 2011)

Since the early years of the twentieth century Christianity has become a new factor in Rwandan society. This book investigates the role Christian churches played in the formulation and development of the racial ideology that culminated in the 1994 genocide.

Julie Ma

Mission Possible

Biblical Strategies for Reaching the Lost

2005 / 978-1870345-37-1 / 142pp

This is a missiology book for the church which liberates missiology from the specialists for the benefit of every believer. It also serves as a textbook that is simple and friendly, and yet solid in biblical interpretation. This book links the biblical teaching to the actual and contemporary missiological settings with examples, making the Bible come alive to the reader.

Allan Anderson, Edmond Tang (Eds)

Asian and Pentecostal

The Charismatic Face of Christianity in Asia

2005 / 1-870345-43-9 / 596pp

(Reprinted 2011)

(Published jointly with APTS Press)

This book provides a thematic discussion and pioneering case studies on the history and development of Pentecostal and Charismatic churches in the countries of South Asia, South East Asia and East Asia.

I. Mark Beaumont

Christology in Dialogue with Muslims

A Critical Analysis of Christian Presentations of Christ for Muslims from the Ninth and Twentieth Centuries

2005 / 1978-1870345-46-0 / 228pp

This book analyses Christian presentations of Christ for Muslims in the most creative periods of Christian-Muslim dialogue, the first half of the ninth century and the second half of the twentieth century. In these two periods, Christians made serious attempts to present their faith in Christ in terms that take into account Muslim perceptions of him, with a view to bridging the gap between Muslim and Christian convictions.

Thomas Czövek,

Three Seasons of Charismatic Leadership

A Literary-Critical and Theological Interpretation of the Narrative of Saul, David and Solomon

2006 / 978-1870345-48-4 / 272pp

This book investigates the charismatic leadership of Saul, David and Solomon. It suggests that charismatic leaders emerge in crisis situations in order to resolve the crisis by the charisma granted by God. Czovek argues that Saul proved himself as a charismatic leader as long as he acted resolutely and independently from his mentor Samuel. In the author's eyes, Saul's failure to establish himself as a charismatic leader is caused by his inability to step out from Samuel's shadow.

Jemima Atieno Oluoch

The Christian Political Theology of Dr. John Henry Okullu

2006 / 1-870345-51-4 / 137pp

This book reconstructs the Christian political theology of Bishop John Henry Okullu, DD, through establishing what motivated him and the biblical basis for his socio-political activities. It also attempts to reconstruct the socio-political environment that nurtured Dr Okullu's prophetic ministry.

Richard Burgess

Nigeria's Christian Revolution

The Civil War Revival and Its Pentecostal Progeny (1967-2006)

2008 / 978-1-870345-63-7 / 347pp

This book describes the revival that occurred among the Igbo people of Eastern Nigeria and the new Pentecostal churches it generated, and documents the changes that have occurred as the movement has responded to global flows and local demands. As such, it explores the nature of revivalist and Pentecostal experience, but does so against the backdrop of local socio-political and economic developments, such as decolonisation and civil war, as well as broader processes, such as modernisation and globalisation.

David Emmanuel Singh & Bernard C Farr (Eds)

Christianity and Cultures

Shaping Christian Thinking in Context

2008 / 978-1-870345-69-9 / 260pp

This volume marks an important milestone, the 25th anniversary of the Oxford Centre for Mission Studies (OCMS). The papers here have been exclusively sourced from Transformation, a quarterly journal of OCMS, and seek to provide a tripartite view of Christianity's engagement with cultures by focusing on the question: how is Christian thinking being formed or reformed through its interaction with the varied contexts it encounters? The subject matters include different strands of theological-missiological thinking, socio-political engagements and forms of family relationships in interaction with the host cultures.

Tormod Engelsviken, Ernst Harbakk, Rolv Olsen, Thor Strandenæs (Eds)
Mission to the World
Communicating the Gospel in the 21st Century: Essays in Honour of Knud Jørgensen
2008 / 978-1-870345-64-4 / 472pp

Knud Jørgensen is Director of Areopagos and Associate Professor of Missiology at MF Norwegian School of Theology. This book reflects on the main areas of Jørgensen's commitment to mission. At the same time it focuses on the main frontier of mission, the world, the content of mission, the Gospel, the fact that the Gospel has to be communicated, and the context of contemporary mission in the 21st century.

Al Tizon
Transformation after Lausanne
Radical Evangelical Mission in Global-Local Perspective
2008 / 978-1-870345-68-2 / 281pp

After Lausanne '74, a worldwide network of radical evangelical mission theologians and practitioners use the notion of "Mission as Transformation" to integrate evangelism and social concern together, thus lifting theological voices from the Two Thirds World to places of prominence. This book documents the definitive gatherings, theological tensions, and social forces within and without evangelicalism that led up to Mission as Transformation. And it does so through a global-local grid that points the way toward greater holistic mission in the 21st century.

Bambang Budijanto
Values and Participation
Development in Rural Indonesia
2009 / 978-1-870345-70-4 / 237pp

Socio-religious values and socio-economic development are inter-dependant, inter-related and are constantly changing in the context of macro political structures, economic policy, religious organizations and globalization; and micro influences such as local affinities, identity, politics, leadership and beliefs. The book argues that the comprehensive approach in understanding the socio-religious values of each of the three local Lopait communities in Central Java is essential to accurately describing their respective identity.

Alan R. Johnson
Leadership in a Slum
A Bangkok Case Study
2009 / 978-1-870345-71-2 / 238pp

This book looks at leadership in the social context of a slum in Bangkok from a different perspective than traditional studies which measure well educated Thais on leadership scales derived in the West. Using both systematic data collection and participant observation, it develops a culturally preferred model as well as a set of models based in Thai concepts that reflect on-the-ground realities. It concludes by looking at the implications of the anthropological approach for those who are involved in leadership training in Thai settings and beyond.

Titre Ande
Leadership and Authority
Bula Matari and Life - Community Ecclesiology in Congo
2010 / 978-1-870345-72-9 / 189pp

Christian theology in Africa can make significant development if a critical understanding of the socio-political context in contemporary Africa is taken seriously, particularly as Africa's post-colonial Christian leadership based its understanding and use of authority on the Bula Matari model. This has caused many problems and Titre proposes a Life-Community ecclesiology for liberating authority, here leadership is a function, not a status, and 'apostolic succession' belongs to all people of God.

Frank Kwesi Adams
Odwira and the Gospel
A Study of the Asante Odwira Festival and its Significance for Christianity in Ghana
2010 /978-1-870345-59-0 / 232pp

The study of the Odwira festival is the key to the understanding of Asante religious and political life in Ghana. The book explores the nature of the Odwira festival longitudinally - in pre-colonial, colonial and post-independence Ghana - and examines the Odwira ideology and its implications for understanding the Asante self-identity. Also discussed is how some elements of faith portrayed in the Odwira festival can provide a framework for Christianity to engage with Asante culture at a greater depth.

Bruce Carlton
Strategy Coordinator
Changing the Course of Southern Baptist Missions
2010 / 978-1-870345-78-1 / 268pp

This is an outstanding, one-of-a-kind work addressing the influence of the non-residential missionary/strategy coordinator's role in Southern Baptist missions. This scholarly text examines the twentieth century global missiological currents that influenced the leadership of the International Mission Board, resulting in a new paradigm to assist in taking the gospel to the nations.

Julie Ma & Wonsuk Ma
Mission in the Spirit:
Towards a Pentecostal/Charismatic Missiology
2010 / 978-1-870345-84-2 / 312pp

The book explores the unique contribution of Pentecostal/Charismatic mission from the beginning of the twentieth century. The first part considers the theological basis of Pentecostal/Charismatic mission thinking and practice. Special attention is paid to the Old Testament, which has been regularly overlooked by the modern Pentecostal/Charismatic movements. The second part discusses major mission topics with contributions and challenges unique to Pentecostal/Charismatic mission. The book concludes with a reflection on the future of this powerful missionary movement. As the authors served as Korean missionaries in Asia, often their missionary experiences in Asia are reflected in their discussions.

S. Hun Kim & Wonsuk Ma (eds.)

Korean Diaspora and Christian Mission

2011-978-1-870345-91-0 / 301pp

As a 'divine conspiracy' for Missio Dei, the global phenomenon of people on the move has shown itself to be invaluable. In 2004 two significant documents concerning Diaspora were introduced, one by the Filipino International Network and the other by the Lausanne Committee for World Evangelization. These have created awareness of the importance of people on the move for Christian mission. Since then, Korean Diaspora has conducted similar research among Korean missions, resulting in this book

Jin Huat Tan

Planting an Indigenous Church

The Case of the Borneo Evangelical Mission

2011 / 978-1-870345-99-6 / 343pp

Dr Jin Huat Tan has written a pioneering study of the origins and development of Malaysia's most significant indigenous church. This is an amazing story of revival, renewal and transformation of the entire region chronicling the powerful effect of it evident to date! What can we learn from this extensive and careful study of the Borneo Revival, so the global Christianity will become ever more dynamic.

GENERAL REGNUM TITLES

Vinay Samuel, Chris Sugden (eds.)
The Church in Response to Human Need
1987 / 1870345045 / xii+268pp

Philip Sampson, Vinay Samuel, Chris Sugden (eds.)
Faith and Modernity
Essays in modernity and post-modernity
1994 / 1870345177 / 352pp

Klaus Fiedler
The Story of Faith Missions
1994 / 0745926878 / 428pp

Douglas Peterson
Not by Might nor by Power
A Pentecostal Theology of Social Concern in Latin America
1996 / 1870345207 / xvi+260pp

David Gitari
In Season and Out of Season
Sermons to a Nation
1996 / 1870345118 / 155pp

David. W. Virtue
A Vision of Hope
The Story of Samuel Habib
1996 / 1870345169 / xiv+137pp

Everett A Wilson
Strategy of the Spirit
J.Philip Hogan and the Growth of the Assemblies of God Worldwide, 1960 - 1990
1997 /1870345231/214

Murray Dempster, Byron Klaus, Douglas Petersen (Eds)
The Globalization of Pentecostalism
A Religion Made to Travel
1999 / 1870345290 / xvii+406pp

Peter Johnson, Chris Sugden (eds.)
Markets, Fair Trade and the Kingdom of God
Essays to Celebrate Traidcraft's 21st Birthday
2001 / 1870345193 / xii+155pp

Robert Hillman, Coral Chamberlain, Linda Harding
Healing & Wholeness
Reflections on the Healing Ministry
2002 / 978-1- 870345-35- 4 / xvii+283pp

David Bussau, Russell Mask
Christian Microenterprise Development
An Introduction
2003 / 1870345282 / xiii+142pp

David Singh
Sainthood and Revelatory Discourse
An Examination of the Basis for the Authority of Bayan in Mahdawi Islam
2003 / 8172147285 / xxiv+485pp

For the up-to-date listing of the Regnum books see www.ocms.ac.uk/regnum

regnum

Regnum Books International

Regnum is an Imprint of The Oxford Centre for Mission Studies
St. Philip and St. James Church
Woodstock Road
Oxford, OX2 6HR
Web: www.ocms.ac.uk/regnum